THE AUTHOR'S TRAVEL ROUTES

To Mr. Harrison Salisbury

with the compliments of the
author and editor/translator

Duan Liancheng

(Chinese participant in
the November, 1986 Sino-
American "supplementary
diplomacy dialogue)

Dec. 7, 1986
Paramus, N.J.

THE AMERICAN KALEIDOSCOPE

— A Chinese View

By
WANG TSOMIN

Edited and Translated by
DUAN LIANCHENG

NEW WORLD PRESS
BEIJING, CHINA

First Edition 1986
Cover Drawing by Mao Guoxuan

Ms. Wang Tsomin's travel within the
United States was made possible by
generous contributions from:

Armco Foundation
Cabot Corporation Foundation
CBS Incorporated
Corning Glass Works
IBM
Intel Corporation
3M Corporation

ISBN 0-8351-1663-8

Published by
NEW WORLD PRESS
24 Baiwanzhuang Road, Beijing, China

Distributed by
CHINA INTERNATIONAL BOOK TRADING CORPORATION
(Guoji Shudian)
P.O. Box 399, Beijing, China

Printed in the People's Republic of China

PREFACE

Since the thawing of Sino-American relations in 1972, people-to-people exchanges between the two countries have been fast increasing. The gratifying growth of mutual contacts has not only increased a popular desire for more knowledge of each other, but also created a hunger for deeper understanding. During the two years I spent in America as the Chinese Ambassador to Washington, I often felt the American eagerness to learn more about China. I will always think of this interest as a clear symbol of friendship. Upon returning to my homeland, I sensed an equally strong desire to know more about America. Apart from the pronounced interest in American science, technology and management, people of all trades and professions want to acquaint themselves with Americans as fellow human beings, not merely as specialists in one field or another. They often ask: How do Americans live and work? What are the salient points of their history and culture? What are their joys and sorrows? What is the American dream?

The average Chinese, I must frankly admit, is less privileged than the average American in being able to seek first hand such mutual understanding. As yet, few Chinese can afford to visit the United States as tourists. Moreover, our media coverage is only approaching technological sophistication, and is not as all-encompassing as we would like it to be. Consequently, though numerous reports are carried in our press on various aspects of American life, many of them tend to be either superficial or academic. A systematic and popular account of the American land and people is badly needed, particularly for the young readers whose interest in the outside world, especially in the United States as a most developed country, is intense.

It is perhaps against this background that Ms. Wang Tsomin's new book, *American Kaleidoscope*, published last October has been warmly received. Many leading Chinese national dailies and magazines have printed favorable reviews. The first printing was quickly sold out and a second printing had to be rushed to meet the market demand.

I have known Ms. Wang since the 1930s when we both attended Qinghua (Tsinghua) University in Beijing. She is familiar with her subject because she lived in America for a few years in the 1940s, received her journalistic training at the prestigious University of Missouri School of Journalism, and since her return to New China in 1949, has been active in the publishing field as a writer. But I am impressed not so much by her expertise as by her sincerity and earnestness. Reading through the pages one can readily feel that she is indeed trying hard to help the reader know about America and the Americans — by reinforcing her personal impressions with research material, by covering such a wide range of subjects that a young Chinese reviewer overzealously praised the volume as a "mini-encyclopedia," and by laboriously "leap-frogging," as she herself puts it, from one place to another for a whole year across the vast American continent. Having interviewed hundreds of people, she brought back voluminous notes, numerous audio-tapes and photographs.

Wang Tsomin has been a candid person since her younger days. She never minces words. I am glad to find that she writes with the same frankness. She freely and easily records what she saw, heard and thought, leaving aside ideological differences because she was, again in her own words, undertaking the project as a private citizen with no official blessings or obligations on either side of the Pacific. She declared that she would "call a spade a spade."

But America is not all that simple. No observer, for his or her professed objectivity, can completely avoid bias. A foreign writer may even make factual mistakes here and there. So I appreciate Ms. Wang's modest statement that she is, to quote an old Chinese saying, "peeping at the sky through a bamboo tube and measuring the sea with a gourd," (*gungui lice*). American society is too complex. Few, if any, can claim to know it all. Even Alexis Tocqueville did not proclaim himself to be an authority. Nonetheless, I see in *American Kaleidoscope* a welcome effort in the right direction. And I hope that the volume will be followed by more works of this kind, popular or scholarly, general or specialized, to enhance Chinese understanding of America. Such an understanding, I believe, is a key element for peace and development — the two paramount issues of our times.

It would be ludicrous to presume that American readers would read this book to learn about their own country. None of them, for instance, needs to be enlightened about the Boston Tea Party, though the author understandably has to explain to her Chinese reader that the Tea Party was not a social gathering, but a revolutionary landmark. However, some Americans may find the book interesting because most people seem to be fond of looking at a mirror and are curious as to what others are saying about them. I think those working for friendship between Americans and Chinese will find the book a useful reflection of their own noble endeavor. And I believe that they, too, will not mince their words if they find any inaccuracy or misrepresentation in the volume. The author says emphatically that she is ready to revise it if there is to be a new edition.

May more Chinese and Americans join in the effort to make "the east meet the west" not only in business but also in mind!

Zhang Wenjin

(ZHANG WENJIN)
Former Chinese Ambassador to the United States;
President of Chinese People's Friendship Association with Foreign Countries

Beijing, July, 1986

CONTENTS

FOREWORD

An unexpected chance has enabled me to live and travel extensively in the United States for one year. The purpose is for me to gather impressions and materials for a book on contemporary America.

The writing project had its inception in late 1979. At that time, a delegation of Chinese economists headed by Mr. Ma Hong (who later became president of the Chinese Academy of Social Sciences) was touring the United States as guests of five prestigious American universities with business management schools — the Massachusetts Institute of Technology, Harvard, Stanford, Pennsylvania, and Indiana. The delegation's American hosts suggested writing such a book for a Chinese audience. The proposal, coming at a time when China and the United States had established diplomatic relations after an estrangement of thirty years and were seeking to understand each other, was timely and worthy.

After eighteen months of preparation, a time devoted mainly to fund-raising, M.I.T. Professor Richard D. Robinson wrote Mr. Ma to say that a Chinese writer could be sent and that "what we envision is not a dull scholarly analysis, but rather a lively, semi-popular account of life in the United States as seen by the writer. Naturally he/she will be free to write whatever seems appropriate." The professor had been entrusted by M.I.T. President, Paul E. Gray, to manage the project. Though the letter of formal invitation was signed by President Gray, it was Professor Robinson who took meticulous care of the project from beginning to end.

Probably because the hosts had made it clear that they wanted an informal, not an academic work, the Chinese Academy turned to my publishing organization to look for a journalist to do the job. I was offered the assignment.

The United States was where I had studied in the 1940s (in the School of Journalism, University of Missouri, Columbia, Missouri). Naturally I was interested in making a second visit to see what changes had taken place in the intervening years. But the job of writing a book on such a vast and complex country made me hesitant.

I consulted senior scholars and journalists as well as my friends. They all thought it was a worthwhile, though arduous, undertaking. They suggested that such a book should cater primarily to a young readership. As China was shifting to a policy of opening up to the outside world, its hundreds of millions of youth were becoming increasingly interested in other countries, particularly the United States. In addition to personal observations, they advised, the book should provide some elementary knowledge of that country, its land and people, its past and present.

The basic approach to be stressed was *shi shi qiu shi* (seeking truth from facts), a tradition undergoing vigorous revival in China after the "cultural revolution" of 1966-1976. During those ten years of turmoil, many basic facts about life were ignored in the midst of ultra-revolutionary rhetoric. People were made to believe, among other things, that there was nothing good whatsoever in Western capitalist society. But then the axiom *shi shi qiu shi* was re-emphasised. When applied to writing, it simply means "calling a spade a spade" or reporting the facts without tarnishing or garnishing. It was also my conviction that only in this way could the book promote genuine understanding and friendship between the Chinese and American peoples.

I then canvassed prospective young readers for suggestions. Having lived behind closed doors for so many years, the youngsters were knowledge thirsty. They said they wanted to know about American history, geography, and all aspects of contemporary life. Their numerous questions ranged from why the United States was nicknamed "Uncle Sam"—the sullen-faced old gentleman they had often seen in caustic newspaper cartoons—to an inquiry on the meaning of the stars and stripes on the American flag. In short, they wanted to know something about everything—an almost impossible job for me!

Nonetheless, their enthusiasm inspired me. It was with their encouragement and the heartening calls from my colleagues and friends that I accepted the assignment and ventured out on the journey, all alone and as a private citizen, without official blessing and without official obligation to either China or the United States.

The tour lasted from May 1982 to May 1983. For technical reasons the publishing of the book is a bit belated. But I am attempting to create impressionistic images of American society and the people I have seen rather than to delineate time-sensitive subjects. Hence the book.

Remarks for the English Edition

Professor Robinson and other American friends have expressed interest in seeing an English-language edition of the book and believe that the American reading public might like to know how a Chinese views their society. Consequently, the present volume is a translation of the Chinese-language edition published by the Social Sciences Publishing House, Beijing, under the title *American Kaleidoscope: Society, Landscape, and People.* Some minor textual changes have been made in the course of translation with the aim of adding explanations of things Chinese to which I referred. I am surprised, for instance, by the high rents in America. Why? Because most Chinese urban dwellers live in apartments heavily subsidized by the government. A brief account of the Chinese housing system will help foreign readers appreciate my reaction and at the same time give them a glimpse of one facet of Chinese life. Such an explanation, obviously, is unnecessary in the Chinese edition. The Chinese "cultural revolution," often mentioned in the text, also needs some elaboration in the English edition. It would be quite superfluous for Chinese readers. In short, I often "measure American corn with a Chinese bushel." A few words about the "Chinese bushel" seem in order so that my comments are more easily comprehended.

For American readers, I wish to add that while I was doing research and then writing this book I tried to keep in mind the idyllic portrayals of China created by some American writers, as well as the muckraking volumes written by others. Neither the sunny side nor the seamy side alone is the true China. The same may be said of America. While conclusions derived from the same observations can naturally differ from author to author, I have conscientiously tried to avoid one-sided distortions.

Acknowledgments

I wish to express my warm appreciation for the generous assistance given by many American friends during my travels. I also must acknowledge the cooperation of my husband, Mr. Duan Liancheng, who edited my Chinese manuscripts and later translated the whole book into English — not simply out of a desire to help me, but with a shared sense of dedication to the friendship of the American and Chinese peoples. He was a classmate of mine at the University of Missouri and, as former director of the Beijing-based Foreign Languages Publication and Distribution Bureau, remains actively interested in publishing for international understanding. In addition, credit goes to Chen Xiuzheng, Deputy Chief Editor, Zhang Xiaojiang, Deputy Executive Editor, and Zhu Penghe of the New World Press; they helped to bring the English edition to light. Last but not least, I thank Frances Chastain and Brian George, American editors working with that publishing house in Beijing. They have carefully revised the English translation.

Wang Tsomin

Beijing, China
April 1986

Chapter I
THE WORLD IS SHRINKING

From Beijing to Shanghai, then to San Francisco and New York — a flight around half the globe takes only a little more than twenty hours. It is my first air trip across the Pacific and the speed makes me feel that America is no longer the faraway land of the 1940s but a neighbor just next door.

I find evidence on the plane of how Chinese and American cultures are intermingling rapidly — so soon after the Chinese Communist Party and government decided in 1978 on a policy of "opening up to the outside world." The jumbo jet operated by CAAC (the Civil Aviation Administration of China) is an American-made "Boeing 747." The films shown on the way are American, while the optional musical program coming through headphones includes classical Beijing operas. A gray-haired Chinese on my right is relishing the opera arias, with his eyes half closed. He tells me that he has been a chef and an American citizen for many years and is thrilled to be able now to re-visit his hometown in China. But he has to ask for my help in filling the customs forms because he cannot write English properly. "I'm all Chinese, you know," he says proudly. On my left sits a Chinese professor, a pediatrician, going to attend a UN's WHO meeting. Born in Canada, he chose to leave his parents there and return to serve New China. There are many other young Chinese men and women, apparently students or visiting scholars going to the United States for advanced studies. The thirty-odd rows of seats, ten in each, are filled to capacity. And in the closed-off first class cabin there are some "big-shots" who must be traveling on official missions. The hustle and bustle aboard testifies to the growing traffic between the two countries.

Two hours after leaving Beijing, we land at Shanghai, China's largest metropolis, where passports are examined and exit formalities completed. Then we are soon over the high seas. Again and again I intrude into the space of my seatmate, trying to get a glimpse of the ocean. But I am disappointed to see only floating clouds. When the clouds disperse, the sea looks more like a yellow-gray desert, dull and motionless.

It is nothing like my ocean voyage in 1947, which I still remember distinctly and fondly. During that trip I spent almost all the daytime on deck. The splendid sunrise and sunset, the sun a huge fireball emerging from or submerging in the distant seas, turning the vast expanse of water and sky golden-red, could never be matched by any master artist's painting. Sometimes I saw flying fish darting out of the water, and floating things as big as a round table but of irregular shape. Old-timers told me they were jellyfish, a Chinese delicacy often served as a cold dish. It took seventeen days of both light and heavy pitching of the ship (the seas were rough at times) to reach San Francisco from Shanghai, and for a few days after landing I still felt my feet unsteady. New York, then as now, was still forty-five hundred kilometers away. It took several more days to get there by transcontinental train and more than a week by bus. There was air service in 1947, but it was uncomfortable, much slower and more risky than it is now and the fare was prohibitively high.

Nonetheless the speed of the sea and land travel amazed me even then for I had learned from a history book that 101 years ago, in 1848, a sturdy and exceptionally lucky American created a memorable record by making the transcontinental trip in 109 days in a covered wagon typical of the days of westward expansion.

In China of the 1940s, to go from the eastern seaboard to the westernmost plateau would have taken almost a whole year including the travel by slow boat through the harzardous Yangtze River gorges and still slower rides on yakback.

But now I am making the seventeen-day trip in about seventeen hours, and another five-hour flight will take me from San Francisco to New York. Even if I had begun this trip in Lhasa, in western China's Tibet, it would take no more than a week to get to New York.

The world is shrinking and becoming a "global village," and the economic, political and psychological effects are deep and far-reaching. It drives home the truth that all must learn to live, understand, and cooperate with one another. And this is doubly true for China and America, two of the biggest "households" in the global village.

Chatting about my sea voyage with an American on the plane, I learn that there are still passenger ships plying the Pacific, but they are luxury liners operated mostly by the Nordic countries for people who have the time and money to take deluxe tours to the "exotic" Orient.

Bad and Good Luck in San Francisco

The Golden Gate Bridge in San Francisco is well-known in China as the "gateway" to America. But for travelers, the airport is the actual gateway where entry procedures are done. The airport is large but there are no escalators in some areas. I stagger along with several pieces of luggage to find myself at the very end of the queue in front of the immigration office. There are two other queues, one for American citizens and another for immigrants, and mine is for foreign visitors.

When my turn comes, a woman officer takes my passport. The application for a visa and other documents had been mailed to me by my American hosts. She looks at the papers over and over again and then disappears, keeping me waiting and worrying. She comes back almost half an hour later and returns the papers to me without uttering a word, leaving me guessing that she might be checking with the FBI or CIA about a dubious guest. Her unexplained meticulousness, however, almost prevents me from catching my next flight. If its departure had not been unexpectedly postponed for half an hour, I would have missed it. Even so, only a few minutes are left and my luggage has not gone through customs. Good luck strikes when the customs inspector, a Black American, fetches my suitcases and instead of searching them, rushes toward the gate while hurrying me along. My first regret on this trip is that I don't even have time to thank the kind-hearted gentleman.

Misfortunes never come singly, as the Chinese saying goes. I run to the gate only to find I have mislaid my boarding pass. A desperate search of my handbag and pockets yields nothing. The conductor looks on sympathetically, saying they have issued eighty-six cards and eighty-five have returned, but "sorry, we can't prove that card is yours." It is take-off time. But good luck strikes again as a man dashes forward with the card, which he has picked up somewhere. Plenty of good people everywhere!

On this leg of the trip, the plane is more than half empty. Veteran travelers have folded away the arm rests and made sleeping areas for themselves, and one gentleman is snoring loudly. It takes some time for me to calm down. There is not much to see through the window now as the plane is flying at a very high altitude.

Evening sets in. A pretty stewardess chats with me and says that planes coming in from the West Coast have to fly over the city of New York because Kennedy airport is in the southeastern corner of the city. Soon a huge pattern of thousands of lights comes into view. The brightest labyrinth, I gather, must be Manhattan Island, where I had a very pleasant time in the 1940s. And then I recognize the Hudson River, clearly marked out by the twinkling lights on the ships moored at its docks. I see the East River, with its bridges looking like sparkling necklaces. And the Empire State Building, whose many stairs I had climbed. Two towers, rising above the other skyscrapers and softly lit as if they were wrapped in Chinese "cicada-wing" gauze, must be the World Trade Center — non-existent while I was in New York. Oh, America the beautiful, a long-estranged friend is coming back after a lapse of thirty-three eventful years! Tears come to my eyes as I suddenly feel nostalgia for my younger days and excitement over the new experiences yet to come.

Sue is at the gate waiting for me. Here, at last, is an old friend to whom I can pour out my mixed feelings.

Chapter II

SEEKING THE ADVICE OF AN OLD FRIEND

Susan Warren, whom I always call Sue, is a longtime friend of China. Years before the victory of the Chinese revolution, her name appeared among those of the board members of *Far Eastern Spotlight*, a monthly published in New York advocating a democratic United States Far Eastern policy. The other board members included journalists Edgar Snow and Anna Louise Strong, the world-famous black singer Paul Robeson and other noted American progressives and liberals. Sue is now United Nations correspondent of the *U.S.-China Review*, a publication of the non-profit volunteer organization U.S.-China Peoples' Friendship Association, which plays an active role in cementing Sino-American relations. Sue's articles in the journal have won the appreciation of both American and Chinese readers. Meanwhile she teaches at Empire State College of the State University of New York and often travels to other parts of the country to lecture on China.

I feel fortunate to have such a friend who will be able to give me a few valuable pointers on how to plan my travels across the nine-million-square-kilometer country, and how to accomplish my mission. "I must have your advice before going to Boston," I tell her earnestly. Boston will be my working base because M.I.T., in direct charge of my writing project, is there.

Sue says that the hosts' idea is clear. They have invited a Chinese writer to the United States to observe, through the eyes of a stranger, the life of the American people and to record her impressions in a book. It is intended that the reader should have a sense of

21

accompanying her throughout the trip. As for "collecting materials," it simply means gathering facts and analyses from books, the press, and interviews so that the writer's inevitably limited personal observations will assume broader perspectives. Providing basic knowledge of the country is important, but too many facts and figures will turn the book into a sort of almanac. A few maps, she suggests, will suffice to show how America expanded from the original thirteen colonies to the present fifty states and how the country is geographically demarcated by mountain ranges, plains, rivers, and economic features. As for the 230 million Americans, I should always bear in mind that their composition is complex. Though most are the descendants of European immigrants, Hispanics are becoming a very populous minority and their share in the demographic chart, as well as that of Asians, is increasing. Besides, there are Black Americans and Native Americans — the Indians — whose past sufferings and present plight must not be ignored. In short, let there be no misunderstanding among the readers that America is "lily-white."

Later, in Boston, Professor Robinson's wife, Carol, tells me that she and her husband both feel that the letters I write home or to friends could form the basis of the book. This, in essence, is a proposal similar to Sue's envisioning a sort of unassuming, chatty account. It is a pity that hopping from place to place and always in a hurry, I find time only to scribble a few lines to my husband and two daughters. But the voluminous notes I take and the tapes I record do form a plentiful source for the projected book, which could be longer if I allow myself to ramble on.

Unemployment and Rent

Fresh from a relatively poor, developing country, I find New York City glittering in abundance. The city seems more beautiful and the society more affluent than in the 1940s. But the next evening after my arrival, while watching television in Sue's home, I have the first personal encounter with a perennial problem that has plagued America — unemployment. The announcer reports grimly that the rate of unemployment the previous month (April 1982) has climbed to 9.4 percent, only 0.5 percent below the 1941 level. Why 1941? Sue explains that 1941 was a record year after the "Great Depression." She then gives me a refresher course on the history of the high expectations of the 1920s — "a chicken in every pot and a car in every garage" was the political slogan. These disintegrated with the "Black Thursday" stock market crash of 1929. Then came soup lines, Hoovervilles and the New Deal, Pearl Harbor, the booming war industry and all-time high employment, and postwar prosperity alternating with cyclic recessions. Things aren't so bad now compared with the worst times.

At this point, a little girl about eight or nine years old, with big beautiful eyes, pushes open the door and comes in silently. Sue asks her to sit down for a meal, and she eats. Sue asks if her parents are still staying home, and she nods. After the meal she disappears without even saying "thank you" or "good night." Sue tells me that the girl's family, longtime neighbors, live upstairs and have been jobless for quite a while. Worried about the lovely girl, I ask Sue what will happen to the family if they are evicted? The conversation then turns to housing.

Sue and her husband live in a two-room apartment, the rooms much larger than we usually have in China. The quality of the building and the furnishings are very good by Chinese standards, and the greatest blessing of all is the round-the-clock hot water supply for bathing, which would be a rare luxury for Beijing residents. Sue has lived here since the 1930s, and the initial rent of $50 a month has risen to the present $250. New York City has a rent law that limits the rate of increase, but sets no ceiling on rent for new tenants. Thus an identical apartment on the second floor has just been rented for $1,150 a month, $900 more than Sue pays. The unemployed neighbor upstairs pays the same low rent as she, and Sue assures me that they can manage because it's a meager sum. $250 a month a meager sum? Almost $14,000 a year for the new tenant — fantastic! I understand that Americans earn high wages and have high expenses. But still the rent seems too high.

I am accustomed to the heavily subsidized state housing system in China under which people are allotted apartments at a tiny fraction of their income — usually three to five percent of an ordinary worker's monthly pay and bonuses of, say, eighty yuan *Renminbi* (one yuan was worth fifty U.S. cents during my visit and has since dropped to about 30 cents). So what Chinese urban dwellers worry about is not high rent but how to get a livable apartment. But the Chinese system is fraught with shortcomings. For one thing, what the state gets back by way of rent is not even sufficient to maintain the housing, let alone start new housing projects. Besides, the allotment system sometimes leads to favoritism or even bribery, dealings known as "going through the back door." These abuses are hated by the public. Reforms of the outdated system are being experimented with and some cities have pioneered in the sale of apartments, with the buyer paying one-third of the cost in installments over a number of years and the remaining two-thirds shared by the government and the buyer's work unit. This will enable the government to get back more money for new building construction. As incomes have risen tangibly in recent years, many Chinese are fascinated by the idea of owning an apartment even though it will cost them more than a low-rent system. With its highly developed building industry and plenty of funds, I often wonder why the United States cannot gradually alleviate the onerous burden of rent, particularly for the under-privileged.

Is rent particularly high in Greenwich Village where Sue lives? The district, she tells me, used to attract the *literati* and still preserves an antiquated look, with old-fashioned buildings and curio shops lining the narrow streets. But rent here is about the same as elsewhere in Manhattan and it is high all over the country.

My sojourn in New York is short and I have to make full use of every minute discussing America and China with Sue. She knows my country very well but this only makes her eager to learn more. She sets aside a whole closet in her none-too-spacious apartment for storing piles of back issues of the English-language journal *Beijing Review* and uses them as an important window through which to watch China. She has lots of questions to ask me and, as an old friend, does not mince words when she thinks something has gone wrong in my country. As expected, she — and a number of other old friends of China I am to meet later — seems puzzled by our complete repudiation of the "cultural revolution," not only its abuses and excesses, but its whole theory and practice. For me and countless other Chinese who personally went through the chaos, there is no difficulty at all in answering these questions. But for outsiders, who are apt to judge by the printed word, a "revolution," which had the professed aim to eliminate the privileged elite, or the so-called new bourgeoisie, seemed quite justified.

In actual fact — I have to explain again and again — there was no question of a new bourgeoisie emerging in China after the old one was expropriated in the 1950s. True enough, there were and are dark aspects in the country's political life; some bureaucrats deviate from the revolutionary tradition of serving the people and misuse their powers for selfish ends. But this is only a partial phenomenon, though it surely needed rectification then, as it does now. The problem, however, had been grossly exaggerated to the point that a "revolution" was whipped up against practically all veteran Party and government officials and intellectuals, as an "anti-socialist new elite." Meanwhile, careerists, self-seeking "go-getters" and social outcasts suddenly popped up as fervent "revolutionary rebels" against this so-called "elite." They went about insulting and injuring honest people while grabbing power and position for themselves. The result was, and indeed could only be, utter chaos.

Sue is theoretically oriented and my practical experience alone cannot answer all her questions. Sometimes we start arguing, until one or the other calls for a ceasefire. But it is heart-warming to debate with a friend whose only wish is to see China succeed in building an ideal society. That goal, I assure her, remains unchanged. But how to achieve it? As most Chinese would put it now: "Let there be no more *zheteng* (creating turmoil in the name of 'revolution' or anything else); let's get down to work — to modernize the country and earn a *xiaokang* (decent) livelihood for the 1.2 billion people by the end of the century. Socialism does not mean poverty."

For my part, I have as many, if not more, questions to ask Sue about America, but it is time to leave for Boston. As it turns out, I do have more time to talk with Sue, for I had left my luggage at Kennedy airport, not knowing that my domestic flight would leave from LaGuardia, clear across Queens. So we have a long ride across the borough from one airport to the other. I keep urging the taxi driver to hurry until he complains he may get in trouble for speeding. How I wish I had time to relax and be just a tourist! But as a reporter, my job is to pester people with questions all the way from New York to Alaska, from Maine to Florida, and I must get on with it.

Chapter III
THREE MONTHS IN BOSTON

Boston, approximately four hundred kilometers to the northeast of New York City, is the state capital of Massachusetts and an industrial-commercial center of New England. In population (1980 census), Greater Boston ranks tenth among American cities. But it is first in its revolutionary and cultural traditions. Not only was the first shot of the American War of Independence fired in Boston, but the first American college, Harvard, was established there.

There are hourly flights between New York and Boston. The passenger simply goes to the airport, buys a ticket and flies as convenient as a bus ride. The plane arrives at Logan airport half an hour later. Professor Richard Robinson is waiting for me at the exit. Smiling amiably, the tall white-haired professor shakes my hand, saying, "Madam Wang, you have come all alone. You are brave!"

"Madam" — the word is a cultural shock for me. I have to digress a little to explain why, and begin with names. Chinese names usually consist of two or three characters, i.e., two or three monosyllabic ideographs, the first being the family name and the other one or two the given name. In old times, girls were almost always given names symbolizing beauty and chastity, while the names of boys often indicated virtue and achievement. *Spring Moon*, a best-selling novel by Bette Bao Lord (wife of the present U.S. ambassador to China, Mr. Winston Lord), quite typically names some of its male and female characters Sterling Talent and Fierce Rectitude, Spring Moon and Lustrous Jade.

As for forms of address, the old way in China was about the same as in America now. People were formally called *Mr., Miss,* or *Mrs.* But since revolution has brought about drastic changes in customs, "comrade" has been used to address everybody, irrespective of age and marital status. A woman would be offended if she were called *Mrs.* together with her husband's name, for that would imply that she was an appendage to her spouse. A young lady would not like to be called *Miss* which sounds like she is a social butterfly. Familiar friends and colleagues call each other by their surnames preceded by *lao* (old) or *xiao* (young) depending on one's age — *Lao* Wang or *Xiao* Wang, for instance, instead of *Comrade* Wang.

In recent years, however, contacts with Westerners have become so frequent that the words *Mr., Miss* and *Mrs.* have been picked up again when meeting foreigners. But a married woman only adds *Mrs.* to her own name and brushes aside her husband's name altogether. As for *madam*, it is exclusively reserved for the wives of visiting foreign dignitaries. Hence the shock when I hear Professor Robinson call me "Madam Wang."

But after all I am not a complete stranger to American ways. Before long I start calling the professor Dick in the informal American way I like, and he calls me Wang Tso, an affectionate nickname my friends gave me in college days.

THE PROFESSOR'S FAMILY

Dick drives through a tunnel under the Charles River onto an expressway. The network of American highways is an engineering wonder. It plays an important role in American civilization by linking all parts of the vast continent into a closely-knit whole. We soon arrive at a town called Newton which is quite a distance away from downtown Boston. The professor's home, surrounded by trees and lawns, is in the town.

Carol Robinson comes out of her kitchen to greet me. She has a very good figure and looks much younger than her age. The couple's sixteen-year-old twins, ninth grade students, are also at home. Julie is twelve minutes older than her brother, Eric. Dick also "introduces" me to the family pet, a fat, slow-moving dog. "He has lived fifteen years and had a good life," Dick says.

I take a quick glance at the house. There are two fairly large sitting rooms, a dining room, a study for the professor, a big kitchen and a bathroom. The bedrooms are upstairs. Susan Warren's apartment in New York appeared to me to be exquisitely furnished and well disposed for the scholar. So does Dick's home, though it also strikes my Chinese eyes as quite luxurious. I had seen similar houses owned by wealthy businessmen and comfortably situated intellectuals in pre-revolution Shanghai and Beijing. Nowadays, in a largely egalitarian society where the general standard of living is not high, even ranking officials in China usually live in sparsely furnished houses or apartments though they are much more spacious than the cramped living quarters of ordinary citizens. But American millionnaires, I suppose, will sneer at me for describing the professor's house as "luxurious."

Carol treats me to a delicious dinner, by candlelight, as is the custom with many other American families. The dinner consists of two courses, one meat and one vegetable, plus salad, dessert and tea or coffee. Fresh from China, I compare everything with the Chinese ways. The dinner makes me feel that the age-old Chinese custom of feting guests with many courses should be simplified. It is not so much a question of money as of time, particularly because Chinese housewives often have to line up to purchase good foods. Over-hospitality has led to the opposite; many Chinese families feel reluctant to entertain foreign guests because they believe that something special has to be prepared but find it too time consuming. I am in no way casting a reflection on American hospitality. In fact, I have long found myself in agreement with some outspoken American visitors to China who complain about the waste of twelve-course banquets.

The professor is very friendly. He carries my luggage from the car to the house and turns a sitting room into a temporary bedroom for me. I find myself resting comfortably in a sort of greenhouse with pot-flowers and mini-landscapes on shelves or suspended from the ceiling, also a sort of curio shop with antique plates, vases, bowls, jars and pots displayed all around. Dick shows me the Chinese, Japanese or Korean markings on the bottoms of these *objets-d'art,* a testimony to his interest in the Orient where, he tells me, he served during World War II. After the war he worked for some time in Turkey and elsewhere in the East. In his study I find an enlarged photo of Edgar Snow, the Missouri-educated American journalist who ventured into the Chinese Communist areas in the 1930s, became a personal friend of Mao Zedong, Zhou Enlai and other Chinese leaders and wrote the book *Red Star Over China*, which is treasured by Chinese till the present day. The photo, Dick tells me, was taken in the 1940s when he, as the correspondent of a Chicago newspaper, met Snow in South Korea. That the photo is hung so prominently in his study, I think, shows the professor's respect for the late Snow, who foresaw victory for the Chinese revolution while it was at its weak beginnings.

Carol is a busy person. She teaches foreigners English in a social studies center, and tells me that the experience may enable her to go to China some day to teach English as a second language. She goes to the market, prepares the daily meals for the family and does the laundering and ironing in the basement.

The basement attracts me because of the small wood shop there. Eric is working in the shop to build a model cabin complete with plumbing and furnishings. The tendency of many young Americans to want to learn a trade while still in the teenage years leaves a favorable impression on me. In China, the Confucian tradition of treasuring book learning above everything else and disdaining all trades and professions except officialdom, has been repudiated. But old ideas die hard. Young students often lack the ability to work with their hands. This has aroused concern among educators and parents.

The basement also attracts me because of a display of many sea shells — like the multifarious watches and clocks in the glass cases of a Chinese watch repairer's shop. They were collected by Dick, who has spent many years on seashores. He was born in the state of Washington and educated at the state university in Seattle on the Pacific coast. He moved to the Atlantic coast to get his doctoral degree from Harvard and then began teaching at M.I.T.

Dick, now a professor of international management at M.I.T.'s Sloan School, is also busy. I often hear him writing at his typewriter as soon as he gets home from work. I have heard people say that American professors are faced with the choice of "publish or perish." It means that failure to produce publishable works will damage their prestige and may even cost the jobs of those who have not been awarded tenure.

The twins are busy, too. After school, Julie works three times a week for two hours at the town library. Her job is to return books to the proper shelves, a task American libraries stress in order that each book can be readily found at any time. The job is rewarding, not for the pay of $2.25 an hour, but for the interest in books the work has engendered in her. Eric, in his spare time, works in his carpenter shop or practices violin while Carol accompanies him on the piano.

My visit makes Dick and Carol busier than usual. He has to take me to M.I.T., arrange for me to see people, and get a card from the library for me, and so on. Carol "provides wheels" for me whenever I go out, making me wonder how America could keep going if all automobiles stopped running for twenty-four hours.

Friendly and Open-minded

Before long the Robinsons and I know each other well enough to be informal. Both Chinese and Americans like humor. While helping Carol in her kitchen I see the batteries of different sized knives, strainers with big, small, and tiny holes, the toaster, the micro-wave oven, the regular electric stove, a great variety of strange-looking cooking utensils, and the piles of dishes after a day's meals. I tease Carol by saying, "We in China can cook a nice dinner with nothing more than a rice cooker, a pot, and a mixing spoon. But look at your American kitchen with all these gadgets! It seems you have to have a big hole for a big cat, a small hole for a small cat and one hundred holes for one hundred cats!" Carol laughs, saying, "Listen to Wang Tsomin jibing at us!" Occasional jokes like this bring us closer.

But more often we discuss serious subjects. I ask, for instance, what exactly is meant by the often-used American term "middle class." Dick says that he belongs to the middle class, and adds after a few moments that he belongs to the upper-middle class. Carol joins in, saying, for example, that rich oil magnates cannot be considered middle class if they have had little education. This leaves me puzzled, because we in China believe that social classes are defined by people's relationship to the "means of production," farms and factories for instance, and not by their standard of living, still less by their level of education. Those who own "the means of production" and derive the greater part of their income by exploiting the labor of workers or peasants belong to the capitalist or landlord class. Those who earn their living by "selling their labor power" are the working people. Dick apparently knows something about the Chinese criteria and says to Carol that her definition is not Marxist.

Dick is not a Marxist either. But he does not consider Marxism a heresy. I find later on my trip that many Americans, like Dick, are open-minded (liberal or "enlightened" as we say in China), ready to hear differing views and to absorb new ones.

Visiting the library where Julie works, I see a poster calling on people to attend a town meeting and vote on a "nuclear freeze" resolution. Before arriving in the United States, I read much about the anti-nuclear movement but did not realize that it had gained such momentum. In Boston I see many cars carrying placards with skull and crossbones painted on them to dramatize the nuclear menace. I tell Dick that I am interested in the town meeting. He tells me that active supporters of the "nuclear freeze" are often condemned as serving Communist interests. "People all over the world want peace," I say. "Why should you limit the privilege of expressing the people's wish to Communists or Soviets?" "I'm not saying that," Dick explains. "You should know that just a few years ago people advocating full diplomatic recognition of China were also branded as serving Communist interests."

Dick says that he would like to accompany me to the town meeting. He is not particularly interested in the "nuclear freeze" drive but has an open mind on the issue. Besides, he is always ready to help me see anything I want to see.

I am also interested in meeting some less fortunate people. Hearing this, Dick immediately suggests that I have a good talk with Ida Uttaro, a domestic worker who comes once a week to help clean their house. "Ida is a woman of very modest income," he says. "Given the fact that her husband is permanently bound to a wheelchair, the church is particularly important to her. It's a place where she receives consolation and social support." Carol explains that she herself could probably take care of the house cleaning, but has asked Ida to help so that she has more time for her own work as a travel agent, and to be with Dick. "Ida is proud, a good worker, and a good friend. She cleans the house almost effortlessly. I am not that able," Carol says. "She is also fun to have in the house."

The Robinson family impresses me as being very friendly and sincere, open-minded, and sympathetic to those less fortunate than themselves. I feel happy that immediately after leaving my old friend Susan Warren in New York, I have come to know these new friends. It augurs well for my trip.

What Is Meant by Middle Class

I return to the question of middle class since I am often told that America is a "middle-class country." To put it more figuratively, American society is like a spindle whose two ends — the very rich and the very poor — are small groups. People also talk about the upper class, the working class, and blue-collar and white-collar workers. What exactly do they mean?

In China we attach great importance to social classes. For instance, whether an urban resident was formerly (before the revolution) a factory owner or a worker, whether a rural resident was formerly a landlord, a rich peasant or a working peasant, made a world of difference as far as his political and social status was concerned. Capitalists, landlords and rich peasants were exploiters, and workers and peasants were the exploited. Intellectuals (professors, teachers, doctors, scientists and others) were considered neither exploiters nor exploited. It was only after the "cultural revolution" that the labels were removed from all but a few surviving landlords and rich peasants, and full, equal citizenship was granted to them.

China's standards certainly cannot be applied to America or, for that matter, to any other country. But then how is American society stratified? I try to find a widely accepted, not necessarily Marxist, classification. Finally I come across an interesting book, *Sociology**, by Ián Robertson. The author provides a general outline which he says "most sociologists would probably accept."

* *Sociology*, 2nd edition, published in 1981 by Worth Publishers, Inc., New York, N.Y.

American society, according to Mr. Robertson, consists of three classes, each containing two elements. The "upper upper" class comprises the "old aristocracy of birth and wealth." Its members tend to know one another personally, to attend the same schools, to visit the same resorts, and to intermarry. The "lower upper" class may actually have more money, better houses and larger automobiles than the upper uppers, but they lack the "breeding" to be accepted into the highest circles. The distinction, however, is not generally recognized by the rest of society, and is of little importance outside the elite circles themselves. The upper uppers and lower uppers combined constitute one to three percent of the American population.

The middle class is sub-divided into two strata. The "upper middle" class consists primarily of high-income managers, professionals and high-level executives with college training and an accumulation of property through savings. They represent about ten to fifteen percent of the population. Members of the "lower middle" class are usually small-business people and farmers, semi-professionals, sales and clerical workers who have a modest income, some savings, and a college or a high school education. They constitute thirty to thirty-five percent of the population.

The "upper lower," or working class, consists primarily of blue-collar workers — small tradespeople, service personnel and skilled or unskilled laborers. They are characterized by low income, some savings and a high school or grade school education. These people represent forty to forty-five percent of the population.

Finally the "lower lower" class, often simply called the lower class, includes "the permanently unemployed, the homeless, the illiterate, the chronic 'skid-row' alcoholic, and the impoverished aged." They represent as much as twenty to twenty-five percent of the population. Although certain members of the upper lower, or working class, earn incomes higher than some lower middle-class members, Mr. Robertson writes, they lack "prestige" in American society and cannot be rated as middle class.

These are my broad generalizations from Mr. Robertson's general outlines of American class structure. I am in no position to judge their merit. I cite the analysis here as "one of the hundred schools of contending thought" as we might call it in China. Nonetheless, it helps me understand why Dick readily classifies himself as upper-middle class, and why Carol takes educational level into consideration in her disdainful reference to the oil barons.

Careful readers may point out that the above percentages don't add up. Let me stress again that it is a rough sketch. The term "middle class" which I use often in subsequent chapters should be understood in its American, not Chinese, context. Standard writings in China regard "middle class" as the lower echelon of the bourgeoisie, "national capitalists" next to the "bureaucratic-compradore* capitalists" who ran both big business and the government with the backing of foreign imperialists in pre-revolutionary China.

JULIE'S HIGH SCHOOL

I tell Dick that I would like to visit a high school. There are more than 13.3 million high school students in the United States and I should get an idea of their school life.

But I feel hesitant. I do not want to appear as an object of curiosity to teenagers and be watched like a monkey in the zoo. In China, *wai bin* (foreign guests) visiting schools often get this treatment from the friendly kids. Julie's high school is in Weston, a town west of Boston. With a population of only 11,500 and no particular sights to see, the small town rarely sees Chinese visitors.

Dick drives me to the school, along with Julie, who has skipped the bus in order to accompany me. Since students live in all parts of the town (none of the American towns are as compact as their Chinese counterparts), there is a free school bus service.

The beautiful school buildings are surrounded by lawns and trees and the atmosphere is exceedingly tranquil. Students rush to their classrooms almost noiselessly. I feel relieved that nobody seems to notice me, a Chinese stranger dressed quite differently, even when I take a seat in a classroom. American society is generally cosmopolitan and even children reveal little curiosity about foreigners.

---

* The word "compradore" originally means a buyer for a foreign business in China and certain other Asian countries.

The wide hall between classrooms is lined with olive-green lockers on both sides. They have spring locks and each has a number painted in white. They look like those in Chinese public bath houses but are made of metal instead of wood. Julie leaves her coat and schoolbag in her locker and leads me to her geometry class. She obtains the consent of the teacher for me to sit in the classroom as a listener. I have forgotten all my geometry lessons and have only a faint memory of the teacher coming in with a big wooden T-Square to draw on the blackboard. But here the teacher pushes buttons and all sorts of circles, triangles and squares appear on a screen as large as a blackboard. It is time-saving and the figures are of course more accurate than hand-drawn ones.

When the class is over, Julie leads me to her second class of the morning — typing. A woman teacher briefly explains the exercises to be done and the students start working on office-size typewriters. The teacher moves around but no student raises any question. She then comes out of the classroom to talk with me. This, she says, is probably the richest town in Massachusetts and most residents here are business executives or professional people. At least ninety percent of the students in the school will go on to college. They are learning typing not as a trade but as an aid to their studies. Julie, however, types very well and can become a professional typist if she wants. I ask how fast a student is required to type in her class. She replies that forty-five words (five key-strokes count as a word) per minute would be rated as superior but "speed with errors is no speed."

Having finished her exercise, Julie shows me the way to the library and says that she will come to meet me at lunch time. The library has large reading tables, all vacant now because students are attending classes. After glancing over the periodical racks, I go to the catalogue drawers to see if there are any books on China. Under the heading of "Mao Zedong", I find three books: *Mao Tse-tung, An Anthology of His Writings*, edited by Anne Freemantle and published by the New American Library; *Mao Tse-tung; Political Leaders of the 20th Century*, a Penguin book written by Stuart Schram; and *Mao and the Chinese Revolution* by Jerome Ch'en, Oxford University Press. Then I look in the author index for Edgar Snow and find four of his books including *Red Star Over China*. I borrow from the librarian a book entitled *Chinese*

Communism, Selected Documents edited by Dan N. Jacobs and Hans H. Baerwald (a Harper Torchbook). On the card attached to its inside back cover, I find names signed by more than ten borrowers. It is impressive that there are readers of such an academic work even among high school students. There are a number of other books on China I would like to look at, but Julie has come to take me to lunch.

The dining hall is also quiet. There are many serving windows where foods are sold for cash. I choose the regular menu of the day and pay only ninety cents for two large pieces of fried chicken with fried potatoes, two small dishes of boiled peas and sliced cabbage, plus dessert, butter and a small bread. A similar meal in a small restaurant outside would cost at least four dollars. Julie explains that the standard menu is subsidized by the government. The diners put their food in a tray, pick up plastic knives, forks, and paper napkins, and then move to the dining tables to eat. Julie's food, an assortment of salads plus milk, costs $1.25. I have not finished my meal when Julie hurries me, saying that the next batch of diners is coming in and we have to make room for them. The students dump everything left, including the trays, the cute little knives and forks, and much food, into a waste can. I am not accustomed to these practices and feel that the Americans are too wasteful.

After the meal I meet James Ryan, a counselor in the guidance department. The department, Mr. Ryan tells me, has a chairman and four counselors who help the students select courses and prepare for fields of study after their graduation. The counselors keep themselves posted on the progress and interests of their students through contacts with teachers and parents, and offer them advice on elective courses so as to give full scope to their talents. There are many electives, among them computer studies. Because expenses for making computer study a compulsory course have yet to be approved by the Town Meeting, Mr. Ryan explains, it remains an elective.

In discussing school finances Mr. Ryan says that at least half the expenses of American public school education are provided by local authorities — by the town of Weston in the case of his school. Forty percent comes from the state government and the remaining ten percent from the federal government. America, Mr. Ryan says, was the world's pioneer in making elementary and middle school education compulsory, and has set up a large number of public schools. There are, however, also some private schools. A town usually derives its income from real estate taxes. The other taxes, income tax and sales tax for instance, go to the state and federal governments as prescribed by law. The town, as the basic administrative unit, supervises the finances of the local public schools. It also appoints and removes the principals and teachers, and determines the guidelines for education. The children of Weston residents attend school free, but non-residents have to pay very high tuition. Mr. Ryan cites himself, a non-resident, as an example, saying that he would not be able to afford to send his children to the school. Is it possible to move the family to the town? I ask. Mr. Ryan says that houses and rents here are too expensive for people of the lower income brackets.

What Mr. Ryan says confirms my earlier impression that disparities exist between different American public schools. Those in poor localities are often short of funds, pay lower salaries to their teachers, and lack adequate teaching facilities and equipment. And this accounts for the lower level of their education. I often hear Americans say that equal opportunities in their country is embodied first in equal educational opportunities. But this seems to be more of an ideal than reality as far as middle school education is concerned. For elementary and higher education, as I shall report later, similar inequalities also exist.

Explaining the goals of the school, Mr. Ryan lists ten points which have been formulated according to state guidelines. The first two objectives are: "To develop the basic skills (reading, writing, speaking, listening, observing, analyzing and computing) needed for communication, perception, evaluation, and conceptualization of ideas; and to provide awareness of man's cultural heritage through study of history, the arts, literature and science."

"Bookworms" Won't Do

To "build a solid college application," Mr. Ryan continues, the school has laid down four points. To put it in a nutshell, the students are required not only to perform well in the study of the academic core and elective courses, but at the same time to participate in activities outside the classroom, in sports programs, publications, student government, and community volunteer work as "evidence of personal competence and commitment." That is to say, the school does not place one-sided emphasis on book learning — a deviation now being criticized in China for it tends to promote students "with high exam marks but low working ability" — bookworms, in short.

Later, I have the opportunity to attend the graduation exercises of Dover's Sherborn High School in the Boston area. A highlight of the ceremony is the recognition of outstanding graduates. Most of the awards are given to students who have been conscientious in one or another kind of work outside the classroom — for abilities as an organizer, or for good performances in the school band or football team, for instance. In comparison, fewer awards are given for purely academic achievements, evidence that they don't care much about "pedants."

Julie has to go to the Weston Public Library and work two hours in the afternoon. Carol picks us up in her car. I thank Mr. Ryan, who has given me a very informative interview.

According to Mr. Ryan, the public school systems vary greatly from place to place in the United States and there is hardly any uniform rule. But in the Greater Boston area, children usually go to kindergarten at the age of four or five and to the first grade at the age of five or six. Some localities rate the first eight years (from first to eighth grade) as elementary education and the remaining four (from ninth to twelfth grade) as high school. But students do not have to sit for entrance exams. Julie is attending the ninth grade, the equivalent to third grade of junior middle school in China.

In China, the system is uniform nationwide: children go to grade school at the age of six or seven, study for six years before they move on to a three-year junior middle school. Some will rise to three-year senior middle schools. Only a lucky few will find their way into universities and colleges. The students have to take exams to qualify for both junior and senior middle schools. Competition for college enrollment is much keener. In recent years, more vocational schools have been opened to replace general senior middle schools.

Chinese children, however, have many more chances to go to full-time nurseries than in America.

Soon after my visit to the Weston High School, I happen to meet an American who knows a lot about Boston schools. She tells me that Weston is one of the best schools, but even then it cannot compare with the two private schools in the town. Only wealthy families can afford to send their children to the private schools because both of them are boarding schools that charge very high prices. She suggests that I should see some poorer public schools to get a balanced picture. One of her friends, a history teacher, recently resigned because she was beaten twice by her students. These incidents took place in a Dorchester school on the south end of Boston. The students, she says, are mostly whites. They have to go through an electronic search at the school gate as passengers do at an airport, so that no pistols or knives will be brought in. Massachusetts, she tells me, ranks among the top ten states granting the largest sums of money to their public schools. Indeed, the average amount per school and student is relatively high. But the trouble is that schools in poor districts get much less than the average.

I met a Black American, Aukram Burton, at the Boston chapter of the U.S-China Peoples' Friendship Association. He had worked for more than ten years as a public school teacher. He tells me that practically all prosperous families have moved from the inner city to the suburbs and the vacancies left have been filled by the poor. "Go and have a look if you don't believe it. All public schools in what we call the inner city are attended by Blacks and Asians. The percentage of whites is very small. The quality of the schools is poor, and it is the same in other major cities."

Before my arrival in the United States, I had read some discussions on the quality of education there. I am struck by two points which Americans invariably emphasize when I talk with them about this question. Tracing fluctuations over the past thirty years, they recall the stimulus American education got from the Soviet launching of *Sputnik* in 1957. Since World War II, the United States had tried to remain unsurpassed in all scientific and technological fields. Consequently, the Soviet lead in space technology came as a shock. As a result, great emphasis was focused on education, particularly in space-related sciences, but efforts have relaxed with the progress of American space technology.

Another point they stress is competition with Japan. International relations are intricate. Politically, Japan is a close ally of the United States, but many Americans seem to regard it as the worst adversary of their business-minded country. Japan is a frequent topic in daily conversation. When it comes to education, people often say that Japan is doing better and that the United States must catch up. This is usually followed by complaints about huge federal military expenditures. They say that a tiny fraction of money which goes to the military, if diverted to education, would lift many American public schools from their sorry plight.

"WHAT TO DO IF YOU'RE SICK?"

This question is repeatedly posed to me by my American friends, soon after my arrival. They keep telling me that a visit to a doctor will cost $60 to $70 and hospitalization will cost thousands. It is not like in China where most workers and all government employees are covered by a public health program under which we pay 10 *fen* (3 cents) to visit a doctor, and pay only for food if hospitalized. In short, they tell me I have to get some kind of medical insurance. Quite unexpectedly this leads me to a personal experience with bureaucracy and red tape in the United States.

Rita Gould of Boston, an American devoted to close relations between our two countries, and who is very kind to me personally, helps to arrange for a salesman from a medical insurance company to meet me in her home. Hearing my circumstances the gentleman tells me that I must get a certificate from the local Social Security office proving that I do not have "medicare" benefits. I explain that I am a new arrival from China, obviously ineligible for any Social Security benefit, but he insists that I must have that written certificate.

Reluctantly I go to the local office of the Social Security Administration to apply for a certificate. They keep me waiting for quite a while and finally come up with the answer that I have to get, first of all, a "Social Security card" and apply for "medicare." I can go back and wait, and the card will be mailed to me in one or two months. I explain that I have no job in the U.S. and have not paid any Social Security tax. How can I draw anything from a bank if I have not deposited any money there? This is only common sense, I point out. What I need is simply a document certifying that I am not eligible for any Social Security benefits. I need no card. They insist that I must have a card and that this is official procedure. Well, what can you do about *official* procedure?

Two months later I receive the card. I go to the office again and the answer I get is that with the card I can now fill out an application for "medicare" and then wait for "a notice of disapproved claim" which will be the official certificate I need. "Be patient and you will get the notice within a month," they console me.

I explain again that I don't need to apply for care, medical or otherwise, because I know as well as they do that I am not entitled to Social Security benefits. What I need is a certificate so that I can pay for my own medical insurance. But that's the official procedure! My voice gets louder as I find it difficult to control my temper. An official, apparently of a higher rank, comes out, invites me to his office and inquires about my trouble. I repeat the story once more, stressing that I don't want to apply for anything but must have a certificate.

The gentleman carefully reads my papers and finds that I am to write a book about America. "A book about America. What are you going to write?" he asks. Unable to restrain myself, I reply: "Everything, including the bureaucracy here!"

"Oh, you speak English so fluently," the gentleman says. After a little while, he suggests that he can write me an "unofficial" notice of disapproval and I may try to see whether it will be accepted. Since I don't want to fill out an application, he says, he can do it for me because all the relevant information is contained in my papers. The only thing I have to do is to sign the form. While saying this, he begins to fill the form for me. Then he tells me that if his "unofficial" notice is not accepted, I don't have to worry because the official one will reach me in about one month. It appears that nobody can do anything about the *official* procedure. But the gentleman has been conciliatory enough, and I leave.

Rita insists on my having a try with the "unofficial" notice and takes me to a downtown building housing a national insurance company, Blue Cross and Blue Shield. A woman there provides me with information about different types of policies under which I have to pay from $60 to $200 a month, depending on the range of coverage. When I have got a rough idea of all the complexities and begun to chose the policy, the woman then tells me that the company will start paying my medical expenses nine months after the policy is taken.

"Nine months," I exclaim, "I'll be back in China by then!"

'That's why I have to tell you," she says politely and explains that this is a safeguard against people who have found themselves affected with a chronic disease and come to take out an insurance policy.

At this point even the most zealous friends advising me to get medical insurance leave me to chance. When I leave Boston two months later, the official "notice of disapproved claim" comes by mail all the way from the northeastern program service center of the Social Security Administration in Flushing, New York. Busy packing my luggage, I throw the letter and the card too, into the wastebasket.

What Is "Social Security"

So much for my story. But my Chinese readers are likely to ask what is "Social Security?"

The American Social Security program has a history of nearly half a century since Congress adopted the "Social Security Act" of 1935. It has evolved and grown so much that today one out of every six Americans is drawing "Social Security benefits" in one way or another. Practically all wage earners as well as their employers are paying "Social Security taxes" to the federal government. Volumes have been written on the subject and I can only cover a few points of particular interest.

To begin with, where does the money come from? The 1935 Act provided that an employee earning $3,000 a year had to pay $30 as "Social Security tax," or one percent of his income. In addition, his employer must pay a matching sum, i.e., $30 for the employee. Likewise, a worker earning $1,000 a year had to pay $10 and his employer the same amount. But $30 was the ceiling. A factory manager earning $30,000 a year, for instance, had to pay only $30 and his employer, the factory owner, the same sum. This was because the 1935 Act stipulated that "Social Security taxes" were set at one percent of "the first $3,000" of an employee's pay. To put it in another way, the tax rate was one percent for people below "the annual earnings base" of $3,000, but lower for those above the base — the higher the income, the lower the rate.

Over the past five decades, the annual earnings base has risen from $3,000 to $32,400 (1982) and $35,700 (1983), and tax rate from one percent to 6.7 percent. The requirement for employers to pay a matching sum remains unchanged. But many American writers on the subject point out that while the tax means actual deductions from the employees' paychecks, the employers can include their matching funds into the cost of their products and services and thus shift the burden onto consumers, that is, onto society at large. In the meantime, critics also underline the fact that people with incomes higher than "the annual earnings base" pay only 6.7 percent of the "first $35,700" of their income and are exempted from levy on the remainder however large it may be. This actually means lower tax rates for those in the higher income brackets. It can hardly be called fair, they point out.

People covered by the Social Security program receive full retirement benefits at the age of sixty-five, and 80 percent if they retire at the age of sixty-two. Beneficiaries over the age of sixty-five are also entitled to "medicare." In addition, the program also includes benefits for the disabled and for the spouses and children under eighteen of the deceased. But there is no "medicare" for people under sixty-five whose health insurance is either arranged by their employers or provided for by private insurance companies — in either case the insured must pay a substantial amount as premium.

Unemployment benefits are another matter. The source of the funds, and the sum and duration of the benefits paid, vary from state to state. Take 1982 for example: There are 11.7 million beneficiaries in the country who receive an average weekly payment of $119.34 for total unemployment over an average period of 15.9 weeks. This may seem a handsome sum in Chinese terms. But it is actually very moderate compared with American wages, and the average time limit — 15.9 weeks — seems very short.

Then there is "welfare," an entirely different program. It would be called "social relief" in China. Under the program, large numbers of poor people, many with no income at all, get various types of government aid. They are usually referred to as people "on welfare," and are often thought to sponge from the taxpayers.

Now let me return to the subject of Social Security. Because of the prolonged recession since 1975 and the steady rise of unemployment to a new peak of 13 million in 1982, the amount of Social Security taxes paid decreased accordingly. In the meantime, with life expectancy lengthening, recipients of retirement benefits and medicare kept on increasing. Consequently the Social Security program came to the verge of bankruptcy in 1982. The question debated in Washington was how to keep it going? The press reported almost daily on the heated debate in and outside Congress. A compromise "package deal" was finally worked out by the Republicans and Democrats.

But many of the proposed formulas which were intended to make the program solvent are likely to create new problems. Gradual increase of the age of retirement from 65 to 67, for instance, seems to be an effective measure to increase the number of Social Security taxpayers while reducing the number of beneficiaries. But as one economist rightly complains: "Armchair professors and bureaucrats who sit behind desks pushing a pencil all day can work until the age of sixty-eight without any serious difficulty while manual workers are too worn out to stay on the job that long." There are other future problems. When Americans born during the postwar "baby boom" years (1947-1964), reach retirement age, a situation ancient Chinese sages warned against — "fewer producers and more eaters" — will emerge. According to demographers, there are now 43 million people born during the peak decade (1955-1964) of the "baby boom" years, and 33 million born during the subsequent decade (1970-1979) of "baby bust." The ten-million disparity between the two figures is big enough to create a social problem. We in China often dismiss imaginary fears as "worries of a man of the Qi kingdom that the sky might fall." American discussions about "a demographic disaster for Social Security beginning from the year 2010" seem better founded than the Qi man's worry. But it is a long-range problem demanding no immediate solution, and the sky won't fall anyway.

CALL THEM "SENIOR CITIZENS"

Unlike the Chinese, Americans don't like the epithet "old." Seldom is an American old folks' home called that. But the name of the one I am going to visit seems a bit too exaggerated. Its name is "Francis Cabot Lowell Mills." A parallel example would be to call the home for the aged housed in the once-famous Shanghai Jiangnan shipyard, "The Shipyard."

For the sake of clarity for my Chinese readers, I take the liberty of calling it the "Lowell Home for the Aged." It is in an Italian district in the town of Waltham, about eighteen miles northwest of downtown Boston. Carol Robinson's domestic help, Ida Uttaro, who is a descendant of Italian immigrants, lives there and introduces me to the institution.

Financed by a private development company, two buildings of the defunct Lowell Mill were renovated in 1979-80 for the present purpose. The home has 258 apartments, most of which consist of a single room plus kitchen and bath. They are all occupied, by more than three-hundred residents. Only one-fifth of them are married couples; the rest are widows and widowers. Citizens below the age of sixty-five are not eligible to live there.

A woman shows us around and answers my questions. The buildings are new, the walls plastered with plastic paper, and the floors covered with plastic carpets. The colors are carefully selected and the whole place is kept spotless. We first look at the public facilities on the ground floor, including a reading room, a recreation room, a hall for festive gatherings, and a laundry room where you drop 50 cents into a machine to wash a load of eight to nine pounds of laundry, and 75 cents to dry in another machine. We also have a look at the outdoor grounds and see people lying on folding chairs and enjoying the May sunshine, and others fishing along the banks of the Charles River that runs alongside the former mill.

The main income of the residents here, I am told, is their Social Security retirement benefits. The sums vary, depending on how much Social Security tax one has paid before retirement. Even those enjoying maximum benefits, however, cannot afford to live here if they do not have extra incomes. The monthly rent for an apartment, the woman says, is $545.

Don't they have to pay other expenses, apart from rent? I ask her. She replies that the rent collected in any case does not exceed one-fourth of the residents' income and they can keep the remainder for other use. The discrepancy is made up by state and federal subsidies. That is why there are many applicants on the waiting list. "They have to wait for perhaps a few years," she adds. At this point I notice that Ida is winking at me, a hint that some "back-door connection," as we would call it in China, is probably necessary to gain admittance.

There is a kitchen in every apartment and the residents are required to be healthy enough to take care of themselves. Therefore no public dining hall is available. Adequate safeguards are provided against any emergency. Every apartment is equipped with two buttons, one in the bedroom and the other in the bathroom, so that the staff will get a signal either in the office or at home in off-hours. Though there is a telephone in every apartment, an old gentleman or lady may suddenly become too sick to dial. In America, it often happens that old people living alone are found dead days after their hearts stopped beating.

In discussing telephones, the lady tells me that the service, as well as electricity for lamps, stoves and fans, are charged separately so that the residents will economize. Running water, hot and cold, is free.

There are special safeguards against intruders, who can easily prey on the old. Any outsider wishing to see the resident of Apartment One, for example, must push the No. 1 button on a board after he comes into the building. The resident is thus notified that somebody is coming, and can push a button to allow entrance into the hall. But to make sure that the visitor is not an intruder, a closed circuit TV can be switched on and the visitor viewed on the screen. The residents keep their apartment doors locked all the time and nobody can get in unadmitted. Fire and other safety measures are all well devised.

Comfortable but Lonely

The woman leads us upstairs to visit Mr. and Mrs. George Caldwell in their apartment. As we pass through the hall, we see decorations on every door, multi-colored plastic flowers, exotic toy animals, and human caricatures. They make me feel that the old people here still enjoy life. Suddenly a door opens and a white-haired, bony old lady comes out. She keeps saying "telephone, telephone," loudly. Ida knows from her accent that she is Italian and starts talking to her in that language. What the old lady wants is some help to phone her family, probably because dialing is difficult for her. Ida follows her into the room, and so do Carol and I.

It is a one-room apartment, adequately furnished with a single bed, a sofa, a dining table, a TV set, an electric fan. The telephone is on a small writing desk. Ida dials and then speaks in English to the person answering the phone: "She will not ask you to take her home, but only wants to say hello to you." She gives the receiver to the old lady, who begins talking loudly in Italian. She does not speak English at all, Ida tells me.

Our guide seems displeased with the unexpected appearance of the untidy and bony Italian woman. I hasten to explain that her's is a quite comfortable home in comparison with the standard of developing countries. I ask her if the old lady is in her nineties. She seems to be pleasant again, saying that the lady is eighty but looks older than her age. What saddens me is that Ida had to assure her kin in the first place that she would not ask for a home visit. Why not take her home once in a while? She must be very lonely.

We then go on to the Caldwell's apartment. It is a four-room flat with good furniture in the sitting room and nice bedding in the bedroom. On the wall hang pictures of their grandchildren. They show me the photos one by one while I keep saying "how lovely" and "how cute," as the children really are. But the guide whispers into my ears: "The trouble is that they don't come to visit them."

In the elevator I meet two Chinese. We start talking in our language. The two gentlemen tell me that they are going to see a Chinese woman living here who has just fallen seriously ill. The guide says that there are three Chinese couples and three singles living here. "They have a good spirit of unity and always help one another," she comments.

In a room downstairs some residents are playing a game of chance called "Bingo." They sit at desks with numbered squares and place markers on them. A caller, like a teacher in a classroom, loudly calls out: "Sixty-three... eighty-five...." I can identify the winners by the broad smiles on their faces. "Bingo," I am told, is a kind of gambling that involves small stakes and is allowed at the home as a pastime.

At the gate I meet another Chinese living here. Learning that I have come from Beijing, he invites me to his apartment. But I have to leave for other appointments. He gives me his phone number and writes down mine, insisting that we must have a talk later. He is Han Guangmin, from Jiangsu Province, a graduate in the 1930s of the well-known National Central University of Nanjing. He mentions many of his professors and inquires about their whereabouts, including Lou Guanglai, a well-known scholar of English literature who has, unfortunately, passed away. Han tells me that he moved from the Chinese mainland to Taiwan before the revolution and later came to stay in America. He is apparently very glad to meet somebody from the mainland because he wants to know what is happening there. He calls several times later inviting me to Boston's Chinatown where 50-cent luncheons are provided for old people. I regret that I have not found time to meet this homesick compatriot again. He tells me over the phone that he goes to Chinatown every day for the lunch. It must be a pastime for him, like Bingo for others, to make the thirty-six-mile daily round-trip. Since he can afford an apartment in Lowell, I don't believe he needs to go to Chinatown just for the cheaper lunch.

On our way out we take a quick look at that part of the Lowell Mill which is being remodeled into an industrial museum. Lowell is regarded as a historical milestone in American industrial development. It was founded in 1813 and was the first mill in the world to use electricity as motive power. It was the most modern textile enterprise of the time. We are shown its boilers housed behind two-feet thick walls, a reminder of once burgeoning industrial might. Ida says that she still remembers how her mother, a worker in the mill, brought her here to see the place. Ida's mother came to America from Italy when she was five, started working in the mill as a child laborer, and grew up to be a spinner all her life.

The story of Ida's mother is not unusual. There had been a great wave of immigration from southern and eastern Europe to America from 1880 to 1920. It led to the adoption of an immigration law by

Congress limiting the influx of people from those regions while giving priority to western and northern Europeans. The Lowell Mill offered jobs to many Italian immigrants and that is why Waltham became practically an Italian town. The mill later grew into the Lowell Company with diversified operations and became so prosperous that it was moved to a site north of Boston. There, an industrial town still named Lowell was founded. It is rightly regarded as a monument — erected by the industrial revolution with cheap immigrant labor.

Diverse Forms of Old-Age Homes

Old-age institutions in America differ greatly from place to place. In Mississippi, in the Deep South, I see one convalescent home. Unlike Lowell, it looks more like a hospital with all its staff clad in white. Most inmates either walk with a stick or move about in walkers. Others lie still in collapsible chairs and stare blankly through the wall-high glass windows. They are all upper middle-class people because monthly costs can run into thousands of dollars per person.

In Washington state on the Pacific coast, I see another institution which sells apartments to old people at the price of tens of thousands of dollars per unit. The residents are provided many services at reasonable charges on condition that they will return the apartments to the corporation when they die. An American friend, Mary Helen Robinson, accompanying me on the visit, introduces me to John and Beth Slingerland, who are living there. The elderly woman had been a pioneer in the field of special education — the American term for education of the handicapped and retarded. Even as an octogenarian, she is writing a book. The couple tell me that this type of retirement home is a good bargain for people who live long. One old gentleman just died, only two years after he moved in. That is tantamount to donating an apartment to the institution.

According to Ian Robertson's *Sociology*, only five percent of all American old people live in homes for the aged; the rest stay in their own homes. I have met many aged Americans and have been impressed by their spirit of personal independence and refusal to become a burden on their offspring. While Americans don't like to be called old, I attribute this quality not to vanity, but to a determination to get to life's finish line independently, as a good sportsman should do.

To avoid the unpleasant epithet of "old," people in the United States who are over sixty-five are usually referred to as "senior citizens" or "the aging." I read in an American newspaper a satire proposing that the word "old" be banned altogether and "old friends" be replaced with "friends of long standing" or "friends who have communicated with each other for a long time." I once personally experienced something of this nature. A relative had accompanied me to a clothing store. Unable to find a coat of the right size for me, he went to a saleswoman whose hair was grayer than mine. According to the Chinese tradition of showing respect to elders, he asked: "Where can we find a suitable coat for the old lady?" The saleswoman said, quite seriously though in a very pleasant tone: "Look, young man, she isn't old, is she? Don't ever call her old lady again, remember."

It was sweet of her, but it made me sense all the more what a rare freedom we have in our society not to feel the need to shun the word "old".

THE BEAUTIFUL CHARLES RIVER

In Boston I stay in a high-rise apartment building called West Gate on the bank of the Charles River. Strolling along the wooded riverbank, I often see scenes which appear exotic to me.

At dusk a car comes and parks at the side of the road along the river. Then another car comes from which a young man or young woman gets out. He or she goes into the first car and immediately starts embracing and kissing the waiting person, not caring whether there is anybody else around. If I happen to be sitting on a bench nearby, I quietly pick up my books or papers and walk away. Though courting in parks is becoming more common in China, the young people are not yet as bold as the Americans.

Sometimes while I watch ducks floating on the ripples, a young man or woman suddenly emerges from a car. He or she gets into another car, and the two cars drive away. Another happy couple have been able to see each other — because of the automobile.

And the couples are not always youngsters. Occasionally I see an old couple driving to the riverbank. They take folding chairs from the roof of the car, seat themselves in a secluded place, and enjoy the summer breeze as well as the serenity of their late years.

The landscape is made more picturesque by the boats with full-blown triangular sails, and the racing shells which dart forward as rowers pull in unison to the call of the coxswain. There are also motor yachts leaving behind them long, white trails of foaming water and stirring up flocks of water birds as they speed away.

What enchants me even more is the night scene. I sit on a sofa and watch the view through the glass windows spanning the east and west side of my living room. The yellow headlights of cars move along the river and the green streetlamps above them are reflected on the water like shimmering silk ribbons. Farther on, beyond the river are two brightly lit high-rises with winking lights on their spire-shaped tops. Together with other buildings, they form a beautiful skyline which all my visitors love to watch from my sitting room. Farther away must be Logan airport, where planes keep ascending and descending with their multi-colored lights. I like the night scene so much that I have never once drawn the curtains during my three-month stay at the West Gate.

Friends from India

This sixteen-story building is owned by M.I.T. and is for the use of students who have spouses and children. When students leave school during summer vacation they may sub-let their apartments. I have a three-month sub-lease through the school housing office from a Finnish student who has gone home with his wife and daughter for the summer, and will return in the fall to complete his doctorate in physics. He has left most of his personal belongings behind and kindly permits me to use his typewriter, TV set and other facilities. The place has become my only "home" during my one-year journey.

Residents of West Gate come from all continents. We often meet in the elevator and the laundry room in the basement or on outdoor lawns. A student from India who has just got his doctorate in physics invites me to dinner in his apartment. We sit on the floor because he has sold all his furniture and is about to leave. The Indian meal his wife cooks is spicy and delicious. Their child, playing around, is cute. There are two other guests, my American friend Richard Pendleton, a black progressive, and a young man from India. The dinner soon turns into a warm discussion on problems of Third World development. My Indian friends' intense interest in China moves me. They say again and again that India and China should be good friends. They have hopes that China will find a way to prosperity and strength, and that India might benefit from China's experience. I tell them that India is also gaining experience which will be of value to us Chinese.

The discussion lasts until 2 a.m. Reluctantly, I have to leave. As a remembrance of this chance encounter, I present them some English language books on China that I have brought from Beijing. Whenever I recall the pleasant days I spent along the Charles River, I remember these friends, and our shared wish for the well-being and progress of our countries.

Two Strange Things

On the right side of West Gate stands a twenty-four-story, gray building provided by M.I.T. as a dormitory for single students. I go to visit a Chinese-American woman, Doris Cheng, who lives there and find to my surprise that she shares a four-room apartment (plus a common sitting room, bath and kitchen) with two boy students and another girl student. One of the boys is American, the other Polish, and the girl is from South Korea. Doris tells me that the Pole is moving out to live with his girl friend who has just arrived from Poland. I ask the young man if they are getting married. He says that he will live with her for a while and see if they can make up their minds. This type of relationship — living together as an unmarried couple — is not unusual in America, and is sometimes called a "trial marriage."

I remember that when I was in Missouri in the 1940s, boys visiting their girl friends in the school dormitory were allowed only to sit in the parlor and the housemother always tried to keep a close surveillance on what happened. She would certainly have fainted if she were to learn that girl students were sharing an apartment with boys. While I don't consider myself a conservative, I still cannot appreciate the advantages of this new "life-style."

The section of the Charles River which winds past M.I.T. is so charming by moonlight that I decide to take a walk alone along the riverbank one evening. I have to give up the idea, however, because my friends seriously warn me that it is not safe. Suchu, a good friend of mine studying at Harvard, once comes to see me in my apartment. It is getting late and I insist that she has dinner with me. As soon as she puts down the chopsticks she takes a hasty leave saying that she must go home now because she has come by bike. "It is too risky when it is dark," she says. She is not overly cautious as only recently she was robbed of her handbag in broad daylight. Although I have finished my one-year journey across the country safely, this fact has not kept me from noticing that many Americans I have visited habitually turn on the radio when they leave their house, switch it off when they come back, and turn on lights when they leave home to spend the weekend elsewhere. Their purpose is to create the impression that the house is occupied. If they leave for a trip, they ask either a relative or a friend to stay as a "house-sitter" or at least hire people to regularly mow the lawn. Some households are equipped with automatic switches that turn lights on in the evening and shut them off in the daytime. Others have "warning systems" with a notice at the door announcing that the house is protected. They pay a monthly charge for this system. They also must remember to turn it off when the house is re-entered, or a false alarm will be set off and the police will come.

Heeding the advice of my friends, I satisfy myself by looking at the moonlit Charles River through the windows. And I gradually come to realize that the beauty of Boston's skyline owes much to the sight of two towering buildings, the John Hancock Building and the Prudential Tower. The Hancock Building was designed by the Chinese-American architect, I. M. Pei, who is well known to Beijing residents for his work, the Fragrant Hills Hotel, built a few years ago.

There is an interesting story about John Hancock, for whom the Hancock Building was named. Mr. Hancock was a leader of the Bostonians and other Americans in their War of Independence. He was also the first man to sign the American Declaration of Independence. He wrote his signature so boldly and with such a flourish that, according to him, "George III can read it without his glasses." That was in 1776 when the outcome of the American

Revolution was still in doubt and there were many bloody battles still
to be fought against the British. But Mr. Hancock was apparently
certain of the final victory. I am told that is why Americans, when
asking people to sign their name, may say: "Your John Hancock,
please" — a worthy tribute to the optimistic revolutionary leader.

SALUTE THE PEACE-LOVING AMERICANS
— A Town Meeting in Boston and One Million Demonstrate in New York

After nearly three hours of heated debate, a resolution calling for a
nuclear freeze has been passed at the Weston Town meeting.
Accompanied by Professor Robinson, I have witnessed the whole
proceedings.

The Town Meeting, as we would put it in China, is the source of a
"grassroots" administrative unit's power. All residents of voting age
each have one vote. Barring special circumstances the Town Meeting
is held once a year to elect public officials, deliberate on reports of the
town's work during the preceding year, pass the budget, and establish
the administrative guidelines for the coming year.

Weston has a population of 11,500 and an electoral body of 7,000.
After a week's discussions, the meeting has finished all its business
except the last item on the agenda — whether to petition the state
legislature for a special law to permit the town to place the following
question on the ballot:

Do you agree that nuclear war is not a survivable means of
settling international conflict, and accordingly we should urge
that the United States and the Soviet Union should immediately
and jointly stop the nuclear arms race, adopting an immediate,
mutual and verifiable freeze on all further testing and production
of nuclear weapons and of missiles and new aircraft designed
primarily to deliver nuclear weapons?

Kenneth Fish, who placed the motion, is the first to take the floor.
He declares that there is no more urgent question before the town, the

country, or the world than the nuclear arms race. He says that he hopes the motion will stimulate discussion so that people would become "better educated."

He yields the floor to Jennette Cheek, a greying woman, who voices support for Mr. Fish and says: "When we are asked to delay negotiations with the Russians in order to build up further our store of strategic nuclear weapons, we inevitably accelerate the arms race, for the Russians will build too. Who can deny this?... Then there is the question of waging a 'limited' nuclear war. In the last few months there has been a mounting opinion that even the smallest beginning of the actual use of nuclear weapons runs an overwhelming risk of turning into the holocaust we dread. Increasingly the verdict is: There is no such thing as *limited* nuclear war."

The speaker has not named anybody, but all know that it is President Reagan and his colleagues' public references to a "limited nuclear war" that has sparked a massive anti-nuclear movement in Western Europe. It has spread from Europe to the United States and Canada.

The second supporter of the motion is Jonathan Moore, a specialist on the question of nuclear weapons. He cites facts and figures to show that American and Soviet nuclear strength is more or less on a par and tries to clarify "the folly" — that in order to reduce you've got to increase first. He maintains that the continued arms race greatly increases the probability of a "massive global nuclear war" and that negotiations for cuts without a freeze won't work. Mr. Moore also makes an interesting point by saying that "despite all the misleading, defeatist talk about the Russians being twenty-feet tall and the United States being weak and puny by comparison, there is virtually no U.S. military leader who would trade forces with them."

The two speakers are warmly applauded. Then two more speakers take the floor proposing an amendment. They talk at length to prove that a freeze at the present level will hurt the United States. Therefore "freeze" should be replaced with a call for American-Soviet negotiations to reduce their nuclear weapons to an equal level.

Mr. Fish will not accept the change. He explains that to define what is meant by "an equal level" will itself lead to endless debate. The United States and the Soviet Union, he says, are, in fact, in a situation of relative parity. Each has its advantages and weaknesses. It is an opportune time for a freeze.

A motion is then raised calling for a vote on whether to accept the amendment. The chairman pounds his desk with a gavel like a judge and announces that those for the amendment should stand up and say "aye," and those against say "no." Scattering calls of "aye" are followed by a chorus shouting "no!"

Debate is resumed on the original motion. Four successive speakers take the floor, all opponents. With often far-fetched argument, they try to convince the meeting that the Russians are not trustworthy.

Somebody proposes that the debate be terminated, a proposal which requires a two-thirds majority to pass. The cry of "aye" is much louder than "no." The procedural motion to end debate is passed by a three-fourths majority. Then the original motion is put to vote. Again, "aye" dominates and the call for a freeze is passed by an overwhelming majority.

On our way back Professor Robinson asks me what I think of the meeting. I say that I am impressed by the citizens' sincere effort for peace. I am also glad to have an opportunity to see the well-known New England " town meeting" in action. But I am sorry to learn that only 475 people, about 6.8 percent of the town's voters, have been present. Moreover, only 351 have taken part in the voting — 235 for, and 66 against. Nonetheless, I believe the meeting reveals a basic trend which will influence policy if what the people say counts.

An Unprecedented Demonstration

A month later, I go to New York from Boston to watch a demonstration. Organizers of the 12 June 1982 march declare that it is "the largest meeting for disarmament in the nation's history."

A few days before the event, I went to Concord in the Boston suburbs to visit Carmelita Hinton, mother of Bill Hinton (known in China by his Chinese name Han Ding). Mr. Hinton, an old friend of China, is author of *Fanshen*, which describes how the down-trodden Chinese peasants freed themselves in the historic land reform movement led by the Communists. Mrs. Hinton (who passed away the next year), was founder of the Putney School in Vermount, a nationally known progressive secondary school. It was at her place that I found the opportunity to join the 12 June demonstration which had been advertised prominently in the *New York Times*. Her daughter Jean and grandson Peter were organizing people of the town to participate, and I immediately signed up. Because Concord (where the first shot of the American War of Independence was fired on 19 April 1775) is twenty-two miles away from my West Gate apartment, Jean invited me to stay at her home the night before. The demonstrators would have to set out early in the morning to reach New York.

I was delighted when that evening at Jean's home I met two old acquaintances. They are David Crook and his wife, Isabel. David, a Briton, and Isabel, a Canadian, have been working as English language teachers in Beijing for many years. They are quite well-known in China's education circles. They happened to be visiting in America and came to join the demonstration. In the company of old friends, I wouldn't need to worry about getting lost in the huge crowds of demonstrators. Together we could form a sort of small "international brigade" or "Beijing detachment."

We set out at 2 a.m. on a chilly night. The streetlamps are few and far between. We walk in quick steps and hear our shoes padding on the road. Passing through the main street, turning at the public cemetery, we make a few more turns and arrive at the assembly point. Many people are already there. They are mostly young, though some are very old. It is still dark and I cannot see very clearly. Then four chartered buses come. With about forty people getting on my bus I figure there are about 160 demonstrators from the small town of Concord alone. Chatting with a few youngsters on the way, I learn that they are high school students and this is their first trip to New York. Worthy successors to the cause of peace, I think.

The buses speed on an interstate highway across half of Massachusetts and then turn south into Rhode Island, Connecticut, and New York. Five hours later (including a stop for breakfast) we reach Queens in New York City. From there we are to go by subway on to the New England assembly point. We meet organizers distributing placards to the demonstrators as soon as we arrive in

Queens. Dave gets one with the word "freeze" in bold caps and two smaller lines reading: "No nuclear war! Nobody wants it!" Isabel buys a small triangular banner for $1 from a man calling out for donations. The slogan on her banner reads: "Demonstrate and rally for disarmament." I also get a small banner for $1 and a button with a peace dove and olive branch pattern for another dollar. Isabel puts the button on my chest and we move on with the crowds into subway trains.

I am moved to find in our midst people carrying babies on their backs, holding toddlers in their arms, or pushing them in strollers. People, from all over the country and perhaps all over the world, are gathering in the streets outside the U.N. building. From there they are to march to Central Park in the middle of the city for a mass rally. How many people are taking part? Nobody seems able to give an accurate answer. The general estimate is one million.

The throngs move on like rolling waves. Multi-colored balloons are flying everywhere. People wearing drumshaped children's masks walk on stilts (it is the first time I learn that Americans also have these types of masks and stilts which are very popular in Chinese country carnivals). Acrobats do their feats while marching. Festively decorated floats are followed by people singing and dancing to fast drumbeats and shrill flute tunes. And then there are the more militant columns of veterans of the civil rights and anti-Vietnam War movements of the 1960s. They march abreast and sing the protest songs that were popular in those days. The broad avenues are turned into a panorama of colors surpassing the most imaginative point painting by French impressionist masters.

Many imaginative slogans are written on the countless placards and banners raised over the marching columns. Some examples: "No nukes," "Freeze the nuclear race," "I hate nuclear war," "Choose life," "Save the People," "For our children, for your children, stop the madness," "Bear babes, not arms," "Arms are for embracing," "Build houses not bomb shelters," "U.S. out of El Salvador," and "Reagan is a bomb — both should be banned."

I am deeply impressed by the solemnity of the demonstration's purpose, and by the good humor and optimism of these Americans who can wage a serious political struggle in such a festive atmosphere.

There is such diversity in the composition of the participants. I later learn from press reports, that the movement is called a "Rainbow Coalition". There are men and women from all trades and professions, Protestants and Catholics, Communists and government officials. They represent the whole spectrum of races, ages, occupations, wealth, religious beliefs and political convictions. Mayor Edward Koch (better known in China by his Chinese name Ko Dexua) joins a contingent of Queens demonstrators to march past the U.N. building.

The sponsors of the demonstration are all grassroots organizations, mostly Christian bodies, but also many secular ones including the New York City Public Employees' Union, popularly known as District Council 37. It is estimated that $700,000 was needed for holding this rally. Many famous artists had given benefit performances to help raise these funds, and a considerably larger sum of money had been collected from private donors. The volunteers organizing it, if they had been paid, would have cost even more. There are more than two-thousand volunteers in the Central Park alone! They wear bright red sweaters with the word "disarmament" on them. Many medical doctors and nurses are also there to provide free service to the over-fatigued or accidentally injured. The organizers are proud of their roles. One declares: "If any of you think that people don't have power, I say you're wrong." Another says: "Until the arms race stops, until we have a world of peace and justice, we will not go home and be quiet. We will go home and organize."

I learn from press reports during my stay in the United States that many prominent people have come to support the nuclear freeze. They include Catholic bishops, close to one-hundred Nobel-prize winning scientists, and different institutions of the print and electronic media. And the movement continues to grow. In 1984, a new wave of the anti-nuclear campaign sweeps Western Europe when deployment of U.S. Pershing II and cruise missiles begins. In America, 100 million people watch the film "The Day After," a good measure of the increasing public anxiety over the dreadful prospects of a nuclear holocaust. The New York rally strengthens my conviction that peace can be safeguarded if the people persist in their struggle.

SOME LIVE BY ODD-JOBS

Ida Uttaro and Bob Freeman—both of them live by odd jobs. And I shall always remember both of them. Ida is a woman with a golden heart, and Bob is a well-educated person in a sorry plight.

Ida is the domestic employee of the Robinson family who arranged for me to visit the Lowell home for the aged. She is a descendant of Italian immigrants.

Ida fell in love with Frank Uttaro and married him in 1947, one year after the World War II veteran was demobilized. Eight years later, in 1955, Frank was struck with a terrible disease—polio. Confined in a veterans' hospital for twenty-one months, he escaped death but was paralysed. He used to be a truck driver who traveled hundreds of miles a day. But since his discharge from the hospital, he has stayed in a wheelchair beside a dining table in the kitchen for twenty-five years. Even worse, he has to be helped by Ida to change posture in the chair or turn around in bed. He eats only one meal a day in order to keep down his weight so that Ida can move him. And he has to refrain from drinking. Sitting still with a urinal bag underneath him is too painful. Ida must go out to work and cannot attend to him all the time. His eyes are somber and his fingers, though numbed, are capable of snatching cigarettes which he keeps smoking, one after another.

"Even Frank's mother could not be as kind to him as you are," I praise Ida while visiting them in their Waltham home. Ida tells me that she had thought the matter over and made up her mind many years ago. "We were very happy in the first eight years of our marriage. He had not done anything unfair to me. He couldn't be kinder to our daughter and two sons. He didn't waste a single cent. He was always tired after a day's driving but would start working the moment he came home. He was not lazy, not at all. Could he be blamed for the illness?"

Of course not. Regardless, it has been hard for Ida. She has done all the work since. Apart from odd jobs here and there and her own household chores, she takes care of her daughter Linda's two-year-old baby girl, Amanda. Linda's work is demanding and she is on the night shift. She can't carry on without adequate rest. Ida has to do the baby-sitting when Linda goes to sleep.

Frank is so depressed that he does not even want to talk. I try to start a conversation about his life story, but to no avail. How old is he? How does the family support itself? I cannot raise these questions directly because it is impolite to ask Americans their age and income. As we become better acquainted, Frank utters a few sentences once in a while. Pieced together, a rough sketch emerges.

Frank's grandparents moved to America from Italy at the turn of the century, his father an infant at the time. Ida's grandparents came at about the same time. Frank says his grandparents died before he was born. His father worked at the Mica Company all his life. The company used to produce electric toasters and miscellaneous home appliances, but it no longer exists today. His mother gave birth to eight children and worked for many years in a plant producing rubber shoes and boots. After work the father busied himself all the time growing tomatoes, cabbages, and potatoes in the family plot. He also grew flowers. In winter time the greenhouse had to be heated. Frank began helping his father with the work when he was very small, sixteen hours a day and seven days a week.

Sometimes Frank got odd jobs to earn a little pocket money. There was a cemetery in the neighborhood and he would dig graves there for fifty cents an hour. A pit was seven feet long, three feet wide and six feet deep. It was not easy to break the hard ground, and even more difficult to shovel the earth out from the bottom. Rest a little while? No. The graveyard keeper was strict with the part-timers. Go slow? Impossible. Fifty cents an hour was pretty good pay and you had to sweat for it. "Now," Frank says, "you can dig a pit in no time with machines."

"Things in America have changed so fast," I say. "Only fifty years ago you had to dig grave pits with picks and shovels." I hit upon the number fifty after some calculations because Frank told me he started working in 1940. At the age of 17 he became a heavy truck driver for Mica, where his father worked. Frank will soon be in his sixties.

He became a G.I. soon after Pearl Harbor. His family made a real contribution to the war by sending four men into the armed forces.

Before the outbreak of fighting his eldest brother joined the army engineers and went to build the Alaska Highway; another brother went to Guam. Frank and one other brother went to Germany, where Frank served in the American occupation forces in Berlin. Later moved to Paris, he came home in 1946, too late to see his father who passed away toward the end of 1945.

Hearing that we are talking about the war, Ida comes with an enlarged photo for me to see. "What a handsome young man! It's Frank, right? And his army uniform, so well fitting!" I point to the insignias and badges on the uniform and ask what they represent. Frank explains that they mean corporal, technician, Ninth Army, European Theater, etc.

The photograph, Frank tells me, was taken by a German photographer and he paid him with two packages of American cigarettes. A pack of cigarettes cost five cents in his army canteen but was sold on the market for German marks equivalent to one American dollar or more. Such a beautiful portrait for two packs of cigarettes! This reminds me of the dire poverty stalking Germany, and indeed throughout Europe and the rest of the world in the immediate postwar years. The United States was the exception.

As I gaze at the picture, Ida suddenly bursts forth with reminiscences. "I saw the picture at the home of Frank's sister-in-law. He was in Europe at the time. I couldn't help saying to myself, 'Oh-o-o-oh, I'm going to get him! I'm going to get him!' ".

"But what a *prize* you got! What a *prize* you got!" Frank says, apparently moved. And he cheers up a little, his eyes gleaming in smiles. He recalls that once his brother drove him and four girls to a beach in New Hampshire for an outing. "And you know what? Ida fell on my lap and sat there all the way."

Ida laughingly retorts: "We were too crowded. Besides, I was light as a feather."

Frank continued the story. "After that she came to see me every Sunday with macaroni and fish or meatballs. She would ride over with her uncle. Oh, it was delicious. I was always hungry after a whole morning's work in the backyard."

"I didn't say I cooked the food. I always gave credit to my mother," Ida replies with a laugh.

I ask Frank if he was too busy at the time for romance. He says that he always found a little time for Ida. Her mother, however, was strict and insisted that she be home before 10:30 p.m. He was busy in other ways, also. Several girls kept calling him on the telephone and would talk on endlessly. Sometimes he would just put the phone down on the table and let these chatterboxes talk.

"That was very mean!" Ida interrupts. "Why didn't you say 'Excuse me'? They would have understood."

Then Ida turns to ask me: 'Wang Tso, wasn't there a shortage of marriageable men in China during the postwar years? There was an acute shortage here." I tell her that we did have a shortage, but it wasn't as bad as in Germany and the Soviet Union.

The couple resume their happy reminiscences. I don't have the skill to describe how Ida finally "got" Frank or the happy years of their life together before his illness. I am only gratified that my visit has enabled them to temporarily retreat from the present to a more carefree past.

But worldly concerns do return. Ida tells me later that Frank gets a monthly disability benefit of $400 under the Social Security program. As for her own income, I only know that she works six hours (including travel time) a week for the Robinson family and gets $40 for it. She must have other jobs to keep the family going. Expenses are high, Ida says. Tax on the house is $1,500 for the past year and she does not know how much more it will be for the next. House insurance is $400 a year, and car insurance another $400. Replacements for two worn-out tires have cost her $180, and for a new water tank, $450.

Trying to change a subject, I ask Ida if she thinks she is a member of the middle class (many Americans say they are). Ida is frank and replies: "No, I'm not. But my brother is." Her brother could drive hundreds of miles to New Jersey to attend the wedding of a close relative. Ida had thought about going also, but had to decide against it because the trip would have been too expensive. She would have had to stay one night in a hotel and eat in restaurants on the way. In addition, there was the cost of gasoline. Her brother, she continues, could take even a one week vacation in Las Vegas. But his wife, unfortunately, is the type of person who takes everything for granted and thanks nobody for her good life.

"Wang Tso," Ida tells me, "don't think owning a car means people are rich. Poor people in America have to have a car, too. They need it to go to work.

"But I am lucky to have this house. My mother was paralysed for ten years after a stroke. I took care of her all along. It would have cost at least $250 a week to send her to a convalescent home. After her death in 1974, my two brothers and I each had a share of the house she left behind. My elder brother said it had been hard on me to attend to our sick mother for such a long time and he let me have his share. I borrowed some money to pay my other brother. I am lucky to own this house." Speaking of her car, Ida says again that she is lucky to have bought it for $2,800. She would have to pay a much higher price now.

I find that Ida, instead of complaining, always feels she is fortunate. With Frank's tragedy to contend with she carries life's burdens calmly and seems to look at the bright side of things whenever possible. But she does have reason to feel this way. Frank's brother, she tells me, is much better off financially but cannot get along with his wife. The couple have not spoken to each other for three months. A few days previous the brother had come to Ida's house and stayed for hours. He said that it had a warmth which was absent from his own home. "We at least respect each other," Ida says. "Whenever we have a chance, the whole family gets together, we cook something for ourselves, and talk and laugh. This is happiness for us."

"I Want Se-cu-ri-ty!"

"Then what is your greatest worry? Don't you have any worry at all?" I ask.

"Oh, yes," she says. "I don't want anything, neither welfare benefits, nor good dresses or jewelry. No, nothing. But I do want security, se-cu-ri-ty."

The greatest insecurity is sickness. Though she pays a yearly premium of $600 for health insurance, a major illness could ruin the family. Moreover, all sorts of bills continue to come. She spends $861 to have her car overhauled. Then the house needs to be repaired. These are necessities.

But, Ida adds, she is more fortunate than people who have no income at all, those who are "on welfare." She recalls that three days ago she met a young woman who had a child with her. It was raining and they were taking shelter under a tree. The woman had been carrying a grocery bag which was now soaked. Ida stopped the car and asked if they were having trouble getting home. The woman said she lived in a housing project about one mile away. So Ida picked them up and drove them home. She learned that the woman's husband had divorced her and then disappeared. She had sent two elder children to a public youth camp in New Hampshire for fear that they might get in trouble on the streets. She was now living on welfare with her three-year-old child. "It's a good thing that the government built those housing projects," Ida says, "but the management is poor and there are plenty of problems."

The grocery bag was broken when they got home. So Ida helped the woman carry some of the things to her door. She got a glimpse inside. "You should see that place, Wang Tso. It's so bare. And her groceries are all marked-down, dented cans, the kind you sometimes find dumped at the supermarkets. She also had a few rolls of toilet paper. Many Americans say people on welfare spend public money buying lobsters and crabmeat. This is a slander on a lot of poor people. There are always a few who are adept at lying and cheating, but not the many. Would that woman drag her child along to buy those miserable articles if she possessed the money to buy lobsters?"

"Ida," I think to myself, "you have a golden heart!"

An Unemployed Teacher

I now tell the story of Bob Freeman. He worked hard for ten years to put himself through college in New York. He has a bachelor's degree in primary education and a master's degree in special education. Today he drives around Boston with a string of keys and opens houses where he is hired to do odd-jobs.

Bob spent ten years instead of the usual four-plus two to get his degrees not because he was slow witted, but because he had to work much of the time. After graduation he did get a job in one of the public schools in Boston as special-education teacher for physically handicapped and mentally retarded children. There were only a few such pupils, but their educational levels differed greatly. Bob taught courses ranging from the first to the fourth grade and, in addition, had to take pains to arrange a curriculum suitable for all.

My Chinese readers may wonder why a person with a master's degree would teach in a grade school, because in China he would be considered an intellectual and be assigned to a higher job. I need to explain that this is not because of employment difficulties. American education is quite developed and only college graduates who qualify in state examinations are eligible to teach in grade schools.

But Bob did run into employment difficulties when he was laid-off four years ago. Not only Bob, but many others. I saw Boston teachers on television meeting to protest their lay-off. Some parents of the students were shown weeping in sympathy. The 629 laid-off teachers had tenure, but it did not help. The problem is that American schools had increased rapidly to meet the needs of the postwar "baby boom." Then came the "baby bust." Now all those born during the boom period, statistically the last year being 1964, have grown up, and there are not enough students to fill the vacancies in primary and high schools. Consequently, there is a "surplus" of teachers and unemployment runs high. Bob had to take any job offered him.

"The longer I'm away from teaching, the less chance I'll go back," Bob tells me. "New methods develop, knowledge expands, and schools prefer to employ new graduates. Teachers staying on the job do get retraining. Many of them, for example, attend computer courses sponsored by the city government." The sources of Bob's depression become more apparent.

I met Bob at the home of my friend Rita Gould. He works twenty hours a week for her at seven dollars an hour, a more stable job than any he has held previously. But he has to take other jobs in addition. For instance, an old lady hires him for the explicit purpose of accompanying her to visit doctors. In that case his old car becomes an indispensable "means of livelihood."

Rita hired Bob by chance. One day she saw him cleaning the house of a friend and asked him to come to her home to do the same. On the day Bob came, Rita's secretary, also employed on an hourly basis, quit. Bob recommended himself because he could type, write letters, and do the usual secretarial work. That was why when I first met Bob at Rita's home she introduced him to me as "my secretary, cook, and Jack-of-All-Trades." Bob is kept busy during the twenty hours at Rita's home and feels he is fortunate to be so employed. Rita's husband, a medical doctor, passed away not long ago. She is establishing a consulting firm called "The China Source" and often goes out on business. Bob understands that she needs a trustworthy assistant at home and tries his best to be reliable.

"I hope Rita's firm prospers so that someday she will take me to see China," Bob says while dusting the exquisite Chinese furniture in Rita's sitting room. I find a painting of lotus flowers by the well-known Chinese artist Huang Yongyu tucked in a corner of the wall. He had written the Chinese name for Rita on the painting in his beautiful calligraphy, showing that it was a special gift to her, and consequently enhancing the value of the piece. I explain this to Bob and he tells Rita. She is pleased and decides to move the painting to a more prominent place facing the windows. This episode seems to bring Bob and me closer, and he begins telling me something about his life and family.

His father joined the army and went to war when he and his sister were very small. Five years later the soldier returned and stayed with Bob's mother just long enough for her to give birth to another boy. The man then deserted her and she had to rear the three children all by herself.

"He had an obligation to support his children. Why didn't your mother take him to court?" I ask.

"She did," Bob says, "but my father did not have a regular job and kept on moving from place to place. My mother had difficulty knowing where he was. She would locate him and he would move again. The little money she got each time was not worth the trouble and emotional distress."

His mother later married a man fourteen years younger than her, who turned out to be jealous of the children. Seeing his mother's plight, Bob and his sister left home one after the other. The youngest brother became a teamster when he grew up. "He earns good money," Bob says. "Besides he will have Social Security benefits when he gets old. Not me though. People living on odd jobs don't pay Social

Security tax. Even if we want to pay, our employers would have to pay a matching sum. That won't work, will it?"

Bob's sister, a nurse, has a son and daughter, both very small. She too has been deserted by her husband. And she also is out of work. Bob baby-sits for her on weekends so she can work as a substitute nurse. This means she works about eight days a month. I presume she is also a welfare recipient. But Bob does not live with her on weekdays. However hard-pressed, Americans prefer to live separately for the "privacy" they so cherish. This, in a way, accounts for the diminishing size of American families. The average number per household was 3.14 in 1970. It had dropped to 2.76 in 1980 and unofficial figures for 1982 show that the trend continues to decrease.

Bob was more ambitious than his sister and brother. He managed to get a good education in the hope of finding a respectable and stable job. But bad fortune appears to have denied him the chance. He is a warm-hearted person who willingly shares the difficulties of his sister. Over forty years of age now, he remains single. Unemployed and with a dependent sister, it must be difficult, I surmise, for him to find a spouse even though he needs the warmth and care of a family.

Whenever I think of Boston, I hope that Bob will see better days. He is an educated and decent man — why should he be deprived of the right to fulfill his potential?

THE SEAMY SIDE OF BOSTON

The Americans are realistic. When I compliment them on how beautiful Boston is, they often remind me that things are not all good. At the observatory on the sixtieth floor of the John Hancock Building, I admire the grand view. But a gentleman points to the south and asks me if I can see any difference at that end of the city. Once I tell a friend that I am now familiar with Route 1 of the city bus and won't get lost. He says disapprovingly: "But you have not traveled to Dudley at the other end. It is another world compared with the M.I.T.-Harvard area you know."

Others are more outspoken. Kermit Robinson, a young engineer, and Professor Robinson's son by his former wife, suggests that I should meet more poor people in order to really know the city. Another friend proposes more specifically that I interview some street-cleaners on the M.I.T. campus who usually work from dusk to 3 o'clock in the morning, and "they have plenty of stories to tell you." I try to find somebody to introduce me to those people, but it is not easy. I am told that they are in a bad situation and don't like foreigners who they believe are competing with them for jobs. There are of course knowledgeable workers, but nobody seems able to help me select the right persons to interview.

The point my American friends have been driving at is simply this: For tourists and visitors Boston means those prestigious universities, the magnificent 19th-century buildings in the Back Bay area, the outdoor concerts at Boston Common or on the meadows along the Charles River, and the garish shopping center at Quincy Market. But Boston also has another face.

As I am to leave Boston in late August, I feel a bit upset at my failure to look closely into the other side of the city. I am not here on a muckraking mission but I know middle-class Boston is not the whole Boston.

Quite unexpectedly I find in *The Boston Globe* a front-page story under the heading: "Boston Is Called a City in Decline." The report is based on an 809-page study by the Brookings Institute entitled "Urban Decline and the Future of American Cities." The Brookings Institute, I should add for the benefit of my Chinese readers, is a respected "think tank" in Washington, D.C. The study has been prepared by three economists after three years of studies of 153 major American cities.

Boston, the Brookings paper declares, is one of the four "most distressed" major American cities. The scholarly report defines strictly the terms used. By "urban distress" it means a city's inability to perform such social and economic functions as providing employment, education, health care, transportation, recreation, and "leadership for groups subjected to discrimination." A "declining city" is defined as one whose "distress" continues to worsen. Boston, according to the Brookings findings, is both "in distress" and "declining."

The study acknowledges Boston's paradoxical nature. During the period under study, it says, the city "suffered from high and rising unemployment and violent crime rates, a high percentage of poor, old housing, a rising city government debt burden, and falling per capita income." Nevertheless, "many people consider Boston a very attractive city with excellent cultural, educational and environmental amenities."

The study also points out that large numbers of white residents have moved to the suburbs and left blacks and other minorities behind. "White flight" has resulted in a great "disparity" between the inner city and the surrounding SMSA (Standard Metropolitan Statistical Area).

The Globe on the same day publishes an editorial entitled "All That Glitters." It declares: "While the description (of Boston as a city in decline) may be news to some of the fortunate who enjoy Boston's numerous pluses in higher education, culture and urban ambiance — the decline is no secret to others. They are the unfortunate who cannot find satisfactory work, affordable housing, satisfactory public schooling, good transportation, or peace unmarred by racial tensions." Listing the city's lagging development, the editorial concludes: "If the Brookings study is a surprise to anyone, it may be because the Brookings scholars sought, unlike the current City Hall administration, to look at the whole city, not merely the downtown glitter [where heavy investments have been made for a 'renaissance' symbolized by Quincy Market]."

"The Two Faces of Boston" is the title of another article by a *Globe* staff writer. A similar duality, I later find, seems to characterize all big American cities — a manifestation of the polarization of American society.

Chapter IV
TO MAINE

Of the six New England states Maine is the northernmost one. Largest by size and smallest by population density, it has an area four times as big as that of Massachusetts. But its population is only one-fifth of that of Massachusetts, averaging 36.6 per square mile as against 737.7 for the latter. While I was studying in the United States in the 1940s, fellow American students had told me that foreigners usually thought Mississippi was a poor state but Maine was actually poorer.

I am going to Maine at the invitation of Roslyn Foner. "If luck would have it, strangers one thousand *li* apart will become friends," as a Chinese folk-saying goes. It is sheer luck that has made me a friend of Roslyn and her husband Philip Foner, a progressive American historian. In early spring 1982 Professor Foner was making a lecture tour in China. I happened to be a listener at his lectures. Introducing him to the audience, the host said that Professor Foner had written and edited close to one hundred books. Classical Chinese writings often describe a prolific writer as "one who has produced books with a combined thickness to match his height," the host said, and this analogy could be literally applied to Prof. Foner. This graphic introduction stuck in my mind.

What was more important, however, was Foner's lectures. They helped me to understand a lot about the history of American labor, particularly the difficulties it has faced in the past two decades. They also gave insight into the civil rights movement of American blacks. His lectures were so enlightening that I hoped to have more opportunities to learn from him.

As luck would have it, my daughter, a student of American

71

history, met Roslyn. Learning that I worked in a publishing house, Roslyn, a book designer, said she would very much like to meet me. So we met in Beijing. As a writer-editor, I did not have much to share with an artist. But I found Roslyn a very warm person and we quickly became friends.

The Foners live in Philadelphia and own a house in Maine where they spend their summer vacations. Soon after my arrival in Boston, they invited me to spend a few days with them in Maine. The cool state derives much of its income from vacationers. There are many villas along its Atlantic coast for rich people to escape the summer heat. The numerous hotels on the sea coast are open only in summer time.

People with a moderate income can afford to get lodging at reasonable prices, usually on lakeshores. Nicknamed "the Pine State," Maine abounds with forests growing around its lakes and hills. The Foner's summer retreat is at a small town called Weld. To help me locate it, Professor Robinson had to find an old large-scale map. Far removed from the coast, Weld is tucked away on Mt. Blue, along the shores of Lake Webb. It has 130 residents, according to the map. But later I find in the Weld post office that the population has increased to 430. The town is not reached by expressway. Roslyn has told me over the phone that she will pick me up at the state capital, Augusta. It will be a ninety minute drive from Augusta to their house.

TRAVELING BY BUS

From my West Gate apartment I walk for thirty minutes across the well-mown lawns of the M.I.T. campus and get to the subway station. The underground train travels much faster than I expected. I arrive at the Greyhound bus depot near a large park in downtown Boston almost one hour earlier than the Maine-bound bus from New York City. It gives me a chance to look around carefully at an American bus station.

Boston is the hub of many bus routes, but the depot is quiet, without the usual hustle and bustle of bus or railway terminals in China. There are a number of ticket windows. Passengers line up along a railing some distance away from the windows. When a clerk behind a window calls out "next," the first person in the line moves out. First come, first served—people proceed in perfect order.

Back in the United States after a long absence, I had forgotten the American custom. One day in the town of Lakewood, New Jersey, I went to the post office. Seeing only one person standing in front of the window I went straight to line up behind him, not noticing that there were a few others waiting behind the railing. My old friend accompanying me stood at the gate and frowned at me. I did not know what was annoying her till she later reminded me that in all public places, from the post office, the bank, to the washrooms at busy airports, the same unwritten rule must be observed. It may seem trivial, but I find the American habit of keeping public order worth emulating. It is an important part of the "civic virtues" being promoted in China after many hectic years.

The waiting room is a long hall with numbered gates on both sides. Passengers wait for announcements over the public address system of the gates they should enter. The Maine-bound bus, for instance, stops at Gate 11. There are two rows of chairs at the center of the hall. At least half the seats are equipped with small black-and-white TV sets on the handles. The sets are turned on by dropping twenty-five cents into the slot. I walk around and find many people watching either football or tennis matches. The Americans are great sports fans.

There are luggage lockers. By dropping seventy-five cents into a coin slot, you can leave your things in a fairly spacious compartment and rid yourself of the burden of carrying them with you. It is an automatically controlled, labor-saving device, available also at airports.

It takes five hours for the bus to come from New York City to Boston. Boston is a big midway station where the bus stops a little longer than at other towns. Many passengers take the opportunity to go upstairs to tidy themselves up in the washrooms where there are hot and cold running water, paper towels and wall-size mirrors. On the bus, too, there is a small toilet, a facility not available in the 1940s. All these, again, seem to be trival, but they combine to make long-distance travel convenient and comfortable. We in China are often told that America has a superb network of expressways totalling 3.95 million miles. The milage is impressive but travel would still be difficult without the other conveniences provided at the bus stops and the many roadside filling stations, hotels, and restaurants for motorists.

The Greyhound bus driver is a symbol of American efficiency. He works also as the conductor and luggage clerk. He checks the tickets of passengers, deposits their luggage in the luggage compartment between the front and back wheels, and returns them to those disembarking. He also stands at the exit and lends a helping hand to senior citizens. He is conscientious, considerate, and always pleasant. All the drivers I met during my travels on the Greyhound and Trailways lines were like this. They must have been carefully selected and trained to live up to the motto written on the driver's seat: "Safe, Reliable and Courteous." One of the rules on the bus is that passengers must use headphones if they turn on their radio. One tourist neglects the rule. The bus driver speaks through his microphone in a polite but firm voice: "Use your headphones, please."

An Interesting Companion

Everything seems fine to me except one thing. Two-thirds of the seats on the bus are vacant while so many cars are racing by on the same expressway. The Americans waste too much precious energy as they waste food, paper, and much else.

I take a seat beside the window to get a better view. As the bus drives northward, there are more and more hotels, restaurants, and tourist resorts visible from the road.

"Are you Chinese?" A man looking like a worker asks me. He takes the seat at my side, though there are plenty of others around. We strike up a conversation. "The Chinese are clever and able, and the Japanese, too," he says. He speaks with a heavy accent but his language is expressive and interesting.

He tells me he is from Oaxaca, near the Pacific coast in southern Mexico. According to his description, Oaxaca has much seafood and fruit. Bananas, peaches, and plums are dirt cheap. Coffee beans sell for only fifty cents a kilo. "Unlike the Americans, we bake and grind our beans. American canned coffee is not pure and tastes awful."

"Our honey is one hundred percent pure," he continues, taking out a bottle from his bag to show me. "Unlike the Americans, we cook the whole fish, complete with the head and tail. The Americans cut their fish into steaks." "Unlike the Americans," he goes on, "we kill our own chickens" and he pulls a finger across his throat to illustrate. "The Americans eat tasteless frozen chickens."

He is Francisco Braco, a Hispanic. Hispanic in America means an immigrant from Spanish or Portuguese-speaking countries, mainly from Latin America. Their number has been growing. The United States conducts an official census once every ten years and the one in 1980 showed that there were 14,605,883 Hispanics in the country, representing 6.4 percent of the population. Some demographers predict that Hispanics will eventually outnumber blacks (11.7 percent of the population in 1980) and become the largest single minority.

Though he keeps on saying "unlike the Americans", Braco was born in America and is an American citizen by law. Every year he works six months as a shoemaker in Lowell, Massachusetts. In that period he is an American. Like a migrant bird, he moves to warm Oaxaca as soon as winter sets in and becomes a Mexican. He tells me that it is terribly cold in New England and the money spent on heating is enough to support his whole family in Mexico. Another reason he works only half a year is the sad experience of his father. Moving to America to work as a mason in his teens, the old Braco labored till his retirement at sixty-five and died two years later. He had paid Social Security tax for many years but enjoyed the benefits for only two. Braco thinks year-round work is not the way to keep fit and live long. His wife and two daughters, both born in America, are in Mexico. The girls have graduated from colleges and are working for higher degrees. "They will become teachers and live a respectable life. They will be clean and never look as dirty as me," Braco says.

I am wondering how Braco can quit his job and pick it up again as he pleases. He explains that he has worked many years for the same shoe factory owner. The boss knows well that he is a good hand, capable of making all types of shoes, for men or women, with high or flat heels. "And every pair is quality made," he says. The factory produces to order for a number of cities. Business was brisk a few years ago and the boss used to ask Braco to work fourteen to fifteen hours a day and paid him by the piece. With the present recession, he was lucky to work eight hours a day. The factory is waiting for new orders and has temporarily laid off its workers. That is why Braco is going to visit a fellow Hispanic in Maine. He knows Lowell inside out and there is no point staying idle there. Workers like Braco are exactly the kind the boss likes because they will come and go at his will. Besides, Hispanics are paid lower wages, Braco says.

I am writing of this chance encounter in order to show my Chinese readers that the composition of the American population of 230 million is complex. They or their ancestors came from many countries and regions. But their vastly different cultural traditions still persist and their connections with their mother countries and towns remain close. Americans often say that their country is a "melting pot." It is true to a certain extent. But assimilation is far from complete. I often joke that what's in the "pot" may be a beef stew, the WASPs (white Anglo-Saxon protestants) being the choicest pieces. Braco is a living example of the other diverse components. Chinese will misunderstand America if they view it as a white mass with just a few black dots.

Reflections at Portsmouth

Braco, an old-timer in this part of the country, advises me to visit Portsmouth, New Hampshire, on my way back to Boston. Portsmouth's "re-creation-of-history" show every May through August is worth seeing. In fact, I have learned from tourist books that Portsmouth, where immigration began at about the same time as in Boston, is trying to attract sightseers with actors dressed in eighteenth century costumes and performing farm tasks of the time.

I decided to stop for a few hours there on my return. Not for the show though, but for entirely different reasons.

Portsmouth was an annoying name to me in my school days. When I entered junior middle school in Shanghai in the 1920s, China was in the midst of revolutionary upheaval. The National Revolutionary Army, founded on the Kuomintang-Communist alliance, had fought its way up from Canton in the Northern Expedition against the imperialist-backed feudal warlords. Patriotism pervaded our schools. Teachers attached great importance to anti-imperialist and anti-feudal education. My history teacher was a zealot. He required students to commit to memory all the unequal treaties imposed on China by the imperialist powers since the Opium War of 1840, as well as the dates and places of their signing. I had a good memory and could rattle off all the names except the Treaty of Portsmouth — a tongue-twister in Chinese.

Trying to help me, the teacher said: "You must hate it if you want to remember it. Just think. The Japanese went to war with the Russians. They didn't fight on their own soil but chose China's Dairen (Dalian) as the battlefield. Portsmouth is the city where they negotiated peace. Hence the Treaty of Portsmouth, signed in 1905, at China's expense. It is another national humiliation for us!"

I looked up history books before my visit to the town. The United States at the time was beginning to assert itself as a world power. Fearful of Czarist expansion in the East, it needed Japan as a counterweight. Influenced by propaganda, many Americans believed that Japan was the "victim" in the Russo-Japanese War. Theodore Roosevelt, the American president from 1901 to 1909, acted as a mediator between the Japanese and the Russians. The Treaty of Portsmouth brought about an uneasy peace between the two imperialist powers fighting over China. The President was awarded a Nobel Prize for his contribution.

Standing on the shores of Portsmouth and having nothing much to do, I give free rein to my personal reminiscences. What a miserable childhood we had lived! Many times a year, often with tears in our eyes, we had to observe the "national humiliation days." When we grew older, imperialist aggression became all the more blatant. Uppermost in our minds was how to save our nation from complete enslavement. We were willing to pay with our lives if necessary. What else could we do? The Portsmouth Treaty was a historic proof of the helplessness of a weak nation, however just its cause might be.

Then I remember the days when I first came to study in the United States. Fellow American students were friendly and sympathetic on the whole. But I once met a few young ROTC officers who told me to my face: "So you are from China, eh? That must be a terrible place." I answered back: "America isn't a paradise, either." But I knew my retort was feeble.

At long last, the days of humiliation were gone!

HISTORIAN FONER AND ROSLYN

I now resume the story of my visit with the Foners. The bus passes Portland, the largest city in Maine (there are many Portlands, Portsmouths, Columbias and other places bearing the same name in the country). When I arrive at Augusta, Professor Philip Foner and Roslyn are at the bus depot waiting for me. Braco is happy that there are people to meet me. He helps me off and wishes me good luck.

Philip is at the wheel. The highway is lined on both sides by thick woods with only a few clearings for farms. We pass by a small town with nice looking buildings. Chinese usually equate America with sky-scrapers and don't know that the small towns are often more beautiful. Roslyn tells me there is a paper mill in the town and some people commute from Weld to work here. In Wilton, another town, there are two shoemaking factories and most residents are shoemakers and their families. We are soon at Weld. The place is sparsely populated but its highways are paved and maintained just as well as those in urban areas.

We continue the drive to the summer house which is six miles from the town. Roslyn stops the car on the way. She and Philip take out some plastic tanks from the trunk and fill them with clear water brought down through a pipe from the hills. We rest for a while and drink the cool water. Getting back to nature is particularly attractive to the citizens of an urbanized country.

As the highway ends, we turn onto a bumpy mud road. The professor tells me that we are on the track made by the former owner's horse wagons. A shack ahead used to be his stable. We are entering the "Foner Estate" comprising three acres (equivalent to 20 Chinese *mu*) of forests and a house built in 1898. Foner bought the "estate" from the granddaughter of the owner.

I poke fun at the professor, who is a Marxist: "With so much land and so many trees, you would be a regular landlord in China, a target of revolution. There was no escaping that."

"The trees are the real 'landlords,'" Foner replies with a laugh. "They have lived off the land since ancient times. I don't use the land as 'means of production.'" The car stops in front of the house before he finishes his retort. Roslyn leads me slowly up a creaking wooden staircase. By the time I enter my room, the professor has already begun clattering at his typewriter. That is the way he writes enough books to "match his height."

During my sojourn I find the professor as punctual as a clock. He is the earliest riser in the house. Every morning he cooks his breakfast, puts it on a tray, takes it down the staircase and eats while watching the sunrise from the lake shore. Then he listens to the morning newscast. After that he starts working in the midst of Strauss or other music coming over the radio. At this time he is compiling an index for a revised edition of his book *Organized Labor & the Black Worker, 1619 to 1981*. And he never misses his morning and afternoon swim in the lake.

But he has not forgotten me. Whenever he has a break, he calls out from downstairs: "Wang Tsomin, do you have any question to ask me? Come on and let's talk."

What I want to know most is about the professor himself, the life of an American Marxist. But he does not like to talk about himself. I try to steer him on the course by asking: "How come you even got Thomas Jefferson involved and caused a ban on his writings?" For I have read from a book that at the height of the McCarthy anticommunist witch-hunt in post World War II America, an investigation probed the U.S. government's information program. The State Department reacted in a panic and directed its libraries around the world to remove twenty books from their shelves. One was *Selected Writings of Thomas Jefferson* edited by Philip Foner.* "It's true," the professor says. And that's all I get.

But the professor becomes eloquent when he talks about American blacks and poor whites, about Cuba and Poland. Asked about long-term trends of the American living standard, he tells me that it ascended steadily for many generations — the son living better than the father and the father better than the grandfather. But the trend shifted downward, he says. I find this view is shared by many other Americans I meet. In Washington D.C., I talk to a group of young

---

* *A People's History of the United States*, by Howard Zinn, published by Harper & Row Publishers, 1980.

people born during the postwar "baby boom." One of them says: "All of us have graduated from college. But what's the use of that? We are not worth as much financially as our parents." The others agree with him. In Iowa City, in the Midwest, I meet a representative of the Iowa state legistature, Jean Lloyed-Jones. She tells me: "We can't help it. The younger generation has to be satisfied with less." Will the prediction prove true — less income, smaller apartments, and so forth? Perhaps only the younger readers themselves will be able to answer.

The Foner house is proof of the past's rising trend. Built at the turn of the century, it has now been modernized. The kitchen is equipped with a four-burner gas stove, a big refrigerator, and many cupboards. A toilet and shower bath have been added. A rubber hose leads lake water into an electric heater which provides plenty of hot water at the turn of a switch.

The professor and Roslyn are an affectionate couple. Phil (as Roslyn calls him) seems to rely on his wife for everything but his writing. He loudly calls "Roz" when his typewriter ribbon needs to be replaced or when he sees some insect on the floor. I soon realize that both the caller and the called thrive within the partnership. But at the same time I am a bit worried. When that unfortunate day comes and one of them has to "go meet Karl Marx" (the jolly way we refer to death in China), how will the survivor bear the blow? And I see clearly that Roz is not in good health.

Roz, on her part, is worried about me. One morning she talks to me seriously. "I couldn't go to sleep last night when I thought of your task. It should have been undertaken by a committee and done in two or three years. Now you are doing it alone in one year. But I advise you to relax, just travel around and see places. An over-strained mind cannot produce a readable book." From her look I know she is really worried for me. I decide to accept her advice. But how can I with so much to see and to learn in the year? That's the way Roz is, always caring for others. I had heard about that in China. Phil was giving lectures and she thought she should do something, too. Many Chinese students read but cannot speak English. To help them, Roz prepared a number of topics, such as "my happiest day" and "my worst day." She asked the students to prepare and then tell their stories one by one in

English. In this way she not only helped them with the language but got to understand them as fellow human beings. It's no wonder the students came to love her.

Lake Webb is secluded and tranquil. Every morning I stand on the shores and allow my eyes to linger on a unique landscape, an oil painting of undulating blue hills and umbrella-shaped trees, veiled in a milky white mist. I am reluctant to leave. But I must.

Roz says that I should go into the town and meet the people there, who seldom see any Chinese. We go together, first visiting the library. It has a good collection of books and is open every Tuesday and Thursday. Its service, to my surprise, also includes measuring blood pressure!

We then go to the post office. It has only a postmaster and all the delivery is done by part-time workers. "There isn't much to do in winter," the postmaster explains, "you can see many lights around the lake in the evening, but it will be all dark as soon as snow begins."

At this point, a woman comes in and we strike up a conversation. She says that her ancestors came from England five generations ago and her family has lived all along in Maine. She is a retired teacher and her grandchildren are seventh-generation Americans. She says that she is very pleased to meet a Chinese in the town. The next summer when I am back in China, Roz writes saying that the teacher had specifically requested that she convey her greetings to me. Americans are a particularly friendly people in these smaller places.

Family History

I meet Phil and Roz again on a number of occasions in Boston, New York City, and Philadelphia. From my chats with Roz I piece together some biographical information about them.

Their parents were poor people who came to the New World in the wave of mass immigration from eastern Europe at the turn of the century. Phil's father was not yet married. He lived in New York City by selling seltzer water, a favorite drink then. He had a horse-wagon to carry the water through the neighborhood in big barrels. Then he had to climb the stairs and deliver the water, many bottles in a bag. It was back-breaking labor. Phil's mother was an orphan taken to America at the age of seven by her aunt. She worked as a maidservant. After marriage she gave birth to four sons. Phil was the elder of twins born in 1910. All four brothers grew up to become political radicals.

As for Roz, her father was also a workingman, a typesetter. She, too, grew up to be a rebel against tradition. It was generally believed in those days that sending girls to college was not of much use. But she would not accept that and worked her way through college.

Phil was diligent in his studies. He also worked his way through college and began writing his doctoral dissertation at the age of twenty-two. His thesis was later published in 1940 as a book, *Business & Slavery: The New York Merchants and the Irrepressible Conflict*. The first of Phil's works, it won wide acclaim from reviewers. Phil met Roz in a May Day parade in 1938. He was a professor at the City College of New York at the time. He and his colleagues joined the demonstration in their doctoral robes. Roz was there as a member of the kindergarten teachers' union. They fell in love and got married the next May Day.

In 1941 the New York state legislature set up a committee to screen the teaching faculties of the city's schools and colleges. Like a bolt from the blue, more than fifty progressive teachers were dismissed overnight. Phil was one of them. The pay checks stopped coming when he needed them most to raise a newborn daughter.

The Fur and Leather Workers' Union hired Phil as "activities director" in charge of workers' basketball, chess and checker games. Obviously misplaced, Phil proposed to the union leaders a few months later that he be allowed to open a course on labor history for young workers, and he was made the union's "educational director." The job gave scope to his talent and enabled him to train quite a few strong grassroots leaders for the union.

In 1942 Phil collaborated with some friends to set up the "School for Democracy." It was forced to close soon afterwards. Then they founded the Jefferson School. With Paul Robeson and other well-known artists and writers on its faculty, it became a prestigious institution. But it was also forced to close soon. Meanwhile, Phil edited books for Citadel Press while continuing his own writing. From 1945 to 1967, Phil was a part owner of Citadel Press and for several years Roz was its production manager.

It was not until 1967 that Phil was appointed Professor of History at Lincoln University, Pennsylvania, and finally returned to teaching, a work he has always loved. The Marxist had paid dearly for his political conviction.

Phil has indeed always depended on Roz to take care of his daily life. But Roz had a revelation in late 1982 when she fell, suffered a bone fracture, and had to lie still with her leg in a cast. I went to see her. With tears in her eyes she told me how Phil was taking care of her. She had used to believe that he could not do a thing but write; but she now found that he would and could do eveything for her.

Before my departure from the United States in May 1983, we made plans to meet again in Beijing because Phil had been invited to make another lecture tour in China later that year. In September when I was anxiously expecting a telephone call from them upon their arrival, the host organization suddenly informed me that he might not be coming because Roz had died on 3 September. She died peacefully of a stroke while asleep. Born in 1913, Roz was young in spirit. She left us too soon.

At a memorial meeting in New York City, daughter Laura gathered the songs Roz liked most as the background music. Ella Mazel, a comrade and close friend of Roz for forty years, and also a friend of mine, made a tape recording and printed a memorial booklet of the gathering. She sent me a copy of each. I turned on the tape and heard Laura say as the meeting began: "This is a song I learned from my mother that she liked a lot. It was written by Lewis Alan and Fred Katz in 1936 for the International Brigade in Spain, and I'd like to ask people who know it to sing it with me." The song:

> *To you, beloved comrade,*
> *We make this solemn vow —*
> *The fight will go on,*
> *The fight will still go on.*
>
> *Like you, beloved comrade,*
> *We pledge our bodies now.*
>
> *The fight will go on,*
> *The fight will still go on.*

Rest here in the earth,
Your work is done.
You'll find new birth
When we have won,
When we have won.

Sleep well, beloved comrade,
Our work will just begin.
The fight will go on,
Till we win,
Until we win.

Chapter V

VISITS TO HISTORIC SITES

Although I have only a rudimentary knowledge of American history, having visited many historic sites, I feel a need to write on some aspects of America's past. Young Chinese readers should take advantage of a wide variety of Chinese and English-language books on the subject if they are seriously interested. I write here primarily for the uninitiated in the hope that my sketchy account will stimulate interest in the rapid development of America so that they will pursue the study further. As the old Chinese proverb goes, I am merely "casting a brick to get a gem" (*pao zhuan yin yu*).

FIRST PAGE OF AMERICAN HISTORY
— An Instructive Exhibit: "New England Begins"

It is a happy coincidence that when I arrive in Boston, an exhibition "New England Begins: The 17th Century" has just opened in the city. New England comprises six states in the northeastern part of America — Maine, New Hampshire, Vermont, Massachusetts, Connecticut, and Rhode Island. Their combined area is not much bigger than that of New York state, but they occupy a very important place in American history. I learn much from my visit to the exhibition.

"House-raising" is one of the "special events" of the opening week. A team of twelve carpenters, dressed in seventeenth-century costumes, using period tools and speaking the dialect of the times, goes into action. They cut down oaks and erect house uprights, cut clapboards with a big saw and climb up to thatch the saddle roof. The event culminates with a seventeenth-century festival meal to celebrate the completion of the house. The visitors are spellbound by the fancy costumes and the crafts which are almost lost now in modern America. A brochure says that the house is a fascimile of a building erected in 1637 in Dedham, near Boston, the only surviving structure of an earlier day.

The exhibit is housed in the Boston Museum of Fine Arts, world famous for its collection of Chinese and, particularly, Japanese *objets-d'art*. The museum building is impressive with its imposing, carved marble columns and beautiful marble floors. It is surrounded by flowerbeds and lawns. There are wide boulevards some distance away on which flashy-colored cars move in endless procession. The modern splendor forms a sharp contrast to the old-style house. But the simple building serves as a reminder to admirers of the prosperous charm of present-day America that the country had a humble beginning only 350 years ago. At that time China was convulsed in the historic peasant revolt against the Ming Dynasty which was led by Li Zicheng. Li captured the imperial palace of the Ming Court in Peking but soon afterwards was defeated. These are quite recent events by the standards of Chinese history. American history, however, was just dawning in the wilderness of a sparsely inhabited continent.

The three-month exhibition includes many other events — spinning, weaving, hurdling, wattling and daubing, etc. Musical performances show that the immigrants, in spite of the hardships besetting them, enjoyed their new life and were confident of a better tomorrow. For me, however, the historical documents and relics displayed in the exhibition halls were more useful for the background knowledge they provide.

A Difficult Start

The first colony in New England, called Plymouth Plantation, was founded accidentally because a ship carrying immigrants from England had lost its way. The time was 1620. The band of settlers boarding the *Mayflower* was to go to Jamestown in today's Virginia, where a colony had been established in 1607. The ship, instead, sailed to the Massachusetts Bay hundreds of miles to the north. Winter was coming and food was running out. The immigrants decided to land at Plymouth. It was December. Of the 102 who landed, only half lived through the severe winter to see the spring of 1621.

Crossing the Atlantic was no easy task in those days. Ordinary people did not have the financial and material resources to make the voyage. And they had no right, either. A colony could be founded only with the blessing of the English king, usually bestowed on chartered companies. Having missed their destination, the immigrants on the *Mayflower* had no authority to manage their colony. They found a way out by drawing up and signing an agreement to form "a civil Body Politick" and elect a leader. The agreement came to be known as the Mayflower Compact and occupied a prominent place in early American history as a model of self-government. Even today there are shops, restaurants, and apartments named after the Mayflower everywhere in the country. The Plymouth "Body Politick" elected William Bradford as its governor. The journal he kept was later published as a book entitled *Of Plymouth Plantation*. It was displayed at the exhibition. By the end of the century (1691), the plantation was amalgamated with the Massachusetts Bay Colony, which forms the theme of the exhibition.

The Massachusetts Bay Colony was founded in 1630. Its elected governor was John Winthrop. He was a somber-looking English aristocrat, as a portrait in the exhibition shows, and a well-educated lawyer from a rich family engaged in trade. In his thirties, Winthrop despaired of the stagnant economy, spiralling prices and rising unemployment in England. He decided to move to the New World. He kept a journal which was later published as a book, *History of New England*. It was also displayed at the exhibition.

The New England settlers considered themselves English. Most came with their families and resettled together in towns and villages modeled on English patterns. Some villages had farmland in the middle surrounded by log cabins. Others had houses clustered in the middle with outlying farmland and pastures. But the settlers soon found the land was rocky and poor. "The chief product is stones," as the old saying goes. But the area abounded in forests which could be used to build ships, a highly lucrative trade. Cod fishing was also profitable. In addition, there was fur trading with the Indians for the European market. Trade enabled Boston to grow into the biggest North American port, while Massachusetts eventually became one of the most prosperous of the original thirteen English colonies.

The many original maps displayed at the exhibit show that the early settlements were concentrated on the Atlantic seaboard. The settlers knew practically nothing of the wilderness to the west. A map drawn by Captain John Smith, leader of the Jamestown colony, after many reconnoitering trips to Massachusetts Bay is prominently displayed. It was the captain who first named the area "New England." Wide circulation of his map resulted in general acceptance of the name among the immigrants including the competing Dutch and French settlers. It was also this map which led the Mayflower pilgrims to land at the place marked out as Plymouth. The name was later carved on a huge rock on the seashore which became a national monument.

All settlers coming to America had to face great ordeals. The first band which came to Jamestown, for example, experienced even greater difficulties than those in Plymouth. Of a total of 144 who set out from England, thirty-nine died on the voyage, and only 38 survived two years after their landing. They were about to return to England but gave up the idea when a new group of immigrants came. The winter of 1609-10, "the starving time," was worse than anything before. The document, *Journals of the House of Burgesses of Virginia*, records that in this deadly winter, people at Jamestown had been

> . . . driven thru insufferable hunger to eat those things which nature most abhorred, the flesh and excrements of man as well of our own nation as of an Indian, digged by some out of his grave after he had lain buried three days and wholly devoured him; others, envying the better state of body of any whom hunger has not yet so much wasted as their own, lay wait and threatened to kill and eat them; one of them slew his wife as she slept in his bosom, cut her in pieces, salted her and fed upon her till he had clean devoured all parts saving her head. (quoted from Howard Zinn's *A People's History of the United States*).

This was an extreme example. It nonetheless throws some light on the tribulations the trail blazers suffered.

Other exhibits testify to the enormous contributions New England made to America's cultural development. The *New England Primer* , which taught the children their letters, shows the importance attached to education. Compulsory primary education was first introduced in New England. A *Commencement Day Broadside* reminds visitors of the founding of Harvard College in 1636, the first American institution of higher learning. But the academic debate at the time, as the broadside shows, was conducted in Latin, and dissertations were also written in Latin.

New England was also the place where a printing trade and library service were first started. A section of the exhibition displays a rich assortment of wooden furniture and silverware. They are as intricately carved as those kept in Beijing's Palace Museum, but the patterns are entirely different and distinctively Western. The colonies of New England were also the cradle of other American crafts and trades.

Their forms of self-government, however, were perhaps the most important contribution New England colonies made to American culture. These forms were different from the governments of those other colonies the English king formed for aristocratic proprietors. This factor helps explain why the first scenes of the great drama of the American Revolution would be eventually staged in Boston.

Plight of the Indians

I am deeply impressed by the exhibition's frank treatment of the history of American Indians. A brochure reads:

Before 1615 a total of 72,000 Algonkians lived between southern Maine and the Hudson River. By 1690 these peoples were exterminated or enslaved. No amount of dwelling on the prejudiced attitude of Englishmen toward tribal cultures, no emphasis on their half-hearted attempts to convert the Indians to Christianity, and no appeal to the legal fiction of purchasing land from Indian leaders — nothing alters this brutal reality. The Puritan leaders were responsible for a systematic, ruthless takeover of Indian lands and a mad, genocidal destruction of Indian populations. They vied with one another in a panicky scramble to grab whatever they could while it was to be had. Trading post was pitted against trading post, colony against colony, the English of New England against the Dutch of New Amsterdam and the French of New France.

What were the prizes? First, they sought control of the fur trade and the production centers of wampum, the shell beads used as money in the trade. Second, once the fur-bearing animals were killed off, particularly the beaver, competition shifted to political control of various tribes and the lands they inhabited. Third, those tribes that would not submit were destroyed, the prisoners of war sold into slavery in the West Indies and the land broken up and distributed among white settlers.

After describing how the Indians' economy of self-sufficiency was undermined, the brochure continues:

Along with trade goods, the Europeans brought diseases to which the Indian population had no resistance. Smallpox, measles, and bubonic plague proved virulent killers. The first recorded plague, from about 1616 to 1619, hit the Massachusett tribe around Boston harbor the hardest, leaving the area virtually depopulated, a catastrophe over which John Winthrop later glorified in God's having "providentially" cleared the area for his group to settle in.

. . . .

Once the English established permanent settlements in New England, the pace of intimidation, acculturation, and outright destruction of Indian tribes was greatly accelerated. . . .

Remnants of the Algonkian tribes dwindled away, victims of poverty, alcoholism and broken dreams.

Why are the American natives called Indians? A brief explanation may be necessary for young Chinese readers. In the 15th and 16th centuries, the great Venetian traveler Marco Polo's glowing account of China had fired the imagination of many Europeans with a dreamlike journey to the East. But the overland route to China was blocked at the time. The theory that the earth was a globe was gaining popularity. People thought they could get to China by going west on a circumnavigational sea route. But nobody in the world knew the existence of the American continents and islands between Europe and Asia except the natives living there. When Christopher Columbus set out on his historic voyage, he had with him a letter of salutation from the Queen of Spain addressed to the Khan of China.

As Columbus's ships approached today's Bahamas Islands in the Caribbean Sea in 1492, the sailors cried out "Land!" in ecstasy, and believed they had reached India, and China was not far beyond. Until his death Columbus still believed that he had arrived in India. That was why the American natives were called Indians. In China we translate the name into *Yindi'anren* just to avoid confusion with our neighbor *Yinduren* , the Indians. The American natives, in fact, had different names for different tribes. They had lived on the land for ten to twenty thousand years (twentyfive thousand years, according to some scholars). Then Ferdinand Magellan started his historic voyage in 1519. His expedition crossed the Atlantic, passed the southern tip of South America and sailed across the Pacific, eventually returning to Europe. Only then did Europeans know that the Americas were not Asia.

By the 1560s, Spaniards and Portuguese swarmed to the Americas. The Dutch and the French followed closely on their heels. The English, however, began colonization only in the 17th century. When New England was first settled, the present city of New York was a Dutch possession named New Amsterdam. The American nation was still in an embryonic stage. The United States is very, very young by Chinse standards.

THE WAR OF INDEPENDENCE
—Boston Tea Party and the American Revolution

Looking east from the John Hancock Building observatory in downtown Boston on a sunny day, you can see the dim contours of islands off the Atlantic coast many miles away. Down below is the large Boston Public Garden with luxuriant greens and a glittering lake. The Boston Common is farther to the east with its monument to the 1770 Boston Massacre, a prelude to the rebellion against English rule. On the east side of the Common is the Old Granary Burying Ground, where the five victims of the massacre are buried in eternal glory along with John Hancock and Sam Adams, organizers of the Boston Tea Party, and their secret messenger, the silver-smith Paul Revere. Farther beyond is the Atlantic coast on which, a little to the south, is the Boston Tea Party Museum. *Beaver II* , a Tea Party ship, is moored at its side. "The Boston Tea Party," as now translated into Chinese, can easily be misunderstood as a social gathering celebrating some occasion. Actually it means the group of patriotic young Americans organized by revolutionary leaders to storm the British ships to dump defiantly their cargo of tea into the Boston harbor. This incident touched off the war to win independence from Britain.

Zigzaging eastward from the Observatory are a number of old streets called the Freedom Trail. So many memorable sites are there that nostalgic tourists have likened the trail to a necklace strewn with priceless pearls. They include Faneuil Hall, where American patriotic leaders made the decision to resist the British-imposed duties on tea and Old South Church (also known as Old Church Meetinghouse), where mass meetings were held to stir up the public against British rule.

During my stay in Boston I often stroll around this part of the town and daydream. Could the Boston Common, so quiet and beautiful now, be the drilling ground of British troops, called "Redcoats" because they were dressed in scarlet jackets, with snow-white trousers and shiny black helmets? Hadn't the Redcoats, armed with deadly muskets and dazzling bayonets, arrogantly trod the Boston streets? History moves fast and inexorably.

The Massachusetts settlers, as I have described in the preceding chapter, had a strong tradition of self-government. For 150 years after their arrival, they had worked to turn the wilderness into a thriving land. But the mother country was determined to extract the wealth they developed. After an abortive attempt to impose a Stamp Act on its American colonies, the British king sought to levy duties on tea and other commodities. The exploitative measure aroused vehement protest throughout the colonies in general, and in Massachusetts in particular.

The British sent two army regiments to Boston in 1768 to garrison the unruly city. They assessed townspeople for labor, and deprived many of their jobs. Popular resentment mounted. One cold winter day in 1770, some fifty ropemakers and other Bostonians whose jobs had been taken away, vented their wrath by throwing snowballs and oyster shells at the Redcoats. A brawl ensued. The soldiers fired, killing five and wounding six others. The killers were given only a token punishment. People were outraged. Ten thousand of them marched in the funeral procession, more than half of the total Boston population of sixteen thousand.

The Boston Tea Party

The Boston Tea Party occurred in 1773, three years after the Boston Massacre. American patriot leaders decided to prevent the British East India Company's tea ships from unloading their cargo in Boston. The British government, on its part, decided that the ships must unload before they were permitted to leave. A deadlock emerged and the British sent naval vessels. Boston's patriot leaders gave the British merchant ships twenty days to depart for London. They called mass meetings in the Old South Church to generate popular support, and petitions for the ships to leave were sent daily to the British-appointed govennor, but to no avail.

The ensuing events are recapitulated with sound and color at the Tea Party Ship & Museum. Apart from historical documents and relics, the museum displays most prominently a wooden chest filled with tea. It is said to be the only one remaining of the 340 dumped into the harbor by the Tea Party. A show of slides goes on continuously for visitors, to recount the anxiety and wrath of the Bostonians at the time.

An American friend accompanying me on the visit tells me the dramatic story in greater detail. Adams and Hancock had secretly organized a band of young men for action. Swearing not to divulge their secret plans to anybody, they were divided into three groups of thirty for each of the three British tea ships in the harbor. The leaders wore for easier identification white handkerchiefs around their necks, and red strings on their wrists. The 21-day limit ended on 16 December 1773. With mass meetings continuing at Old South Church, one more petition was submitted to the governor and was rejected. Sam Adams then spoke up in the church and declared that "this meeting can do nothing more to save the country." It was a countersign for action. Whistles were directed at where the young patriots hid. These were answered by Indian war whoops and such cries as "Boston Harbor a teapot tonight," or "Hi, Mohawks, get your axes and pay no taxes!" A band of "Indian warriors" appeared, their faces smudged with soot and painted red, and rushed to the dock where they boarded the ships. With the captains and crews ordered to stay quiet or else in their cabins, the "Indian warriors" then seized the tea chests, broke them open and flung them overboard. The operation proceeded almost noiselessly except for the crash of axes into the chests. Thousands of people gathered on the wharf to watch silently. It was near dawn when the work on all three ships was done.

Beaver II is a facsimile of the *Beaver*, one of the three tea ships. I wonder how such a small brig could sail across the Atlantic. My friend assures me that it is true to the original. And he asks if I have seen the slogan "Taxation without representation is tyranny," saying that it was the real heart of the issue. In fact, he explains, only three pennies were to be levied on a pound of tea and it would not have been much of a burden on the colonies though people in those days drank tea twice a day. Going deeper into the matter, he says, the tax issue was a struggle for the right to rule. It was why the British government reacted angrily to the Tea Party. It demanded compensation. The Bostonians refused to pay. The British then brought in more warships to impose a blockade on the city in a bid to force it into submission.

The high-handed repression, instead of bringing the Americans to terms, brought the thirteen often jealous, indifferent, and separate colonies together. But it was hard for the Bostonians. The British government replaced the governor with a general and fresh reinforcements were dispatched to the city. My friend mentions that because there were so many British in the town figures of speech such as, "one out of every three is a Redcoat," or "Be careful not to tread on the toes of Redcoats" invaded the language.

The Bostonians were confronted by the choice of either surrendering or fighting. They chose the latter course and began organizing militia in the towns and countryside. Militiamen took an oath to be ready "at any minute," and became known as "Minutemen." My friend asks if I have seen the statue of the Minuteman at Concord. He is referring to the town west of Boston where American Minutemen and British regulars fought the first battle. After the initial confrontation, the colonists convened the second Continental Congress in Philadelphia and sent George Washington to Boston as Commander-in-Chief of the American forces. In Charlestown, north of Boston, Washington led the first major duel with the British — the Battle of Bunker Hill.

Where the First Shots Were Fired

A visit in Boston without going to Concord would be tantamount to visiting Beijing without going to the Great Wall. I had gone to Concord twice, but on business. A real journey into the past is arranged by the hospitable Robinsons.

We are about to leave West Gate when a thunderstorm strikes. I am afraid that we will have to cancel the trip. "If you don't like the weather in Boston," Dick says, "just wait a minute." The saying means that Boston has a very changeable climate. True enough, the sky soon brightens up, vegetation becomes greener and the sweltering summer heat has been subdued. We drive to Concord, twenty miles west of Boston.

In the eighteenth century Concord was a small village. On the night of 18 April 1775, a British expedition of some seven hundred men set out quietly from Boston in a surprise move to seize the American militia's arms and ammunition, and arrest Adams and Hancock. They ran into Minutemen in Lexington on their way to Concord, however, and a shot rang out from a Redcoat's musket. Others followed, eight Americans died, and the American Revolutionary War had begun. It was dawn, 19 April.

The striking statue of the Minuteman at Concord arouses my interest. His look and clothing bear a remarkable resemblance to the Chinese guerrilla during the war of resistance against Japan (1937-45).

Perhaps this is because both were "farmers" who could raise a rifle to fight, or lay down his arms to plow.

It is summer vacation for schools in the United States. A group of youthful students are looking up at the statue on its pedestal while a young man, a volunteer guide, explains. I have seen many of these after school activities in America. In the Tea Party Ship & Museum, for instance, there is a two-hour special program for students and pupils leading them into history by ingenious devices instead of dull textbooks. The kids are allowed not only to board *Beaver II*, but are provided with a chest which they can fling into the harbor in imitation of the Tea Party "warriors." I appreciate these resourceful ways to help youngsters learn and remember history.

The battleground at Concord remains largely as it was, with thick bushes and grass. At the far end of it is an ancient house which, Dick tells me, was used by Minutemen as a sentry post to watch the Redcoats. The Concord River flows close by. The British troops coming from Lexington crossed the North Bridge over the river to seize the American military stores. The bridge remains intact today. At the center of the open ground stands a monument on which the names of the war dead are inscribed. I stand in silent tribute to the heroes who had laid down their lives for national liberation. The fighting at Concord and Lexington, though not a big battle, showed the Americans that their farmers could beat British regulars.

Many other historic sites have been preserved in the vicinity. The Colonial Inn attracts many tourists. We have tea in its cafe. The Wayside Inn is a hotel with a restaurant, antiquated in appearance, but inconspicuously equipped with all modern facilities. Visitors flock to the place for a memento lunch or dinner. I wouldn't have had the luck to eat there if Carol had not reserved seats a few days earlier.

We drive back from Concord on an old post road. It was along this route that the secret messenger Paul Revere rode out from Boston to Concord in the night. His mission was to report to Adams and Hancock that the British were coming and to give the alarm to the Minutemen there. On the way he was intercepted and taken into brief custody by the British, though his mission was accomplished by another secret messenger. The place of his detention has also been preserved. The British troops, in fact, were watched on all sides by hostile Americans. To keep troop movements secret, only their officers were told where they were going. But with the local people on alert, American spies were able to get exact information about the location of the British.

There is not much to see at the Lexington battlefield. But on 19 April every year, Dick tells me, history is recreated. Seventy men acting as Minutemen line up to meet seven-hundred acting as Redcoats. A shot is fired and then followed by a barrage. Eight Americans fall as if they had been shot.

The actual sequence of historical events was that after the skirmish at Lexington the British marched westward to Concord six miles away. Some one thousand Minutemen had assembled there, and fighting broke out. The Americans fired from behind stone walls, stables, trees, and bushes. The Redcoats began to retreat. Back in Lexington more Minutemen went after them to avenge their eight fallen comrades. The British had to fight all the way back to Boston because there were Minutemen everywhere. If fresh reinforcements had not rushed to their rescue, most of the seven-hundred Redcoats probably would have fallen to the continuous attack.

Why did those colonists fight so valiantly? A brochure provides a good answer. It says: "When asked decades later why he had taken his musket and gone out to face the soldiers, one man who had turned out that day said simply, 'We had always governed ourselves, and we always meant to. They didn't mean we should.'"

The flame ignited at Lexington-Concord spread. But the Americans still had a hard and protracted war to fight before they would finally win independence in 1783.

Battle of Bunker Hill

Before my departure from Boston for China the next spring, I make a special point of visiting the Bunker Hill Monument in Charlestown, north of Boston. It is the site of the first major battle of the American Revolution. The monument is 220 feet high and the visitor has to climb a 294-step staircase to its apex. The exhibition hall beside it displays many paintings depicting the battle that took place about two months after Lexington-Concord.

To ensure that their garrison in Boston would not be threatened, the British dispatched 2,400 men to launch a fierce attack on Americans positions on Bunker Hill. George Washington came to assume command of the American forces after the battle began. The Americans ultimately retreated, although in good order, after the British launched their third attack. But it was a costly victory for the British. One of their generals said that Great Britain could not afford another such "victory." An American leader said, "I could sell them another hill at the same price." The price was, in spite of their superior arms and cannons, 476 Redcoats dead and many more wounded. The loss of 89 British officers who were either killed or wounded was a particularly serious blow.

Washington found his men so steady that his officers could order: "Don't shoot till you see the whites of their eyes!" The men followed instructions and made the most of their meager ammunition.

I see houses in the vicinity of the battle site flying the American flag of the time, thirteen white stars in a circle symbolizing the thirteen colonies, rather than the present fifty stars in a square for the fifty states. The residents are obviously still proud of what the old flag stands for—an independent America. The Minuteman's words on self-government represent a homely but great truth still valid today. People everywhere want to govern themselves.

THE BIRTH OF A NATION
— Independence Hall and Washington Square, Philadelphia

Philadelphia is the fourth largest city in the United States after New York, Chicago and Los Angeles. It is better known in China as Feicheng ("the Phil city") because the full name is rather difficult to pronounce. Seen from the air, the metropolis looks like a mammoth bat sprawling on the Delaware River, the old city being its body and the later extensions its wings.

At the time of the American Revolution, Philadelphia and New York were the only two American cities with a population exceeding

20,000. Philadelphia was the largest and New York second. From 1790 to 1800 the city was the temporary capital of the newborn nation. Washington D.C. took its place in 1801.

Philadelphia is unquestionably historic. The well-known Independence Hall, Liberty Bell Pavilion, and Washington Square are all situated close to the Delaware in the old city.

Many streets in this section of the town are paved with pebbles or stone blocks. The buildings, however refurbished inside, keep their original outward appearance. Old-timers can tell offhand which were built in the eighteenth century and which in the nineteenth century. The tick-tack of horse carriages and the jingling of their bells add to the atmosphere of antiquity. Tourists vie for a ride in them though the fare is about ten times higher than a taxi. The city is proud of all these, and rightly so.

Though the first shots of the War of Independence were fired in Lexington, Concord, and Boston, the United States of America was born in Philadelphia. The Declaration of Independence, "birth certificate" of the nation, was signed here on 4 July 1776. The date has been designated Independence Day, an equivalent to our National Day. Chinese readers may still remember reports of the American Bicentennial celebrations in 1976. It was the two-hundredth anniversary of the signing of the declaration which announced that the thirteen English colonies* had decided to unite and fight to establish a republic, independent of British rule.

Unknown Heroes of the Revolution

One sunny morning I come to lush green Washington Square. The Tomb of the Unknown Soldier of the American Revolution is there. A written declaration, as the experience of all colonial people shows, does not bring about independence by itself. The pen often has to be backed up by the gun. The American Revolution was a harbinger of

---

*The thirteen colonies are, by the order of their ratification of the Declaration of Independence: Delaware, Pennsylvania, New Jersey, Georgia, Connecticut, Massachusetts, Maryland, South Carolina, New Hampshire, Virginia, New York, North Carolina and Rhode Island. They became the first thirteen states of the United States of America.

this truth. The tomb reminds visitors of the bloody eight-year war and the enormous difficulties the Americans overcame to turn their Declaration of Independence into reality. The tomb is also a monumental tribute to the contributions of George Washington, Commander-in-Chief of the American forces and the first President of the nation.

The tomb consists of a bronze statue of Washington standing behind a stone coffin. An eternal flame burns in front of the coffin which bears the inscription: "Beneath the stone lies a soldier of Washington's army who died to give you liberty."

A wall-size granite tablet stands behind Washington's statue. A passage from Washington's Farewell Address when he retired after serving two terms (1789-97) as President is inscribed on the tablet. It is early in the morning and there are few visitors. No noise except the chirping of birds can be heard. Quietness enhances the solemnity of the place. With a feeling of respect I copy down the inscription, which reads:

> Freedom is a light for which many men have died in darkness in unmarked graves. Within this square lie thousands of unknown soldiers of Washington's army who died of wounds and sickness during the Revolutionary War. The independence and liberty you possess are the work of joint councils, and joint efforts — of common dangers, sufferings, and success.

The tomb, without the pomposity of feudal mausoleums, is memorable. Washington and the other heroes deserve perpetual reverence. When they founded the first modern republic, China was still in the midst of the Qing Dynasty's monarchic rule, and Europe continued to be parceled into possessions of large and small royal courts. Theirs was a contribution not only to America but to all mankind.

Sunrise or Sunset

Within walking distance of Washington Square is Independence Hall, on Independence Square. I join the many visitors already assembled there. Visitors are admitted into the hall group by group to avoid congestion. The meeting hall on the ground floor is the place where the founding fathers gathered to make their momentous decisions.

The Chinese translation of the words "founding fathers" tends to evoke the image of aging, sagacious statesmen. In fact, with the exception of Benjamin Franklin, they were mostly middle-aged or young men. Thomas Jefferson, who drafted the Declaration of Independence, was thirty-three at the time. John Hancock, who presided over the Second Continental Congress when it passed the declaration, was thirty-eight.

The meeting place witnessed many great events. Here, George Washington was appointed Commander-in-Chief on 15 June 1775 and immediately left for the New England front. Here, the Declaration of Independence was passed and signed. Here, the American Congress accepted the captured colors of the British army after General Cornwallis's troops laid down their arms to surrender.* And here, the Constitutional Convention adopted, after heated debate, the United States Constitution, thus resolving the paramount question of whether the newborn nation was to be the "United States of America," a unified country that was to grow in strength.

Visitors listen attentively to the guide as she points to a chair and says: "It is the seat of George Washington when he presided over the Constitutional Convention. It is called the 'sunrise chair.'" She goes on to explain the origin of the name. After seventeen weeks of often acrimonious debate, the convention finally adopted the Constitution. Washington and the other delegates, impressed by the solemnity of the moment, sat in grave meditation. Eighty-one-year-old Franklin, with his usual sagacity, pointed to the half-sun painted in brilliant gold on the back of Washington's chair and said: "I have often and often in the course of the session, and the vicissitudes of my hopes and fears as to

*Cornwallis's army surrendered on 17 October 1781. This prompted the British government to terminate the war. Peace negotiations were started in April, 1782 and lasted until November when a preliminary accord was reached. The treaty was formally signed in Paris the next year. Actual fighting had gone on for six years, though the War of Independence is usually chronicled from the Lexington-Concord encounter in 1776, to the signing of the peace treaty in 1783.

its issue, looked at that behind the President, without being able to tell whether it was rising or setting: but now, at length, I have the happiness to know that it is a rising, and not a setting, sun." Hence "the sunrise chair."

Facing the President's seat are thirteen long tables covered with dark green cloth, six to the left and seven to the right. There is a candlestick on each table with an unlit candle. But, the guide says, one of the tables was vacant at the Constitutional Convention because Rhode Island, the smallest of the thirteen original colonies, refused to attend.

Many historic documents and relics are displayed on the second floor. It would take at least a whole day to look at them carefully. I follow the usually fast-moving Americans out of the hall to an open ground outside. There is a hustle and bustle as more visitors join lines to enter the hall. Pupils are coming group after group, escorted by their teachers. A team of filmmakers with a camera mounted on a big tripod are photographing the Liberty Bell Pavilion on the side. When the Declaration of Independence was first read to the public after its adoption, I am told, chimes from the belfry rang out and reverberated all over Philadelphia. This made the pavilion historic. I find a bench in the shadow of an ancient tree to sit and have a good look at the hall and the pavilion from a distance.

A vigorous elderly gentleman passes by. I ask him to snap a photo for me. Returning my camera, the gentleman tells me that he has brought his granddaughter here for a visit. The small girl is now playing with her young friends and he has to wait for a while. Seating himself on the bench, he begins a conversation with me. I ask if he can explain to me the basic cause of the American Revolution. Apparently an educated man, he answers after a brief pause: "I have read a book which puts it this way: 'When the people in power can neither keep the consent of the governed nor keep down the dissent of the governed, then there will be a revolution.' It was so with the American Revolution."

I ask again why the young nation was menaced by a possible "sunset." After another pause, he explains that the thirteen colonies, like sisters-in-law in a big household who had just got rid of their overbearing mother-in-law, would not like somebody to take her place. That is to say, they did not want a powerful national government to rule over them as the English king did. They finally came to realize, however, that the nation could survive only in unity, and would perish if divided. This made it necessary for them to accommodate each other and accept a national constitution. In fact, he recalls, dissention among the thirteen colonies was already apparent at the time of the signing of the Declaration of Independence. He cites some examples. The declaration contains the oft-quoted statement: ".. that all Men are created equal, that they are endowed by their Creator with certain unalienable Rights, that among these are Life, Liberty and the Pursuit of Happiness." But some states, when writing their own constitutions in pursuance of the declaration, replaced "the Pursuit of Happiness" with "the acquisition and protection of private property." Condemnation of the slave trade, written into the draft declaration by Thomas Jefferson, was deleted in deference to the slave holding southern states. Likewise, the United States Constitution, adopted later, provided only the termination of slave traffic by 1808, but shunned the issue of slave-holding. These are reasons why, the gentleman adds, some historians say that the Constitution was a product of three principles — "compromise, compromise and compromise" — compromise for the sake of survival. He then adds that he is just chatting and it would be best for me to go to the library and read the differing views of historians.

Fundamental Statute Adopted

After victory in the War of Independence, according to history books, controversies among the thirteen states assumed alarming proportions. Each of them tried to promote its self-interest at the expense of others. There were disputes over state boundaries. Trade was another source of acute friction. New Jersey, for instance, had to pay high export duties and dock fees to ship and sell its vegetables in New York City, just across the Hudson River. Slavery was a strong centrifugal force because the southern states feared that the national government might move for its abolition. Worse still, some states were bypassing the union to negotiate with foreign governments. Nine states had founded their separate armies and some had their own navies, too. Independent currencies were put in circulation in a number of states, resulting in great financial chaos. The situation was so bad that something had to be done.

In 1787, upon the proposal of several states, the American Congress called on all thirteen states to send delegates to Philadelphia for a meeting to amend the Articles of Confederation. The Articles, adopted by the Second Continental Congress in 1777, did provide for a unified government. But it took four years for the states to ratify them. Even then the articles had so little binding power that Washington called them a "rope of sand." At the 1787 meeting called to amend the articles, delegates soon found that mere amendments could not remedy the situation. To unite the states, it seemed imperative to create a federal government presided over by a head of state, and to have it rest on the foundation of a federal constitution. In this way, the meeting evolved into a constitutional convention. States supporting the idea sent their delegates promptly. The vacillating ones stalled. Small Rhode Island refused to attend.

The convention opened on 14 May 1787. Washington was elected to preside. Sixty-five delegates were named by twelve states, but ten failed to show up. The fifty-five who came to Philadelphia often absented themselves from sessions. The Constitution was finally adopted on 17 September. Only thirty-nine delegates signed, and some did so with reservations. The other sixteen refused to sign at all.

In order to take effect, the Constitution had to be ratified by two-thirds, or nine, of the thirteen states. In 1788, New Hampshire voted fifty-seven to forty-six to become the ninth ratifier, thus establishing the fundamental statute's validity. Rhode Island procrastinated until May of 1790, when by a narrow margin (34 to 32), it voted to ratify. The birth pangs of the new nation were over and the danger of a "disunited states of America" was finally warded off.

The bicentennial of the United States Constitution will soon come. During the past 200 years, enormous changes have taken place in America and the world. At the time Washington retired from the presidency, the United States was a small agricultural country with a population of four million, including 700,000 slaves. Now, with a population of 232 million, it has become one of the world's two superpowers.

American independence was an event of worldwide significance. The Declaration of Independence, called by Karl Marx the first declaration of human rights, was a clarion call to all peoples to rise against colonial rule and feudal oppression. It is regrettable to note, however, that since it has become a world power, the United States has not always adhered to the spirit of its own declaration in the conduct of its international relations.

TWO BATTLEFIELDS OF THE CIVIL WAR

— Antietam and Vicksburg

The American Civil War, also called the "War Between the States," began in 1861 and ended in 1865. In China it was the period when Empress Dowager Cixi of the Qing Dynasty, who built the famous Summer Palace in Beijing, began her reign. In America, a great statesman, Abraham Lincoln, became President and guided the country through a bloody war to abolish slavery.

After independence the United States saw the rapid growth of capitalism propelled by the industrial revolution. On the eve of the Civil War its industrial economy ranked fourth in the world and was superceded only by Great Britain, France, and Germany. Capitalism thrived on wage labor in the North, while the agriculturally based economy of the South depended significantly on black slavery. Conflict between the two different economic systems ultimately brought war.

The slave-holding states of the South, which seceded from the United States to form the Confederate States of America, were on one side. The remaining states were united in their determination to preserve the Union by forcing the rebelling southern states back into it. In the process, they would ultimately abolish slavery throughout the country. Washington, D.C., was the Union capital, while Richmond, Virginia, was the capital of the Confederacy. The secessionist government had its first, and also its last president —

Jefferson Davis. Its territory comprised eleven* of the thirty-four American states at the time and had a population of nine million, forty-percent of them black slaves.

The Bloodiest Day

About sixty miles northwest of Washington D.C. is the site of an important battle — Antietam Creek. While I am visiting the American capital, my hosts Dick and Martha Bernhart take me to visit the national monument there. It is September. Exactly 120 years have elapsed since the battle on 17 September 1862. During the one-day duel more than 25,000 men on both sides fell dead or wounded. It came to be known as "the bloodiest single day of the Civil War."

The monument is a towering structure and the exhibition hall is also impressive. Visitors keep coming in a steady stream. A short film interpretation of the battle is shown to visitors at thirty-minute intervals. Dick says that though he has seen the film many times he still likes it for its lyrical recitation, harmonious background music, and vivid portrayal of the human sufferings in that fratricidal conflict. After seeing the film I find Dick's casual comment to have been appropriate. But what attracts me more are the old paintings of the battle scenes. The artists' brush had greater freedom than the camera's lens. They could combine a panoramic view with precise details, giving at once a realistic and romantic presentation. On a faraway hill in the background southerners are seen swarming down with muskets. Fighting is already raging between the advance contingents in the foreground. The northerners' muskets are firing, shown by the small puffs of white smoke at their muzzles. Some soldiers are falling from horseback. Some have been cut down. Medics are running with stretchers. Officers look around anxiously from their steeds. One

---

* The eleven states, in order of their secession from the Union, were: South Carolina, Mississippi, Florida, Alabama, Georgia, Louisiana, Texas, Virginia, Arkansas, Tennessee and North Carolina. South Carolina announced its secession on 20 December 1860, after the election of Lincoln, who was dedicated to anti-slavery, to the presidency. Six other states followed closely on its heels. The southerners opened fire on 12 April, 1861. President Lincoln issued a call to quell the rebellion. Four more states then seceded from the Union.

cannon, the mightiest weapon of the time, blows out a huge ball of smoke.

While I am still engrossed in the scenes, Dick reminds me that we must go now to visit Harpers Ferry, on the Potomac River. We are in Maryland and Harpers Ferry is in the neighboring state of West Virginia. On the way, Dick explains to me that the Confederates, trying to end the war quickly, marched northward in a bid to capture Washington. They thought if they were to succeed, they might be able to obtain international recognition. The great European powers of the time all had developed textile industries and hoped to retain the American South not only as a source of cotton, but as a market. After Antietam, however, they hesitated to recognize the Confederacy. Antietam was also a turning point because five days after the battle, Lincoln issued a preliminary edict which freed all black slaves in the rebelling states and, on New Year's Day, 1863, the formal Emancipation Proclamation. The war began to take a favorable turn for the northerners, or Federals.

Harpers Ferry also saw battle during the war. But it owed its fame primarily to the abolitionist movement prior to the war. In 1859, twenty-one people, including five black slaves, took part in a revolt led by John Brown. They seized a federal arsenal at the ferry. In the ensuing battle most of them were killed. Brown was captured and sent to the gallows. American historians differ in their appraisal of Brown but all agree that he persisted in his conviction and believed truth was on his side at his death. The Brown uprising, though small in scale, nevertheless showed that smoldering hatred for slavery was about to explode.

Harpers Ferry today keeps the appearance of a small mid-nineteenth century town. The cramped shops, their wooden counters and displays of goods, all remind me of the small Chinese towns south of the Changjiang (Yangtze) River familiar to me in my young days. To pay tribute to Brown, a projection room has been set up where visitors, without the help of a guide, can turn on the projector and see historical scenes on a screen. Tape recordings play simultaneously to narrate the story. It is an economical and effective way of disseminating historical information.

The Vicksburg Battle

Later, when I visit Mississippi, in the Deep South, I have an opportunity to see another important Civil War battle site at Vicksburg. Close to one thousand miles southwest of Antietam, Vicksburg is proof of the wide extent of the war.

It is late November when I arrive at the town. The Christmas season has begun. Colorful garlands are hung on lampposts at intersections. Shop windows are decorated with Christmas trees, colorfully tinselled and spread with imitation snow. In stark contrast to the battlefield I am to see, it is a serene sight.

Roving the country from one place to another, I always have to rely on the guidance and help of my American friends. Margaret and Bryan McLemore (better know as Mag and Mac) of Hazlehurst, Mississippi, both well advanced in years, readily drive me a long distance to the Vicksburg National Military Park and Cemetery.

The forty-eight-day battle at Vicksburg in 1863 was a decisive campaign in the Civil War. Situated on the east bank of the Mississippi River, Vicksburg was a strategic stronghold known as "the Gibraltar of the West." The Confederates vowed to defend this fortress which controlled the Mississippi River, a primary artery of inland navigation. The Union forces initially mounted fierce frontal attacks and suffered serious casualties. They then shifted to a siege by land and naval forces. The defenders, reduced to eating mules, dogs, and even rats, were finally forced into submission.

The large military park is in the western suburbs of the town. All states involved in the war, north and south alike, were apportioned a tract of land or a hillside on which to build their own monuments. As we drive along, we see bronze statues of soldiers (some on horseback and others presented in busts), granite sculptures, towering tablets, Roman columns, and carved arches. Inscriptions on bronze plaques record heroic feats performed during the war. We soon arrive at the cemetery. It is lined with row upon row of tombstones as far as the eye can see. Battlefield foes now dwell as eternal neighbors.

We then come to the *USS Cairo*, now restored, and a museum. Sunk in the battle of Vicksburg, the warship was salvaged a few years ago after resting on the riverbed for almost a century. The ship is placed on wooden supports and protected by a large overhead roof. Visitors can look from a staircase behind railings. Everything found on the ship, from weapons to articles of daily use and a few coins, is displayed in glass cases at the museum. I am amazed by an intact black shirt which, according to the caption, is made of Chinese silk.

The Civil War raged on for nearly five years. In early April 1865 the Federals captured Richmond, and shortly afterwards, Robert E. Lee of the Confederate forces surrendered what was left of his battered army. At dawn, 10 April, Washington, D.C. reverberated with a three-hundred-gun salute and people went into ecstasy over the end of bloodshed. Of the population of thirty-million, over 600,000 died (many due to sickness). Property losses amounted to $15 billion. But the deep wounds inflicted in people's hearts could not be expressed in figures. The soul-stirring conflict has since become the topic of so much creative imagination that some people say books on the subject could "fill the Grand Canyon."

Slaves Emancipated?

My Chinese readers may ask why the black problem has remained since the slaves were emancipated more than a century ago. The answer is complex.

To begin with, it is not exactly right to say that the blacks were emancipated. They played an important part in emancipating themselves. One historian argues, "the North could not have won the war as soon as it did without them, and perhaps it would not have won at all." Many blacks rose in revolt in the South. Of those who fled to the North, 200,000 joined the Union army and navy. They fought with great valor and 38,000 of them died. When the Thirteenth Amendment to the Constitution, which abolished slavery, went into effect in December, 1865, the black slaves became legally free, and this undoubtedly represented a giant step forward morally for the United States.

But what the four million blacks in the South lacked was "freedom from want." For generations most had known nothing but how to grow cotton and other agricultural staples. They now asked for forty acres of land, plus a mule for each household. Since the plantations had been, in the first place, established by their labor or the labor of their ancestors this was a modest request. Moreover, many plantation owners had fled or died during the war and the land had been cared for by the slaves.

Blacks had been granted small plots of land during Lincoln's presidency. When the great man was assassinated, however, much of this land was taken back and the former slaves were forced to accept the "sharecropping system." Under this system, harvests were shared on a half-and-half basis between the landowner and the farmer. Share cropping, however, only seemed fair. The blacks, for example, did not even own their bodies before emancipation. Consequently, they were so poor that they had no food, money, or draught animals and farm implements. Landowners were able to give credit at extortionate rates to blacks so they could purchase these necessities; in exchange, they took much of the harvest. When accounts were finally settled after the harvest, blacks were more destitute than ever. If they ran away, they were pursued and "righteously" punished for debt delinquency. The black slaves had been emancipated only to be plunged into a new form of bondage.

The sharecropping system virtually ended many years ago with farm mechanization, but there is still a long road ahead before black people, in general, are completely integrated into a realistic chance at participating in the mainstream of American prosperity. The civil rights movement which swept the country in the 1960s was only a dramatic chapter of the unfinished struggle. I shall continue the story in my report on Atlanta, Georgia.

RECALLING WESTWARD EXPANSION ON THE MISSISSIPPI

—From 13 to 50 States

Everybody has an attachment to his *alma mater*. Soon after my arrival in Boston, I make a trip to the Midwest to visit the University of Missouri School of Journalism in Columbia, Missouri.

Columbia is a small college town. I have to transfer to a smaller plane in St. Louis, the largest city of the state. I had been to St. Louis many times in the 1940s. This is a welcome opportunity to revisit old haunts. The city straddles the Mississippi River which flows from north to south down the American continent. The "Great River" or "Father of Waters" as the Indians used to call it, the Mississippi was once the western boundary of the newborn United States. It witnessed the legendary westward expansion of the country, and "Old Man River," an affectionate name for this important geographical entity, would tell a whole epic if it could speak.

Changing Notion of the "West"

The history of the expansion of the United States is composed of the experiences of settlers pushing steadily westward from the east (the Atlantic) coast to the west (the Pacific) coast. Consequently, the idea of "west" kept changing with the times. When English immigrants started colonizing the New World in the 17th century, the "west" began practically on the Atlantic seashore. In the Massachusetts Bay Colony, when a settler saw his daughter off to visit relatives in another settlement several miles to the west, he wrote in his dairy: "I did greatly fear for Abigail's safety, as she is gone into Duxbury. It is her first journey into the West, and I shall pray mightily for her early return."* Wherever a new clearing was opened up in the virgin forests and a log cabin was built in the early times, it usually meant another step toward the west.

As more and more immigrants came from Britain, thirteen English colonies took shape on the Atlantic seaboard extending from Maine in the north to Georgia in the south, and fenced in by the Appalachian and Allegheny Mountains to the west. Before the American Revolution, farmers and hunters already followed the tracks of wild animals and Indians and crossed these mountains to seek a livelihood on the other side. Then Britain issued its Proclamation of 1763 declaring areas west of the mountains to be royal property inviolate

---

* Quoted from *Alistair Cooke's America*, published by Alfred A. Knopf, Inc., New York, 1982.

and flatly prohibiting settlement there. "Going west" became a dream for many Americans who hoped to acquire land beyond the Appalachians.

The War of Independence broke the British-imposed limit and American frontiers pushed beyond the mountains to the Mississippi. Over one million people negotiated the steep range to settle in the wilderness between the Appalachians and the Great River, some farming and some hunting. Much of their produce had to be floated down the tributaries of the river and then carried to the port of New Orleans. New Orleans, as well as the territory east of it loosely called Florida, were Spanish possessions. Though Spain allowed the unloading and transit of American goods at New Orleans, Americans were worried about the possibility that the doorway might someday be closed. It would be economically disastrous because three-eighths of their produce had to go through New Orleans.

American apprehensions eventually led to something like a fairy tale — a real estate transaction unprecedented in history and known as the "Louisiana Purchase." The purchase touched off a massive westward migration, with the pioneers' covered wagon as its hallmark. St. Louis, in mid-continent, was the staging point for people trekking to open new frontiers.

The Territory Doubles

No sightseer in St. Louis will skip the Gateway Arch, a unique colossus of stainless steel. Non-existent in the 1940s, it is a great new attraction for me, too. An elevator zigzags visitors up to the top of the 630-foot arch where they are greeted by a panoramic view of the Great River and the big city. The arch was erected to commemorate St. Louis's role as the main point of departure for pioneers bound west.

The arch reminds me that when I was studying in Missouri, older Americans would proudly tell us foreigners that their state was bought by President Jefferson from Napoleon Bonaparte of France for three cents an acre. An acre is equal to 6.07 Chinese *mu*, good enough to support a peasant household in old China. And for three cents! When I was told the story, a coke or a cup of coffee in the snack bars near the campus cost five cents.

But the Louisiana Purchase was not legend, it was history. The whole territory ultimately comprised parts of fifteen future American states extending from a border with Canada to what is the present state of Louisiana. It was hailed by many Americans as a "godsend" and called by others a "windfall."

The story had its background in the secret diplomacy and intricate political and economic manoeuvers of the ninteenth century. Spain, a leading colonial power at the time, decided to cede the immense Mississippi region of Louisiana to France. A secret intelligence report on the transfer reached American President Thomas Jefferson. The fall of Louisiana into the iron fists of Napoleon would spell great peril for the young United States. Senile Spain was not so difficult to deal with, but ambitious Napoleon promised to be anything but an accommodating neighbor. Reports of the transfer were confirmed in 1802. President Jefferson immediately instructed his minister in Paris to negotiate secretly for the purchase of New Orleans and the adjacent area for a maximum of ten million dollars. If the French would not sell the whole lot, he should try to buy New Orleans for no more than 7.5 million dollars. With France then locked in a struggle with Britain, Jefferson hinted that if the United States could not get New Orleans, it might have to enter into an alliance with its old foe Great Britain.

The American minister paid numerous visits to the French Foreign Ministry but obtained nothing. Jefferson sent a special envoy to help him. While the envoy was on his way to Paris, however, the minister was suddenly summoned to the French ministry and asked how much he would pay for the whole of Louisiana. Events moved so dizzily, the story goes, that the minister, at first unable to say anything, blurted "four million dollars." After much haggling treaties were signed in April 1803 ceding Louisiana to the United States for fifteen million dollars. Nobody had precisely delineated the territory so the natural terrain, such as the Mississippi in the east and the Rocky Mountains in the west, were cited as boundaries. The purchase doubled American territory overnight. The United States was a winner. As the proverb goes, "Two dogs fight for a bone, and a third runs away with it."

Later on my trip to the Deep South, I spend a few days in New Orleans. It is situated near the mouth of the Mississippi as it drains into the Gulf of Mexico. The estuary is wide. There are more ships plying the channel than we would see at the mouth of the mighty Yangtze in Shanghai. Ship whistles reverberate over rolling waves. Jumbo ferries carry passengers and their cars across the river free. My host, curio shop owner Tom Dean, leads me to the highest deck of such a ferry for a full view of the city and its French architecture — a reminder of its former owners.

The Louisiana Purchase was signed in the Cabildo (formerly the seat of French, Spanish, English, and finally American rule in the Louisiana Territory, it now houses a collection of historical articles) in New Orleans. A cheerful-looking bust of Thomas Jefferson stands there. It is only natural that the President should look pleased with his clever diplomacy. Jefferson, it is said, acted so hastily that he did not bother to obtain Senate consent before making the deal. His envoy, too, hastened to offer the price of fifteen million dollars and close the transaction without the President's prior authorization. It was lucky for the Americans that the capricious Napoleon did not change his mind.

Immediately afterwards, President Jefferson sent an expedition to explore the newly acquired territory. His detailed instructions specified that a way be found to the Pacific Ocean. This indicates that even then Americans were dreaming of pushing their frontier to the west coast. Setting out from St. Louis, the expedition, helped by friendly Indian guides, trudged along the muddy Missouri River to the foothills of the Rockies. They then trekked over rugged mountains to find a wild river, the Columbia, descending into the Pacific. They eventually reached its estuary and the coast. The whole trip took eighteen months, from 1804 to 1806. A wealth of data was collected and brought back by the expedition. The mission ultimately formed the basis of the American claim to the Oregon Territory, another huge region, in the Northwest. And that was why the route, taken by early Pacific-bound settlers, came to be called the "Oregon Trail."

In 1805 a second expedition set out from St. Louis. It ventured northward along the west bank of the Mississippi to reach its source. Returning to St. Louis, the team turned southwest and again reached the foothills of the Rockies. It then embarked on a southward trip and arrived at Santa Fe, now in New Mexico, a Spanish possession at the time.

The next step was to encourage Americans to settle the new territories. There were already some Spanish and French living there. For them and the black slaves in their possession it was only a question of "naturalization." But for the native Americans, the Indians, the real owners of the land since time immemorial, the tragedy of forcible removal from their homelands would begin to unfold.

Push to the Pacific

After the Louisiana Purchase American territory grew to half the size of Europe. Economic growth was a strong force that motivated further expansion. The United States, as some expansionists put it, must "marry" Texas, a vast, once-independent republic in the southwest. Texas was compared to a bride with a huge dowry waiting to be taken to her wedding. The United States must also obtain the rich valleys of California in addition to the Oregon territory. These and other territorial claims became part of the election platforms of mid-nineteenth century American presidential elections. Successive annexations were achieved by negotiated purchases or, when necessary, by force. In the war with Mexico, 1846-48, for example, the United States gained an immense region which included the present state of California. As one historian puts it: "The war marked an ugly turning point in the relations between the United States and Latin America as a whole. Hitherto, Uncle Sam had been regarded with some complacency, even friendliness. Henceforth, he was increasingly to be feared as the 'Colossus of the North.' Suspicious neighbors to the south began to condemn him as a greedy and untrustworthy bully, who might next despoil them of their heritage."*

As a result of these annexations the whole North American continent with the exception of Canada was incorporated into the United States. The next step was to admit the new territories into the Union as new states, when conditions were ripe. An important condition was that they had to be adequately populated. They were so vast that some Americans predicted it would take five hundred years

*The American Pageant, A History of the Republic, by Thomas A. Bailey, published by D.C. Heath and Company, Boston, 1966

to turn the wilderness into inhabited land. History, however, proved that their prophecy was too conservative. By 1912, slightly over one-hundred years from the Louisiana Purchase, the last two states on the continent, the forty-seventh and forty-eighth had joined the Union.

While I was in Missouri in the 1940s, the American flag had forty-eight white stars representing forty-eight states. It now has fifty because outlying Alaska and Hawaii gained statehood in 1959. Alaska, the largest state, was purchased from Czarist Russia for $7.2 million. It is still sparsely inhabited by a population of 488,999 (1982 figures). Hawaii used to be an independent kingdom and was then a republic. It was annexed in 1898. The state, a chain of islands in the Pacific, is 2,500 miles away from San Francisco.

*   *   *

According to prevailing views in China, the United States began moving from the stage of free capitalism to imperialism by the mid-1850s. The brunt of its expansion was then extended overseas as frontiers closed on the continent. By the 1898 war with Spain the United States seized the Philippines, Puerto Rico in the Caribbean Sea and Guam in the Pacific Ocean. The war marked a complete American entry on to the stage of imperialism.

The two World Wars followed. As the flames of these conflagrations did not spread to continental America, American economic and military strength grew spectacularly. Consequently, the "American era" followed World War II in which Washington virtually dominated the capitalist world. American supremacy, however, began to decline with the Korean and Vietnam wars. But the country still remains one of the world's two superpowers.

These are recent events familiar to my Chinese readers and there is no need for elaboration.

A THOUGHT-PROVOKING CHRONICLE

After reading the preceding chapters, young Chinese readers might like to have a quick recapitulation of outstanding American events compared with corresponding periods in Chinese history. After my return to Beijing I happen to find a booklet entitled *This Is America,* edited and translated into Chinese by the U.S. Embassy in China. It contains just such a chronicle. I take the liberty of including parts of it in my book with special reference to the advance of American technology.

The chronicle shows at a glance that the United States is a very young country. When the first English colony was established in Jamestown, it was in the last years of the Ming Dynasty in China, second to the last of the many feudal dynasties in the country's recorded history. The American Revolution and the birth of the United States corresponded in time to the reign of the traveler-calligrapher Emperor, Qianlong of Qing, the last dynasty in China. The subsequent two hundred years saw the rapid emergence of the United States as a world power.

The chronicle also shows the quick pace of American technological development. The first telephone exchange, for example, was opened in 1878. Thomas Edison invented the first electric lamp in 1879. The first successful airplane flight was made in 1903. Less than six decades later, man-made satellites were rocketed into space. And another decade later astronauts landed on the moon. The application of scientific and technological innovation has been a powerful force propelling the rapid development of America.

It is natural to compare. During my stay in America, I often mused on the past and future of my country. China has an ancient civilization of undisputed greatness. Prolonged feudal rule, however, impeded a modern transformation, while the United States and other Western countries changed rapidly with their capitalist political economies. Social and economic progress in China was hindered even further — to the point of stagnation — when the country was reduced to a semi-colonial status following the Opium War in 1840. An upward trend came only with the revolutionary victory in 1949, and particularly with the historic Third Plenum of the Communist Party's Eleventh Central Committee in 1978 which brought the country on track after years of political turmoil, trial-and-error, haste-makes-waste mistakes. But the wide gap resulting from a centuries-old standstill or even retrogression, cannot be closed overnight. The question is how to catch up with America and the other developed nations. I believe a long period of concerted effort and hard work is needed. But not only that will do. In the present-day world of increasing international interdependence, the task cannot be accomplished in isolation. I believe that we must keep China open to the outside world in order to assimilate the strong points of others, and yet to avoid their pitfalls. In short, self-reliance is essential. But self-reliance does not mean groping in the dark behind closed doors. These thoughts kept coming to my mind as I observed the American scene and compared my country with it.

Now the chronicle, or rather selections from it:

- 1492 (Fifth year of the Reign of Hongzhi, Ming Dynasty) — 12 October, Christopher Columbus lands on San Salvador Island in the Bahamas.

- 1607 — First permanent English settlement established at Jamestown, Virginia.

- 1619 — 30 July, House of Burgesses, America's first elected legislature, meets at Jamestown.

- 1620 (First year of the Reign of Taichang, Ming Dynasty) — Mayflower Compact establishes government by majority will in Massachusetts settlement.

- 1636 (Ninth year of the Reign of Chongzhen, Ming (Dynasty) — 28 October, America's first college, Harvard, founded at Cambridge, Massachusetts.

- 1647 — Massachusetts school law lays foundation for free public education.

- 1774 (Thirty-ninth year of the Reign of Qianlong, Qing Dynasty) — First Continental Congress opens 5 September in Philadelphia, Pennsylvania, "to consult upon the present unhappy state of the colonies."

- 1775 (Fortieth year of the Reign of Qianlong) — 19 April, first shots of American War of Independence fired at Lexington, Massachusetts.

- 1776 (Forty-first year of the Reign of Qianlong) — 4 July, the thirteen colonies sign the Declaration of Independence from England.

- 1781 — 17 October, General Cornwallis surrenders his Army.

- 1787 (Fifty-second year of the Reign of Qianlong) —

Constitutional Convention meets in Philadelphia to draft a new constitution.

• 1789 (Fifty-fourth year of the Reign of Qianlong) — George Washington elected first President.

• 1793 — Eli Whitney invents the cotton gin to separate seeds from cotton.

• 1801 (Sixth year of the Reign of Jiaqing, Qing Dynasty) — Federal capital moves to Washington, D.C., from temporary quarters in Philadelphia.

• 1803 (Eighth year of the Reign of Jiaqing) — Purchase of Louisiana Territory from France doubles land area of the United States.

• 1804 — Lewis and Clark Expedition starts exploring the northwest.

• 1807 — Robert Fulton makes first successful steamboat trip.

• 1819 (Twenty-fourth year of the Reign of Jiaqing) — United States buys Florida from Spain.

• 1828 (Eighth year of the Reign of Daoguang, Qing Dynasty) — First railroad is begun.

• 1833 — Hussey reaper, followed by the McCormick reaper in 1834, revolutionizes harvesting of grain crops.

• 1844 — Samuel F.B. Morse sends first telegraph message from Washington D.C., to Baltimore, Maryland.

• 1860 (Tenth year of the Reign of Xianfeng, Qing Dynasty) — Abraham Lincoln is elected sixteenth president.

— 20 December, South Carolina, followed by six other southern states, secedes from Union in reaction to election of Lincoln, whose views on slavery they fear. The seven southern states organize the Confederate States of America.

• 1861 (Eleventh year of the Reign of Xianfeng) — First guns are fired in a war over question of southern states' right to secede.

• 1863 (Second year of the Reign of Tongzhi, Qing Dynasty) — President Lincoln issues Emancipation Proclamation granting freedom to slaves in southern states.

• 1865 (Fourth year of the Reign of Tongzhi) — Civil War ends with surrender of Confederate states.

— 14 April, President Lincoln is shot while attending the theater in Washington; he dies next morning.

- 1867 (Sixth year of the Reign of Tongzhi) — Territory of Alaska is purchased from Russia.
- 1869 (Eighth year of the Reign of Tongzhi) — 10 May, golden spike unites Central Pacific and Union Pacific Railroads at Promontory, Utah, forming first transcontinental railroad.
- 1878 — First telephone exchange opened.
- 1879 (Fifth year of the Reign of Guangxu, Qing Dynasty) — Thomas A. Edison invents first electric lamp.
- 1898 — War with Spain, declared in April, ends in July. Peace treaty signed in December cedes to the United States Puerto Rico and other islands under Spain in the West Indies, Guam and the Philippines in the Pacific Ocean for payment to Spain of $20 million.
- 1902 — The Electric Theater, America's first movie house, opens in Los Angeles, California.
- 1903 (Twenty-ninth year of the Reign of Guangxu) — 17 December, Orville and Wilbur Wright make first successful flights in heavier-than-air mechanically propelled airplane near Kitty Hawk, North Carolina.
- 1908 — 1 October, Henry Ford introduces efficient, low-cost car, begins era of mass production, and "puts America on wheels."
- 1914 (China has overthrown the Qing Dynasty and established the first republic by the Revolution of 1911) — 15 August, Panama Canal opens, permitting ships to travel from Atlantic to Pacific oceans without rounding the South American continent.
- 1917 — 6 April, United States enters World War I, declaring war after German violations of American neutrality.
- 1927 — 1 January, first coast-to-coast radio network broadcast, the Rose Bowl football game, is made by National Broadcasting Company.

Charles A. Lindberg makes first non-stop solo flight across the Atlantic from New York to Paris.

- 1928 — Warner Brothers' "The Jazz Singer," first feature sound film, revolutionizes film industry.
- 1929 — 29 October, stock market crash marks beginning of America's worst economic depression.

- 1933 — Under President Roosevelt, government launches "New Deal" program to provide work for unemployed, raise farm prices, and stabilize banks in the wake of the depression.
- 1935 — Congress passes Social Security Act, providing old-age and unemployment insurance, and aid to needy, elderly persons, the blind, and dependent children.
- 1939 — As Europe plunges into war, President Roosevelt declares American neutrality.
- 1941 — 11 March, Congress passes and Roosevelt signs Lend-Lease Act to aid foes of Nazi Germany.
— 7 December, attack by Japanese on Pearl Harbor, Hawaii, brings United States into World War II.
- 1942 — 2 December, physicists at University of Chicago, Illinois, achieve first nuclear chain reaction.
- 1944 — June, Allied forces land on coast of Normandy.
- 1945 — 12 April, Roosevelt dies of cerebral hemorrhage.
— 7 May, Nazi forces surrender, ending war in Europe.
— 14 August, Japan surrenders, ending war in Asia.
— 26 June, United Nations Charter signed by United States and Forty-nine other nations in San Francisco, California.
- 1951 — 20 December, first electric power is obtained from nuclear energy.
- 1953 — 27 July, armistice is signed after two-year talks to end fighting in Korea.
- 1958 — 31 January, United States sends up first satellite, Explorer I.
- 1959 — Alaska becomes the forty-ninth state, Hawaii the fiftieth.
- 1963 — 22 August, more than 200,000 march in Washington D.C. in support for proposed civil rights legislation.
— 22 November, President John F. Kennedy assassinated.
- 1964 — 2 July, President Johnson signs Civil Rights Act of 1964 barring discrimination based upon race or color in public places.
- 1968 — 4 April, the Rev. Martin Luther King, Jr., civil rights leader and winner of Nobel Peace Prize, is assassinated in Memphis, Tennessee.

- 1969 — 20 July, Apollo 11 astronauts Neil Armstrong and Edwin Aldrin land on moon's Sea of Tranquility. Two-hour walk collecting rocks and soil samples is televised 400,000 kilometers to earth.

- 1970 — 15 December, United States gross national product (GNP) reaches $1,000,000-million mark for the first time.

    Bureau of Census figures show U.S. population at 203,235,298 (first time above the 200-million mark — *Author*).

- 1972 — President Nixon travels to Beijing in February for meetings with Chinese leaders.

- 1973 — 27 January, a four-party agreement on ending the war and restoring the peace in Vietnam is formally signed in Paris.

- 1974 — 9 August, President Nixon resigns office of Chief Executive, first President to do so.

- 1975 — President Ford visits the People's Republic of China and talks with Chairman Mao Zedong and Vice-Premier Deng Xiaoping.

- 1976 — 4 July, the United States celebrates its Bicentennial.

    — 20 July, and 3 September, Viking I and II, respectively, land on different parts of Mars. The unmanned spacecrafts take pictures of the terrain and run analyses of soil.

- 1979 — 1 January, full diplomatic relations are established between the United States and the People's Republic of China.

- 1980 — 4 November, Ronald Reagan is elected fortieth President of the United States.

- 1981 — 12 April, the United States launches the first flight of the space shuttle Columbia. For fifty-four hours the craft orbits the earth.

Chapter VI
THE DAYS IN NEW YORK

Kitchen is almost synonymous with *home* in Chinese, as *hearth* is in English. In this sense I have a home in Boston, though for only three months. I have to leave now, however, and begin to lodge in hotels and eat in restaurants. It will be difficult even to prepare a cup of tea with boiling water, which we Chinese sip all day long. There is plenty of ice water in American hotels, but none of the thermos flasks available everywhere in China.

American schools commence on 1 September. The Finnish graduate student who has sublet his apartment to me for the summer is returning with his wife and daughter. I must leave the place spick-and-span for him. The "Eighth Route Army" (forerunner of the present Chinese armed forces) tradition is cherished by all Chinese, and part of that tradition is to clean thoroughly before departure the places they have billeted. I must adhere even more strictly to that tradition in a foreign land.

I get up at five o'clock in the morning. It is a beautiful dawn. The distant Harvard Bridge stands out against the background of a rosy eastern sky. The bluish street lamps are reflected on the Charles River like shimmering ribbons of silk.

But I can only take a quick glance as I bid farewell to the scene which I have enjoyed watching so much. Laundry is the first thing to be done. I load the sheets, pillow cases, towels and other things in a cart and take them by elevator to the washing machines in the basement. I then come back to work. Half an hour later I go to the basement again to put the laundry into a dryer. One hour later I fetch them back, fold them , and put them into the chest of drawers. The big curtains and carpet had been cleaned a few days earlier, but there is mopping to do in the bedroom, sitting room, bath and kitchen. Then, the packing. My whole morning is taken.

Cable, Post, Train and Automobile

The telephone rings. It is my old-time colleague Suchu, who has just come back to New York from Beijing. She tells me that my family in Beijing has not heard from me for one month and is very worried, and suggests that I give them a telephone call right away. It is easy to put a call through to Beijing and the voice is always clear in spite of the enormous distance. But it is past noon in Boston and would be in the small hours of the morning in Beijing. I am afraid of disturbing people at home. Suchu then suggests that I send a cable.

Professor Robinson, who has come to see me off, is in my apartment. He opens a telephone book and tells me that I can send the cable by phone. I hesitate because I doubt very much if the operator can accurately get the romanized Chinese name and address. Besides, there is the problem of paying the bill, as I am leaving. Dick says it is simple. Just leave a note to the Finn asking him to charge all unpaid phone calls and cables to Professor Richard Robinson of the M.I.T. Sloan School. That's all.

America is divided into four time zones: eastern, central, mountain, and Pacific time. Noon in Boston on the Atlantic coast is nine in the morning on the Pacific coast and midnight in Beijing.

I dial the international cable office. The operator with a soft voice asks my name, address, phone number, and under whose name the phone is listed. She then begins to take down the name and address of the cable, letter by letter, and the message. She does it almost effortlessly and reads it back for me to check. Not a single slip and the whole business takes less than five minutes. I feel pleased and compliment her: "You are marvelous. You really know your work. I appreciate your efficiency." She laughs sweetly and says: "Thank you, have a nice trip."

Sending a cable seems so easy as to be insignificant. I mention it just to show that, on the whole, American service personnel are well trained, proficient, efficient, and courteous to customers. Our service industries should learn from them. The postal service is another example. To send books to China by ordinary mail costs forty-five cents a pound. Books are defined as printed matter in bound volumes. Loose leaves are much more expensive. Books must be packed in bundles not exceeding fifteen pounds each. But postal clerks will not turn you away for surplus weight or faulty packaging. In the small town of Lakewood, New Jersey, the postmaster gives me a regular postal bag free, dumps my eighteen-pound cardboard box into the bag and sends it away. In the big southern city of Houston, I go to the post office with two boxes of books weighing forty-five pounds. Knowing the difficulty for me to repack, the postmaster also gives me a canvas bag free and puts the whole package into it for dispatch.

Americans, I must add, are usually dissatisfied with their postal service for what they consider to be inefficiency and frequent errors. Some people have exaggerated the issue to prove that the public sector must of necessity be inferior to the private sector of the economy. The American postal service is operated by the government. Private postal service for package delivery has appeared in the country in recent years and one of them is called United Parcel Service. Some friends tell me that they prefer to send their Christmas gifts by "U P S" because its delivery is faster, and it guarantees against damage to the usually exquisite wrapping and packaging of American gifts.

I leave by train. This is to be my first railroad trip in my current visit to America. I have bought two tickets, one from Boston to New York City and another from New York to Washington, D.C., The date of booking is stamped on the tickets and will be valid for one month. You can take any train on any date during that period. There is no question of seating according to numbers because over half of the seats are unoccupied.

Dick accompanies me to the station. He repeatedly asks me to phone him every week. From his appearance I sense he is worried I might not cope with the nine-month journey.

The conductor checks each passenger's ticket and then hangs it on the light luggage rack at the side of the coach. It is very quiet in the coach. The only noise everybody can hear is the announcement over the public address system prior to each stop. There is no music incessantly coming from loudspeakers, as there is in China. Passengers talk in subdued voices. I look around the coach and find that practically all passengers are sitting alone. The few seated in pairs must be couples or friends. All seats face forward like those in Chinese buses and the facing seats commonly found on Chinese trains are absent.

The buildings along the railway are generally old and weatherbeaten. Some structures, perhaps former factories, are only skeletal and appear ready to collapse at any time. Others have their windows sealed with wooden planks. The dilapidated look is a sharp contrast to what you will find along the interstate expressways. The golden age of American railroading has long since passed.

It was in 1956 that the United States legislated federal subsidies to build interstate expressways into an extensive network. Industrial growth is always closely linked to transportation. With greater accessibility to an interstate highway system, many plants moved away from the railways.

One history book recalls vividly: "By the 1890s a few daring American inventors and promoters ... were developing the infant automotive industry. By 1919 there were sixty-nine companies, with a total annual production of 181,000 horseless vehicles. The early contraptions were neither speedy nor reliable. Many a stalled motorist, profanely cranking his balky car, had to endure the jeer: 'Get a horse' from occupants of a Dobbin-drawn carriage."*

Today, however, licensed American "horseless vehicles" total 159,760,000, including cars, buses and trucks. Out of a population of 230 million, 145,299,000 have driver's licenses, according to the Federal Highway Administration's figures for 1981. There are few places one can visit in the United States where an automobile cannot be seen. While many towns on the Boston-New York railway appear to be built on hills, cars are still visible ascending or descending undulating streets. There are numerous rivers and lakes, ideal sites for recreation, easily discernible with their boats, yachts and colorful amusement park facilities, and all accessible by automobile.

At nine o'clock in the evening the train arrives at Rye, a small station where I get off. While I stand at the exit, my friend Bernie

---

* *The American Pageant*, by Thomas Bailey, published by D.C. Heath and Company, Boston, 1966.

Mazel has seen me and is running up to the coach. I met him once in Boston and we had lunch at the home of his daughter and son-in-law, Julie and Jerry Sussman. Just turning thirty, Jerry is already an associate professor of engineering at M.I.T., and an internationally known computer expert.

Bernie tells me that Philip and Roslyn Foner are staying at his home. It is very good news for me.

Bernie's home is in New Rochelle, a town in the wealthy suburbs of New York City, just as Professor Robinson's home in Weston is in Boston's upper middle-class suburbs. Bernie has a large house with walls built of big rectangular stone blocks. As I meet Ella, Bernie's wife, at the gate, I say: "You are living in a castle!" Ella hastens to explain: "Not all Americans have houses like this. I feel guilty to live here." I understand she is referring to the more than thirty-million Americans under the official "poverty line," many of whom live in slums and ghettos or are "bag ladies" and tramps.

Americans are often frank, and they freely admit that many people don't share the plenty of the land.

A PUBLISHER ON HOW TO GET RICH

— And Loneliness in America

Chirping birds break the morning quiet and wake me up. Looking out through the windows I see tall trees on both sides of Bernie's house. Alighting on higher branches, the birds seem to be singing especially for the bedrooms on the second floor. The absence of urban noise pollution must be a characteristic of this high-class district.

I go downstairs and find a spacious and gorgeously furnished living room with a grand piano. Pianos seem to be a must in the homes of all comfortably situated Americans. On the opposite side is a smaller living room called a "den"; it is furnished with a television set. Bernie is in the kitchen. He tells me that preparing breakfast is his job because Ella sleeps late. I have rarely seen as large a kitchen. Beside it is a small dining area and then a bigger one.

I chat with Bernie over a cup of coffee. He tells me his parents were Russian Jews who came to America in at the turn of the century. Almost penniless, they worked very hard and saved some money to open a small shop selling clothes and sundry goods. His mother worked as a saleswoman, and Bernie and his older brother, both born in America, helped her. The shop was open from eight in the morning till nine in the evening and somebody had to be there all the time.

Ella's parents were also Russian Jews who came to America at about the same time. As young intellectuals, they had been involved in the unsuccessful 1905 revolution. After they married and emigrated to the United States in 1909, Ella's father studied engineering at night while working during the day. He was far from wealthy, but he eventually earned enough money to support Ella and her brother through college.

Bernie was able to study in France because the City College of New York granted him a fellowship after his graduation there. Upon his return Bernie went into publishing in 1938 and worked in a mail order sales company. He would, for instance, send catalogues of new books to prospective readers, which is an important method of promotion. Marketing is a specialized field of learning in America and Bernie was good at it. He learned about the trade and began to have his own clients. As consultant he helped a number of magazines to start or build up, including the widely read *Scientific American* and *New York Review of Books*. His efforts began to make him prosperous.

He then set up a publishing company in the field of business, even though it was not a subject which really interested him. Consequently, he sold it and opened his present publishing house which specializes in psychology, psychiatry, and professional books in these fields. "It is not giant business," Bernie says. "But the American economy is so big. There is room if you can pick your specialized area. You are not competing with publishing giants like Macmillan. You make special products not worth the trouble to the big companies which are interested in making enormous profits. But your products will sell well and small companies with a few employees — mine has about twenty — can make money. So the chance to earn more makes people work harder and look and find special areas where they can produce something that will contribute to the economy. It will be part of the whole economy, and will create jobs. People want work and fear unemployment. You contribute to the whole economy by creating jobs."

"Me First"

But all this, Bernie says, is built on the idea of "every man for himself." "Me first." People worry about their own family and don't care about the next person — this leads to two very serious problems. First, some people are concerned solely with their own profit. They just don't care about the life or death of others. Even though they know that what they are doing is harmful to others, they keep it secret in order to maintain their profits. This is one danger. Secondly, people feel more alone in the world because everybody is working for himself. "This can lead not only to selfishness and destructive forms of competition, but to a sense of loneliness. People feel separated from each other. It is a torment."

At this point, Philip Foner comes in and joins the conversation. He asks if I have read in the daily newspaper about the asbestos company Johns-Manville's filing for bankruptcy. Philip says that here is a classic example of profit seeking at the expense of workers' lives.

I reply that I have read Johns-Manville's full-page bankruptcy announcement in *The New York Times* but confess I don't understand what it means. He explains that exposure to asbestos can lead to asbestosis. This was recognized way back in 1927. The role of asbestos in lung cancer was proven later, perhaps in the 1930s. But the American asbestos industry kept the information secret for many years because the long latency period of the disease makes the hazards difficult to ascertain.

"Then how was the secret discovered?" I ask.

Philip says that it is because more and more victims have filed suit for compensation in recent years. It has become such a big issue that the court had to subpoena the secret correspondence between the company owner and his attorney. Under American law, he explains, the court can subpoena evidence. "You have probably heard that Nixon had to submit the tapes he made in the White House upon subpoena."

Philip has to leave on business and the conversation is interrupted. Resuming our talk on loneliness, I ask Bernie if he has read in a recent issue of *The New York Times* Sunday Magazine an article called "Alone — Yearning for Companionship in America." The article says that people can be lonely in isolation or lonely in a crowd. I ask if Bernie agrees.

"Absolutely. I have read the article," Bernie says.

"Why?" I am puzzled. "Americans have so many social activities. They seem always to be inviting each other to dinners and parties."

"The social activities are very superficial," Bernie explains. "I would guess there are very few real friendships. For instance, people join the local church, the Jewish temple or other religious organizations, not so much for religion but because they are centers for social interaction where people can meet people. Yes, it is a form of getting together. But at the same time, you are alone. That is why there is a great increase of mental illness. Alone in a crowd. Big parties, celebrations, friends, and yet alone. When everybody leaves, you can't get away from yourself. Plenty of wealthy people have committed suicide, you know. Competition, not cooperation, is the basis of this society. Failure in this competition can lead to becoming an outcast. Our society pays dearly for this."

Bernie goes on to say that thirty million Americans remain outside the economic mainstream of society. In fact there are some families who have not had a steadily employed person for generations. These people have subsisted on welfare or public assistance. While necessary, these measures lead to a sense of fatalism and helplessness. Who doesn't want to do something, to live in a better house, to send his children to a better school, to have a better television, and, in short, to live better? Bernie asks if I have heard of the word "anomie." It means the personal alienation and disorganization experienced by individuals in a capitalist society — and in America, of course.

"But China has her own problems," Bernie adds. "Your problem is not the ruthless competition we have here. It is how to encourage and arouse people to greater effort. This is called 'incentive' in English. You can't do without material incentives, either."

Progressive Publishing

Our conversation then turns to Bernie's lecture in China. He is going to talk on progressive and Marxist publishing in America, of which, he says, there is very little. There are probably hardly half a dozen publishers who can be called progressive or Marxist. They publish a small number of books which reach a limited audience. Yet other advanced capitalist countries, such as Japan, France and Italy, have a much more flourishing leftist publishing industry.

Seeing that I am interested in the subject, Bernie lets me see the notes of his lecture. I have time only to leaf through the pages and find that he mentions a few books that are particularly interesting. The first is, *The End of Prosperity — The American Economy of the 1970s,* which is composed of a collection of ten essays selected from the *Monthly Review*. The magazine is edited by the leftist economist, former Harvard professor Paul Sweezy, who is quite well-known in China. The book analyses the American economic decline of the 1970s and tries to prove that though Keynesian solutions granted temporary economic relief, these remedies are no longer applicable. It develops the argument that the dominance of monopoly capital and the continued pursuit of profit have created the present economic situation, and predicts that it will worsen. "The permanent answer to capitalist problems is socialism."

Another book is *The Deepening Crisis of U.S. Capitalism*. Also a collection of essays, the book discusses how and why the long post-World War II economic prosperity in America has come to an end.

A new publication, *The Left Academy, — Marxist Scholarship on American Campuses*, attracts my attention. It says that there are now over four-hundred courses given on Marxist philosophy, whereas there were hardly any in the 1960s. This growth of Marxist scholarship was stimulated in part by the political activism of the 1960s, and was fueled by political struggles over civil rights and against the Vietnam War. In addition, more and more younger scholars became disillusioned with the prevailing thinking in their disciplines and are exploring new methodologies. Bernie says that the book is especially useful for the long bibliographies that are given for different disciplines. They are an invaluable guide to further work in each field. But he also points out that without a connection to the working-class movement, Marxist studies do not represent the slightest danger to capitalism. And that is why the book can be published by one of the biggest private publishing houses in America.

The Asbestos Tragedy

Now let me come back to the "asbestos tragedy". One week after our talk about it, the event becomes a sensational subject in the American press, to be found on the news, editorial and feature pages. It is called "one of the worst industrial health tragedies in history" because "from now until the end of the century, there will be an estimated 8,500 to 10,000 deaths a year from asbestos-caused disease." "That is the price of having allowed 27.5 million workers to be exposed to asbestos over the last 40 years" and "documents brought to light in litigation. . .raise disturbing ethical questions." *

These documents contain a file code-named "Dust" found in the personal safe of asbestos magnate Sumner Simpson. It is the correspondence between Simpson and the general attorney for the Johns-Manville firm, Vandiver Brown, concerning the advisability of reporting asbestosis in the trade journal. In 1935, several years after the first major study of the disease had appeared in Britain, the editor of the journal *Asbestos* asked permission to mention the problem. Discussing the request with Brown, Simpson wrote that "I think the less said about asbestos, the better off we are." Brown concurred: "I quite agree with you that our interests are best served by having asbestosis receive the minimum of publicity."

The truth has gradually leaked out. A number of victims have sued the company for compensation. In some cases, they win large claims after protracted legal proceedings, but lawyers have taken their fat cut. With more and more people filing suit, Johns-Manville is now trying

*The New York Times, September, 1982.

to take refuge in the bankruptcy courts. Once it is declared bankrupt, it may emerge whole, having washed its hands of the whole business.

HOW THEY GO TO COLLEGE

— Basics and Problems in American Higher Education

Thousands of Chinese are studying in America and more may follow. American higher education is a topic of wide interest among my Chinese readers. During my stay at Ella's quiet and comfortable home, I spend some time reading up on the subject.

I shall dwell on three questions which many Chinese youths have asked me. One: how do American colleges enroll their students? Two: how do American college students support themselves financially? And three: why enrollment in the two-year junior or community colleges has surpassed that of the four-year colleges and why have part-time students sharply increased?

American education is not nationally standardized. The federal government has a Department of Education. But the office does not set up, or even have supervision over, the individual schools throughout the country. Its function is mainly the gathering of information and statistics and the regulation, through the granting or withholding of funds, of federal orders. The basic control is in the hands of the departments of education of the separate states, and at the local level, in the boards of education of individual communities, whether in cities or in groups of small towns that have district boards. Textbooks, for instance, are sold by competing private publishers and are selected by the local school boards at their own discretion. Management is so decentralized that there is hardly any uniform system. This is a basic point of departure in discussing American higher education or, indeed, education at any level.

Some Statistics

There are 1,325 accredited four-year colleges in America, and a number of them have graduate schools granting master's or doctor's degrees. "Accredited" means the school has been certified by the state or city as meeting certain minimum criteria. In addition, there are 1,200 two-year colleges in the U.S. Of the total of 2,525, only about 300 describe themselves as being to any degree selective. All the others follow an "open door" policy. In Chinese language, the 300 should be called "key schools". They have a large applicant pool of outstanding calibre. But their enrollment is limited. So they are highly selective and competitive. The others are open to all high school graduates. The United States has had, and still has, the largest ratio of college students to population of any country in the world. Of every 100,000 Americans, 5,650 are going to colleges. Of all American high school graduates, 60 percent move up to institutions of higher learning.

Children officially start school at the age of five, in what is called kindergarten. They usually attend for about two hours in the morning or afternoon for one year. Daycare or full-time nurseries like we have in China do not exist to any significant extent. All children are guaranteed, by the states, the right to a public school education, and attendance is compulsory until the age of 16. The elementary school level, sometimes referred to as primary school, usually consists of six years after kindergarten. This is followed by six years of high school. The average high school graduate is 18 years old.

But there are dropouts from both primary and high schools. The reason is that many students are not adequately motivated. Children of people who have not had a steady job for generations, for instance, tend to believe that it does not make much difference whether you go to school or not. As for those above 16, they can freely discontinue their studies because they are no longer covered by compulsory education. Among college students, half quit before graduation. In America, a college diploma helps in finding jobs but it is certainly not a guarantee, as is the case in China, where there has been "an iron rice bowl" — promise of a job whatever your performance. It is nothing very unusual to find Ph.D.s working as taxi drivers in America.

College graduates who go on to study in graduate schools are mostly highly intellectual students whose great joy in life is learning. M.I.T. Professor Robinson told me that in the eyes of the people in his hometown he is "crazy." He was brought up in Yakima, a town of about 50,000 in Washington state, where people make good money growing apples or raising cattle. In terms of material remuneration, the work he puts in as a professor is not very rewarding. But in the meantime I find American professors are widely esteemed and enjoy a high social status. This, I suppose, is out of respect for people who value intellectual pursuits above monetary gains.

As for American primary and high school education, I have heard many complaints, particularly about the great disparity among schools. One disturbing result is that there are 20 million functional illiterates among American adults, averaging one in every 11.5 of the total population.

How the Selective Schools Enroll

In China we often hear about getting "admission," a prerequisite for going to study in America. How then do the American students get admission to college? In China, we had in the past formal entrance examinations given by separate universities, the kind I had to sit for in the 1930s. And now there is the nationally standardized entrance examination held every summer, a nerve-racking event for college-aspiring youngsters. But none of either kind seems to exist in America.

American students are "tracked" after the ninth grade, equivalent to graduation from junior middle school in China. That is, they are channeled into either a college-bound program or a vocational or business curriculum. This tracking is based on a combination of factors such as scores on certain standardized intelligence, aptitude and achievement tests, grades achieved in school work, teacher recommendation, the interests of the student, and the economic situation of the family. Non-academic students are permitted, however, to switch to the college-bound program by making up certain courses required for college admission — three years of English study; a certain amount of science; a certain amount of social studies, that is, history, geography and government; and a certain amount of foreign language, usually Spanish or French.

College-bound students usually begin to apply for admission in the second semester of the 12th year, equivalent to the third or last grade in a Chinese senior middle school. The far-sighted ones begin choosing their colleges one year earlier, in the 11th grade. This is also the time for students to take two tests. These are nationwide standardized tests, but are administered by private, non-profit organizations and are not in any way binding on anyone. They are given so that students can determine how they rank scholastically compared with all the others of their level of education throughout the country, and they are frequently required by the colleges for their admissions procedures.

One of such national tests is called the SAT: the Scholastic Aptitude Test. It is not intended to test specific knowledge of facts, but rather, the ability to reason, to use and comprehend the English language and to solve problems. The test is divided into verbal and mathematical sections. The other test is the American College Testing program, known as the ACT. Both tests are so prevalent now that many colleges will accept the results of either one. However, they are accepted only as reference and not as criteria as to whether a particular student may or may not go to college.

How do the students decide on which colleges to apply to for admission? In China, a student has to list his choice of schools from the first to, say, the eighth in order of his preference, before he sits for the national examination. For American students, only about half have any choice. An important factor is the financial situation of the students' families. The only way about half of them can go to college at all is to attend institutions close to them so that they can live at home and don't have to travel to and from school for summer and winter vacations. The luxury of choice applies to the financially better off.

Then do all students who can afford to choose try to get into the most prestigious universities? Not necessarily. They must consider how strongly they are motivated. Schools "on top of the pyramid" are very demanding. As we would say in China, "One who stands out as the first in a country school may be the last in an urban school." The best students in American high schools, too, often find themselves in the lower group of their college class, with a devastating effect on their self-esteem and self-confidence. They would do better to match themselves to a level where they will best fit in. The SAT and ACT tests play an important role here.

Of the 300 selective colleges, 100 are the most competitive ones, including, for instance, Harvard, Columbia, Princeton, M.I.T., Yale,

Cornell and Stanford. They are most sought after by the very brightest students and a large problem of selection occurs. Here we get figures like 15 percent of applicants accepted at Harvard, or 20 percent at Princeton or Yale.

How is the choice made when virtually every applicant is overqualified scholastically, has excellent recommendations by teachers or others, plus perhaps an outstanding record of leadership activities? The selection is usually done by a committee on admission. Its members think in terms of not only individual students, but of the student body as a whole. They want national representation — a student body that reflects all the different areas of the country and a mixture of ethnic and economic backgrounds so that the students may broaden their horizons.

Also, they are interested in character and personality, which is why most require personal interviews. They look for students who may have overcome some great handicaps, whether economic or physical. This means that they expect students to be not only academically talented but strong-willed and unyielding before adversity.

The committee hopes that applicants will answer its questions openly so that they may learn as much about themselves by answering as the school learns about them by asking. The questions are not factual ones. The applicants are asked to write one or more essays which are supposed to convey something about their personality. The qualities looked for, besides honesty, are originality, imagination, the ability to express oneself — anything that will set one student apart from the others.

"Applicants go through a lot of torment to write these compositions," a friend tells me in a conversation. "I know, because I lived through it with my four children." And she cites a few examples of topics:

"List three adjectives that accurately describe you and briefly explain why you chose them;

"Please comment on a book or motion picture you recommended most enthusiastically to your friends during the past year;

"Describe your hometown in 50 years;

"Write a review of a concert, movie, dance or theatrical performance in the year 2000;

"Describe a difficult experience you have had in your life and how you dealt with it;

"A local, national or international issue may be of great concern to you. Share your ideas and commitments on the issue or issues."

It is evident from all this that the selective colleges make a special point not to admit and graduate those whom we would call in China "bookworms with high marks but low ability."

As competition is very keen, fine points of distinction are often made in the final selection. An applicant may be chosen because he plays a musical instrument for which there is a vacancy in the school orchestra, or because he can strengthen a weak team in a particular sport.

The result of application is so unpredictable that students have to apply to probably a minimum of four or as many as ten or more colleges to make sure of at least one acceptance. This naturally leads to difficulties and even chaos for the schools. Often the colleges have to offer admission to a larger number of applicants than they have places for. Then they may be over-accepted and end up with crowded dormitories and other disorders. Colleges which have under-accepted and don't fill the number of vacancies usually have a waiting list that they can draw on. These questions occur only in the most competitive colleges. Many of them are private institutions.

Public Colleges

Public institutions are usually state colleges. The four-year state colleges and universities exist to serve the residents of each state. The two-year community colleges are devoted primarily to residents of their immediate geographical districts. In most cases, virtually every high school graduate meeting certain minimum academic requirements is automatically assured of admission. This makes application much simpler. Many of these schools are interested in out-of-state students as well, although they do charge them higher tuition. Some state colleges are very well known and much in demand. Take the University of Michigan, for instance. Though there is a Michigan state law limiting the number of out-of-state students to 20 percent of the student body, the applicant pool is still so large that the university has had to switch from "open door" to a "selective" policy of admission.

I have had a personal experience in this regard. While I was going to the University of Missouri, tuition for students of the state was $45 per semester. The same was charged foreign students as a preferential treatment. For out-of-state students tuition varied depending on how much Missourians had to pay to attend a college in a particular state. A schoolmate of mine from the state of New York, for instance, had to pay $90 a semester because a Missouri student would pay that much to go to a New York state college. The Missouri School of Journalism was the first of its kind in the world and had many out-of-state students at the time.

At present, New York and California are the two states boasting the most extensive network of institutions of higher education. Both have many state colleges in different cities and towns. The University of California at Berkeley is a famous one and cannot open its door to all native Californians. Applications of students who cannot be placed there are passed along to a second-choice campus.

How Students Support Themselves

The cost of college is high. At least $12,000 is needed annually to go to Harvard, for instance. The first responsibility for college expenses rests with the students' families. There are indeed many families that can manage even the highest expenses. But the majority of working- and middle-class families cannot afford the charges at even the least expensive institutions, much less at the most expensive. Even attendance at the lowest-priced community colleges, with the cost of maintaining the student at home — food, clothing, carfare, medical expenses, and so forth — may be impossible.

This reminds me of a Mississippi doctor I met some time ago at a dinner party. All his family were present on the occasion, including his son, a college student. Perhaps the host had talked to him about my interest, as the doctor said to me: "I have heard you would like to meet some poor people. You may interview him. He has no more than five dollars in his pocket." He pointed to his son. The doctor was of course joking. I asked him nonetheless, "I have heard that American youths are very independent. When they graduate from high school at 18, they earn their own money to go to college and will no longer depend on their parents, however wealthy they may be. Is that true?" The doctor laughed and pointed to his son again, saying, "Ask him how much of my money he spends a year." The young man tells me shyly: "My father is supporting me through college." American doctors, I should add, are usually wealthy.

But there is an important point to be made. Among American youngsters, including those from wealthy families, I have found none disdaining menial jobs. While I was at the University of Missouri, the librarians were fellow students. The large mess hall was staffed almost entirely by students, including those who punched your cards at the entrance, who carried the food from the kitchen to the steamtables, and who attended to the big dishwashing machines. The same is true today. But it seems that part-time work usually plays only a supplementary role in meeting the students' expenses.

Another source of student income is scholarship awards. Until about the 1950s it was traditional for poor students to attend colleges they couldn't afford by getting scholarships based on exceptional ability. Today there are still many sources of private scholarships, so many in fact that listing information about them takes a 1,000-page book.

Government aid is another source of student income. While Eisenhower was President (1953-61), the federal government started a massive program of assistance to needy students. By 1978, this was expanded to include low-interest loans to students from families with incomes up to $25,000 a year, the loans to be repaid over a period of ten years after graduation. Under the Carter administration, all students, regardless of family income, were made eligible for loans.

But all these programs are being cut drastically. According to the Reagan administration's latest proposals, federal financial aid will be available only to those from families earning less than $7,500 a year. And these are the very families who need their children's earnings to exist and can't spare them for college education. Recent studies have shown, in fact, that as many as half the students from families earning less than $12,000 a year would probably not continue their education at four-year colleges without federal aid.

Two-year Colleges

This leads to the question of why enrollment in two-year colleges has sharply increased in recent years. These institutions are more responsive to the needs of young people today, for a variety of reasons. First, most of them are commuter schools which students can attend while living at home. Second, most have lower tuition charges. Third, most are vocationally oriented, offering training for higher-level jobs than high school vocational programs. And fourth, many of them provide good basic academic programs from which students can transfer into the third year of a four-year college. The last means that the students are in an advantageous position where they can, to put it in a Chinese saying, "advance to attack or hold the line in defense."

Why has the number of part-time college students increased sharply? The reason is again economic. From 1966 to 1979, while total full-time college enrollment increased 53 per cent, part-time enrollment increased 145 per cent. Looking at it another way, whereas in 1966 part-time enrollment represented 30 per cent of the total enrollment, in 1979 it had grown to over 41 per cent. In fact, at some colleges, or in some programs, part-time students outnumber full-time ones. Under the present conditions, this trend may continue to rise.

Plenty of Problems

American education is well developed. But it also faces many problems. The subject is so controversial with respect to every level of education that a hundred experts would give a hundred different points of view.

One authoritative assessment, however, is to be found in a report, "A Nation at Risk," prepared by the National Commission on Excellence in Education. *The New York Times* (April 27, 1983) highlights it in a front-page story under the heading:"Commission on Education Warns 'Tide of Mediocrity' Imperils U.S." The paper lists the 18 members of the commission — nationally known educators including a Nobel Prize winner, presidents and professors of universities, members of state educational boards and a high school principal. There is also a parent representative, a mother of four from Michigan. Also on the panel is Jay Sommer, a high school language instructor and the 1981-82 National Teacher of the Year, whom I have had the honor to meet for a lengthy discussion at Ella's home.

I have read the excerpts of the report. Since China is attaching so much importance to education, I think it fit to quote some salient points:

> Our nation is at risk. Our once unchallenged pre-eminence in commerce, industry, science and technological innovation is being overtaken by competitors throughout the world. This report is concerned with one of the causes and dimensions of the problem, but it is one that undergirds American prosperity, security and civility. We report to the American people that while we can take great pride in what our schools and colleges have historically accomplished and contributed to the United States and the well-being of the people, the educational foundations of our society are presently being eroded by a rising tide of mediocrity that threatens our very future as a nation and a people. What was unimaginable a generation ago has begun to occur — others are matching and surpassing our educational attainments.

The report lists many indicators of the risk. For example, international comparisons of student achievement reveal that on 19 academic tests Americans were never first or second and, in competition with other industrialized nations, were last seven times.

The report stresses that these deficiencies come at a time when the demand for highly skilled workers in new fields is accelerating rapidly. For example: Computers and computer-controlled equipment are penetrating every aspect of our lives — homes, factories and offices. One estimate indicates that by the turn of the century millions of jobs will involve laser technology and robotics. Technology is radically transforming a host of other occupations, including health care; medical science; energy production; food processing; construction; and the building, repair, and maintenance of military equipment.

It looks like a strong wind of change is sweeping the world as what we call in China "a new technological revolution" gathers momentum. Far-sighted people even in America, which can rightly take pride in its educational attainments, are worried about the loss of its superiority. Isn't it, then, an equally, if not more serious, challenge to us Chinese? And shouldn't we do more, much more, to accumulate and develop our own font of talent?

A KALEIDOSCOPIC DAY
— Excerpts from a Diary (2 Sept. 1982)

Bernie comes to bid me farewell in the morning. He is going off to work.

Ella takes me from New Rochelle to New York City, where I plan to stay for a few days.

We are driving on an expressway at high speed. All is quiet except the whizzing of the car. Suddenly there is a loud bang and the car rocks terribly. Ella makes a sharp turn and brings the car to a small triangular plot off the roadway. She looks very tense and breathes heavily. I seem to hear her heart pounding. Calming down a little, Ella says, "Lucky I got it under control." We were indeed lucky to be in the outermost lane where there is a little room to stop on the side. Otherwise we would have been hit by cars coming from behind. We get out and find the left front tire is flat after a "blow-out."

"Heaven helps the blessed." A pedestrian appears. There are few pedestrians in America except in busy urban centers. People always drive and seldom is anybody seen walking along expressways. Ella beckons to the man. He says there is a gas station just beyond the low hill ahead. Ella leaves me behind, tells me to explain to police if they come, and hurries to find help at the gas station.

A black policeman comes in a car about twenty minutes later. I tell him what has happened. A white officer comes in another car. They consult a little and one drives away. A few minutes later the white policeman says he has phoned for a truck to come and tow us, and he will be leaving. Ella comes back with a boy. He is a short, blond kid with a childish look and oil stains all over his clothes.

Teenagers Learn Trade

John, with his name-tag on his chest, is smart. He opens the trunk, takes out a spare tire, and tools. He then lifts the left front wheel with a jack and begins to replace the tire. "Look at this!" he says. "You should have had a new tire long ago. Lucky the cop didn't see it. He would have given you a ticket* if he had." Yes, we are fortunate.

I ask John what place this is. I wish to find out. It's where I have narrowly escaped death.

"Yonkers, you'll soon be in New York. Riverdale is next on the way. Have you heard about Riverdale, on the Hudson? Luxurious apartments over there. It's in the Bronx."

Luxurious apartments? I know the Bronx has the worst slums. Ella explains that the slums are at the southern end. John is speaking about the northwestern part. He is right.

I praise John for his efficiency. He is proud, saying: "I know everything about cars."

The boy is energetic and open. I ask him about his family. He is eighteen, has been on this job four months, and works eight to nine hours a day, six days a week. He is paid $200 a week. Tips vary, and average about $25 a week. His parents came from Ireland. John's father is a bus driver on a route from south Bronx to a small island called Rikers in the East River. There are two prisons on Rikers Island. The bus riders are mostly poor people going to visit prison inmates. They are bad-tempered and often brawl or pick fights. "Father hates his work," John says. His mom does housecleaning in the neighborhood, going to work at fixed hours, or by telephone appointment. One sister is a nurse. Another is a secretary in "a big firm" on Wall Street. John is particularly proud when he says "a big

---

*Notices of fines are called "tickets," which seem to haunt motorists all the time. Traffic control in America is strict, as it should be. Policemen hand out tickets to law violators, but don't accept the money. You write a check and mail it to a designated place. And you'll get into even greater trouble if you don't do this. I was fined twice and paid $15 and $20 respectively. I was not driving but felt I should pay when friends driving me got a ticket. Tickets are very easy to get. You will be fined, for instance, if your car is parked at a parking meter longer than you have paid for.

firm." He also has twin sisters, aged fifteen, and a young sister, thirteen.

There are quite a few American families with many children. But on the whole population growth has been slow in recent decades. (There were 232 million Americans by January 1983, an increase of 29 million over the 203 million in 1970.) Demographers predict a continuing decline in the birth rate, a population of 250 million by the year 2000 and a drop to 200 million by 2080. But immigrants come to the country in large numbers every year. They will help to boost the population to 270 million by 2000. Factors determining birth rate and immigration, however, are complex and these predictions represent just one of "the hundred schools of contending thought," as we would call it.

Ella is completely calm by the time John finishes replacing the tire. She pays him $10 plus a tip of $5. The young man is overjoyed and keeps saying "good luck" to us. He then races away in leaps and bounds like rabbit.

We resume the drive. Ella tells me that most Irish are Catholics who like big families. Though John looks like a boy of fifteen, he is now making a reasonable wage — more than the minimum of $3.25 an hour set by government.

As the only son among six children of the family, John would have been pampered in China. Yet he works hard in the United States. Americans begin in their teens to learn skills, such as driving (which is a necessity for everybody), carpentry, painting, general maintenance and repair, and so on. Many boys earn pocket money as newsboys or mowing lawns. Most of them learn to be adept with their hands. Parents, on their part, encourage their children to be independent. Youngsters are imbued with the tradition and learn to rely on themselves whenever possible.

We are soon crossing a bridge over the Harlem River and entering Manhattan. New York City is divided administratively into five districts, or boroughs — Manhattan, Queens, Brooklyn, the Bronx, and Staten Island. But Manhattan has become the symbol and synonym of New York. When people talk about New York, they often have in mind Manhattan, a small island where real estate is the most expensive, and population density the highest in the world.

Ella proposes that we make a detour to see an exposition of medieval West European artifacts, housed in The Cloisters. On the way, Ella tells me, we can also see the George Washington Bridge on the Hudson River. This bridge was built by "work relief" during the Great Depression in the 1930s and was completed in 1938. Renovated and with a new tier added in 1962, the bridge has fourteen parallel lanes and is a unique structure in the country.

The Cloisters is worth seeing. It is a modern structure in medieval style and represents the best architectural designs of Western European monasteries of the middle-ages. It has a special collection of French and Spanish religious art that dates from the twelfth to the fifteenth centuries. These priceless exhibits make The Cloisters an important part of the Metropolitan Museum of Art, which houses the largest collection of its kind in the country.

We mount the staircase and enter The Cloisters, which is shrouded in trees. The thick stone walls, the round marble pillars, and the arches give the feeling of taking a real journey into the European Middle Ages. The slow, soft chiming of bells adds to the atmosphere of tranquility and solemnity. There is a courtyard surrounded by a covered walk. Trees and lawns in the yard are laid out in the style of medieval monasteries. Music is playing in a low tone, which, Ella tells me, is also medieval. On all sides of the courtyard, called Cuxa Cloister, are romanesque and early and late Gothic halls, and a dimly lit chapel so antiquated that one seems to see shadows of praying, black-robed medieval monks.

In the northern and eastern wings of Cuxa Cloister is an exhibition of arts. Many exhibits are from twelfth century Europe. The period corresponds to the late-Northern Song and early-Southern Song Dynasties in China. Song Dynasty relics are valued in China, even though there are those which are considerably older. It is not surprising that exhibits of the same period win such acclaim in a young country like America.

Ella is full of ideas. Leaving The Cloisters, she says she will take me to see Spanish Harlem. Rectangular shaped Manhattan is intersected by twelve avenues running from north to south, and has over two-hundred streets which go from east to west. All avenues are parallel and so are the streets, forming a chessboard pattern. The southernmost is First Street and the number increases with each street to the north till they exceed two hundred. Avenues are likewise named by numbers. For example, famous Fifth Avenue runs down the center of the island. Broadway is probably the only exception which is neither numbered nor parallel, but cuts diagonally through Manhattan.

Spanish Harlem is in the northern part of Upper Manhattan. All shop names are in Spanish. Some small restaurants put their names in both Spanish and Chinese, offering Chinese cuisine to Hispanic gourmets — a living example of the American "melting pot." Streets are littered with paper and garbage and look dirty and old. Pedestrians are untidily dressed, a match with their surroundings.

Ella tells me that we'll soon reach the Puerto Rican district and she would like to take me to see her aunt. Puerto Rico is a Caribbean island annexed by the United States after its war with Spain in 1898. Many Puerto Ricans have since come to live in the United States and form another minority discriminated against in American society. Ella's aunt, though an immigrant from Russia, lives in the district.

The Elderly Cherish Independence

The old lady is very pleased to see Ella and me, a Chinese. She is "listening to a book" on China. The United States Library of Congress lends talking books to blind, handicapped, and elderly people. The "books" are discs or tapes which are loaned together with players. The book is called *Spring Moon,* a novel depicting the vicissitudes and eventual disintegration of two mandarin families in Suzhou (Soochow) and Peking since the end of the ninteenth century. A best-seller in the United States in 1981, it has been reproduced as a "talking book." The old lady gives me a copy of "The Library Notebook" which is a catalogue of the "talking books." Distributed free, the "notebook" says that the service began fifty years ago in 1931. At present 162 libraries across the country are collaborating with the central library to serve an audience of over 700,000.

Ella's aunt tells me that she came from Russia in 1907, when she was twelve. "Oh, you'll know my age right away." "You certainly don't look your age," I say to the eighty-seven-year-old lady. Not just a compliment, I mean it. She lives alone in the two-room apartment with kitchen and bath and takes care of everything for herself. Besides, she goes once a week to a children's hospital in the vicinity and works as a volunteer — telling the children stories. "I am happy to be with children though I have had none," she says. I admire this American spirit of independence. Young and old alike, always try to stand on their own feet.

"Auntie worked all her life as a nurse," Ella says. "She now lives on a Social Security check plus interest from some savings," she adds. Ella is kind-hearted, and, I presume, she must be helping her financially. But it would be indiscreet to ask.

Leaving Ella's aunt, we continue sightseeing. The city becomes more plush as the street numbers get smaller. Ella drives along the Hudson River and then turns into Central Park, which is so-named because it is at the center of Manhattan. A huge strip of green in the heart of the city, Central Park is a treasure in such a densely inhabited place . It undoubtedly plays a great role in ameliorating the weather, purifying the air, and beautifying the environment. Unfortunately, it is also known for its dangers. A popular guidebook explicitly advises readers not to go there after dark.

As I open my diary in the hotel room, the day's experience seems to be a kaleidoscope of so many colors and patterns I don't know what to write. Of all the sounds, one voice is most distinct. It is Ella saying, "look, look!" The voice is permeated with the friendly warmth of an American who wants to help me see and know America, without missing a minute.

I think back to earlier in the day when Ella parked the car at the intersection of Broadway and 80th Street, and said that I had to see the Zabars grocery store. I view a delicatessen selling a huge assortment of cakes and breads to endless lines of buyers. Then there is a section specializing in Chinese foods which makes me hungry for its abundant supply of rare seafood and wild game, as well as the ordinary preserved beancurd and vegetables. The shop, of course, sells a wide variety of American foods, as well as specialties of a number of European and Asian countries. Ella then leads me upstairs to see cooking utensils, including all imaginable pots, pans, and dishes — even a whole battery of big and small Chinese *longti* made of thin bamboo strips to steam buns. Consumer economies are so well-developed in this country that whenever there is a product, there is a place that will sell it.

Ella starts chatting with a silver-haired lady at a counter. She is talking to Ella about a new kind of bread. Ella introduces me to her, saying that I have come to write a book about America. The lady says to me earnestly: "You must write about ordinary Americans, men and women, young and old. Please be kind. We Americans are a good people." Shaking her hand to say goodbye, I tell her equally in earnest: "I agree. Americans are a good people. And I am interested in ordinary Americans." I might add that during my one-year visit I seldom visited dignitaries, but tried to mix with middle- and lower-class Americans. It is not that the rich and powerful will keep a foreigner at arm's length, but because I believe that the America of ordinary Americans is closer to the true America.

AROUND MANHATTAN BY BOAT

A Chinese scholar once wrote that if a tourist in America skips New York City, he would be visiting a dragon without seeing its pearl. The most precious pearl, according to Chinese legend, is to be found on the *Li* Dragon which wears it under its jaw. *U.S. News & World Report* (1983/4/18) puts it in a more prosaic way: "What do foreign visitors want to see when they come to the United States? New York City is attracting more of them than any other American city."

Five boroughs make up New York City, but Manhattan is clearly the center and the chief reason to visit New York. I don't have the time to go to all boroughs, nor a guide to show me around quickly. Besides, I don't want to spend money just sightseeing. Then how can I get an overview of the whole city? Americans love efficiency and there must be an efficient way to do it. It happens that I live at West 42nd Street and on the other side of the street is Pier 83, the starting point of "Circle Line Tours." You pay a fare of $8.50 for a three-hour cruise around Manhattan from tip to tip. At the same time you catch a glimpse of the other four boroughs.

Tourists board the boat and sit in chairs on the deck where there is an unimpeded view in all directions. As the boat moves on, a guide calls attention to the sights and tells their stories through a megaphone. He claims to be an octogenarian and his nostalgic, mellow voice certainly leads one to believe he has witnessed everything he says. Change, continuous change — this is the keynote of his reminiscences, comparisons, and frequent jokes.

Manhattan is an island shaped like a long bag. It faces the Atlantic in the south and is separated from the continent by the Harlem River in the north, the Hudson River in the west and the East River in the east. Across the East River lie Queens and Brooklyn. The Bronx is on the other side of the Harlem River. Staten Island is much to the south.

Overview of Manhattan

As the boat leaves Pier 83, I look back and see a massive cluster of towering skyscrapers. They make you wonder how people can live in such a place, so crowded that even the breeze from the river cannot seem to penetrate the thick forests of buildings. That is the busiest section of Manhattan, the most glittering part of the "pearl under dragon's jaw."

The octogenarian guide is speaking. "Look at that sixty-story building," he says. "It's the Woolworth Building, once the tallest skyscraper in the world." Woolworth is a familiar name to me. In the 1940s there were Woolworth stores in almost every American city, "dime stores" selling low-priced commodities. But many youngsters now don't even know what "dime stores" are, a result of years of inflation. Woolworth seems to be falling into oblivion. Then there is the Empire State Building. Why the grandiose name? Every American state has a nickname and New York is called "the Empire State" because George Washington, visiting here in 1783, had remarked that New York would become "the center of the new American empire." A few days before the cruise I had visited the observatory on the 86th floor of the building and then went to the top floor, the 102nd, by elevator. The automobiles moving on Fifth Avenue down below looked like the car-shaped pencil sharpeners Chinese pupils like to use. Many of them were yellow and looked like beetles; they were taxis. New York City has probably the world's largest number of cars for hire. The Empire State Building was completed in May 1931 and was the tallest skyscraper in the world when I visited it in 1948.

Then the guide shows us the twin towers of the World Trade Center whose 110 storys rise above the Empire State Building. The tallest building now, he says, is the Sears Tower in Chicago; the Empire State Building is only the fourth-tallest.

The old man has everything at his finger tips. He says that the view in this section will change drastically by 1986. There is a construction project in front of the World Trade Center to "create" a piece of land on the Hudson River. Its area will come to 100 acres, or 600 *mu* by Chinese measurement. Not much, but it will be a veritable treasure in a place where "an inch of land is worth an inch of gold," as we would put it. Named Battery Park, the place will accommodate sixteen-thousand households plus thirty-five thousand people in various service trades. Obviously, it will be for the wealthy only. The project is so designed as to make use of the many obsolete docks on the Hudson, a good idea to save time and money. In fact, a number of high-rises have already appeared on the newly created land.

Statue of Liberty

As the Hudson widens, we come close to the sight which more than anything else is symbolic of the New World. Practically all aboard are aiming their cameras at it — the Statue of Liberty. In 1948 I had climbed the 167-step staircase from the ground to its pedestal and then another 168-step staircase inside the statue to its top. The statue is having a complete facelift for her centennial, and the staircases will be replaced by elevators.

While visitors are still watching the statue, the "octogenarian" reminds them to have a look at Staten Island. "You may not have the time to visit it. It is the only predominantly residential borough, and the only borough connected with Manhattan by ferry (instead of a tunnel or a bridge)." "And please look at the small island not far away from the Statue of Liberty," he goes on. "It is Ellis Island, the 'gateway to America.' For half a century, from 1892 to 1943, immigrants coming across the Atlantic to America were cleared there for entry."

Passing by the southern tip of Manhattan, we see the Brooklyn Bridge, once the world's longest, which connects Manhattan with Brooklyn. Historical records say that close to 10,000 people came to watch the ribbon cutting when the bridge was commissioned in May 1883. A stampede followed in which twelve people died.

Before we reach the bridge, the guide points to another cluster of skyscrapers and tells us that Wall Street is in that direction, on the southern tip of Manhattan. Except for the New York Stock Exchange, the world's financial center, Wall Street cannot be seen from the river. But I had been there and found it to be quite a narrow street, dim and somber, fitting more for its infamy than its fame.

Twenty years after the completion of the Brooklyn Bridge, the Williamsburg Bridge was built on the East River. It became the world's longest at the time, with its span of sixteen hundred feet, five feet longer than the Brooklyn. By rough count I have seen nineteen bridges on this cruise, most of them spanning the East River and the Harlem River.

Queens is adjacent to Brooklyn; both are on the western end of Long Island, off the Atlantic coast. The "octogenarian" summarizes: "Now you have seen all boroughs of the city except the Bronx. The four boroughs are all on islands. But you may not feel it because there are so many bridges and tunnels linking them." He is right. Both the John F. Kennedy International Airport and La Guardia Airport are on Long Island. I came to New York from San Francisco via Kennedy airport and left the city for Boston via La Guardia. But I never felt I had been to Long Island. The beautiful bridges and convenient tunnels "misled" me into thinking I had only been in Manhattan, and that Manhattan *is* New York.

United Nations

Of all the sights on the East River, the United Nations is the best known. The tallest building of the group is the site of the U.N. Secretariat. A library is behind it. The General Assembly Building is an old acquaintance to all because it appears so often in the media. I have visited the world organization several times. It is probably the place with the world's highest "mountain of documents" and largest "sea of meetings" as we would say in Chinese. Over the decades papers produced or originated here would have weighed megatons, and the resolutions and declarations adopted have probably mounted into the tens of thousands. Though not always successful in its efforts to resolve major international issues, the United Nations nevertheless plays an irreplaceable role.

There also is a Roosevelt Island on the East River, the most unusual of all American residential districts, and perhaps a prototype of future living styles. A "city within a city," it comprises four groups of apartments which accommodate two thousand households. Each group has its own public school, stores, park, playground, and day nursery so that traffic is reduced to the minimum. There are cable cars commuting between the island and the center of Manhattan in five minutes. It is quiet, luxurious, comfortable, convenient, and almost free of pollution out there — a secluded paradise in a bustling world. All is fine except that it's expensive. It reminds me of John, the boy who repaired our car in Yonkers. Isn't the prisoner-infested Rikers Island his father hates also on the East River? I would like to see Rikers, too. But the "octogenarian" guide has perhaps forgotten to mention it.

Facing Roosevelt Island on the other side of the river is the well-known Upper East Side, another glistening gem. The huge meadow in front of Gracie Mansion, home of New York's mayors, looks like an emerald carpet. Behind it are deluxe apartment buildings overlooking tree-lined Riverside Drive. The Upper East Side is also the site of superb art galleries. This part of the city is another reserve of the rich. A subway rider tells me that as the train goes north from the Upper East Side, more and more passengers will be of a different type. Well-clad ones will gradually vanish till you find shabby people all around. Small wonder that a guidebook assents: "Near W. 97th Street much of Manhattan's opulence ends with a bump."

Our cruise boat is now on the Harlem River. I find on both sides a continuous scene of wretchedness and squalor. The white slums in the Bronx and the black Harlem ghettos on Manhattan resemble the Hispanic and Puerto Rican districts I have seen earlier. The Bronx, separated from Manhattan by the Harlem River, is the only borough not on an island.

There are many other sights I must omit. Overall, I have seen a huge metropolis at once affluent and destitute, elegant and dilapidated, glittering and glaring. One of the glaring examples: There is a high-rise with an eye-catching sign at the top: "Dogs' Hospital." I love dogs but feel miserable at the thought that so many humans around the world, Americans not entirely excluded, are languishing in poverty and disease.

NEW YORKERS CELEBRATE LABOR DAY
— Impressions and Reflections

The first Monday of September is Labor Day in the United States, falling on September 5, 1982, while I am in New York City. On that day I find West 42nd Street, where I live, turned into something like a country fair. Milling crowds of holidaymakers pick their way through an endless row of street stalls. Food venders sell, in addition to the ordinary run of hot dogs and soft drinks, specialities like broiled beef. Big chunks of meat sizzle on iron racks over charcoal fires, turning brown, oozing fat and smelling good.

Many others sell an array of ordinary clothing including blue jeans and rubber-soled canvas shoes, some similar to Chinese tennis shoes and others with tilted tips and fancy patterns of white, red and blue bands. There are also stalls selling miscellaneous things, even curios or imitation artwork. The scene reminds me vividly of the bazaars thriving at Beijing's Longfu Temple and Shanghai's Town God's Temple half a century ago. It is doubly strange to see all these near modern Times Square and the plush Rockefeller Center.

A number of stalls sell books. One of them specializes in "revolutionary literature." I find there English translations of many works by Marx, Engels, Lenin and Mao Zedong including the well-known "little red book," *Quotations from Chairman Mao.* Printed portraits and photographs of Marx, Lenin and other revolutionary teachers are pinned to the draperies, with price tags. While I am attentively leafing through some volumes, the stall keeper leans forward and asks: "Are you from the People's Republic of China?" I nod. He asks further. "Why aren't you selling Mao's quotations any more?" He follows this up with more questions about China's foreign policy, particularly Sino-American relations in a way that can hardly conceal his disapproval.

No doubt he is a leftist. The encounter reminds me of a comment made by a Chinese-American friend on the American Left. There is a saying in China: "four-way division and five-way disintegration" to describe grave disunity. My friend said sorrowfully that the phrase can literally apply to major American Left organizations if you change "four" to "three" and "five" to "four." The three-way division means the mutual estrangement of the old U.S. Communist Party which is pro-Soviet, the Progressive Labor Party which regards no one but its own members as genuinely revolutionary and socialist, and the Revolutionary Communist Party, which used to be pro-Chinese. The three-way division became a four-way rift when the Revolutionary Communist Party split after the overthrow of the Gang of Four in China. Those for the overthrow quit and formed a new organization while those against remained. This is a very broad generalization, my friend stressed, and the whole situation is very complex.

The bookseller sounds like one who has remained, because he apparently esteems the "little red book," a hallmark of the "cultural revolution" which supporters of the Gang of Four still hanker after. The book has fallen out of use in China. We have discarded the *Quotations* because, quoting Mao out of context, it has proved to be an instrument of dogmatism.

Nonetheless I feel grateful to the bookseller for his interest in China and I don't blame him at all for his ignorance of the real facts of life in a faraway country. There were so many attractive slogans in those years. "The workers, peasants and soldiers must be masters of the land," for instance. What's wrong with it, particularly to the ears of the toiling masses abroad? But those slogans could only be taken at face value. No, I don't blame him. Instead, I have misgivings about his safety for his radical views. I have in my hand a tabloid bought a few minutes earlier for 25 cents which contains a report on how thugs have smashed a store selling revolutionary books. Hooligans and their behind-the-scenes bosses don't care which faction you belong to if you are against the Establishment.

I think of citing my personal experiences in the "cultural revolution" by way of explanation to the bookseller. But a bustling market is certainly no place for a serious political discussion. I can only smile to him and walk on to the next stall.

There a woman, clad in a bright red shirtwaist and beaming with smiles, comes up and gives me a leaflet. "Vote for me, please," she says and hurries away. The leaflet, slightly larger than a postcard, shows her picture with the words "FRAN SCLAFANI for Attorney General." On the opposite side are her biographical notes and the kind of catchphrases we in China would see only in commercial advertisements. For instance, "New York State needs Fran Sclafani" and "Fran Sclafani will be an Attorney General that New Yorkers can be proud of—for she will truly serve ALL OF THE PEOPLE." I guess all politicians running for public office in the coming November mid-term election are out today electioneering in the crowds. Later I learn that the position of attorney general is an important office with a $60,000 annual salary, the same as a lieutenant governor. Of course I don't mean to imply the lady is out for money instead of justice.

I move through four crowded blocks and get to Eighth Avenue, which looks even more festive. There are makeshift stages on platform trucks where people beat drums, blow trumpets, play music, sing behind microphones, play rock and roll, or twist and grimace like circus clowns. Spectators often join in the spree, rock-n-rolling "like mad" to my Chinese eyes.

I walk on to Fifth Avenue. This thoroughfare running through the middle of Manhattan is the east/west dividing line. It is the equivalent of Wangfujing in Beijing and Nanking Road in Shanghai, and at 42nd Street it is a commercial center much more garish than its Chinese counterparts. The Labor Day parade proceeds on Fifth Avenue from 26th to 52nd Street. Newspapers have predicted a turnout of 500,000 marchers and 100,000 spectators. There will be "hobos" selling apples along the line of march (reminders of the unemployed workers who tried to make a living that way during the Great Depression), for the theme this year is "unemployment." There will be more than 150 bands and 125 floats in the parade. The reports say Broadway stars will be there, marching along with other representatives of the 500 unions affiliated with the New York Central Labor Council.

Unseemly Origins

Having watched the fanfare, I cannot help asking an American friend, a veteran trade unionist, how the U.S. Labor Day originated and why it has evolved into this sort of merry-go-round. For us Chinese and most people of the world, May 1 is labor day, a militant day of working-class solidarity. And it is widely known that May Day's origin goes back to the American workers' demonstration for an eight-hour workday in Chicago in 1886 and the general strike staged in other parts of the country.

The friend, who has for years worked in meat-packing unions, gives me a book called *Haymarket Revisited*. You will find the answer there, he says. Here are a few passages:

> In 1894, Grover Cleveland [the 24th U.S. President] suddenly announced that the first Monday in September would be Labor Day in America, and he signed a bill to make this a national holiday. Peter McQuire [a trade union leader] and other trade unions had been lobbying for this bill since 1882, and now, perhaps as a way of calming the American labor movement's enthusiasm for May Day, Cleveland gave in to the September date. Beginning in the 1950s, the American Bar Association sought to have May Day referred to as "Law Day" in the United States.
>
> Today only Canada and the United States use the September date, while the rest of the world uses May Day as the workers' day. The French Canadians have rebelled against the September day in the last few years and have begun to use May Day. In recent years it has become increasingly evident that the September date is not a purely union workers' day, but also a holiday for businessmen, bankers, lawyers, and stockbrokers.

The book adds that even Peter McQuire, who is known as the "Father of Labor Day" (the September one), later favored having May Day adopted throughout the world.

The following sequence of events will further clarify the question:

—**May 1, 1886:** "Eight-Hour Day Movement" began as workers in Chicago marched up Michigan Avenue while 340,000 laid down their tools across the country.

—**May 4:** "Haymarket Massacre" occurred in Chicago when police attacked workers. Four died and dozens were wounded.

—**1889:** A delegate of the American Federation of Labor to the International Labor Congress in Paris asked that May Day be adopted as an International Labor Day. Workers would march on this date for the eight-hour day, for democracy and the right of workers to organize. This day would also be a memorial to the "Martyrs of Chicago."

—**1892:** At an international socialist conference in Geneva, a delegate from the American Knights of Labor made a similar resolution and it was adopted. Founded in 1869, the Knights of Labor was a fast-growing and powerful union at the time, drawing no color lines.

—**1894:** President Cleveland made the first Monday of September Labor Day and a national holiday.

The whys and wherefores are clearer in retrospect. We have a saying in China — *tou liang huan zhu,* "stealing away with the beam and pillar to topple the house." It might well be used as the heading of the story. If May Day, which American workers had shed their blood to establish, is eventually proclaimed "Law Day," as the American Bar Association wishes, the ingeniously-devised metamorphosis will be complete. And three cheers for the Establishment!

Present Labor Movement

American labor has had a glorious and militant tradition. But unionists I have met admit that the movement is getting weaker. Why? I sought enlightenment from Professor Philip Foner, a progressive historian I met in China and again in Maine. He made the following points:

One, many giant American corporations are transnationals with subsidiaries in Europe and Third World countries. They transfer capital to places where labor is cheap, to reduce costs. A sizeable proportion of what they produce overseas is then shipped back to the

American market. In the process they have closed many plants in the country and deprived a lot of workers of their jobs.

Two, traditional industrial areas in the northeastern and midwestern states are losing their dominance to the southern and western states (often called the Sun Belt). Unions are stronger in the old industrial bases but weak or non-existent in the south, therefore goods can be produced more cheaply there.

Third, the heavily unionized steel and auto industries are in serious trouble. An important reason is the stiff competition from Japan and Federal Germany where equipment has been updated in the postwar years. America is technologically capable of restructuring the industries, but many profit-minded capitalists resist that. The giant U.S. Steel Corporation, for one, closed two major plants in Youngstown, Ohio, and Bethlehem, Pennsylvania, a few years ago. Workers were laid off permanently without any prior notice.

Fourth, the use of robots is increasing in the mills. They work 24 hours a day, do not organize and never strike. And robotics is fast reaching out into new fields.

Fifth, the numbers of workers in strongly unionized basic industries — steel, auto and rubber for instance — are decreasing while the much less unionized service industries have been expanding fast. Union membership in retail trades — shops, supermarkets, fast-food industries, etc. — constitutes only 7 percent of the total work force compared with 45 percent of the total in steel, auto and other basic industries. Increasing employment by service industries coupled with decline of basic industries means a falling percentage of union members in the overall work force.

Sixth, more and more illegal immigrants are entering the labor market. They are paid far less than the $3.25-per-hour minimum wage prescribed by the U.S. government and will accept the heaviest and dirtiest jobs. Union membership is out of the question for these people who are always wary of deportation.

Seventh, employers have new means to sabotage unionization. In the past, they hired thugs and hooligans to prevent workers from organizing by brute force. Now a new business called "management consultancy" has appeared and is booming. College-educated "specialists" and "psychologists" make intensive studies to devise union-busting tactics. They might, for instance, intimidate prospective union members by spreading the word that the boss would move the plant to the south if a union were formed. They seize every opportunity to publicize the corruption of union leadership. The unfortunate part of the story is that such corruption does exist in some unions, whose bosses draw fat salaries, accept bribes from the bosses or collude with mafia-type organizations.

Back in my hotel after watching the celebrations, which are ironically gay against the background of a recession-mired economy and 10-percent unemployment, I read in the day's *New York Times* a lengthy analysis entitled "Frustrated and Wary, Labor Marks Its Day." The article says: "Their [the union leaders'] anxieties are fed by the proliferation in recent years of management consultants specializing in sophisticated methods to persuade workers there is nothing a union can do for them that the boss is not doing better. These services have revived, on this centennial of Labor Day, an age-old anxiety in the minds of many top unionists about whether the bulk of the nation's businessmen are reconciled to the existence of unions and want them to survive at all." The article also reveals that unionized workers now make up only 20 percent of the labor force. I remember that the percentage in 1947 was 35. A sharp drop of 15 percent in 35 years is indeed a serious challenge to American labor.

Will the American labor movement continue to decline? Professor Foner and many other Americans believe it won't. Wherever there is oppression, there is resistance, as we often say in China. If and when an economic crisis gets out of hand and workers find it impossible to carry on, there will be a blow-up. Labor Day then will probably not be the kind of gala fair blessed by Big Business.

CLOTHING, FOOD AND HOUSING
— A Letter to My Daughters

This morning I saw on New York City's Fifth Avenue a middleaged man wearing a multi-colored hat in the shape of the type of nylon umbrella that Beijing children like. I thought that if anybody cared to put on his head a double-eared Chinese cooking pot he wouldn't attract any curious stares in Manhattan, where novelty is the norm.

This has prompted me to write you this letter which may later form part of my book. Remember what you said when I asked you, as a prospective reader, what I should write? "American clothing, food, and housing," you answered so promptly. "And how they find jobs, apartments and spouses. Everything about their daily life."

Hats and "Liberation"

Let me begin with clothing and makeup. On the whole, Americans are much more "liberated" than when I was a student here. What I mean is that they feel freer to pick and choose their own personal styles. They can be as fancy, or even odd, as they like. For example, don't believe that every American girl must wear a bra and use lipstick. They might dispense with them altogether, depending upon the social occasion. This "liberation" from the dictates of fashion and conventional morality is perhaps an outcome of the youth revolt against tradition which swept the country over a decade ago.

I'll give you a few more examples of oddity. When I took my first stroll on New York streets upon my arrival, I was amazed, almost shocked, to see a white male wearing a T-shirt, blue jeans and tennis shoes tilted at both ends like a canoe — nothing very unusual except for three bold Chinese characters, written with Chinese brush and ink, on his shirt which read, believe it or not, "I love her." If he were a Chinese walking on Beijing streets, public-spirited citizens might offer to help him to a mental hospital. He is not unique, however. Soon after, I saw in downtown Boston a young white woman wearing a sweater with the big Chinese ideograph "love" in the center of a heart pattern on her chest. And on her short right sleeve was another Chinese character: "*mei*" meaning "younger sister." My friend Rita Gould was with me and I explained to her what those characters mean. She smiled and told me: "The woman might be gay" — since she openly proclaims love for women.

I also saw a pair of extraordinary trousers when I was visiting a high school with Julie, Mrs. Carol Robinson's daughter, in Boston. A girl student walked up with a group of schoolmates. She wore a pair of snow-white trousers, one leg decorated with a pattern of bright flowers running from the waist through the knee to the foot. They were all similar in shape, but each was different from the others in color. The other pant leg was completely white.

When I first saw women in sweaters made of a mixture of blue, purple, white, and red knitting wool without any pattern whatsoever, but with sleeves much shorter than their shirts, I thought they must be thrifty housewives making do with odds and ends of used wool. I found later I was terribly mistaken because such sweaters are a new fad. They are hand-made and therefore expensive in this country where labor costs are high. The coarse wools, selected deliberately to unmatch in color, are readily available in shops. The absence of any set pattern is intended as proof that they were made only by hand.

But don't think that all or most Americans are dressed like that. I have cited the examples just to show that they can dress as strangely, or as scantily, as they like in public places and nobody will make a fuss of it.

Do they still differentiate between casual and formal dress? Yes, they do. You have seen many American tourists in China. Most of them are dressed very informally. But they will dress up for banquets or other formal occasions.

I carefully watched what people wore at a commencement at Harvard University and at a town meeting in Weston. Men usually wore suits and neckties and women wore suits or dresses of good-quality materials. But there were also some very unconventional ones. A lady mounted the rostrum to speak at the town meeting, in blue jeans and with spectacles lifted to her forehead — a proof of "liberation" even on serious occasions.

Do women still wear evening gowns with flowing skirts that they must lift up a little when moving about, the kind that are often seen in movies? Yes, sometimes they do. One evening I went to the Lincoln Center in Manhattan with two American friends. The opera there happened to be at intermission. I saw through the big glass windows of the checkroom hall many ladies in that type of gown, with glittering necklaces and other jewelry. The theater was presenting Japanese *kabuki,* an event for "highbrows." But in the midst of people dressed like old-time nobility, I also saw some who were very casually dressed.

This is quite different from what I experienced in the 1940s. On an Easter weekend I went to St. Louis to spend the holidays. There was a Mass in a famous Catholic cathedral I wanted to see. But I was refused admission because I didn't wear a hat. Luckily I had a silk scarf with me and improvised by wrapping it on my hair, thus gaining a reluctant admission. In those years, rules, though unwritten, were very strict as to what to wear on different occasions. I thought then that women's headgear must be a headache. Middle-class ladies had to have a veritable storehouse of hats, some broad-brimmed and some narrow-brimmed, some with flowers and some with feathers. I saw in San Francisco a few old ladies wearing hats with small cages atop and several feather-made birds perched inside. The hat departments in big stores had such a wide and highly priced variety of women's hats it made me dizzy. But few women wear hats now that they are "liberated."

Is clothing expensive? Well, it depends on your pocketbook. Women's fur coats costing thousands of dollars and men's suits selling for hundreds of dollars are found everywhere in shop windows. There are even luxury stores where items such as these are priced much higher. Poor people, however, can get very cheap second-hand garments at the Salvation Army or other thrift stores. When I first heard of the Salvation Army, I thought it was a church turned into a shop. Actually it has, amongst the various services it performs for the poor, a chain of stores located throughout the country which sells used goods at very low prices. Much of its stock, I am told, is donated by individuals. You have to pay sales tax for everything you buy in America but second-hand wares are tax-free.

Besides places like the Salvation Army, there are frequent "garage" or "yard" sales where people can buy used clothing. To dispose of their junk, a family, or some families together, put a small ad in the local newspaper announcing a sale. Almost all American towns, even very small ones, have their newspapers financed largely by advertisements from local businesses. Such a sale is usually held on a Saturday, and is a single-day affair whether business is slow or brisk. Things unsold by late afternoon can be dumped into big plastic sacks and offered to customers at a dollar a sack. People can drive around in their cars on Saturdays and find good bargains at such sales.

I may have dwelt too much on details. What is the general situation regarding clothing and fashion trends? There was a good report in *The New York Times* a few days ago under the heading "Recession Changing Clothes-Buying Habits." It generalized: "Leaders of the American apparel and fashion industry in New York City and across the country say that buying patterns are changing and that they are facing their most difficult challenge since the recession of 1975."

What is meant by the "challenge?" The most serious part of it is that "middle-income buyers are rebelling at higher prices caused by inflation and are making do with the clothing they have." These people are the mainstream of American consumers. The report pointed out, however, apparel in three general categories is still selling well: "The highest-priced merchandise, such as elegant evening clothes; clothing of lasting quality that is generally conservative in style; and merchandise that is called 'exciting' — retail terminology for clothing that looks fashionably new without being 'extreme.'"

Let me interpret a little. The highest-priced evening clothes are selling well because people in the highest income brackets are not much affected by recession. While middle-income buyers tend to make do with what they have, the upper middles would buy clothing "of lasting quality that is generally conservative in style," i.e., apparel that will hold out longer. Fashion-minded customers prefer moderate styles because the "extreme" ones can easily fall out of vogue. That's the general pattern. But keep in mind that the American scene is fast changing. Bell-bottom trousers and mini-skirts still believed by some Chinese pursuers of Western ways to be the current craze, have long ago lost popularity and have been replaced by a succession of styles. What will be the craze at the next turn of fashion? Nobody can tell.

Chinese Cuisine, Health and Fast Foods

I have found a lot of new things, too, in American eating habits. The first weekend after my arrival was spent with Susan Warren in her New York home. It is her family's custom to dine out on Saturdays. The couple took me to the Hunan Restaurant in the neighborhood.

They insisted that I order. But I found it very difficult to choose because everything on the menu appeared so expensive to me; I was still preoccupied with the Chinese price scale. Finally I ordered a hot-sour soup, the only course under two dollars. They ordered three more dishes. When the soup came, I found it was for me alone, in a thick bowl that held only as much as a Chinese tea mug. Sue paid $25 for the dinner including about three dollars of change left on the table as a tip. A fifteen percent tip is customary here. Sue told me that there were more than twenty Chinese restaurants in Greenwich Village where she lives, and this is a moderately-priced one.

As we were about through eating, the waitress laid a plate on the table with the bill placed under three "fortune cookies." The cookie is a tiny triangular-shaped biscuit, hollow inside. When you open it, you find a two inch paper slip telling your fortune — hence the name. The slips are passed around for everyone to enjoy, though nobody takes them seriously. Still, a soothing prediction such as "all the troubles you have will pass away very quickly" is nice to see when I am just beginning to write a difficult book!

Soon after I got to Boston, Carol Robinson told me one day that "Dick will have something unexpected for you in the evening." It turned out to be a dinner given by his graduate students for their professor, to which I was also invited. It was a rich banquet, including even a Beijing duck. The place is at another Hunan Restaurant. Don't misunderstand and think it is part of a chain of restaurants. It is called *Hunan* perhaps because the name sounds more authentically Chinese. Many restaurants not named Hunan also claim that they offer Hunan cuisine. Others advertise themselves as specializing in Hunan, Sichuan, Canton and Shanghai dishes — an almost complete spectrum of Chinese culinary arts.

Chinese restaurants already abounded in major cities while I was studying here in the 1940s. They can now be found in small towns too. There are two of them in Columbia, Missouri, where none existed in the earlier years. While most Chinese restaurants in the forties were called "Chop Sueys," today, most are "restaurants." Hunanese and Sichuanese cooking, I am told, have become more popular than Cantonese foods.

It is only natural that America, which calls itself a "melting pot" of immigrants, has a highly heterogeneous culinary culture. Americans will eat anything that tastes good without the least regard for its origins. Chinese cuisine, however, is far more popular than the three-per-thousand ethnic Chinese ratio in the American population would lead one to expect.

Still it's difficult to generalize when you can find well over eighteen thousand kinds of foods in supermarkets. The subject can be analyzed, however, from three different perspectives: eating habits as conditioned by health considerations, by personal economics, and by the quickening tempo of life.

First, health considerations. One set of vital statistics shows that heart and circulatory problems, cancer, strokes, and diabetic complications are the leading causes of American deaths. The big family of antibiotics that has appeared since the Americans developed penicillin during World War II has conquered most infectious diseases. Consequently, the above-mentioned four have become the most deadly enemies.

The diets of many people are now shared by consideration of these four enemies. It is now known that being overweight makes one more susceptible to heart disease and stroke. The Metropolitan Life Insurance Co. has been publishing desirable height and weight charts since 1959 on which height is matched by ideal weight. Americans keep scales in their bathrooms, a reflection of their concerns. They try to discipline themselves against eating excess fat, cream, or sugar. That monster called cholesterol seems to haunt everybody.

Fresh vegetables in salads, replacing the over-cooked mash I dreaded in the forties, fresh fruits which have almost eliminated canned fruits and juices, and leguminous foods — with bean-curd in the limelight — are considered amongst the most healthful foods. Skim milk and yogurt are thought better than whole milk, margarine often substitutes for butter and meat must be lean. Bacon, ham and sausage contain too much fat and nitrate salts for many, while cakes and sweets are becoming suspect for their high calorie and fat content. Drink your coffee black or with sugar substitute if you must, but don't add cream. Americans, according to some nutrition experts, take far too much salt, three teaspoonfuls a day containing five-thousand milligrams of sodium. With this in mind, those conscious of the dangers strive to keep it below two thousand milligrams — much better for normal blood pressure.

This increasing concern has led to the popularity of "health foods." According to one estimate, supermarkets with "health food" departments totalled 1,000 and sold $146 million worth of such foods in 1970. The number has jumped to 6,600 with a total turnover of $1.6 billion in 1982. But there are many people who are critical of the fad. *Public Employee Press,* published in New York, for one, has warned its readers that prices of health foods or "natural foods" "are unnaturally high" and "there is no need to go to a health food store and spend three times as much for an item."

U.S. News & World Report (16 August 1982) in an article entitled "How People Seek Relief from Soaring Food Prices" spotlights another new eating trend. It reports: "More and more Americans are turning away from the supermarkets this summer in a search for cheaper and better food. All sorts of ways are being tried — most of them aimed at circumventing the middleman, who is now taking sixty-five cents of every food dollar." Out of the dollar, according to the report, thirty-five cents go to the farmer, thirty-one cents to the processor, nine cents to the wholesaler, six cents to the transporter and nineteen cents to the retailer.

An effective way to bypass the middleman is "U-pick:" select and buy foods on "pick-your-own" farms. I haven't had a chance to do that, but I tasted peaches and berries picked by friends. They are very fresh and just ripe, and the price is seventy percent lower than that at supermarkets. There are also roadside stands selling fresh produce at farm prices, a good bargain for lower-income people.

The most effective way, however, is perhaps "U-grow." Many Americans are doing just that. People gardening in the suburbs have increased to record numbers. "Community gardening" is becoming more popular in urban centers. In New York City, about 120 families and one thousand school children are working in one such garden at 90th Street and Columbus Avenue. They raise crops on small plots and swap them among themselves. "Many of our families depend on vegetables from the garden," one grower tells the reporter.

In addition, fast foods are growing fast. The trade has been thriving because people often have little time and want to have an occasional change from homemade foods. MacDonald's hamburgers and Kentucky Fried Chicken have popularized fast-food eating places. There is now a wide variety of different chains throughout the country. The customer picks from a menu posted on the wall, puts it on a plastic tray and chooses a table to sit at. There are no waiters or waitresses. The used plastic containers are dumped into a big can and the tray is returned before the customer leaves. There are take-out services with foods and plastic knives and forks packed in paper boxes which save the trouble of both cooking and dishwashing. Some shops supply only take-out meals.

The first friend introducing me to a fast food restaurant is my oldtime schoolmate, now an American citizen. She said it's a very common lifestyle that I must learn about. Fast-food restaurants not only cater to transient travelers but are frequented by neighborhood families with small children. I ask why. A sociology student, she rattled off figures to explain. More women have joined the labor force over the last twenty years, she said. The number of married working women accounted for thirty percent of the total employment in 1960 and increased to fifty percent in the 1980s. A great portion are mothers under thirty-five. They are often tired after a day's work and fast-food restaurants free them from the time-consuming chore of cooking, and give the kids a welcome change. Young people, too, like fast foods. They often run around but don't have much money to dine out. A bag of French fries plus a soft drink saves both money and time, though it hardly fulfills any nutritional needs!

My limited experience makes me feel that fast foods are often greasy, full of sugar, and other carbohydrates. A ready-made meal contains very little fresh vegetables — a small dish of sliced cabbage for instance. While good for a change, fast foods can hardly be the basis of a healthy diet according to American standards.

Americans are perhaps the most favored people in the world in terms of the percentage of their disposable income spent on food. Statistics for 1979 showed that out of every one hundred dollars, 16.6 went for food, while the figure was about twenty percent in other developed countries. In developing countries consumers spent fifty percent or more of their income for food. One American food dollar, according to *U.S. News & World Report,* comprised thirty-three cents for meat, poultry and fish, nineteen cents for fruits and vegetables (including potatoes), twelve cents for milk and milk products and five cents for fats and sugars; eleven cents for flour, cereals and bakery products, and the remaining twenty went for miscellaneous items. Proportionately, the less spent on staples, the better the diet; and the less spent on food means more spent on clothing, housing, recreation, tourism, etc. — a sure sign of a higher standard of living.

Still, statistics are sometimes more deceptive than revealing. The 16.6 percent of American income spent on food, as well as the twenty percent in other rich countries, is only an average; it includes families which may spend as little as one per cent of their income on food, and those who have to scrape up every cent, plus food stamps, to feed all mouths. Polarization is growing in America, and this is a fact most fair-minded Americans admit and deplore.

Condominium

The most important new development in American housing is the condominium. Abbreviated as "condo," it was practically unknown to most Americans ten years back.

My former schoolmate, Chiu, the librarian, introduced me to this new lifestyle. Lakewood, New Jersey, the small town where her home is, also has condos and she herself lives in one of them. I asked her to snap a picture of me in front of the building to illustrate a condo. She did but explained that there were many other types.

Later I see other condos: economical, median, and luxurious ones. Chiu's condo, as I see it, is a modest one. It consists of a living room, three small bedrooms, one with shower minus tub, and the other two sharing a bath that has both shower and tub. Closets are in the hall. A washing machine is in the basement. There is a bright kitchen spacious enough for a dining table. We often sit and talk in the kitchen because food and drinks are within easy reach, and the telephone is also there.

Chiu has a son and a daughter, both college graduates now working on the West Coast. Her husband had found another partner and they were divorced several years ago. I tried to persuade her to sell the apartment upon retirement and move to where her son or daughter live. She would be lonely remaining in the small town, I stressed. I didn't mean that she should go to live in the house of her son or daughter, even if they were still single at that time. Grown-up children in practically all families I know choose to move away and live independently, though their parents usually have rooms to spare. This is an ingrained American lifestyle which Chiu has apparently assimilated. We in China often think that American parent-child relationships are cool. But we should not forget the contradictions inherent in our own extended families. The soul-stirring novel *Family* by Ba Jin (a leading contemporary Chinese writer) is a good illustration. What was good about that kind of big family in old China, beset with overt and covert rivalries among siblings and in-laws? If the traditional family was purely good, why has the idea of the modern nuclear family spread so quickly following the May Fourth Movement of 1919? There is no rose without a thorn.

Well, daughters, I have digressed. Let me return to the condo. How to define it? It is a project comprising many housing units which may be apartments in one building, or separate houses in a group, and *owned* by the residents. Ownership, instead of lease, is the essence of a condominium.

As I write this letter, the American economy is going through the worst slump since World War II. Construction is one of the hardest hit industries as far fewer people are buying houses. There are at present about forty-two million Americans around the age of thirty, those born during the postwar "baby boom" and now in the prime house-buying age. Part of the classical American dream is to own a home with lawns and trees behind a white picket fence. But it seems that today the young have to be satisfied with less.

The price of houses doubled in the 1970s and the interest rate is high, making it more difficult for most people, who buy houses on credit instead of with cash. An independent house, I am told, costs at least $70,000 and is beyond the means of most young people. So the idea of owning an interest in a piece of land in conjunction with others has caught on. People are "going condo" which economizes on both land and building costs. Besides, the condo has a "built-in social structure" which frees the residents from the chores of maintenance, management, heating, hot water supply and the like. Condo owners simply write a check and pay a certain sum each year and don't have to worry about the upkeep. I have seen condos with children's playgrounds, tennis courts, swimming pools and assembly halls. Residents pay for all but the children's playgrounds.

The "built-in social structure" has attracted many wealthier people, particularly elderly couples. They would sell their houses and buy a condo to save trouble. Luxurious and median condos have appeared as a result. Many of the usual household chores have been socialized in America, and a further socialization of work contributes to the condo boom, apart from the lower sales prices.

The sociologist Ian Robertson, whom I quoted earlier, predicts that most Americans will have moved into condos by the turn of the century. I don't believe so. There are many beautiful private houses I have seen across the land, distinct from each other in architectural style. Americans value individuality and uniqueness too much to abandon the dream of an individual home if it can be economically affordable.

This appreciation of the unique is exemplified in the attention to both the interior decoration and environmental beauty of their houses. They try to achieve a harmony of setting and color, as they do with their clothing. A woman, for instance, would take pain to match her dress with her stockings and shoes, with her purse and necklace. It is part of an aesthetic perception acquired through education, a point worth noting by young women like you who often talk about beauty. Beauty is often not a result of expensive dresses or furnishings, but merely a show of good taste. For those Americans who are driving thousands of miles from the northeast to the "Sunbelt" in search of jobs and who have to shelter in parks, however, aesthetics is just so much talk. But that is another problem. What I am saying is that many Americans put in a lot of work to beautify their living quarters.

The small home is another trend in housing. The "mini-home concept" is appearing primarily in condominium projects in the "Sunbelt" where condo supply has fallen behind demand. It is said that the new "small home" looks better than it sounds. These units are often designed by visionary architects who specialize in the efficient use of limited space. Their designs include built-in cabinets and tables, light colors and huge windows to provide the illusion of extra footage. And "Murphy beds" (folding sofa-beds) are enjoying their best sales in twenty years. *The Washington Post* quotes a resident of such a house as saying, "It's funny, but the longer we're here, the bigger it gets."

Small-house living, in its turn, is leading to such other lifestyles as smaller wardrobes and fewer major purchases, giving simpler entertainment to visiting friends, and spending little time at home. Save money for recreation and travel. Not a bad idea, I say.

IMMIGRATION: THE PAST AND PRESENT
— Reflections Stimulated by the Statue of Liberty

Edouard de Laboulaye, a nineteenth-century French historian, suggested that France present a monument to the U.S. to commemorate the friendship between the French and American peoples. The French approved the idea and preparations were made in the 1860s. At that time the doorway to America was open to immigrants from most parts of the world.

The monument turned out to be a colossal, 151-foot statue weighing 225 tons which took the celebrated French sculptor Frederic Auguste Bartholdi ten years to complete. It was finished in 1884 and two years later, on 28 October 1886, it was dedicated at Bedloe's Island at the entrance of New York Harbor as the "Statue of Liberty Enlightening the World." A poem by Emma Lazarus was graven on a tablet within the pedestal. The last lines proclaim the oath of the "Mother of Exiles":

> Give me your tired, your poor,
> Your huddled masses yearning to breathe free,
> The wretched refuse of your teeming shore.
> Send these, the homeless, tempest-tost to me,
> I lift my lamp beside the golden door!

The United States Congress, however, "amended" the oath six years earlier by adopting the "Chinese Exclusion Act" and the oath from the very beginning didn't mean much to the "wretched" Chinese sweating away in America. Still when Laboulaye put forward the idea of the monument, America's "golden door" was truly open to all.

Discrimination and Restriction

For almost one hundred years after American Independence (1776), there were virtually no laws governing the admission of aliens. Throughout the nineteenth century, the vast majority of immigrants came from northern and western Europe. The peak immigration years of 1880 through 1920 — consisting predominantly of southern and eastern Europeans — caused concern in Congress. By 1921 a system of quotas for different countries was introduced and a drastic limitation was imposed on the total number of immigrants. This had the effect of favoring northern and western Europeans over immigrants from southern and eastern Europe and other regions of the world. Henceforward even Europeans were treated differently by the "Mother of Exiles."

Restrictions based on national origins continued till 1965 when Congress amended previous immigration laws and shifted to a system of priorities based on family reunification and needed skills and professions. The amended act contains, roughly speaking, the following major points:

A total of 270,000 people a year are allowed to enter the United States as legal immigrants, with no more than 20,000 from any one country. Preference is given to six general categories of applicants, i.e., unmarried sons and daughters over twenty-one of U.S. citizens, spouses and unmarried sons and daughters of resident aliens, married sons and daughters of U.S. citizens, brothers and sisters of U.S. citizens twenty-one or over (first, second, fourth and fifth preference, respectively); members of the professions or persons of exceptional ability in the sciences and arts whose services are sought by U.S. employers (third preference); and skilled and unskilled workers in short supply (sixth preference). Spouses and children of preference applicants are entitled to the same preference if accompanying or following to join such persons.

In addition to the 270,000 limit, according to the 1965 amendment, immediate relatives of U.S. citizens — their spouses, children and parents—are allowed to come for reunification as an "unlimited category." Small special groups, such as former U.S. citizens, missionaries and certain aliens employed by the U.S. government over a long period, may also be admitted over and above quotas. Immigrants in these categories average well over 100,000 a year, thus bringing the annual total of legal immigrants to some 400,000.

Who are the main beneficiaries of the immediate-relatives clause? I presume they must be Asians and Hispanics long discriminated against in the past. When I arrived in San Francisco from Shanghai, I saw many Chinese women, children and elders coming on the same CAAC plane. They were obviously being admitted as immediate relatives.

Chinese Immigrants

My Chinese readers may be interested in learning more about the "Chinese Exclusion Act," the historical background of its adoption and its repeal. In the 1860s, cheap Chinese labor was in great demand to cultivate swampy lands in California and build the trans-continental railroad. So much so that under the Burlingame Treaty concluded in 1868 between the Qing Court and the U.S., "free migration and emigration of their citizens and subjects" was prescribed as well as the "reciprocal rights and freedom" of the immigrants. As China had already been relegated to the status of a semi-colony after the 1840 Opium War, "reciprocal rights" were just so much empty talk.

At the time of the Burlingame Treaty, the Chinese people were living through a great ordeal. The "Taiping Heavenly Kingdom," a historic peasant uprising, had been crushed. Many Chinese had to flee their homeland in search of a livelihood abroad. Others were inveigled into signing work contracts as virtual slaves or simply "shanghaied" to unknown destinations. Those coming to America lived and worked under extremely difficult conditions and significantly contributed to the development of the land.

On 10 May 1869 the "Golden Spike" united the Central Pacific and Union Pacific railroads at Promontory, Utah, forming the first trans-continental rail artery. A period of quicker westward expansion began with rail transportation. So did a period of Chinese expulsion. Anti-Chinese riots planned by racists occurred on ever larger scales, during which many Chinese laborers were expelled or even murdered.

The anti-Chinese campaign culminated in the adoption of the 1882 "Chinese Exclusion Act." In its final form the act provided, among other things, prohibition of Chinese immigration for ten years. The ban was extended for another ten years in 1892. And in 1902 it was again prolonged — this time indefinitely. It was the Japanese who eventually blasted away the restriction with bombs. They attacked Pearl Harbor in 1941. America joined the war and thus became an ally of China. Almost as an afterthought, Congress repealed the Chinese Exclusion Act in 1943 and graciously permitted China an annual immigration quota of 105!

After the war, six thousand Chinese women married to American servicemen were admitted under the War Brides Act. Another legislation in 1948 gave permanent residence permits to 3,465 Chinese students, visitors and seamen in America.

In 1949, the United States government decided to make better use of part of the huge sum of money appropriated as aid to the tottering Chiang Kai-shek regime. The fund was diverted as subsidies to Chinese students studying in America at that time. Some students, however, returned to the mainland to take part in building the newborn People's Republic. Those who stayed later became American citizens. Many are now PhDs, specialists, and scholars. On my visit I met many former fellow students. All of them retain a deep attachment to their homeland, and many have made contributions to China's reconstruction and to a new friendship between the Chinese and Americans.

Refugees and Illegal Immigrants

Beginning in the late seventies, America admitted large numbers of refugees, mainly from Southeast Asia and the Caribbean. They could apply for permanent residence status after one year and for citizenship after four more years. As citizens, their immediate relatives will receive preference for immigration to the United States under the 1965 amendment. During the late seventies and early eighties, an average of 200,000 refugees were admitted each year. Added to the

400,000 legal immigrants, they bring the annual total of entrants to 600,000.

In addition, there is a continuous entry of illegal immigrants, or "undocumenteds." Specialists estimate that the net inflow is now roughly 500,000 a year. Newspaper reports have quoted an official of the U.S. Immigration and Naturalization Service (INS) as saying that 819,919 persons were apprehended in 1982 while illegally crossing the United States-Mexican borders. They were mainly Mexicans, and Central and South Americans. Despite its considerable effort and sophisticated equipment, the INS has not been able to stop the influx.

When added to the 400,000 who immigrate legally and the 200,000 average refugee level, the 500,000 "undocumenteds" push annual immigration above the million mark. This is the crux of the immigration question bothering the United States in recent years. The country started counting immigrants in 1820 and recorded 8,385 in that year. Since then there were six years topping the million mark — 1905, 1906, 1907, 1910, 1913 and 1914. The massive migration in those years was caused by unsuccessful revolutions against the Czar in Russia, by turbulent political situations in eastern and southern Europe and then the First World War. As noted before, the predominance of eastern and southern European immigrants led to legislation in favor of western and northern Europeans. The new peak level in recent years is a result of an influx from Latin America and Asia, including the "boat people" from Vietnam. The changing pattern of immigration is shown in the following charts reproduced from *Population Bulletin* (Vol. 37 No. 2) published by the Population Reference Bureau, Inc. in June 1982.

Immigration is one of the major topics under nationwide discussion during my visit. Congress is debating a bill introducing amendments to the 1965 act. Meanwhile, much is being written in the press. Speaking on behalf of the illegal immigrants, Hispanic papers point out the ways they are exploited: they are paid much below the minimum wage while doing the heaviest or dirtiest jobs, and they don't dare claim social security benefits. It is unfair, the papers say, to accuse them of adding to the burdens of American taxpayers. As for job opportunities, they are not really competing with American citizens. They merely fill the vacancies American workers won't take up. But these pro-immigration voices are weak.

There have been calls for reducing the number of immigrants. But conservatives who like to portray themselves as the protectors of "free American institutions" find themselves caught in contradictions of their own making. Even so, many are outspoken and some even declare bluntly that "one more is too many." I have seen, for instance, in *Readers' Digest*, a mass circulation magazine selling 17.9 million copies per issue, a cartoon of a stern-faced Statue of Liberty. Her torch has vanished. Holding the Bible in one hand, she extends the other to keep people at arm's length.

The debate will continue through the 1980s. Its outcome will certainly shape the way America is perceived by other peoples, not to

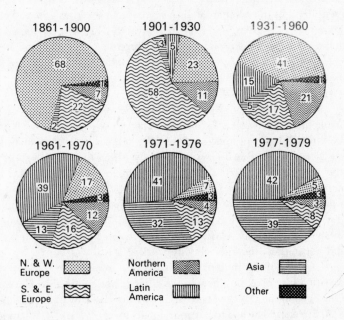

LEGAL IMMIGRANTS ADMITTED TO THE U.S., BY REGION OF BIRTH: 1861-1979 (numbers in percentage of total)

mention its own traditional self-image as "a refuge for the homeless and oppressed" —however tarnished that image has become since Emma Lazarus's words were carved on the Statue of Liberty.

VISITING HARLEM
—A Conversation with Two Black Americans

Manhattan's 125th Street was once the busiest spot in Harlem, as Nanking Road is in today's Shanghai. A friend driving me through this part of the city slows down the car so that I can have a better look at the world-renowned black community. When a red light stops us at a cross street, a gush of soapy water suddenly rains down on our windshield. My friend quickly rolls open the window but only wide enough for him to stick out a dollar bill. A dirty little hand snatches it away and I see it's a black boy who has already collected a small stack of dollar bills in his other hand. A few more black boys come up and start mopping, rinsing and rubbing our car in a flurry. When the green light shines, we move on and the boys retreat to the sidewalk with their mops and buckets. I look around and find they have buddies at all four corners, ready to "serve" you whichever direction you are travelling.

My friend tells me that his car did need a wash, but the boys have made such a mess that the windshield is now even murkier than it was before. While saying this, he drives to a real car wash. A man at the entrance collects five dollars and starts pushing buttons. As soon as the car moves onto the conveyer, bubbling soapy water is automatically showered on it, followed by high-speed mopping, rinsing and rubbing, also by machines. In five minutes the car comes out the other end clean and shiny. It may have been my friend's intention to show me a good example of American efficiency so that I did not mistake the kids' shoddy work as a real wash.

I ask him if this kind of unsolicited help is unique in Harlem. He says that it's something new in the city but not confined to Harlem. One evening he was "rubbed" four times on Broadway at 42nd and 43rd Streets and he had to pay four dollars for the "work." "What can you do?" he adds. Both of us fall into silent thought, knowing that it's only a tiny aspect of a much bigger problem — the problem of the urban poor.

Tete-a-Tete

"Harlem is to Black America what New York City is to the United States." This is what I have read in a history book. Just one drive through there cannot satify my curiosity about this place which has now become a living example of ghetto America.

A good chance comes when an enthusiastic black friend, Basir Mchawi, offers to take me for a visit to the home of a black artist, Shelton Alkamal Duncan, in Harlem. I have a two-hour chat with Shelton and then stroll around the streets. It is a much more meaningful day for me than ordinary sightseeing and street browsing.

Both Basir and Shelton are thirty-five and my new acquaintances. But the strange thing is that there seems to be neither "national barrier" nor "generation gap" between us. We talk freely. This is probably because all of us have personally known what discrimination and oppression mean. I, a Chinese, who saw in my young days notices posted at Shanghai park gates announcing "no Chinese and dogs allowed," can readily understand their bitter feelings.

Basir and Shelton had visited China together a few years back. They still relish their memories of the trip not so much for the sights but for the reception. At dawn, they recall, they took a walk on Beijing streets and saw many people shadow-boxing. They joined the exercise, mimicking the movements. The Beijing people gave them a spontaneous and warm welcome. In the ancient city of Xian, a large crowd of pedestrians gathered around their bus and heartily applauded them probably because this was the first time they had seen so many black people in a group, says Basir. He and Shelton were astonished and felt honored by the friendliness everywhere, a contrast to their experience since childhood in a society where "Jim-Crowism" used to dominate and racial prejudices still remain strong. "It's unbelievable," they say repeatedly while telling me about their China visit.

This almost innate feeling of mutual respect enables us to chat as old friends on whatever subjects we pick up. Shelton tells me his personal vicissitudes in relation to the rise and decline of enthusiasm for black history. The American Civil War contributed much to black emancipation but fell far short of accomplishing it. The struggle for equal rights for blacks continued throughout the ensuing century, surging and ebbing from time to time. A new climax came in the 1950-60s. Ten years of continuous fighting culminated in the adoption by the United States Congress of the 1964 Civil Rights Bill banning segregation and discrimination. The struggle focused attention across the country. As a result studies in the history of American blacks were inaugurated at almost all college campuses. Shelton, through his father's activities, was influenced by the civil rights movement early in his life. Personal experience going back to the age of ten, plus a disciplined commitment, enabled him to become a teacher of black history at Northeastern University in Boston when he had just turned twenty. In the mid-1970s, however, the enthusiasm for black studies faded in some parts of the academia. Shelton lost his teaching job and has had to eke out a living as a free-lance writer and painter. Life is hard and unsteady for him.

Our conversation turns to discrimination against colored people in America. Shelton's mother-in-law is an ethnic Japanese born in America. After Pearl Harbor, 130,000 Japanese-Americans were rounded up and herded into detention camps in Arizona. Now they are demanding compensation from the federal government for the losses they incurred. Why should the Japanese be singled out for such unconstitutional treatment especially since ethnic Germans and Italians were not? No Japanese was found spying, while many Germans and Italians were arrested for espionage during the war years. Shelton shows me a recent magazine article written by his mother-in-law on the subject and says that the Japanese-Americans have organized to fight for redress through the courts.

We then talk about juvenile delinquency in Harlem. Shelton is critical of the sex-and-violence shown on television. His sister, in order to keep her son from being influenced by it, has refused to buy a television set. One day, Shelton says, she asked the boy to name three of his heroes. To her chagrin, the son rattled off in one breath three TV gunmen. He knew them thoroughly because the other kids had told and retold their stories, or he had seen the programs at the homes of his friends. The influence of the media is so strong, so pervasive, that no quarantine can succeed, Shelton says.

"Harlem Is Dying"

I ask Shelton what he thinks of the prospects of Harlem. "Harlem is dying," he says tersely. Why?

Look at housing, he explains. The buildings have not been properly repaired for close to a hundred years. Some of them were destroyed by fires, others crumbled, and still others, with doors and windows boarded up, are likely to collapse pretty soon. That's why you'll find so many vacant lots on both sides of the streets.

Look at social services. There are no hospitals, no supermarkets and no public high schools. Buses, too, have stopped running and people must take the subway.

And then look at the economy. There are no jobs. People living in Harlem are either unemployed or are commuters working elsewhere. More and more residents are moving away. "And let's wait and see when I, Shelton Duncan, will be forced out," he says in a husky voice.

There is nothing much to regret, I think, for him to leave this place. By American standards his apartment is quite humble. I have not seen a more cramped one. As soon as you enter the door, you find a dining table almost blocking the hall. Crossing a cooking corner which could be called a kitchen, you see three doors in a close row. One opens into a dark and tiny bathroom. Another leads to the bedroom for Shelton, his wife and their ten year-old daughter. And the third room is where we are talking. It is his studio, jammed with easels, books and chairs. I wonder how the painter can retreat a few steps to examine the perspective. All windows have iron railings outside and make the rooms dimmer.

"You live on the third floor and what's the use of those railings?" I ask. "It has been like that since I moved in," Shelton says. "Theft and robbery are rampant and drugs have changed the whole nature of crime," he adds. Shelton is apparently not in good health. He is often short of breath and even more so when he talks rapidly.

He then explains aspects of "drug culture" in America to me. Marijuana, he describes, is a sort of enlivening, non-habituating stimulant. Cocaine is different. It is expensive and poor people can't afford it. Prostitutes are not rich but they need it to keep them going. New York City has supposedly banned drug trafficking and adult sellers are liable to severe prison terms. But the mafia is the chief trafficker and little seems to be done about it. Organized crime even uses teenagers as street corner vendors. These kids, if caught, will be sent to juvenile camps for a few years. But they make thousands of dollars a week, much more than grown-ups can possibly do. How do they spend the money? They themselves become drug addicts. Some of Shelton's grade school friends have died as a result. Once habituated, Shelton explains, you can't get away from it. If you don't have the money, you will steal and rob. That's why drugs have changed the whole nature of crime. Who are the chief victims of the criminals? The blacks in the neighborhood within easy reach.

I ask Shelton what he thinks of the 1964 Civil Rights Bill. He says that the present situation is "more dangerous." Before the bill, segregation and discrimination ruled supreme and everybody saw that social injustice was responsible for the blacks' miseries. But people now are saying to the blacks:"All doors are open to you" and "you have every opportunity." Yes, a small number of blacks are fortunante enough to avail themselves of opportunities and manage to rise to middle-class status. But most remain at the bottom of society, have nothing, and are desperate.

Take "affirmative action" for instance, Shelton continues. Blacks had won it the hard way. But what kind of "action" has it turned out to be? If there are, for example, five job openings and a larger number of applicants, "affirmative action" would award three of the jobs to white females, one to an Asian or Hispanic, and the fifth to a black. "I'm not exaggerating. White women are the chief beneficiaries." "Affirmative action," as Shelton interprets it," lumps white females together with minorities and lets them compete for whatever vacancies are left unfilled by white males. There are just so many jobs and you fight for them." It's a clever way, I think, to make people scramble for a few crumbs and thus forget the basic cause of why they must fight for bread in a land plagued by "food overabundance."

Young Chinese readers may wonder why white women are placed in the same category of discriminated minorities. I am not discussing women's questions here but should add that sex discrimination still persists in America. Women account for 51 percent of the total American population and men 49 percent. Obviously, women are not a minority. But unequal pay for equal work is prevalent and employment discrimination is not at all rare. That's why women need protection. American women did not have the right to vote until 1920 when a long and arduous fight by feminists finally won universal suffrage for them. As a woman, I appreciate the protection given females by "affirmative action." But I can also understand Shelton's negative response. It sounds good in theory. In practice it has a divide and rule effect.

Shelton's view that the present is "more dangerous" reminds me of my talk with a black woman in an entirely different situation. She is Phyllis A. Wallace, associate professor at M.I.T. and author of the book *Black Women in the Labor Force*. I visited her at her Boston home in a good apartment building in a wealthy neighborhood. She had an exquisitely furnished living room and a study lined with floor-to-ceiling bookshelves. I chatted with her while helping her prepare lunch in the kitchen. Her food, mainly fresh vegetables, seedless grapes and other fruits, meets the American standard of a "healthy diet." She lives alone and doesn't have to support a family. She is obviously one of those blacks who have become part of the middle class.

I asked her what she thought of the Civil Rights Bill. Her attitude coincides with Shelton's. She said that, legally speaking, segregation and discrimination had been abolished and a section of the black population had benefited. But two-thirds of America's blacks still remain in financial difficulties, and many of them are in dire straits. Like Shelton, she said that in the past all blacks believed social injustice was the basic cause of their plight. But now, seeing some blacks enjoying a much better life, the poor have to ask themselves: "Am I not as hardworking as they are? Are they brighter and smarter?" This, the professor said, is a great difficulty facing the blacks.

I tell Shelton about the professor's views. He says that she is completely right. But at this point Basir interrupts, reminding me not to misunderstand and think that blacks have stopped fighting. "Only

you will not see it reported in *The New York Times* or on TV screens,"
he says.

Street Scene

Basir and I take leave of the host and go to a bookstore to buy some
books Shelton has recommended to me. The store on Lenox Avenue,
called "Liberation Books," is the only one of a dozen or so Harlem
bookstores remaining open. But it is well stocked. There are China-
produced English editions of *Selected Works of Mao Zedong* as well as
illustrated translations of Chinese "revolutionary model operas" so
dubbed by Jiang Qing, Mao's wife and "cultural czar" in the "cultural
revolution." When I go to the counter to pay, the cashier, the only
shopkeeper in the store, asks me where I come from. She says she
would like very much to have a talk with me since I am the first person
from the People's Republic of China to visit her store. And she
immediately puts a question to me; "Why did you stop selling the
book *How to Be A Good Communist* some years ago? I had read it and
found it to be a good book." I explain to her that the book became
taboo as its author, Liu Shaoqi, was framed and persecuted during the
"cultural revolution." But it is again available because Liu, who had
been the chairman of the Chinese People's Republic for many years,
was posthumously rehabilitated. She asks further: "Is it true that the
people out there must do what the higher-ups tell them to and are not
allowed to say anything different?" I try to explain the situation to her
briefly and she appears to be intensely interested in continuing the
talk.

But a few customers have come to pay. I also must leave for other
appointments. Short as the encounter is, the black woman has left a
deep impression on my mind for her serious interest in my country and
her well-educated, elegant manners.

Basir shows me around. I find the streets littered with wastepaper
and garbage everywhere. People in shabby dress either lean on walls or
sit on doorsteps with blank stares. They appear bored and dispirited.

There are small groups of teenagers playing with portable
taperecorders, some singing, some twisting and turning in dances.
Their poor clothes remind me of the car "washers" I saw on my

previous visit. I try to make out what they are singing and find it to be Loretta Lynn's country music, *Coal Miner's Daughter, There Is No Way Out* and *I'm Tired of This Dirty Old City.* The songs fit the surroundings. The boys sing in subdued melancholy and husky voices to the slow twangs of the guitar on the tape. It is so depressing I think the music could be called "derelicts' lament." The scene brings to mind an aptly written passage from the travel book *Let's Go USA:**

> New York City is many worlds. To the artist, it is the Sacred Mountain. To the businessman, it is the bazaar to end all bazaars. To the European immigrant, it was the land of freedom and opportunity; to contemporary Latino immigrants and blacks, it is mean streets and unemployment. No other city provides such contrasts ... the slums of Harlem are only minutes away from the extravagant cooperatives of the Upper East Side.... You may well be excited, saddened, fascinated, frustrated, amused, angered, drained and rejuvenated — all in one visit.

Heydays

Manhattan is an expensive place "paved with gold." Why would blacks make it their home? There is a story behind it.

Beginning in the 1870s, land developers forced out the shanties, squatters, and goats that composed Harlem over a century ago. Luxurious houses and apartment buildings were put up so that Harlem would become a fashionable address for the rich and powerful.

The construction of a subway system to Harlem in the 1890s triggered a terrific wave of land development and speculation. Harlem was almost completely developed by 1904. For twenty years around the turn of the century, real estate owners speculated madly, anticipating that the subway would bring them fabulous profits. Land changed hands monthly and speculators made millions from soaring prices. The artificial boom led inevitably to the bust of 1905. Too many houses had been built and steep rents resulted in a high vacancy

---

* *Let's Go: The Guide to Budget Travel in the U.S.A.,* written by Harvard Student Agencies, Inc. and published by St. Martin's Press, New York, 1982.

rate. Faced with financial ruin, Harlem landowners saw rental to blacks, who needed a place to live however high the rent, as the only solution. Harlem therefore became the first place in America where blacks had access to decent housing. In response, whites kept on moving out. By 1915 opposition to black settlement had ended. And Harlem in 1917 was predominantly a black community. By 1920 all major black institutions had moved from downtown New York to Harlem.

Harlem became the capital of black people in America and, indeed, all over the world. Though the community was poor and beset with problems, the 1920s were a uniquely vital and creative period in Harlem's history. Art and literature flourished. Jazz, which many Chinese youth know, filtered north from the American South and developed into a sophisticated musical form in Harlem which then spread to the whole world. A galaxy of black writers, artists and political thinkers had gravitated to Harlem — which would be too long a story to tell here.

The Great Depression in the 1930s hit Harlem like a nightmare. Since then it has been sunk into poverty and despair and has never regained its former vitality and glamor. Still, blacks continued to flock to the place from the American South, the Caribbean and Central America. Conditions in Harlem have continued to change for the worse over the decades. But the "low wage and high rent" pattern set by people controlling its economic lifelines remain unchanged up to the present.

To cope with the onerous rent, black tenants often share their apartments with other families. The "warm bed" system has emerged for bachelors who rent a place to sleep in shifts. Landowners concern themselves only with collecting rents and don't bother about maintenance and repair. Neglect for many decades has left Harlem so dilapidated that the houses are worth only a fraction of the value of the land. Whatever housing remains intact is now inhabited by far more and far happier rodents and roaches than black tenants. Shelton has good reason to say that "Harlem is dying."

Chapter VII

WASHINGTON, D.C.

I have mixed feelings for Washington, D.C., the political nerve center of the U.S.A. These go back to 1948.

One morning in that year I was rushing to class after a cup of coffee at a snack bar off the University of Missouri campus. A man stepped out into my path and abrasively pointed to a headline in the morning paper. "Have you seen it? It's all American taxpayers' money," he said angrily.

I was angered even more and sharply snapped: "Go to hell with your money! Without it we wouldn't have had our civil war."

I had read the report. It was about Congressional testimony on Washington's China policy. At that time, the Chinese People's Liberation Army was winning sweeping victories over the American-propped Kuomintang regime. There were acrimonious charges from Capitol Hill that Washington's aid to Chiang Kai-shek had been inadequate. The administration, trying to defend itself, had to disclose how it had meddled in China's internal affairs and how much military and economic aid it had doled out to Chiang. In fact, there was human "aid" too, because United States military personnel did not stay aloof from that bloody war. While huge sums of American dollars had indeed been thrown down the drain, the rude man shouting at me should have directed his anger at the men in power in Washington, D.C.

I have recounted this quarrel in chats with American friends on my present visit. "It's fortunate that the folly is gone," they placate me. Not completely gone, I say to myself. I then think of Washington's handling of the Taiwan question, the Central American crises, and a few other questions still casting clouds on the Chinese mind.

On the other hand, I have admiration for Washington, D.C. as the center of American leadership. Selection of the capital itself was a testimony to their wisdom. Following the hard-won War of Independence, the thirteen American states each acting individually had almost turned the country into a congeries of competing states. After those masters of the art of political compromise, "the Founding Fathers," managed to bring into being a constitution in 1789, a permanent capital was to be chosen to replace Philadelphia. How to choose the capital was as much a result of clever compromise as the Constitution. George Washington was empowered to select a place which must not be too far to the north or to the south, nor should it be within the exclusive domain of any state. Finally a decision was taken to requisition one hundred square miles of land from Virginia and Maryland at the price of about sixty-six dollars per acre. The site for the capital was named the District of Columbia, and was abbreviated as D.C. Later, the city was named after Washington, hence the name Washington, D.C.*

George Washington appointed the first architect for the city and personally laid the cornerstone for the north wing of the Capitol. But he didn't have the chance to live in the White House, the American presidential mansion. At that time, the U.S. was a small agricultural country with a population, according to the first official census in 1790, of four million. The War of Independence had greatly drained the nation financially, and construction of the capital proceeded at a slow pace. It was not until 1800 that John Adams (in office from 1797 to 1801) became the first President to live in the White House. Throughout American history, with the sole exception of Franklin D. Roosevelt who served as President from 1933 to 1945, no American chief executive has occupied the White House for more than two terms (eight years). This was a tradition established by Washington's

---

*   Chinese readers may ask why it is not simply called Washington. The difficulty is that there are at least six other places in the country called Washington. A well-known one is the northwestern state on the Pacific coast. Washington, D.C. is the formal name to avoid confusion. Sometimes people simply call it D.C.

example. Without life tenure,* masters of the White House changed quite frequently. But there has been no lack of mature and outstanding statesmen there. Though the rapid development of America is largely due to its rich natural endowment and hard-working people, the caliber and wisdom of many leaders who have guided the country from D.C. have also played an important role.

THE CAPITAL AT NIGHT

As soon as I leave the train, I am glad to see a man waving to me. For many times on my one-year journey, people whom I have never seen before find and meet me in this way. There has never been any difficulty because I am always a lone traveler dressed in plain and rather conservative Chinese dress — very easy to recognize even at busy railway terminals on airports.

The man is Dick Bernhart, Professor Robinson's long-time friend. He had told the professor that I am welcome to spend a weekend with his family at their home in the Virginia countryside where there are many interesting people wishing to meet me.

I have traveled from flashy and noisy New York City to the American capital. My first impression is of the quietness of the tree-lined, softly-lit streets and the view of an open sky unimpeded by high-rises. Dick says that to get to Virginia we have to drive through the northwest quadrant of D.C. that contains Capitol Hill, the White House and many other sights. Soon the Capitol comes into view. Its familiar dome of multi-tiered windows, illumined from all sides, stands out gracefully against a dark blue sky and projects a shimmering image in a nearby pool.

Dick tells me that he works in downtown D.C. with a consultant firm involved in Third World construction projects. He has visited

---

* Speaking about the absence of life-tenure, federal judges are an exception. To protect the independence of the judiciary branch of the government, the U.S. Constitution provides that judges "shall hold their offices during good behaviour," which usually means tenure till their retirement, death or resignation. The federal courts are comprised of the Supreme Court, 11 circuit courts of appeal, 91 district courts and three courts of special jurisdiction. Federal judges are appointed by the President with Senate consent.

China twice, in 1977 and 1980, and has seen for himself how reforms in China's agricultural policies are changing people's lives. He came back convinced that the Chinese, who contributed so much to the ancient world, will do likewise in the future. He ardently hopes that Americans and Chinese will become better friends. Later, I read his article, "China's Spring," which emphasizes these themes. We soon drive past the White House. Well lit, it is a majestic structure but bears no resemblance to the palaces of kings. The standard Chinese translation, *Baigong* (meaning literally, White Palace), does not fit, but I cannot think of a better alternative. Dick recalls that when Lyndon Johnson was president, the White House was blacked out in the evening because the chief executive wanted to economize on electricity. People took L.B.J.'s well-intentioned but trivial economy as a joke. The White House is fenced off from the outside by low iron pickets instead of the usual palatial high walls and deep moats. Meadows and trees in the compound are clearly visible. The whole place occupies an area equal to one-hundred Chinese *mu*, not very large.

Turning south from the White House and then to the west, we come to the Lincoln Memorial. A huge statue of the famous President, mounted on a high pedestal, stands in front of a hall with ten imposing granite columns. There is a very long rectangular pool nearby. An image of the brightly lit Washington Monument spire on the other end ripples in the long pool like glistening gold streamers. The night scene of the capital is impressive.

The Potomac River flows by the Lincoln Memorial. Crossing a long bridge spanning it, we are in Virginia. There are no lamps on the bridge, but the yellow-coated parapets and lane markings show distinctly in response to the car's headlights.

Dick says that there will be another hour's drive to his home. It would take two hours when traffic is at its morning and afternoon peak. People who work in town but live in outlying areas usually commute by train. They drive from home to the railway terminal, leave their cars in a huge parking area, take the train to the city and then transfer to a bus. Dick calls Lovettsville, where he lives, a "bedroom" of D.C. Bernie and Ella Mazel also called New Rochelle a "bedroom" of New York City. It is no coindence that I always lodge in such bedroom communities. A growing trend in American urban life is to move to the far suburbs for a quieter and better environment — if you can afford it. This has given rise to the concept of SMSA (standard metropolitan statistical area) to denote a city together with its immediate and far suburbs. There were only 169 SMSAs in 1950 when the term first came into use. The number had almost doubled to 323 by 1981, at least one in each of the fifty states. The 1980 census showed that seventy-three percent of the American population, or 165 million, lived in SMSAs, a mark of the high degree of urbanization. This is a process similar to the mushrooming of what we in China call "satellite towns" near major cities, though China is trying to have small towns spread out in its vast countryside instead of clustering around already swollen metropolises.

Dick talks about his wife, Martha, a person who does not know how to rest. After retirement she hit upon the idea of opening a restaurant. It is called the Village Inn of Lovettsville and Dick dubs it the "Lovettsville Branch of the To Hell with Retirement Club." Martha seriously believes that retirement is not an end, but "a change to another set of interests." We pass by her inn. Dick tells me that it is attracting more and more customers because of its good food, good setting, lighting and music.

The highway is cutting through a wooded area. Dick suddenly brakes the car to a stop. I look out and see a young deer standing dumbfounded in our way. Dick quickly turns off the headlights. If the little animal runs down the highway, Dick says, it will not be able to escape the three dogs at his home just beyond.

When the lights are turned on again, the deer has disappeared. Dick drives slowly in order not to scare it any more if it is still around. Soon we are home. The dogs come by leaps and bounds to greet their master. We feel relieved the deer has fled into the the thickets.

Martha has just come back from the restaurant. The inn closes at 8:30 p.m. but she has a lot more work to wind up the day's business. Small wonder that Dick shows little love for the "To Hell with Retirement Club." While courteously apologizing that she could not go to the station to meet me, Martha leads me to a bedroom and tells me to rest and prepare for a busy weekend.

RANDOM NOTES ON COUNTRY LIFE

The natural beauty and tranquility of Lovettsville makes me nostalgic. Whenever I think of the place, a landscape painting of the American countryside appears in my mind's eye. A small bridge spans a meandering brook and leads to the other shore dotted with small trees, each different from the other in shape and color, but all buoyant in the flush of summer and emitting a mild fragrance. It would take a lyricist to recreate the picture in writing. A prosaic reporter, I only hope my random notes will give Chinese readers a few glimpses into American country life. In China people tend to believe that Fifth Avenue is America.

The vast American land is thinly populated. Houses in the countryside are few and far between. Dick or Martha has to drive me to visit their neighbors.

Disabled But Respected

Everybody in the community knows that Mr. Greene used to be a smart worker. But he has lost much of his memory since he accidentally fell from a high place while working and suffered serious concussion. Since then he has had to live by the simplest odd jobs. People in the neighborhood are very sympathetic and always think of him whenever they need some help. Dick tells me the story on my first morning in Lovettsville when Martha goes out to get Mr. Greene to carry some horse manure to her garden. Both Dick and Martha call the man Mr. Greene. In a country where people usually address each other by abbreviated first names, "Mr." and "Mrs." are often used to express politeness or respect. Though disabled Mr. Greene has apparently not become an ugly duckling. Indeed, because of the sympathy extended by his friends and his determination to work hard, he has maintained the respect of those around him through his misfortune. This is one of the commendable American mores, I think.

After telling Mr. Greene what she wants done, Martha drives me to see his parents. When we drive into the courtyard, the car sets off a flock of cackling and wing-flapping leghorns who flee in all directions — vividly reminding me of country scenes in China. The eighty-year-old Mr. Greene, a retired railway worker, sways in a rocking chair in the living room. The seventy-eight-year-old mother is busy preparing a snack. She says that I am the first Chinese to visit her home and that I must eat something. A big cake has already been placed on the table in the kitchen and coffee is boiling on the stove. I have just had my breakfast. Martha has a tough job of helping me to decline the treat. The lady then shows us around her vegetable garden and the hogs she is raising. It looks like retirement benefits plus the small garden are keeping the family in pretty good condition. To my Chinese eyes their housing is ample and quite comfortable.

Why don't they have their disabled son live with them? We would certainly do that in China. There are probably unoccupied bedrooms upstairs. Even if there are none, the living room or dining room could easily be converted into one. But I refrain from asking the question because I know I am thinking in Chinese terms. The highly individualistic Americans, even the disabled, cherish their personal privacy and freedom. Mr. Greene would probably prefer to live alone even if his parents offered him a room.

Martha then takes me to the house where Mr. Greene is collecting stable manure for her. The lady of the house, all smiles, greets me at the gate. A four-year-old boy looks at me shyly from behind his mom. The boy is starting early as a horseman, the mother says. He owns a white horse which is kept in the stable. His father works in D.C. with the U.S. Department of Labor. The family is obviously well-off and has six horses, one for each member of the household. There is plenty of stable manure and everybody is welcome to take it away free. The hostess explains that most people who raise horses in the United States do it for pleasure, while gardeners prefer natural manure to chemical fertilizers.

Butcher and Country Ham

While America has a big meat-packing industry, I have always believed that all meat on the dining table, whether beef, pork, fish, or fowl, came from distant places. This is not completely true. Small individual enclaves still exist within the vast domains of the Swifts and Armours. Martha takes me to Mr. Burtner's butcher shop in the neighboring state of Maryland, where her restaurant gets its meat supply.

Post-technological America still retains the traditional county, state, and even national fairs. The farmers meet at the fairs and compete with each other for the best steer or hog, the biggest pumpkin or melon, etc. Mr. Burtner is getting ready to go to a local fair with a big load of freshly made ham sandwiches for sale.

The shop is both a slaughterhouse and a processing plant. John, a young worker, shows me the whole place from the first to the second floor. Mr. Burtner asks another partner to get me a ham sandwich and a package of thinly sliced ham. He shows me the firewood with which he smokes the ham on a specially designed stove. He tells me that it is the sassafras wood that gives his ham its unique flavor.

The peach-colored country ham is tender and delicious. It is very different from the mass-produced products of big companies.

Is He a "Nongmin"?

Later, Dick replaces Martha as my guide and takes me to visit Mr. Shaeffer, the first farmer I meet on my present visit. A question crops up in my mind — how to properly translate "farmer" into Chinese. We call people who live by farming *nongmin*, which is translated into English as "peasant." Then "American farmer" is translated into Chinese as *Meiguo nongmin*, "American peasant." It is a misnomer because for historical reasons the term *nongmin* still evokes associations with poverty or even boorishness. What about calling him a *nongchangzhu*, a farm owner? That is closer, but the name would sound like the boss of a big corporate farm or of an old southern plantation.

Anyway, farmer or peasant Shaeffer meets us at his house surrounded by 375 acres (2,276 Chinese *mu*) of land. This would be considered a huge amount of land in China. Corn, the main crop, has been harvested and the field seems to be drowsing in the setting sun. Shaeffer uses part of his corn to raise 150 milk cows and sells the remainder.

Seeing his friend Dick, the farmer begins complaining that the current $2.1-a-bushel price for corn is ruinous. He would have preferred to buy feed from the "elevators" instead of growing it, if he had foreseen the trouble.

While talking, he leads us to see the milk parlor. It has two platforms for cows and a pit deep enough for the milker to reach the udders without stooping. A herd of twelve cows comes in from one end of the parlor and they stand, six in a row, on the two platforms. Milking starts through pipe-connected teat cups. When it is done and the cows move out from the other end, the milkers wash the concrete floor with a hose and let in another herd. The two milkers, boys about fifteen years old, are students who work after school and are paid by the hour. They work conscientiously without a moment's interruption. A continuous measurement is made of the milk flowing into tanks.

Shaeffer tells me that milking is done twice daily, in the morning by himself and his son. The young man is married, lives in the vicinity and is paid for the work — quite unimaginable in China where a son is duty-bound to help his parents. Obviously Shaeffer is the only main laborer on the farm. It is a lot of work to till so much land and raise so many cows even though all labor has been mechanized.

The host then leads us to his machinery shed. He has the exact prices of all the tools at his fingertips and lists them one by one as he shows us around. Altogether, they cost at least $600,000.

We are then ushered into an ancient, but newly renovated, two-story house with high ceilings. Shaeffer and his wife live here. The kitchen is completely modernized and compares favorably with Martha's, or Carol Robinson's in Boston, perhaps larger. There are chandeliers and very good sofas in the spacious and carpeted living room. Another living room, and three bedrooms are upstairs, one for the couple and two well-furnished but unoccupied ones for their two married daughters who visit periodically. Though household chores have been made much easier by all sorts of home appliances, I can still imagine how much time Mrs. Shaeffer has to spend everyday to keep the big house clean. The house is certainly old. Mrs. Shaeffer opens an unoccupied small room at one end of the balcony and tells me that it used to be the living quarters of black slaves.

I compliment Mrs. Shaeffer on keeping the house so clean and orderly. It is no easy job for a couple approaching their seventies. "The work keeps me busy all the time and I have little time to enjoy what I have done," she says. If there is anything that can be called an American trait, hard work is certainly a most prominent one. It impressed me deeply in the forties and remains unchanged now in the eighties.

On our way back, I continue to ponder terminology. Mr. Shaeffer can rightly be called a *nongmin*, inasmuch as he earns his living by his own hands and works hard all year around (cattle raising has no slack season). But he owns land, machinery, cattle, the house, all worth well over a million dollars, and is certainly not the kind of *nongmin* we know in China. In America, farmers like him sometimes call themselves "self-employed family farm owners." That is a more accurate description but it would be a mouthful in Chinese. So I shall continue to call them *nongmin* in the sense that in China, too, more and more peasants are becoming prosperous and educated, and are no longer the bumpkins looked down upon by urban elites.

Hard-working and Proud

Dan Fleming is another "self-employed family farm owner" though he employs three other people. A robust farmer in his early forties, he also complains about the falling farm prices and says that in spite of the good harvest he has lost $28,000 this year.

Dan, by Martha's arrangement, kindly comes to meet me at the Village Inn as soon as he finishes chopping cornstalks at 3:30 p.m. I feel sorry that he has lost so much money after a year's hard work. What's wrong?

Dan owns two-hundred acres and rents an additional fifteen hundred, including pastureland. He cultivates corn and hay, and raises beef cattle. Only hay brings in profit because many wealthy people in this part of the country have pleasure horses and buy hay for fodder.

Dan, I calculate, works on 10,319 Chinese *mu* of land. Apart from the three employees, his son works for him during summer vacations. Dan's wife is a grade school teacher. She often teases him saying that he can't afford to be a farmer without her salary to support the family.

Is his loss a result of high wages? I ask. No. The three men are each paid $130 a week, very little by American standards, plus a year-round free supply of beef. They have a heavy load of work and cannot have supper before 10 p.m. in busy seasons. But the working hours are much shorter in winter because feeding and breeding don't take so much time. The trouble, Dan explains, is that rents and prices for machinery, seed, fertilizer and pesticide keep rising. Only prices for farm products are declining. The federal government buys part of the yield at subsidized prices but the subsidies are not even enough to pay the electricity bills.

Dan Fleming explains further, recalling that American farmers began switching from horsepower to mechanical power from 1936 to 1940 before he was born (he is 42). When he grew up and took over the farm from his father, though he was fortunate to have a complete assortment of horse-drawn implements, machinery had to be bought on credit because other farmers were using tractors. The bigger the machinery, he says, the more it costs. And the farm has to expand its size to fit the investment. Thus production keeps on increasing on his and other farms but the market for farm produce has not expanded correspondingly. That's where the trouble arises. Dan is trying to sell part of his corn for money to build a bigger bin so that he can store the grain and wait for better prices. When will better prices come, or will they ever come? "God only knows," he says.

Dan tells me that there are very few big corporation farms on the east coast. Most of them are in the West, Midwest, and South. As far as he knows, "Virginia Beef" is the largest one in this part of the country. It plants as much as 10,000 acres of corn and 7,000 acres of soybeans. But the giant is also operating in the red.

Perhaps to correct my impression of American farm life which may result from his complaints, Dan adds: "But it's good to be a farmer, you know? I'm self-employed and free to use my time as I want. I can go fishing or hunting whenever I like."

"This is probably true only in theory," I say, smiling. "Actually you don't have the time to go fishing or hunting."

"That's right. There are financial considerations. And then you know you can't go."

Our meeting ends in laughter. All American farmers seem to take great pride in their freedom as self-employed workers. Roger Wheeler, an Iowa farmer whom I meet later, says exactly the same thing to me.

Today while I sit writing in Beijing, I feel sympathy for American farmers like Dan who are caught in a web of financial pressures. Life isn't as easy in the American "paradise" as many might want to believe. You have to work hard and even then, hard work does not necessarily bring happy returns. I also wonder when and how that hideous paradox of a huge farm surplus in America, while there are food shortages and mass famine in many countries, will be resolved.

Ready to Help and Striving for the New

The weather vane as I know it, is always shaped like an arrow with a fish tail. But the one Ralph Ives has in front of his house is a big bird painted in bright colors. Mrs. Gunnie Ives tells me that it's Ralph's handiwork. And the house itself was also designed by him. It is a unique building in which you feel as if you are on board a luxurious yacht sailing on a sea of green. There are five thousand pine trees around the house which you can see waving in the summer breeze through windows on every side. If the house were in pine-loving China, most probably calligraphers would have inscribed a board on its gate calling it something like "Pavilion on Rustling Pine Waves".

Mr. and Mrs. Ives have invited me and the Bernharts to lunch. Talking and laughing, we take seats in the dining room and feel as if we are picnicking in a pine forest. Ralph asks me what I have seen in Lovettsville and what other places I am going to visit. Hearing my itinerary, Gunnie says sympathetically, "It must be pretty hard on you."

"Yes, particularly because I am a foreigner and traveling alone." I then tell them of a difficulty I encountered a few days earlier which does have humorous undertones. I had phoned my friend, the poet Paul Engle, who is to meet me at my next stop — Cedar Rapids, Iowa. I told him that I had confirmed with the airlines and the time of my arrival wouldn't change. Paul, however, insisted that I come to Cedar Rapids three hours earlier so as to join in a welcome for a Chinese writers' delegation due to arrive there. He said that changing flight schedules is routine in America and there would be no difficulty. But I was worried, saying that I was in a foreign country and didn't know how to make the change. I wouldn't mind missing the welcome and would stay one night in Cedar Rapids waiting for him to come back the next day from Iowa City to pick me up.

Gunnie asks with concern: "Then you haven't changed the schedule?" I point to Dick and say, "Yes, he helped me." "Dick is always ready to help," Gunnie says approvingly.

"But there are nine months ahead," I say. "And I don't know what other difficulties will arise"

"Haven't you found the way out?" Dick laughs. "You simply cry out, 'it's too difficult for me' and there will be people to help you."

It is really not a joke. My experience in the following months bears out that American people are always ready to lend a helping hand. It may have been my unique luck to have found help whenever I was in need. Nonetheless, the memory is pleasant. The habit of helping others, some Americans explain, was formed in the early pioneer days when mishaps were frequent for those traveling alone on horseback across the vast continent. At the same time, my friends caution, fierce competition, individualism, and outright selfishness are also quite prevalent.

When lunch begins, I am surprised to hear long, shrill siren sounds, reminiscent of the air-raid alarms I abhorred in China's wartime capital, Chongqing, during the anti-Japanese war. Ralph explains that it's a fire alarm and all registered fire-fighters on hearing it must stand by the telephone waiting for a call. Unlike cities which have tax-paid fire-brigades, all the men are volunteers. The volunteer-fireman has also been a long tradition. Ralph and Dick are probably exempted from the service because of their age, I presume.

While we are speaking of traditions, I ask Gunnie why it is that when they entertain a guest with the traditional grilling of beef on a metal grid over charcoal fire, it is always the man who does the grilling, while the hostess and guests sit and eat. "Well," Gunnie laughs at Ralph and Dick, "they always like to slip away to steal a few more drinks."

When I depart, Dick tells me that Ralph is in the same trade as mine — publishing and journalism. He runs a plant in Baltimore, Maryland, which prints the newly-created newspaper *USA Today*.

Ralph immediately goes to get me a copy of the inaugural issue, which appeared only three day earlier. Under its masthead is printed "via satellite" meaning the paper is to be relayed by satellite for reproduction in fifteen American cities.

I thumb through the thick bundle of about forty pages and find the paper is quite a venture. The color photos, charts and diagrams are eye-catching. The column on the front page called "Newsline" gives a quick run of the day's major events in one or two sentences each. Only one story in each issue is allowed to carry over on other pages, Ralph tells me. It suits the quickening tempo of life.

The big-bird weather vane, the unique house design and *USA Today* leave a strong impression on me that Americans are always striving for something new and unconventional. It is not incidental that the circulation of the new paper has climbed to sixth place among national dailies by the time I leave the United States in May 1983.

ABORTION, SCHOOL PRAYER AND SENATE DEBATE

— Some Observations on the "New Right"

Sexual revolution, or sexual liberation, is a *fait accompli* in America, like it or not. If abortion is outlawed, isn't it obvious that women, particularly unmarried girls, will suffer? This is a question I put to Dick on our way back from Lovettsville to D.C. At that time a debate is going on in Senate on abortion and school prayer. For almost five continual weeks, one speaker after another has taken the floor of the Senate to prevent a vote. The delaying tactics are called "filibuster," often translated in Chinese press as "wearing-out bombing," a derivative from the Japanese tactic of sending a few planes to harass a Chinese city for days on end.

I had intended to try the blue-and-white commuter train out of Lovettsville, but a paralyzing strike by 28,000 engineers across the country makes it impossible. We have to travel by car, driving slowly and stopping frequently as traffic piles up. The trip turns out to be a good chance to talk, even on serious political questions.

Dick does not answer my question directly but speaks about the filibuster tactic. It used to be employed by "conservatives" against "liberals," by southern Senators, for instance, to stall a vote on the abolition of slavery and, in later years, to ward off civil rights legislation. But it has been reversed now and the "liberals" are for the first time using "filibuster" against the "conservatives."

I have learned from the press that as soon as anti-abortion was brought up on the Senate floor, one of the lawmakers produced a four hundred-page manuscript on the history of abortion in America and declared that he would read it aloud word for word to prove that abortion should not be banned. If the Senate wishes to stop these tirades, it has to "invoke closure" by a two-thirds majority. The "conservatives" had made five attempts at closure on this issue but failed to muster a wide enough margin. So the speechifying continues with furor.

Origins

The United States Constitution is the supreme statute of the land. The states have their separate constitutions and can enact laws, as long as they do not contravene it. But the Constitution is tersely worded and it is often hard to decide whether a law violates it. The Supreme Court is therefore vested with the power to rule on the constitutionality of laws. The first Ten Amendments to the Constitution, known as the Bill of Rights, for instance, provide that no person shall "be deprived of life, liberty, or property." The right to life could be cited to oppose abortion, while the right to liberty could mean that women are free to decide on their childbirth. Likewise, conflicting constitutional grounds can be found for or against school prayer.

The current quarrel in the Senate revolves around a ruling handed down by the Supreme Court in 1973. It explicitly provides that a state cannot prevent a woman from having an abortion during the first six months of pregnancy, thus invalidating the anti-abortion laws in Texas and Georgia, and, by implication, overturning restrictive abortion laws in forty-four other states.

The 1973 ruling was adopted by an overwhelming majority of

seven to two. The Supreme Court is composed of nine judges appointed by the President with Senate consent. Once appointed, they have life tenure unless they are removed for misconduct.

As for prayer in public schools (referring to grade and high schools), the Supreme Court had ruled eight to one in 1963 that laws requiring "recitation of the Lord's Prayer or Bible verses" in public schools are unconstitutional. The ruling is based on the First Amendment, which provides that "Congress shall make no law respecting an establishment of religion, or prohibiting the free exercise thereof."

"Liberals" point out that though sixty-four percent of Americans believe in Christianity, the rest include followers of all religions existing in the world, and three percent declare themselves to be non-believers. If formal prayer led by teachers is prescribed by law, what should the non-Christian minority in the student body do? Besides, it cannot be taken for granted that all teachers are Christians. Public schools are financed by government money, the "liberals" contend, and should follow the long-established tradition of separation of church from the state. Though proponents claim that the prayers will be voluntary, can seven- or eight-year-old children truly exercise free volition? If a child joins the prayer simply to get along with the majority, a contradiction may arise with his family belief. If he does not join in, he may feel bad for being different from the others. Furthermore, religion is a personal matter of conscience and nobody has the right to ask others, especially teenagers, to make public their beliefs.

These considerations are the origins of the Senate debate.

Issues Shelved

In its nearly two hundred years of history, the U.S. Constitution has admitted only twenty-six amendments. The first ten, collectively known as the Bill of Rights, were adopted while the Constitution itself was being ratified by the original thirteen states. The Bill of Rights is historic for its provisions of freedom of religious belief, speech, the press, and the freedom to assemble, petition, bear arms, *etc.* The Constitution took effect in 1789 upon ratification and the Bill of

Rights, two years later in 1791. Since then only sixteen more amendments have been adopted in the 191 years up to 1982. Any constitutional amendment must be approved by a two-thirds majority in both the Senate and House and then ratified by two-thirds of the states — a very complicated process.

Both anti-abortion and school prayer involve the Constitution. The "conservatives" are well aware that if they bring up the questions as constitutional amendments, they don't have much chance of rallying a two-thirds majority even in the republican-controlled Senate, let alone the House, which is in the firm grip of the Democrats.

The "conservatives," however, hit upon a clever idea. Led by Senator Jesse Helms, they tucked the two highly controversial issues as "riders" in a completely irrelevant bill on raising the ceiling of the national debt. The bill was to be passed before 30 September 1982 when the Senate was scheduled to adjourn, or else the federal government would be left insolvent. The "liberals" started filibustering. Eventually they forced the "riders" to be withdrawn. So the issues are temporarily shelved.

In the course of the Congressional debate, President Reagan came out openly to support the "right to life" of "the unborn," and "voluntary" prayer in schools. "Conservatives" on Capitol Hill, for their part, make it clear that they will not take the defeat lying down. Later, in 1983, the Supreme Court reaffirmed its ruling upholding women's freedom to have abortion without any constraints in the first three months of pregnancy. But the issues are still far from dying.

In America, abortion is a major question affecting over one million families. According to authoritative statistics, legal abortions alone numbered 744,600 in 1973 and increased to 1.55 million in 1980. Over the period 1973 to 1980, one-third of the women who had abortions were under twenty years of age, and three out of every four were unmarried. Some Americans believe that a ban on abortion will have serious social consequences. As it is, ummarried mothers and fatherless children are already numerous. A great number of them are struggling under the poverty line. Illegitimate children born by young girls (called "children's children"), particularly of blacks, are the particularly disadvantaged. The extreme "conservatives," however, will not tolerate abortion even if pregnancy is a result of incest or rape.

If their demand prevails, the resultant increase of fatherless children is bound to aggravate social problems.

The "New Right"

Dick asks me if I have heard about the "New Right." Yes. And indeed I have read a book entitled *The New Right: We're Ready to Lead**. A scholar in Boston gave it to me and said: "Read it. It's equivalent to Hitler's *Mein Kampf*."

The much-debated abortion and school prayer are actually minor issues in the ongoing rivalry between "conservatives" and "liberals." Since the mid-1970s, the "New Right" has appeared on the American political scene. This group is more conservative than their predecessors and farther to the Right than the traditional Right-wingers. Like the old guard in pre-liberation China who lamented "disintegration of the time-honored order," the "New Right" in America poses itself as champions of "traditional values." They believe that anti-abortion laws can curb loose sexual morality and rampant pornography. They want school prayer for the young so that, with God's help, they will be immunized against anti-traditional ideas and behavior. Americans, as I see it, are correctly impatient with their growing social maladies, and the "New Right" is trying to take advantage of this feeling of discontent by assuming a tough stance on these issues. But they want much more than morality. Their ultimate aim is power. "We're ready to lead," as the book declares.

As my American friends summarize it, the program of the "New Right" consists mainly of: One, rabid anti-Communism. They call for bigger defense spending, more and better arms, and undisputed American military superiority. They not only want to "contain" Communism but to turn the whole globe into their so-called "free world." They send out tens of millions of letters a year to warn of "the danger of Communism."

Two, they are against "big government," a government that does

---

**The New Right: We're Ready to Lead* by Richard A. Viguerie, published by The Viguerie Company, Falls Church, VA.

too much. Programs like social security and medicare, they argue, all breed laziness. They want to slash drastically, if not completely eliminate, the government's social expenditures.

Three, they call for tax cuts to stimulate investment and invigorate the economy. I have read many articles in the American press pointing out that the tax-cutting formulas of the "New Right" will first of all benefit big business. Reduction of social expenditures, on the other hand, will further impoverish the poor. In 1983-84, in spite of a buoyant economy, the number of people living under the official poverty line has increased from 30 to 35 million and the situation will worsen if the "New Right" economic proposals prevail. That's why some of my American friends characterize the "New Right" platform as one of starving the poor to fatten the rich. Apart from anti-Communism, attacking the government's social expenditures is another theme of the "New Right's" gigantic direct mail operations.

Four, they stress "personal freedom and dignity" and advocate a restoration of traditional morality. "American pioneers were strong, God-fearing and family-oriented. They built houses and families to last. They lived, worked and died together," "New Right" writers nostalgically recall.

Five, they bitterly attack the "liberals." In their eyes, 'liberalism" comprises a very wide political spectrum ranging from blacks and other ethnic minorities, trade unions, women's movements and family-planning organizations, to such political figures as Franklin D. Roosevelt, the Kennedys, and Nelson Rockefeller — who was described as "the high-flying, wild-spending leader of the Eastern Liberal Establishment," before his death. They categorically place the blame on the "liberals" for all social evils like homosexuality and pornography, family dissolution, drug addiction, and increasing crime.

They call themselves the "New Right" to distinguish themselves from their predecessors. The "old Right," they say, are mere talkers and pamphleteers who don't know how to get into power. The "New Right" also claims to be a completely voluntary group without bosses or "godfathers." But many people are quick to point out that Senator Jesse Helms of North Carolina is their "generalissimo."

The "New Right" believes that its support of Mr. Reagan, a well-known conservative, was crucial in electing him to the White House in the 1980 election. It was particularly effective in raising and spending funds to shape public opinion and win votes. But they now criticize the President for not being far enough "Right" in his actual performance, and for failing to appoint many of their young leaders to public office.

They make it plain that to get a conservative President elected is only part of their aim. Their larger goal is to win leadership in both the Senate and House, in all states and at local levels. The "New Right" is comprised mostly of ambitious young and middle-aged people. They have formed a multiplicity of political action comittees like NCPAC (National Conservative Political Action Committee)," the Heritage Fund, the Moral Majority, the Congressional Club, and others, as well as many "single-issue" groups which lobby for such diverse causes as "right to life," school prayer, and gun ownership. They are trying to cover the nation with a vast "conservative" network. The weekly news magazine, *Time*, (14 September 1981) says that Jesse Helms, "the New Right's righteous warrior" and his Congressional Club are "the very model of modern, high-technology politics, a shrewd mating of computers and direct mail." "The Helms machine has perfected the techniques of turning fear into funds and piety into profits."

Some Americans, like the Boston scholar who gave me the book, seem worried by the increasing aggressiveness of the "New Right." Many opposed to it, however, think it will engender the kind of mounting opposition that eventually can lead to the decline of the ultra-conservatives. "This country will muddle through to a middle course," an elderly American who has witnessed the swing of the political pendulum for decades tells me.

On the specific issues of abortion and school prayer, however, there is much concern over possible changes in the Supreme Court alignment. Of the nine justices on the court, only one — Sandra Day O'Connor — was apointed by President Reagan, in 1981. She is the youngest, born in 1930. The other eight are much older, including one born in 1906, two in 1907 and two in 1908. Vacancies are likely to appear during President Reagan's second term which expires by January, 1989. In that case new judges will be appointed by the President with the consent of what may be a Republican-controlled

Senate. There is a distinct possibility that the Supreme Court could reverse its former verdicts on the two issues still on everybody's lips.

CAPITOL HILL AND THE WHITE HOUSE
— How the Congress and the President Are Elected

When I come to the west gate of the Capitol, two of my most respected American friends are already there waving to me from the high staircase. They are Roy Fisher, Dean of the School of Journalism, University of Missouri, and his wife, Anne. Roy is on a one-year sabbatical leave in Washington, D.C., to write a book. I am lucky to have them as my guides or else I would get lost in the labyrinth of the complex.

"Capitol" means the building where the U.S. Congress meets. The site is often called Capitol Hill because it is on a piece of high land. The outward appearance of the political hub is more like a botanical garden with lush lawns, blazing flowers, fountains, and pools. Small wonder that some people call it an oasis in the midst of urban bustle.

The interiors of the Capitol look like an art gallery with magnificent paintings and murals on walls and ceilings, as well as many marble statues erected in gorgeously carpeted corridors and halls. The whole place had been carefully restored for the nation's Bicentennial in 1976 and gained added luster and color. There is a steady stream of visitors moving through. I feel sorry that I don't have time to linger and enjoy the treasury of art as I must go straight to the Senate. After depositing my camera and tape-recorder, as requested, we walk to the gallery where visitors can see the Senate chamber and hear its debate. Some tourists are leaving and we take their place in the front row so that we can lean over the balcony and get a closer view.

People are free to come and listen to Senate debate without producing any certificate or paying admission. But most of them are tourists who leave after a quick glance and there seem to be very few, if any, serious listeners. So the gallery is always busy with people coming and going. Roy knows the names of many Senators who sit in semicircular rows. Most names are unfamiliar to me. But Senator

Edward Kennedy, brother of the assassinated President and a well-known "liberal" Democrat, is easily recognizable because I have often seen his pictures in newspapers. On the side close to our balcony is another senator heard more often in China — Barry Goldwater. A longtime "conservative," he doesn't like "Communist China," though on this day he happens to be wearing a bright red jacket. I have just read a gossipy newspaper report that the senator and his wife are unhappy because the endless debate in the Senate is keeping him from going back to Arizona to celebrate their wedding anniversary.

I find that most seats are empty and that of the few senators present, many are whispering to each other. Only secretaries (or pages) are rushing back and forth on the floor. I ask Roy why. He explains that many senators are in their own offices, busy meeting constituents, receiving telephone calls and attending to other business. They cannot afford to sit here all the time. Somebody is speaking on the dais and occasional laughter bursts out in the gallery. The filibuster on school prayer is still going on.

I propose that we hurry to the House of Representatives for a quick look. When we get there, my first impression is that the chamber is considerably larger and the Congressmen much younger. The atmosphere also appears to be livelier than in the Senate.

Chinese readers will probably ask why. When the United States formulated its Constitution in 1787, a provision was made that each state would be represented by two senators in order to ensure equal rights for the smaller states. The number of states increased from the original thirteen to the present fifty, so there are now one hundred senators. They are elected to a six-year term and there is no limit to re-election. Even new senators are usually politicians with long experience and the re-elected ones are of course veterans. That is why they are less numerous and older than the representatives. I still remember a professor teaching American government wisecracking that the Senate has a committee on foreign relations and its House counterpart is called the committee on foreign affairs because "relations" are for the old and "affairs" are for the young.

While accommodation is made for the small states, consideration of population also is given. That is why the Constitution apportions House seats to states in proportion to the size of their population. In

1787, there were sixty-five representatives. A decennial national census was started in 1790 which formed the basis for future redistribution of House seats. With the growth of population the number of representatives rose to 435 in 1910. If more seats were to be added in step with population increase, representatives might someday be counted by the thousands and the legislature would be too unwieldy to work. So a law was made fixing 435 as the maximum number and giving each state a share commensurate with its population. Each representative has a largely equal constituency (The present ratio is about one for every 500,000 people). Special accommodation is made for small or thinly populated states as each of them is guaranteed at least one seat. Representatives have a tenure of two years but they can be re-elected. The Senate, however, has one-third of its members re-elected in every two years. That is why in a year of Presidential election (always the leap year with a 29 February), American voters also re-elect all representatives and one-third of the senators. There is a "mid-term" election in between two Presidential elections in which the whole House and another third of the Senate are re-chosen. The faster revolving political door to the House enables more younger people to get in.

An important demographic trend in America in recent years is a population shift to the South and the West. Corresponding changes have occurred in the number of House seats allotted to different states. New York, which had the largest population from 1810 to 1960, was surpassed by California in 1970 and further outstripped by it in 1980. As a result, representatives from New York state decreased from thirty-nine in 1970 to thirty-four in 1980, while California had its share increased from forty-three to forty-five. In the same period, representatives from the southeastern state of Florida increased from fifteen to nineteen, while Missouri in the Midwest got one seat less, nine instead of the previous ten.

As in the Senate, visitors keep on coming and going in the House gallery. I, too, have to satisfy myself with what we would call in China "a look at flowers on horseback" because it is getting late. Thanks to Roy and Anne who know the way so well, we zigzag back to get my camera and recorder, descend to the basement by elevator, and get on a small train. We are soon off Capitol Hill.

How to Enter the White House

On the next day I go to visit the White House by myself. As in the buildings on Capitol Hill visitors line up in a queue and are admitted freely. But only a few sections are open to tourists. I have no complaint because bombings and other terrorist activities are on the increase. The White House, I am told, is protected by stringent security measures. But sophisticated high-tech safety devices are not easily discernible, so the atmosphere remains free and easy.

I follow the other tourists into the compound and see the well-known Rose Garden. In the halls inside the house I find many beautiful porcelains displayed in glass cases. Some of them are distinctly Chinese, which I can recognize at a glance.

Speaking of the White House, my Chinese readers would probably be interested in knowing how one can become its master, that is, to become the U.S. President. Most Chinese are aware that the presidential election held every four years is full of color and sound, and TV scenes of national conventions are almost like a circus. But what is the electoral procedure? It is rather complex and I can draw only a rough outline here.

For many years now, the American presidential election has been a contest between two parties, Republican and Democrat, though other small political parties participate in it. Whoever has realistic aspirations to the highest office in the land must first get the nomination from either of the two major parties as its presidential candidate. A federal law stipulates that the election shall be held "on the first Tuesday following the first Monday in November" in the fourth year after the previous presidential election. In fact, electioneering begins one or two years before the date. The aspirants travel from place to place across the country, making speeches, meeting the press, expounding their political views and attacking potential opponents. Hand shaking, baby kissing, telling a few jokes, and passing some homely remarks are also important to make people feel that the hopeful candidate is one of the "people," a nice guy, a good fellow. At the same time he tries to enlist support from the local party machines. When conditions are propitious, he publicly announces his intention to seek the nomination of his party.

After much maneuvering and a complex procedure including state primary elections, the two parties hold separate national conventions in the election year to select their presidential candidates. These conventions, attended by large numbers of delegates and marked by intense competition and backstage dealings, are full of glamor, suspense and imaginative publicity stunts. They can attract even more TV watchers than the most spectacular sports events.

Fervor heats up further as election day draws closer. Debate and quarrel, public opinion polls, commentaries and analyses, predictions and forecasts fill the "media" — the press, radio and TV. The race also becomes a frequent topic in daily conversations.

The climax comes on election day. Voters across the country go to the designated places and cast their secret ballots in election booths. I've had the chance to witness only the 1948 election. The 1984 one, as I learn from the press and American friends visiting in China, was by and large the same, though the omnipresence of TV and the adoption of high-tech audio-video devices have heightened the excitement. Radio and TV give round-the-clock coverage on election day, continuously reporting the initial returns and trends nationally and locally, until the final results. Even in the forties, vote counting was fast enough to reveal the outcome by the early hours of the morning. I remember that in the 1948 race between Thomas Dewey and Harry Truman, practically all political forecasters predicted a Dewey landslide. One major paper, the *Chicago Daily Tribune*, wanting a "scoop," announced in a headline, "Dewey Defeats Truman" even before the outcome was official. To the "Trib's" great dismay, Mr. Truman overcame Dewey's lead and was declared the winner after the paper was already on the newsstands. The episode has long been remembered as an object lesson for the media.

Many Chinese think that American voters cast their ballots directly for a presidential candidate. The votes they actually cast in November are for electors who will elect the President. The number of electors in each state is equal to the total of senators and representatives from the particular state. Electors from all states and the District of Columbia combine to form the Electoral College. With 100 senators, 435 representatives, and three "electors" from Washinston, D.C., the total number of presidential electors comes to 538. The President is chosen by a simple majority, i.e., 270 or more electoral votes.

Electors are publicly committed to vote for the presidential candidate of one party or the other. In this sense American voters are choosing their president when they cast their ballots. There is, however, an important "catch" here. The presidential candidate who wins a majority of the electoral votes of any state "carries" the entire state's votes in the electoral college. California, for instance, has forty-seven electors. If twenty-four or more of them representing a certain candidate are "chosen," that candidate will get all the forty-seven votes. This rule often results in a candidate's being defeated by a wide margin of electoral votes though the number of popular votes may be very close.

In the 1984 election, for example, Ronald Reagan of the Republican Party won fifty-nine percent of all valid popular votes while Walter Mondale, the Democratic nominee, got forty-one percent. But Reagan won 525 of the 538 electoral votes against the latter's thirteen, because Mondale "carried" only his home state Minnesota, plus Washington, D.C. The "landslide" for President Reagan actually means the overwhelming majority of electoral votes that he won. In history there were even three elections (1824, 1876 and 1888) in which the presidential candidate winning more popular votes turned out to be the loser.

In spite of all the fanfare in presidential elections, turnout of eligible voters is often low. In the 1984 election, only 52.9 percent of voters went to the polls. Some of my American friends deplore the poor performance, attributing it to a trend toward political apathy. Many voters, they say, are indifferent because they believe the Republicans and Democrats are like "two peas in a pod" and there won't be a basic change whoever gets into power.

Purse and Government

The U.S. Constitution provides that any American citizen born in the United States who has attained the age of thirty-five and been a resident of the United States for fourteen years, is eligible to be elected

President. The most important qualification, however, is unwritten; that is money. In America you need money to do anything anywhere. Campaign tours, TV debates, advertising in the press, direct mail operations, to name a few, are all very costly. Even more sophisticated methods are being developed to popularize candidates and belittle their adversaries. To run for any public office of significance, it is necessasy either to have a lot of money, or have access to it. A brief commercial appearance on TV, I am told, costs tens of thousands of dollars.

According to Federal Election Commission estimates, total expenditure for the 1984 Presidential and Congressional elections exceeded $1 billion. A political scientist placed the total at $1.8 billion for the White House and local government races in that period.

U.S. laws provide that candidates meeting specific requirements are entitled to a certain amount of federal subsidy. But it is generally believed that these subsidies fall far short of the actual expenditures. Huge funds are privately donated or raised by a multiplicity of "political action committees." These committees, which have emerged as political forces just within the last two or three Presidential elections, are special-interest lobbies and many of them are founded by private corporations or manufacturers' associations. According to data published by the United States Information Agency, these committees have increased to about 3,500 in recent years, and the money they spent in 1981-82 mid-term elections for administrative and legislative posts, including Congressmen and state governors, added up to $200 million. Of that sum $86 million was donated directly to competitors for Congressional seats.

My visit to the White House is short and I don't have much to describe. In brief, the place is quite lovely in its simplicity. The column "Washington Talk" in *The New York Times* (April 27, 1983) says: "It takes a full-time staff of ninety servants to keep the White House operating smoothly, and that doesn't include the pervasive forces of the Secret Service or the meticulous ground crews of the National Park Service." A number of curators, florists, and calligraphers who produce documents and invitations, "along with forty maids, waiters and cooks, thirty-two maintenance people and six supervisors, will cost the taxpayers $4.5 million in the 1984 fiscal year." This is not too extravagant for a rich country that spends hundreds of millions for a couple of unlovely missiles. The simplicity of the White House, I surmise, is deliberate to symbolize a republican regime distinct from monarchical rule. But form is less important than substance. America, after all, is no longer an alliance of New England-type self-governing towns, but a colossal dollar empire, however unassuming the White House may be. There is an English saying that whoever controls the purse controls the government. American "liberals," let alone "radicals," often discuss and freely admit that the dollar, to a large extent, controls the White House and the Capitol. To be fair, however, I wouldn't go to the extreme and assert that the American public is completely powerless.

BOATS ON THE OCEAN OF LEARNING
— Big, Medium and Small Libraries

Of all modern American institutions, I admire most the libraries. When chatting with friends back in China, I always praise it, and to such an extent that an old acquaintance jokingly calls me "a worshipper of things foreign". This was a stigma during the "cultural revolution" and was often pinned on people who once studied or worked in Western countries. What deserves admiration, I insist, should be admired and emulated.

The Library of Congress

One morning, Roy Fisher takes me to the Library of Congress by subway. The Washington subway is clean and beautiful, a sharp contrast to its counterpart in New York. But unlike New York where you pay a fare of seventy-five cents and may transfer as many times as you like, here you have to buy separate tickets for different routes. The street network of Washington is complicated, with avenues radiating from the center, unlike the usual chessboard pattern of American cities. Without an old-timer showing the way, I would certainly get lost.

We come to the library situated beside the Congressional buildings on Capital Hill. Roy goes straight to the reading room and I wait for the usual conducted tour.

We tourists are first ushered into the tall, vaulted central hall, with statues of Socrates, Galileo and other Western "cultural giants" looking down from above as if they were guiding the readers seated in circular rows. The spacious hall is exceedingly clean and quiet.

After seeing a film on the history of the library, I leave the group to meet Roy who then leads me to one of the catalogue rooms. There are numerous cabinets in the room, each with many drawers, and each drawer has hundreds of cards. When the cards in all rooms are added up, I am told, they represent a wealth of eighteen million volumes of books, plus eight million photographs, three million maps, thirty-one million manuscripts by well-known writers and four million music books. Since the mid-fifties, the library's bookshelves, totaling 540 kilometers in length, have become increasingly cramped, and the librarians are eagerly looking forward to the new building being erected on the other side of the street.

In spite of their huge numbers, the deposits are easily accessible, thanks to a scientific system of cataloguing. And computers have made the search-and-find process much simpler.

Roy introduces me to a staff worker in the computer room. Learning that I am writing a book about America, the lady becomes all the more helpful. I admit with regret that I don't know yet how to use the computer system, and ask her to show me. She points to a number of books thicker than telephone directories, explaining that they contain the codes. I ask her to find for me new books about China. She says that would be too many and I should specify the fields — politics, economics, geography or history, for instance — as well as the period of publication. I ask for books on Chinese politics published in the 1980s. She taps on the keyboard and a list appears on a screen complete with the names of the authors and publishers, the number of pages, ISBN (International Standard Book Numbers) and the library's cataloguing numbers. Then she pushes a button and a printout comes from the machine on the side. There are about sixty titles on the list, mostly in English and some in French and German.

I make another request for her to find books by Hu Qiaomu, a leading Chinese Marxist theoretician. A few more taps on the keyboard plus a push of the button produce a list of foreign language editions of Hu's *Thirty Years of the Communist Party of China* published in China and other countries.

I recall how relieved I felt when microfilm was introduced in the University of Missouri library, so that I no longer had to move those bound volumes of *The New York Times* and sift through the pages. Enormous progress has been made since then. But even now only a few Chinese libraries have microfilm and microfiche materials open to the public. Fortunately the Chinese government is now attaching great emphasis to updating the library and other cultural services.

I ask the librarian why the list does not include Chinese-language titles. She explains apologetically that though the library does have many Chinese volumes, an ideal way has yet to be found to computerize the complex Chinese ideographs. It is we Chinese who should feel sorry, I think to myself, but I am quite sure that a plausible way will be found before long because many Chinese scientists are working on the problem.

I then remember my conversation with Professor of Chinese History Ping-ti Ho in Chicago. A schoolmate of mine at Qinghua University in the 1930s, he later came to the United States and became a Fellow of the American Academy of Arts and Sciences. An early work establishing Professor Ho's fame was his study of the imperial examination system in the Ming and Qing dynasties (1368-1911). He delved into archives kept by the Library of Congress and other institutions and made twenty thousand cards on the family histories of *jinshi*, the scholars who passed the highest level of the imperial examination.

Another question that puzzles me is that the list of books on China does not include those published by the Beijing Foreign Languages Bureau's affiliate publishing houses. The library claims its collection to be "extensive but selective," excluding "propaganda materials." Leaving the question of different ideologies aside, many of China's foreign-language publications, those on political subjects in particular, were admittedly propagandistic in earlier years. Much change has occurred in the 1980s. But perhaps some time is needed to dispel the old prejudices.

The Library of Congress is also a treasure-trove of tens of thousands of records of folk music, dances, art performances, folklore, folk sayings, and even riddles. There are many invaluable rare books kept in underground stacks where a constant temperature and humidity are maintained all year round. The library also collects films. And it boasts the largest collection in existence of gramophone discs, braille publications, and special tapes and records for the blind. It is also collecting major radio and TV programs produced since 1976.

The Library of Congress, as the national library, is entitled by law to copies of every book copyrighted in the United States. In the meantime, it keeps constant contact with book dealers in the world's major cities in order to acquire foreign books.

Why is it called the Library of Congress? I learn that since its establishment in 1800, the library's primary function has been to provide reference materials and study reports for Congress and the congressmen. At present it still has a congressional service department staffed by eight hundred people responsible for answering the congressmen's inquiries. While Congress is in session, the department answers some 2,000 questions a day covering an almost infinite range of topics. A computer system has been installed so that congressmen can get the necessary data on terminal screens in their offices. Rules provide that only congressmen, government departments, foreign embassies, writers and libraries undertaking research projects can take out books and other materials. But the reading rooms are open to all. Attendance totals 1.5 million every year.

The Library of Congress is the largest in the United States, and perhaps only the Lenin Library of the Soviet Union can match it in the number of books collected. But any library, however big, can hardly claim to be all-embracing. The Library of Congress tries to make up for this by publishing catalogues of all books kept in eleven-hundred American and Canadian libraries. All important works which have seen light since the mid-fifteenth century, I am told, can be found in those catalogues. Altogether around five-hundred joint catalogues have been distributed to thousands of large or small libraries.

It is about noontime. Roy and I go to lunch at the self-service cafeteria. Though old acquaintances now, Roy and I pay our respective bills at the counter. This is an American custom unless a friend has made it clear that he will be the host—a much more straightforward practice compared with the Chinese tradition of *keqi* (courtesy) which requires people to vie in paying or else one might be considered stingy. Roy asks me about my impression of the library. I quote the Chinese saying that "the ocean of learning is vast and books are the boats," adding, "you have made the ocean easily accessible."

In a Small Town Called Brick

"No coincidence, no story," as another Chinese saying goes. I have a college classmate, Mrs. T. C. Chiu, who is head librarian in a small town called Brick in Ocean County, New Jersey, on the Atlantic Coast. A by-product of our reunion is a closer look at the American public library system. The population of Ocean County numbers 400,000. Nevertheless the county has a central library with twelve branches in smaller towns, including Brick.

Chiu takes me to the central library which boasts a collection of 284,719 volumes in addition to microfilms, records, tapes, popular science films and reproductions of famous paintings. Like other American libraries, its bookshelves are open to readers so that they can pick up books by themselves. I look around in the periodical room and find, to my surprise, three English-language magazines published in Beijing—the *Beijing Review, China Reconstructs* and *China Pictorial*, all arriving in good time and kept in good order. The city has no particular connection with China but its library subscribes to Chinese magazines. In some other libraries, I have also found the same Chinese publications, sometimes the English-language *Chinese Literature*, too. In a way this shows the open-mindedness and wide-ranging interest of Americans. But I have also heard complaints that English publications produced in China are not easily available to the public and that greater efforts are needed to help the Americans better understand China.

The town of Brick has a population of fifty thousand. But the town library, to describe it with another Chinese saying, is like "a sparrow, small but complete with all living organs." It has 30,421 books on its shelves, many national newspapers and magazines, in addition to microfilms, tapes, records and reproductions of famous paintings. The paintings are lent to people who may hang them in their homes for a period of twenty-eight days. The readers can get a card permitting them to take books or other materials out, but everybody can come to the library to read.

America is a thinly populated country compared with China, and one seldom sees teeming crowds anywhere, still less in libraries. Chiu says that the readership comprises mainly two age groups: children and the aged. I see many lovely toddlers accompanied by their mothers in the reading room. Senior citizens come mainly for "how to" books — how to reduce, how to fish, etc. These books constitute a high percentage of American publications. To cater to the elderly readers, the library buys a lot of the books they like, especially large-format editions, in spite of its financial limitations.

The library has a staff of ten in addition to some youngsters working on an hourly basis. The services it provides include discussions of books, film shows, and such summer vacation activities for children as puppetry and handicraft groups. Like many other libraries, it has a xerox service which the reader can use simply by dropping a few coins into the machine. The fee varies from place to place, five cents per sheet in major libraries and as much as twenty-five cents in culturally less developed areas. I find the occasional sales of old books by libraries particularly interesting. Limited by space, they have to dispose of the less important books once in a while at a price of fifty cents or a dollar for a hardcover book and twenty cents each — less than you pay for a cup of coffee — for paperbacks. Book lovers can accumulate a "fortune" for themselves at bargain prices.

Americans work five days a week, but the Brick library opens a few hours on Saturdays and Sundays, too. Its staff is kept on duty over the weekends by rotation.

While American business often operates on the principle that "the customer is always right," for American libraries, "the reader is always right." Chiu tells me that her library has an information-by-telephone service, but some parents unwilling to help their children with their homework simply dial the library for answers to the children's math questions. I sympathize with her overworked staff, but at the same time admire their spirit. In China, cold or even rude treatment of customers in shops and other places of public service remains a constant subject of complaint in the press and daily conversations, though the situation is improving gradually.

The Brick library also provides mobile service with a van carrying books to different neighborhoods. Readers can order books they don't find in the van, which will be delivered on its next trip. Mobile service, Chiu tells me, is provided by most town libraries.

Academic Libraries

Public libraries, the kind I see in Ocean County, are financed by the local government and serve the local reading public. There are also "academic libraries," mainly in universities and colleges. The finest and largest ones are found on the campuses of well-known institutions. According to 1980 statistics, there were 14,653 public libraries and 4,618 academic libraries across the country.

I try to visit the academic libraries wherever I can. In Boston, there are over forty libraries at M.I.T. alone, among which the Dewey Library specializes in social sciences and literature. I am issued a card with which I can take books out. Nothing is necessary for just reading in the library. The reader is allowed not only to select books straight from the shelves, but to take books out without filling a form such as we have to do in China. You simply show your card and the librarian stamps a sheet attached to the back cover and demagnetizes it. At the same time, the card number of the borrower is also recorded. If anybody walks out with an unprocessed book, a machine at the gate will buzz and catch him red-handed. Returning books is easy. You don't have to hand them over to a clerk, but simply leave them at a designated place. The Brick town library makes things even simpler by placing two containers bigger than mailboxes at its gate so the readers can return books in off-hours.

"There are scum even among scholars," as we say in China, and this seems to apply to America, too. Book stealing, I am told, is not rare despite the buzzing gadget. It is even more difficult to prevent people from tearing out a few pages of nice pictures or valuable texts. Then there is the universal trouble of books being returned past their "due date" despite repeated notices. "You can't sue over such a trifle," complains a librarian. So, once in a while, the libraries grant "amnesty" to all procrastinators, and it works miracles. The public library in a small town in Washoe County, Nevada, according to an A.P. dispatch I happen to see, had $46,275 worth of books returned in one such "amnesty."

Harvard University is two stops by subway from M.I.T. The number of libraries at Harvard exceeds one hundred. The Harvard-Yenching Library there will be of particular interest to Chinese readers. Hugh Deane, an old friend of China whom I have met in New York, suggests that I read a book on China written by a 19th-century American author whose detailed and vivid description I may emulate. To find the book, Hugh recommends that I see Harvard-Yenching's librarian, Eugene Wu (a graduate of the National Central University of China who later became an American citizen). Mr. Wu is busy, preparing for a lecture tour on the Chinese mainland, and he introduces me to his associate, John Yung-hsiang Lai, an American-Chinese scholar from Taiwan, where his family has lived for seven generations. Mr. Lai is glad to meet a writer from the mainland, and he shows me the collection. The library is a treasure house of 610,000 Chinese, Japanese and Korean books, of which 370,000 are Chinese. Mr. Lai gives me a brief account of the history of the library. Founded in 1928 by the privately-financed Harvard-Yenching Institute (Yenching was a well-known missionary university in old Peking), the library has received many visiting Chinese scholars. During the years when Sino-U.S. relations were severed, all the scholars came from Taiwan, but now most of them are from the mainland. Mr. Alfred K.M. Qiu, one of the first graduates of the Wenhua School of Library Science in Central China's Wuhan, was invited to catalogue the first collection of Chinese books when the Yenching Library was established. Seeing the rich collection now, I feel a great amount of respect for Mr. Qiu; "water drinkers mustn't forget the well-diggers" is a Chinese tradition.

I carefully look around the stacks of rare books and try to find a book by the well-known Chinese sociologist Fei Hsiao Tung. There is a special reason for my search. Back in the 1940s, I had read Fei's *First Visit to the U.S.* and found it insightful. Before my departure for the United States this time, I tried in vain to find a copy of the book and finally got one, through some personal connections, from the

Guozijian storehouse of the Beijing Library, China's national library. It is a photostat copy produced years ago and many pages are illegible. But here, in a foreign country, I find several editions of the book and a fairly complete collection of Professor Fei's other works. I don't need to say how I feel about the contrast. But I am pleased at the thought that a magnificent new building with computerized equipment is being constructed for the Beijing Library.

The periodical reading room has all the important Chinese newspapers and magazines from both the mainland and Taiwan.

In Chicago, Professor Ho, the American-Chinese historian I have mentioned, accompanies me on a visit to the University of Chicago library. It has a huge reading room partitioned into small compartments. They are neat, softly lit, and as quiet as the scripture depositories in secluded Chinese Buddhist temples. The seclusion, however, is coupled with convenience. Many sets of encyclopedias and an assortment of dictionaries are close at hand. There is a big lounge nearby with rows of sofas in which overworked readers can drowse off for a while. And in the basement there is a cafeteria where vending machines serve cold drinks, sandwiches, and hot dogs. In short, everything is arranged so that the reader can stay and work for long hours.

There is also a rich collection of Chinese publications in the library. The latest works are displayed in glass cases. The periodical room has, in addition to Chinese-language newspapers published in America and Taiwan, *People's Daily, Guangming Daily* and other leading journals from the mainland. Row after row of shelves hold Chinese books and contribute to my reluctance to leave. "Redological" works alone fill up many shelves (the most celebrated Chinese classical novel, *A Dream of the Red Mansions* written by Cao Xueqin of the 18th century, has given rise to a branch of study called "redology"). I also find many antiquated volumes of official chronicles of Chinese prefectures and counties issued over the past centuries, printed by woodblock, and thread-bound in an exquisitely Chinese way. They are essential for Chinese historians, and a prize for book connoisseurs. So much money and labor has been spent on this collection!

On another day I go to the Chicago city public library. To enable readers to borrow books from the nearest place in the sprawling metropolis, there is a computer system by which one can easily find out which book is available in which local library. A reader too busy to go to the central library can get the answer by telephone.

It's Superb — But Costly

But American library service is expensive. Take the Library of Congress, for instance. It employs five thousand people and spends $115 million a year. Its tiny counterpart in the town of Brick spends $400,000 a year of which $180,000 are wages.

But the money is well spent. My feeling is epitomized in a Chinese proverb I have scribbled on a book list I got at the Library of Congress: "An inch of time is worth an inch of gold; no amount of gold can buy back a minute of lost time." I have the same feeling at Hinds Junior College, in an out-of-the-way town in Mississippi. There I request recent magazine articles on American labor. The computer produces a list in a matter of seconds. Then the librarian, a charming young lady, finds and xeroxes the materials for me in a few minutes. How much time it would have taken to sift through all those magazines!

As China's modernization drive gathers momentum, a slogan has become very popular: "Time is money and efficiency is life." In the library service I have found an exemplary proof of how Americans increase their efficiency and save their time.

Chapter VIII

OUT IN THE CORN BELT

From Washington, D.C., I proceed to Iowa. Professor Hualing Nieh, a noted American-Chinese writer, and her husband, well-known poet Paul Engle, live in Iowa City, a college town in that midwestern state. I met them in Beijing a few years earlier and they have offered to help me with my visit. Hualing has told me over the phone that a Chinese writers' delegation is coming to Iowa under the "international writing program" of her school, the University of Iowa, and I am welcome to join the activities arranged for the Chinese guests.

I fly from D.C. to Chicago, catch a small 20-seat passenger plane to Cedar Rapids and transfer by bus to Iowa City. The town is not connected by airlines and has a population of only 50,000. I like the quietness here, particularly Iowa House, a university-sponsored hotel where Hualing has arranged for me to stay. With the Iowa River flowing just outside the window, the landscape is fascinating. Besides, Iowa House charges only $22.50 a night, about half the price of ordinary hotels, and it has a good self-service cafeteria. It is economical and also safe. So I decide to stay for a month or so to "ruminate" on the impressions and materials I have so far gathered and to see some nearby places.

In the first few months of my visit, I have been travelling on the northeastern seaboard including major coastal cities like New York and Boston and remote parts of the northernmost state of Maine. Geographically, Iowa belongs to another region known as the Central Basin which is comprised of the whole or parts of ten other states. Iowa is the heartland of the region. The Central Basin is separated from the East Coast by the Appalachian Mountains.

After the thirteen English colonies took shape along the Atlantic coast, Britain issued in 1763 a proclamation prohibiting immigrants from crossing the Appalachians, in order to protect the English king's monopoly of the vast virgin land beyond the range. The unpopular ordinance was a constant irritation to the colonists. Consequently, after the American War of Independence, the territory of the newborn nation was extended in one stroke to the east bank of the Mississippi River, which runs from north to south down the continent. Now free to push west, frontier farmers carrying bread and bacon scaled the Appalachian heights and edged forward along paths made by wild animals. They finally reached the end of the dark forest and came out into sunny, open grasslands which rose and fell in low, graceful slopes. Geographers later named this region the Central Basin. Hundreds of thousands of hardy and diligent settlers gradually transformed the grasslands into a rich granary.

YOU CAN HEAR THE CORN GROW
— Progress and Problems in American Agriculture

Early October is golden autumn in Iowa. On the boundless plains you see vast patches of deep brown corn interspersed with smaller patches of low-stalked soybean. On some plots the corn has been harvested. Here and there you also see luxuriant green pasturelands where cattle are grazing and hogs are grubbing. There are almost no trees on the land except for those planted in and around towns. Iowa is known throughout the world for high-yield hybrid corn, its main crop. A high percentage of Iowa farmers are engaged in agriculture and animal husbandry simultaneously — growing crops while raising hogs or cattle for meat or milk.

It is said that on hot and silent midsummer nights you can hear the corn grow. I believe it because while I was working in northeast China's countryside in the fifties, I often thought I heard creaking sounds from the cornfields. The corn crop in Iowa grows fast, sometimes five centimeters during a night. By late summer it may be six or eight feet high. It is easy to get lost in the "green gauze nets," an affectionate name Chinese guerrillas coined for the cornfields which they used for cover in their hit-and-run warfare against Japanese invaders.

Not only Iowa, but a number of other states on the middle and lower reaches of the Mississippi are good for corn cultivation and are known as the "Corn Belt." One of the most important geographic boundaries in the United States is the fifty-centimeter rainfall line which runs north and south almost through the middle of the country. West of the invisible line are the Great Plains, almost flat and rising imperceptibly for hundreds of miles until they suddenly meet the Rocky Mountains. Rainfall is so scarce in this region that early settlers found only short grasses growing on the prairies, markedly different from the Central Basin with its profusion of tall grasses. The arid Great Plains, however, have also been transformed into farmland, growing mainly wheat. The southern states on the lower reaches of the Mississippi are the chief cotton and tobacco producers and have come to be known as the "Cotton Belt." Further west of the Great Plains is the vast mountain and desert region which now boasts a great number of good ranches. The banana-shaped southeastern state of Florida and the western state of California are the country's "fruit and vegetable baskets." These are the broad outlines of America's main agricultural regions.

Americans don't know *wotou* (corn flour buns which used to be the staple food of north China peasants). But corn is their most important crop. One out of every four cultivated acres is corn. The annual crop is greater than the nation's wheat, rice, and other small grains together. Except for a small amount of sweet corn eaten either fresh, frozen or canned, and popcorn which the Americans learned from native Indians to make and is still much loved today, most American corn — some three-fourths of the yield — is used as animal feed and reaches the table in the form of meat, egg, and milk products. Much of the remainder is processed into oil, syrups, and starch.

Speedy Growth and Chronic "Disease"

Before my departure from Beijing, I had sought the advice of a veteran Chinese scholar of American studies. He told me that agriculture and education are the two mainstays of American society. Agriculture is indeed the foundation of all national economies. In America, its high-speed growth has not only fed the population but provided raw materials, a market and surplus labor for the other sectors of the economy. Farm production is also an important source of capital accumulation and still accounts for two-fifths of U.S. foreign exchange earnings in recent years.

· More than a century ago, two-thirds of the American population lived in rural areas. By 1930, the ratio had decreased to one-fourth and the farm population numbered about thirty million. In 1980, the number had further dropped to six million, only 2.7 percent of the population, and the total farm labor force was only 3.7 million. American population numbered 226 million in 1980, which means that each farm laborer was feeding sixty-one Americans. And this is not the whole story. The country exports huge amounts of farm produce. It provides one-half or more of the soybean, paddy rice, wheat and cotton, and nearly one-third of the animal feeds sold on world markets. One American farm laborer, therefore, is feeding a much larger number of people than sixty-one.

American farms, however, have been steadily decreasing. In 1930, there were approximately 6.5 million of them with an average of 151 acres per farm. By 1980 the number had dropped to 2.4 million, averaging 429 acres per farm. This represents a process of smaller and less competitive farms being annexed by larger ones which keep on expanding the scale of production. And the amalgamation has been synchronized with a continuous rise in the level of mechanization and labor productivity.

The high-speed growth, however, is accompanied by a chronic dislocation which waxes or wanes from time to time. The malady is farm "surplus" or "cheap grain price harming the peasants" as an old Chinese saying puts it. For many years the U.S. government has taken various measures to limit acreage under cultivation and to stimulate and support export. But the trouble has persisted. The year 1982, when I arrive in the United States, happens to be a period of high production, falling prices, and consequent heavy pressures on farmers. Although new storage facilities are being built at a record rate, they are not enough to hold the year's harvest. Empty barges and railroad hoppers, airplane hangars, even high school football fields and city streets are being pressed into service as makeshift granaries. Still one billion bushels have to be left outdoors, protected only by tarpaulins. Competition is fierce on the international market. The strong dollar makes American-produced goods more expensive and results in a decline of exports. The situation is quite serious. "Grim reapings: a record crop buries farmers" is the dour but realistic heading of a popular magazine report.

In 1980, the Carter Administration had imposed a partial grain embargo on the Soviet Union in retaliation against its invasion of Afghanistan. President Reagan, in spite of his extraordinarily tough stance towards the Soviets, moved to restore the trade soon after he took office. At the same time a new federal payment-in-kind (PIK) program was introduced to bolster existing measures to reduce planting. Under the program, farmers who agree not to plant up to half their land normally used to raise wheat, cotton, corn or rice would be compensated with grain or cotton from government surplus stocks. Farmers would receive the "payment-in-kind" at the usual harvest time for their commodities and be free to sell or store them, or, in the case of grain, feed it to their livestock.

PIK plus a drought helped to ease the situation in 1983. But the drastic cutback of planting hit hard at industries producing agricultural machinery, chemical fertilizers, pesticides, seeds, fodder and feeds. "The west wall crumbles when you prop up the east," as we would say in China. PIK petered out in 1984 and the year's bumper harvest turns into a headache for the farmers as glut causes prices to further plunge.

Farm Bankruptcies and Fruit "Over-abundance"

Mammon rules supreme in capitalist America. If a business runs a bad deficit and there aren't enough savings to make it up, bankruptcy will ensue. American farmers are not like Chinese peasants who, in the event of crop failures, can muddle through by tightening their belts and borrowing some food or money from the "collective" or from relatives and friends. American farmers produce in a capitalist way and usually get loans by mortgaging their fixed property to buy machinery, land, and house, and to defray major production costs. Interest rates are high. If they cannot pay the debt in time, the creditors will sue, and the courts may rule a "foreclosure" which means depriving the debtor of the right to redeem his mortgaged property. The mortgaged farm will go on the auction block and its owner may sink from middle-class status into abject poverty overnight. I see many news reports of such foreclosures in late 1982 and early 1983. One photo published in the *Los Angeles Times* (15 January 1983) has left an indelible impression on me. Captioned "Doug Dailey hears his farm being auctioned as his wife, Pamela Sue, and her mother shout 'No Sale,'" the picture shows the young man standing dumbfounded and the two women uttering tearful cries in subfreezing cold. There are also reports of farmers banding together to surround courthouses in protest, or bearing arms to threaten prospective buyers at the auctions. Many family farm owners, facing a bleak future, are seeking work off the land. Cases of excessive drinking, maltreatment of wives, and suicides are on the increase in farming areas, reports say.

There is also an over-abundance of fruits. Later, in San Francisco, I read in the *San Jose Mercury News* (12 February 1983) a report saying: "Thousands of people turned out...to receive free fruit donated by farmers to protest federal rules requiring them to feed much of their crop to cows or use it as fertilizer to keep prices artificially high." The report quotes a consumer union spokesman declaring: "It's a classic economic cartel. They meet every week to limit the supply to get the price they want. The result is hundreds of thousands of pounds of fruit wasted, left to rot on trees, be fed to cattle, [plowed] under while there is rampant hunger throughout the inner cities of this country." I have a personal experience with the artificial price. Before coming to citrus-rich California, I thought fresh orange juice, my favorite drink, must be cheaper there. But it turns out to be the same as elsewhere — 80 cents for a small glass at breakfast in a restaurant. I am even more puzzled to find at the Harris Restaurant at Clovis a bigger glass which costs $1.95. A few hours earlier I had seen rotting oranges littering the ground at nearby orange orchards.

The perennial problem of "surplus" doesn't mean that Americans can't eat more, or better, than they do. Looking around the world, moreover, people are distressed at the sight of roadside corpses and bony, malnourished babies in famine-stricken Africa. Of course one can't ask the Americans to feed the hungry everywhere. But the paradox is still there — huge production and low distribution. This world of ours has gone awry and is full of uncommon things contrary to common sense.

From Steel Plow and Hybrid Corn to Laser

The "surplus" problem notwithstanding, Americans have good reason to say that the continual growth of their agricultural productivity is a miracle. What has made it possible? Natural endowment — a vast and sparsely populated territory and an abundance of fertile arable land — is undoubtedly an important factor. But without scientific and technological progress, nature, however benevolent, cannot be fully tapped.

Iowa and the whole Central Basin are a case in point. At the beginning of the nineteenth century when the first batches of frontier farmers arrived, they settled at the edge of the forest, adhering to their fathers' experience and believing that the only good soil was the soil in which trees grew. They felled trees, dug out the roots, cultivated the land, and built log cabins. After some years, the more adventurous began experimenting with the grasslands. But the wooden and cast-iron plows could not cut through the deep, thick prairie sod. Someone invented a much larger and heavier plow which could break and turn the soil. But then the soft soil stuck to the iron, making the plow so heavy that a team of six oxen could hardly pull it. In 1830, an Illinois mechanic, John Deere, invented a sharp steel plow which solved the problem. By 1850, Deere was producing thirteen thousand such plows a year. The Basin began turning into a granary.

It is not possible to trace briefly the complex story of American farm mechanization. To put it in the simplest terms, tractors came into use in 1910 and mechanization was generally achieved by 1940. The use of machines has coincided with new discoveries in agronomy. Corn production, for instance, registered a dramatic increase in the 1940s. The widespread introduction of hybrid corn helped to raise the per-hectare yield from one thousand liters per hectare, to fifteen hundred in 1948. By 1972 it had reached thirty-four hundred liters and

Iowa chalked up a record of seven thousand liters. Instead of saving the year's best crop for next year's planting, farmers began to buy new seeds from specialized developers of better strains. This has been described by some Americans as "a quiet revolution."

In recent years, computers, lasers and other high-tech devices have found their way into agriculture. The largest tractors now have at least four-hundred-horsepower engines. There are a proliferation of new developments which only writers who know the trade can itemize.

While in Iowa, I make a special trip to the town of Ames to visit the College of Agriculture of the University of Iowa. Dr. J.T. Scott, assistant dean, kindly talks to me about the college's teaching and research programs which are closely integrated with practical farming in the state. The overall impression I get is that American agronomic science keeps progressing and major new breakthroughs may not be far off.

I also join the Chinese writers' delegation on a visit to the John Deere Company in neighboring Illinois. Named after the innovator who developed the steel plow, and an offspring of his simple mill, the firm is now the largest American manufacturer of farm machinery. It has plants throughout the country. We are received in its headquarters and are shown a maintenance training class. The offices, with floor-to-ceiling windows, are plush and bright. There is an indoor garden in the building with artificial rockeries and brooks in the midst of flowers and greens. The cafeteria for the staff is also very nice. Looking around, you can sense the wealth and power of a multimillion-dollar business even though the farm "surplus" and planting cutback have done it great harm. A high ranking company executive entertains us at lunch and then leads us to an exhibition hall of John Deere products. A salient feature is the company's never-ending search for the innovative, the great importance it attaches to developing and perfecting new products to enhance its competitiveness in home and foreign markets.

The maintenance training class is run for persons who sell John Deere machinery in America and abroad. It is a workshop instead of a classroom. Trainees come to learn the structure of the machines so they will be able to use and repair them properly. The training program has woven a vast web linking John Deere with its buyers in many parts of the world. We are then shown a film called "Chinese Agriculture," but much of its footage is given to scenes of John Deere machines running and operating on Chinese land — machines with the distinct deer logo which are sometimes seen on Chinese TV screens.

Soiree on the "Old Man River"

Our visit to the John Deere Company culminates in a ride on the Mississippi River on a yacht called the "J.D." Accompanied by a company vice-president, the public relations director and two company journal editors, the Chinese delegation, Hualing and I assemble on the deck. Correspondents of *Huaqiao Ribao (Overseas Chinese Daily* in New York City) and the *Voice of America* are also with us. Hosts and guests chat while enjoying the scene. The evening glow appears and everybody is busy snapping pictures of the beautiful sunset. On the river, long trains of wide-bodied and flat barges are sailing downstream, with corn bulging out from their holds, like mythical dragons bringing in good harvests. The moon slowly rises from the distant horizon. A pleasant surprise comes when the hosts produce from a hidden trunk on the deck many small folding tables "lying in ambush," as a Chinese guest says. Dinner is served on the tables. Some entertainment is surely appropriate on such a delightful occasion. By repeated applause the Chinese writers urge the novelist *Jiang Zilong* (whose stories on factory life, including *Director Qiao Assumes Office* and *Rainbow*, have been translated into English and are well-received abroad) to contribute something. The jolly middle-aged storyteller rises and says that he will sing a folksong from Shanxi province. He first gives the words for Hualing to translate simultaneously and then sings out in a good voice:

> *You're my sweetheart, everyone knows*
> *But doubt within me grows and grows*
> *When I visit your house your mother bellows*
> *That you are out!*
> *Oh, out, out, out. . . .*

> *The second time your big yellow dog*
> *Jumps up at me just like a frog*
> *And bites my belt,*
> *Oh, belt, belt, belt. . . .*
>
> *The third time that I come to call*
> *Your mother isn't nice at all*
> *She knocks me twice across the head*
> *With an iron pot lid,*
> *Oh, lid, lid, lid. . . .*
>
> *The fourth time, oh the news is bad*
> *Your mother tries to look so sad*
> *She says you died and lay on your bier*
> *Oh, bier, bier, bier. . . .*

The folksy tune and earthy words make us almost laugh our sides out. The Americans are also laughing and then, in their turn, entertain us with their old folksongs.

As the boat moves along the river bank, we can see electric lights, dense or sparse, on the shore, against a string of red lamps twinkling on faraway towers — perhaps the lattice-like towers of power lines. This is a scene often found in America, where electric power abounds. The flat terrain, however, is similar to what we would see on the lower reaches of our mighty Changjiang (Yangtze) River.

The vice-president rises to speak. He says that the yacht "J.D." has received many Chinese people. "The guests have come to talk about farm machines and regard us as machine makers. But it's different tonight. Your profession and interests are different from ours. We gather here as fellow human beings. And you treat us as such, not as machine makers." His good humor evokes a warm response.

When I bid farewell to the two American editors, they warmly urge me to return. It is already past ten when I get back to Iowa House. Till midnight I still feel intoxicated with the soft breeze and bright moonlight on the "Old Man River." Thoughts throng my mind. We Chinese have been farming since time immemorial. But I realized what primitive tools we were using when I was sent several times to villages to "remould myself through physical labor" in the 1950s and 1970s. We are now catching on. And how good it is to forge ties with American farmers, farm manufacturers, and agronomists who have a wealth of experience for us to assimilate! Besides, they are good people.

A VISIT WITH FARMER WHEELER

I met Dick and Martha Bernhart in Washington D.C. and became quite well acquainted with them. Martha told me before my departure: "Now I'll let you know something I didn't intend to tell you. I own 350 acres of land. You don't like landowners, I suppose."

Three hundred and fifty acres! That means 2,124 Chinese *mu* and would make Martha a very big landlord in pre-revolution China (Chinese peasants in densely populated areas now have less than one *mu* per capita). Actually, however, China did not classify landlords simply by how much land they owned, but by how much of their income was derived from rents, usury, and the labor of hired farm hands. If the amount constituted the greater portion of his or her total income, he or she would be classified as a landlord. Martha has worked all her life and even now runs her restaurant after her retirement. She has apparently misunderstood our classification and thought we were against all landowners.

Anyway, Martha not only told me that she owned land but had telephoned her tenant, Roger Wheeler, in Iowa about me. In her wish to help me know the country, she thought that I should visit a farm family. She knew that my next stop was Iowa City, Iowa, where I would meet the noted American-Chinese woman writer, Professor Hualing Nieh Engle. "Roger is our old partner," Dick said. "They welcome you to stay in their home as long as you wish." He explained further, "Martha's land was left by her father. She has retained it as a keepsake."

Soon after my arrival in Iowa City, I set out to visit the Wheelers. "Wa-ter-loo," the bus driver announces. It is dusk and few people are to be found at the bus depot. A tall, sturdily built man in a scarlet jacket comes up to meet me. He is Roger Wheeler, and is accompanied by his wife, Mary. They lead me to the car and tell me that there will be an hour's drive home.

The car whisks away across the great plains. The flat farmland extends all the way to the horizon, only dotted here and there with round grain bins and rocket-shaped fodder silos. "You know what the Indians used to call this place?" Roger asks. "It was 'land under the vast sky.'"

American farmers do not live in compact villages as Chinese peasants do. Their houses, usually surrounded by large farms or grazing grounds, are very scattered. Motor vehicles are a necessity for visiting neighbors. Shopping or doing business in town would be virtually impossible without a car.

Roger points to a house on the way and tells me that it is the home of Mary's mother and that Mary had been born and brought up there. They want to stop for a while to see her because her brother, Mary's uncle, had died that morning. I follow them into the house, expecting to meet a sobbing old lady. But Mary's mother was very calm, saying merely, "They are gone, one after another. Few of my generation are left now." She looks very tidy and keeps the house quite clean. I simply cannot believe that she will soon be an octogenarian. Her husband, Mary's father, already passed away and she is the only soul living in the big house.

From their conversation I learn that Mary's uncle had gone to the fields in the morning, come back to his own house, and shot himself. "He had been ill for three years," Mary's mother mutters. "He didn't want to go to an old-age home. But then who would take care of him?" Apparently the uncle was a widower living alone.

When we are back in the car, I cannot help asking Roger, "Why must American grannies and grandpas go to old folks' homes? You Americans love your children very much. Why don't you live with your sons and daughters when you get old? We in China always remember the love and care of our parents and wouldn't even think of sending them to old-age homes. Only childless widows and widowers live there."

This commonplace comment seems very new to Roger. Later I

hear him tell people repeatedly, "Now listen, Wang says they don't want their elderly people to live in old-age homes."

Pious Christians

"Uncle was a good man," Roger says when we leave the house. "Now he has gone to heaven. Mary and I and all in our families are Christians. Wang, do you believe in religion in China?"

"We may believe, or not believe. I am not a believer, though. But I have read parts of the Bible."

"Bible? I haven't read it very carefully. But Christianity is pretty simple. Let me tell you. All of us are sinners. Jesus Christ died for us sinners — for the salvation from our sins through His sacrifice. Those who believe in this will go to Heaven after their death. Those who don't will go to Hell."

I try to turn the converstion by a question I often ask: "Where did your ancestors come from? How many generations ago?"

"I don't know exactly how many generations. They came from Scotland. And my grandfather moved from the east coast to Iowa as a homesteader."

Roger's family history is quite typical in this part of the country. With the Louisiana Purchase doubling the size of U.S. territory, Congress passed in 1862 the historic "Homestead Act" alloting the land to pioneers. In the ensuing three decades, 960,000 families moved from the east to the midwest. By their hard work they opened up this vast expanse of fertile land. This marked a period of rapid agricultural growth in American history.

Further on our way, we make another stop at the house of Roger's mother. She also lives alone.

We are soon home. The color TV in the sitting room is on. But Roger's youngest son, thirteen-year-old "Baby," has fallen into a sound sleep in the sofa. Our arrival wakes him up. He stands up, his height already reaching Roger's shoulders, and mutters while scrubbing his eyes, "I must go and dump the corn in the truck to dry." And he walks away with a big flashlight in his hand. A hard-working boy!

A "Millionaire"

Mary lets me sleep in her eldest daughter's bedroom. I rise very early the next morning and find that Roger, in blue jeans, has come back from doing his chores. At the breakfast table he gives me a "briefing" about his family. Twenty-two-year-old Lisa, the eldest daughter, works in a bank in town and comes home only on weekends. The second daughter, Lynne, twenty, is married to a farmer in the vicinity. The oldest son, David, eighteen, studies at a technical school. The second son, Randy, sixteen, is an eleventh grader. The youngest son, Roger Jr. (Baby), is an eighth grader. Mary is forty-one and works at a nearby school. Finally, Roger says humorously, "There is myself, Roger Wheeler, forty-eight, self-employed. By 'self-employed' I mean I work only when I want to. I don't have to go to office or school as they do."

"It's fine that you don't have to work when you don't want to," I reply humorously. "But American farmers I have seen seem to feel like working all the time. They rise before the sun and rest only after it goes down, seven days a week."

"You are right, but not completely. Iowa farmers go vacationing in the south in the wintertime, because it's very cold up here. But not me though. The hogs have to be fed, snow or no snow."

Wheeler does not own his crop land. In addition to Martha's 350 acres, he rents fifty more acres from a widow. He pays the widow a rent of $90 a year for every acre, and shares on a half-and-half basis with Martha the main cost and crops from her 350 acres. The present cost of seeds, fertilizers and pesticides is $90 per acre. Martha gets fifty per cent of the bushels harvested. She asks Roger to sell it when she finds the best market price. It's Martha who decides when to sell, not Roger. Roger has bought from Martha the house and the surrounding six-acre plot, and has expanded the house, and built on the plot sties for seven-hundred hogs, sheds for farm machinery, bins, silos and other installations.

Hard-working Wheeler is a rich man by Chinese standards. He leads me to the sheds. Pointing to a big harvester combine, he says, "I bought it two years ago. It's now worth $85,000." Then he shows me the tractors, trucks and other machines while reporting their prices. I keep on adding till I cry out, "Now Roger, you are a millionaire!" He bursts out in laughter.

Then he shows me ten calves which, he says, are Baby's "private property." The boy raised six calves last year and, more experienced now, he has ten this year. The breed is a fast growing one and Baby can sell them in one year's time to be butchered for tender beef. Roger also shows me Randy's "private property" — 130 hogs. By "private property" he means that the kids do all the work and get all the money. There is also a poultry barn with one hundred chickens, providing the family with eggs and meat. "We'll kill twenty and treat you to an all-family dinner on Sunday."

The hog farm is a modernized one. It has a population of seven hundred pigs. A total of sixteen hundred hogs are raised in a year. Roger buys forty-pounders, feeds them for 120 days and sells them when their weight increases to 240 pounds. There is no worry about finding buyers because he has a standing contract with the meat-packers.

Roger's share of the corn harvest is used as hog feed, as is the soybean crop, too, after oil has been extracted. The other half goes to Martha who sells it through Wheeler's help. He plants half his land in corn and the other half soybeans and rotates the crop every other year. Good seeds and fertilizers, plus rotation and hog manure, give him a much higher yield than the one-hundred-bushel-per-acre average in Iowa. "Mine is 150 bushels," Roger tells me very proudly.

"We Are All Conservatives"

Friday evening in America is the beginning of weekend holidays (we in China still work six days a week). All but the married daughter have come home. Roger as the family head leads a prayer at the dinner table. "Oh Lord, thank Thee for our food...for the good rain today...for the nice time we are having with Mrs. Wang...Amen!" A pious speech, attributing everything to God's blessing. I snap a picture of the happy family gathering and have kept it as a special souvenir.

We move to the sitting room after dinner and continue chatting. Talking about Iowa farmers, Roger says, "We are all conservatives."

"What do you mean by 'conservative'?"

"What do I mean? All of us believe in Jesus Christ. All of us are Republicans. And when we marry, we make up our minds to live together all our life. We are not like those people on the east and west coast. They are practically prepared to quit at the time of marriage." Passing to me a copy of the newspaper, he continues, "Now look at these wedding announcements. You'll see who have lived together before marriage. They list only one address for the man and the woman. And look at these birth notices. Some have only the mother's name. They are announcing illegitimate births. What a shame!"

I glance over the paper and do find quite a few notices of the kind. But, ironically, the paper is the *Waterloo Courier*, a local paper from neither the east nor the west coast. Conservative Waterloo, apparently, finds difficulty in keeping itself immune to these "unholy" influences.

Need for Better Understanding

Roger asks me many questions about China. "Do your people still smoke opium?" I give him a brief account of how Lin Zexu, the patriotic mandarin official, burnt opium imports, how the colonialists seized upon the chance to start the Opium War, how they had groomed Chinese warlords to divide and rule our country, and how, finally, we eliminated opium smoking and prostitution, too, after the revolution in 1949.

"So you threw all opium smokers and prostitutes into prison, right?"

I have to explain a little further on how we "reformed" those unfortunate people and helped them turn to a new way of life.

Roger asks another question: "I have heard that in the Soviet Union all children belong to the state and it's up to the government to decide who will be soldiers and who will be farmers or workers. Do you do the same in China?" I have to give him some basic information about Chinese youth, their life and work, their joys and woes.

The chat continues late into the night. I am impressed by the Wheelers' unadorned hospitality to a Chinese. But at the same time I feel sorry that they know practically nothing about contemporary China. This makes me feel strongly the need for more, and deeper, people-to-people exchanges. It also adds to the purposefulness of my trip which I hope will produce a book helping to lessen the ignorance on the Chinese side.

I rise very early again Saturday morning and go out to have a look around. Hard-working Baby is already feeding his calves. He shows me the feed — ground corn mixed with granulated nutrients. Baby tells me that they deposit all their corn in a kind of "feed bank" known as a grain elevator, and get processed feed from it when they need it. The high degree of socialized production and specialization of work undoubtedly plays a great role in increasing the productivity of American farms.

Roger's mother comes in the morning to help prepare the chicken dinner set for Sunday. Mary is attending to the washing machine and preparing lunch. All the others follow their grandmother to the basement to dress the chickens. I join them for a chat with the old lady. She is full of praise for Roger who, she recalled, was a smart boy and later a good student at the University of Iowa at Ames where he studied for one year. Roger was born in January, she says, and his father died in December of the same year. At the time she was working for a telephone company and earning $15 a month. With everything else added, the monthly income of the family was $30. And she had to rear four children. "It was very hard," she says.

Incentive and Competition

"Roger chose to be a farmer probably because he was brought up on a farm," I comment. "Young people in cities wouldn't come to work on farms, I suppose."

"You may say so," Roger replies. "But urban workers don't have much chance to become farmers even if they want to. Farm machines cost a lot of money. I had $1,500 when I started farming, just enough to buy a tractor and a plow. I had to borrow my brother's machines. My equipment has been bought piece by piece over the years. Even now I don't own my land."

Roger is outspoken. He talks freely about his family finances. He is

MEIGUO (America,
the beautiful country) and
MEIGUOREN (the Americans)
—In the author's eyes

America the melting pot: white, black and Asian children at a Denver school ask author to give them Chinese names.

America the changing scene: Marveling at new sights on revisiting alma mater at Columbia, Missouri.

America the beautiful: Nature-endowed grace and man-created splendor blend on the Charles River, Boston.

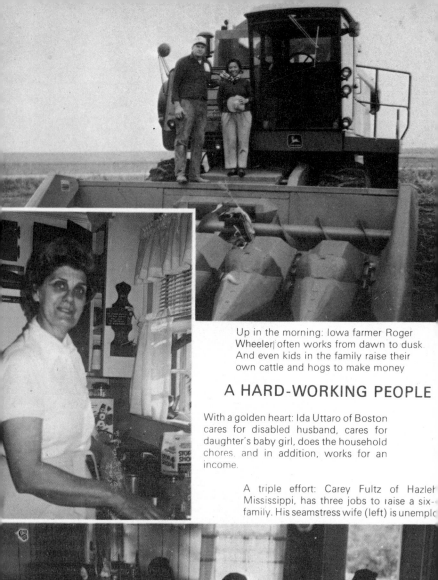

Up in the morning: Iowa farmer Roger
Wheeler| often works from dawn to dusk.
And even kids in the family raise their
own cattle and hogs to make money

A HARD-WORKING PEOPLE

With a golden heart: Ida Uttaro of Boston
cares for disabled husband, cares for
daughter's baby girl, does the household
chores. and in addition, works for an
income.

A triple effort: Carey Fultz of Hazleh
Mississippi, has three jobs to raise a six-
family. His seamstress wife (left) is unemplo

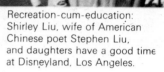

Recreation-cum-education:
Shirley Liu, wife of American
Chinese poet Stephen Liu,
and daughters have a good time
at Disneyland, Los Angeles.

A FUN-LOVING PEOPLE

Strange place to relax:
Like the Chinese, New Yorkers
enjoy a roadside game of chess,
but they have to pay for it.

ee the world:
awyer Mac Shelton and wife
rauke Rynd of Seattle
n a bicycle tour
o the Great Wall, Beijing.

asino-hopping:
as Vegas' Strip claims to offer
satisfaction to every
onceivable desire''.

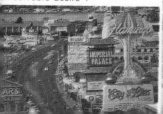

Early start: Children are taught to be independent masters of their own rooms (upper left) and pupils are encourged to express themselves freely in class (right).

DEMOCRATIC SPIRIT
AND
PERSONAL INDEPENDENCE

Tolerant: Genesis-
Professor Sandra V
Junior College gra
author's atheist di
discussion in deep

Old independence:
Many senior citizens are
like 83-year-old retired teacher
Ray Miller of Yakima,
Washington,
who drives his own car,
repairs his own house,
and proudly stands on his own
feet. With Ray is wife Ruth.

Open-minded:
A lecture sponsored by
ten institutions in Juneau,
Alaska, shows American
eagerness to meet new
people and hear new views.

Articulate:
The one-million-strong
demonstration in
New York City
(12 June 1982)
testifies to freedom of
expression. But how much
the popular voice is heeded
is another matter.

...nds
...ens to
... free
..., Mississippi.

From
China

Writer/Editor
Wang Tsomin

LECTURE / DISCUSSION

Saturday • March 12, 1983
Alaska State Museum • 2:00 pm

A tea will follow hosted by:

Juneau Adult Education Center, English As a Second Language
Students, ANS Camp #2 Sisterhood, Poetry Society of Alaska,
Juneau Community Schools, University of Alaska-Juneau, Juneau
School District Bilingual/Bicultural Program, American Ethnasis
Day Committee, Juneau World Affairs Council, and Alaska State
Museum

Wang Tsomin is in this country for a year to collect
materials and impressions for a book on the United States
for publication in China for the Chinese reading public.

Members of the U.S.-China Peoples' Friendship Association always lend a helping hand. Sylvia Fischer of Chicago, an early leading member of USCPFA, and husband Charlie arrange for author to cover Harold Washington's election as the city's mayor.

M.I.T. Professor Richard Robinson, in charge of author's writing project, spares no effort to help.

A FRIENDLY PEOPLE

Dr. M.E. Ensminger, an internationally know animal science specialist and a devoted friend of China, shows author around some California's ranches and farms.

Dean Roy Fisher of Missouri University's Scho of Journalism, Who came Beijing to initiate the Edga Snow fellowships for Chir students, visits Snow's tomb at Beijing University L. to R.: Duan Liancheng authors' husband, editor and translator of this book Fisher; Wang Xi, chief edit *Beijing Review* and Roy's wife Anne.

Studs Terkel is among the noted writers and journalists who took time out to brief the author.

Whitman Severinghaus of Shreveport, Louisiana, who served in the U.S. Army in China in the 1940s, prepares a pot of tea for author every morning and keeps it warm with typical Chinese quilt cover

inority Americans show a special affinity th the Chinese. Author chats with USCPFA ember Richard Pendleton of Boston (above) d attends a party given in her honor Tlingit Indians at Ketchikan, Alaska (below)

Bill Powell of San Francisco is one of the time-tested Americans who have been steadfastly sympathetic with the Chinese people's cause even in the witch-hunting and red-baiting 1950s.

It is **INSPIRING** to see
America's fast progress
(Johnson Space Center, Houston);
GRATIFYING to note increasing
Sino-American links
(Temple of Heaven at Disneyworld's
EPCOT, Orlando);

and **DISAPPOINTING** to find old social
maladies either persist or be aggravated
(job seekers pack Youngstown's
employment office as unemployment
rate reaches double digits).

Courtesy of *Youngstown Vindicator*

doing quite well. And everybody else in the house is earning some money. His eldest son David works two night shifts a week at a bakery and gets $102. Baby makes $100 for every calf he raises and will get $1,000 this year. He owns a motorcycle worth $900. The second son Randy has a motor-bike and a mini-truck worth $3,000. And David has a much better motorcycle worth $3,000, plus a mini-truck. The boys have bought all these "toys" with the money they themselves make. In short, all are doing well.

"I admire the hard-working spirit of you American farmers," I say.

"Well, you are not quite right," replies Roger. "Who wouldn't want to work less and have more leisure? We work because there is incentive. The harder you work, the more money you make. Besides, you have to use your brains and learn skills. In our factories, skilled workers earn several times as much money as office workers on administrative jobs. That's incentive."

I find Roger to be a firm believer in "rugged individualism." He has confidence in the American dream of getting rich by free competition. Stressing the importance of "free enterprise," he cites his seeds as an example. They are bought from a company which guarantees that the farmer will have a good seedling for every seed. "If I don't, I won't buy any more from them. Neither will my relatives, neighbors and other farmers. And the company will be finished. Competiton is fierce. Every company has to win customers. And this means better quality."

An unexpected change in my schedule denies me the pleasure of attending the Sunday dinner. I have to leave Saturday afternoon and feel very sorry about it. To prepare a special lunch for me before my departure, Mary telephones Martha in Washington, D.C., to inquire about my favorite food. She cooks a bowl of Chinese noodles for me. Holding her hand and then Roger's, I don't know what to say to express my thanks.

Roger and Mary take me to the bus depot. I sit in the car, holding a bouquet of roses Lynne brought especially for me from her farm, and wearing a cap Lisa has spent several hours sewing, with the words "Wheeler's Farm" over the sun-shade.

Since then I have become intensely interested in the American farm situation. I feel unhappy whenever I read reports about falling farm prices. A few weeks later, however, I find in *The New York Times* (October 16, 1982) a disturbing report under the heading "Recession Dimming Future of Family Farms." The reporter has interviewed a Missouri farmer, J.B. Grothaus, and writes: "The 16-hour work days, he [Grothaus] says, are the easy part. The discoveries he makes over his books at night are the most painful. After careful computations, he recently found that the corn he was feeding his hogs had cost more to grow than it would have cost to buy at the grain elevator down the road. The tractor tire that cost him $489 in 1974 now goes for $1,775 while his soybeans bring half what they did then."

The article goes on: "Mr. Grothaus is not alone. Among the various occupational groups, people who earn their living on farms around the United States have suffered the greatest decline in income in recent years, according to Census Bureau figures." In these circumstances, the report concludes, "more and more people have been finding or seeking work off the land." May god bless the Wheelers!*

---

* As I was finishing the book in late 1984, I received a letter from Dick Bernhart in Washington, D.C., saying, to my dismay, that in spite of the upturn in the American economy, farmers were hard pressed and Wheeler was in pretty bad shape.

Chapter IX
GLIMPSES OF THE SUN BELT

Back from the Wheeler farm and in Iowa City, I am to end my stay in the Corn Belt and proceed to the Sun Belt. But the landscape and life in the small college town makes me reluctant to leave. It is late autumn. I often sit on a long bench on the bank of the Iowa River, basking in the mild sunlight and watching pale clouds floating casually on the clear blue sky and equally clear blue waters flowing calmly through the plains. The season has made the leaves more colorful — some fiery red, some deep or light brown, and some remaining green. It's all quiet around except for the ocasional cackling of wild ducks. In the evenings there are often theater performances or concerts of classical music.

I feel reluctant, too, to part with Hualing and poet Engle. I met them as an editor of some of their works and we have since become friends. But I have not had much chance to talk with Hualing during my present visit. She is fully occupied with the international writing program. According to what she once wrote about her writing experience, Hualing becomes all engrossed with her characters once she starts writing a story and would often forget to eat and refuse to meet people. But this time I find her to be a most active and sociable person, as organizer of the gathering of writers from many countries. I admire her exceptional ability but hesitate to bother her with anything more than a request to forward my correspondence. When I am about to leave, both of us feel that there is a lot to tell each other. We talk all the way as she drives me from Iowa City to Cedar Rapids. She tells me that she will soon begin writing another novel in Chinese. She has decided on a poetic title — *Qian Shan Wai, Shui Chang Liu* which literally means "Water Flows Eternally Beyond One Thousand

243

Mountains." (The fascinating story, later published by the Sichuan People's Publishing House, tells of an upright young American wed on his deathbed to a Chinese girl student in the 1940s, and the ordeal of his wife and daughter in the subsequent decades for their "illicit relations" with American "imperialists." The story also covers the conflict of American and Chinese values when the daughter eventually comes to America and meets her grandparents).

My destination is Houston, Texas, a state which is one of the "three giants of the Sun Belt." The other two are California and Florida. "Sun Belt" is a loose term coined by journalists, not geographers. It has come into popular use in recent years as the antithesis of the "Frost Belt" or "Snow Belt" in the north. Climatically, the states in the southern part of the country from Virginia in the east to California in the west could all be called the "Sun Belt." But the term is actually used to indicate areas witnessing an economic upsurge and outstripping the developed northern states. The new growth areas also include a number of snowbound western and northwestern states.

Whichever way you put it, an important trend in current America is the shift of the demographic, economic, and political center of gravity from the northeast to the southwest. The 1980 census showed that for the first time in history, population in the east and north (108 million) had fallen below that of the west and south (118 million). According to U.S. Department of Labor statistics, two-thirds of the jobs newly created in the country in 1968-78 (12.3 million out of a total of 18.4 million) were in the west and south. At the same time, traditional industries in the north and east — steel, auto, textiles, etc. which are disparagingly called "sunset industries" — are on the decline. Some people have said that the traditional New York-Chicago economic and financial axis is being replaced by a rising Los Angeles-Houston one. Politically, distribution of seats in the House of Representatives has changed in relation to the population shift. The three "giants," Florida, Texas and California, have gained four, three and two more, respectively, while New York, a traditional industrial base, now has five seats less than before. Some writers have further pointed out that the last American President from the east coast was John Kennedy of Massachusetts, elected in 1960, and all his successors have been from the west or south. President Lyndon Johnson (elected in 1964) was from Texas, his successor Richard Nixon (elected in 1968 and again in 1972) from California, Jimmy Carter (elected in 1976) from Georgia and the incumbent President, Ronald Reagan, is again from California.

Why this shift? Is it because of the warmer climate in the Sun Belt? The once-menacing energy crisis sparked by spiralling oil prices did give the south a better environment for investment because of its proximity to petroleum-rich Texas. But a more important reason seems to be the decline of traditional industries in the north and east, the moving of many plants and the exodus of job seekers to the new Sun Belt industrial centers.

Several scholars I have interviewed stress that factory owners like the south better because union strength is weaker. The American trade union movement used to be very powerful and had won "closed shop" status in many trades, which means that only union members can be hired. Then in 1947 conservative forces managed to have the "Taft-Hartley Act" adopted by the Congress. Innocuously named a "right-to-work" act, it stipulates, among other things, that non-union workers can be employed. This has greatly weakened the unions' bargaining position. After the act was passed, about a dozen southern states enacted similar laws. Not only is unionization more difficult, but trade unions don't exist at all in some new Sun Belt enterprises. Moreover, the attractiveness of the south and the west to entrepreneurs was enhanced by the less densely populated area and the lower real estate prices. These factors contributed to the industrial shift.

The primary factor causing the Sun Belt to thrive, however, is the rise of what are known as "sunrise industries"—electronics, information, space technology, etc. A prevailing view in America is that the mushrooming of "sunrise industries" is an important mark and necessary phenomenon in the ongoing transformation from an "industrial society" to a "post-industrial society" or "information society," as some writers choose to call it. The well-known futurologist John Naisbitt in his best-selling *Megatrends—Ten New Directions Transforming Our Lives*, lists the transition to an "information society" as the first of the ten directions. The ninth direction is from north to south which, he explains, means "really a shift to the southwest — and Florida" — "a trend that is virtually irreversible in our lifetimes."

THE ERA OF ELECTRONICS AND SPACE FLIGHT
— Houston, Austin, Miami and Orlando

Flying over the Corn Belt at low altitude, you will see on the ground many tall, silvery, cylindrical fodder storage solos and round grain bins, which are lower and thicker. When the plane is over Texas, particularly over the areas adjacent to Houston, the most common sight becomes the dazzling silvery oil tankers, an unmistakable sign of petro-chemical industries.

On the way from the airport into the city of Houston I see many empty plots and building sites and there is disarray. Many high-rises are shooting up and most of them are fashionable steel- and -glass structures without much architectural ingenuity. Trees and greenery are scarce. Streets are broad but very few buses are seen. All pedestrians seem to be in a hurry. When I ask some people to show me the way, none of them gives me a ready answer. The Houstonians are not very friendly, I think. But later I come to understand that many people here are new residents or out-of-state job seekers who are not yet familiar with the expanding and fast-changing city. In short, the first impression Houston gives is of fast growth in great confusion.

I laughingly complain to Louise de Young, my friend in Houston, that the city is ugly. A longtime resident, she wouldn't accept that and drives me to see the downtown area which, like other major American cities, is clustered with skyscrapers and glittering with well-stocked shops. I further complain that the city needs more vegetation. Louise then drives me to the area around Rice University, which is covered by towering old trees and luxuriant meadows. Behind hedges or fences are tall, antiquated-looking, but architecturally distinctive buildings which, Louise says, are houses or clubs for rich people. They remind me of a story the Iowa writer Hualing Nieh has told me. Once when she came to Houston to raise funds for the international writing program, a millionaire invited her to stay in his house. She felt ill at ease there because even the bathroom was profusely decorated with precious things and she had to be careful all the time not to topple and damage them. Louise tells me that this area is part of the well-built old Houston and she agrees there is confusion elsewhere. The house Louise bought twenty years ago when she moved here is now worth ten times more, she says. Soaring real estate prices show that the city is thriving. Before long it may become another "gold-paved" Manhattan.

Search for Wealth

The economic growth of Houston and of Texas brings to my mind a line from a completely irrelevant ancient Chinese poem: "Sweeping through the blue of the immense universe and the darkness of the lower world." In it poet Bai Juyi was describing the legendary search a lovesick emperor ordered for the soul of his beautiful concubine who had been strangled by mutinous soldiers. I borrow the line to describe an equally frenetic search for wealth in Texas.

To trace the history of Texas I make a special trip to Austin, the state capital. A museum is housed in the quite imposing granite state capitol there. Since the beginning of the sixteenth century, Texas had successively belonged to Spain, France, and Mexico. In the 1830s it declared independence and unfurled its national flag of a single white star. Ten years later it was annexed by the United States. Every American state has a nickname and Texas is known as the "Lone Star State" because of the flag. The strange thing is that even now the "lone star" is still flying shoulder to shoulder with the Stars and Stripes. I have even seen a pageant of six flags flying abreast — those two plus flags of Spain, Mexico, France, and the short-lived Confederacy of the Civil War which Texas had joined. The Americans are not very strict with protocol.

Texas is a richly endowed state with an area larger than France. But its growth was slow in the early days. Two explorers who landed near Houston from the Mexican Gulf in 1840 and 1853 left their impressions in writing. What they saw were bayou canes ten to fourteen feet tall and in between the forests a thick cover of grass four to six feet or even taller with water and swamp underneath. As they proceeded west they found vast grasslands with countless buffalo, prairie chickens, and whooping cranes. The time corresponded approximately to that of the Opium War in China and was quite recent. The early settlers went in for agriculture and animal husbandry. The King Ranch, the largest of its kind in present-day America, still has its headquarters at Kingsville, southwest of Houston. It is now a multi-national giant corporation that claims to own facilities "on every continent except Asia and Antarctica." It is interesting to recall that its earliest owner, one Captain King, made the first purchase of 15,500 acres from a Mexican for $300 — less than two cents per acre!

At the beginning of the present century, some Texans accidentally struck oil when they were sinking water wells. A frantic search of the "lower world" began for the "black gold." Oil, gas, and petro-chemical industries emerged and grew rapidly. With them appeared the "oil barons." Even now, many northerners still retain a disdain for those upstarts. "Want to get rich quick? Go to Texas and marry an oil man," young women jibe at each other. The gushing oil also gave impetus to the rise of a number of manufacturing industries.

By the late 1950s, the search for wealth began to extend to "the blue of the immense universe" — outer space. A display of the achievements in this new field is found at the Lyndon Johnson Space Center south of downtown Houston, named after President Lyndon B. Johnson. Louise takes me to the center. Its door is wide open to visitors and there seem to be no security measures whatsoever, quite unlike the secrecy which would shroud similar installations in other countries. But experts say that you can't see any real secrets there anyway. Besides, it is important for the development of space science to arouse public interest and popularize the relevant knowledge. The security risks, if any, are worthwhile when you weigh the pros and cons.

Several colossal carrier rockets are set outside the gate. Inside there are a number of exhibition halls. We take a quick look around and see a documentary film recapitulating man's space ventures. A real space suit used by American lunar explorers is on display and almost every tourist wants to have his or her picture taken in front of it. There are not many visitors and no guide is around to explain things. When we come to a space vehicle, a man who looks like a distinguished guest is entering it, accompanied by an escort. I follow them into the vehicle and "overhear" some explanations. The bottom of the vehicle is dotted with small triangular dents. It is said that there are matching bumps on the astronauts' shoe soles so that they can move in a state of weightlessness. The escort points to the rows of small drawers built into the wall, repositories for food packed into tubes like toothpaste. These drawers look very much like those we have in Chinese herbal medicine pharmacies.

I know little about space technology and the exhibit which impresses most is the space suit, because it is real. In Washington, D.C., I had a more real "feel" of outer space when I touched the moon rock mounted on a piece of granite at the gate of the National Air and Space Museum. It is said that over ten million hands have patted the rock. The earliest real spaceship, and Kitty Hawk, the earliest airplane, are also kept in the Washington museum. The Wright brothers performed their historic feat on 17 December 1903, when they rode the propeller-driven machine into the air. The height they attained was 852 feet and the flying time a mere fifty-nine seconds. The earliest use of planes was for the sole purpose of delivering mail.

How rapidly things have advanced since then! Less than seventy years after Kitty Hawk, man had "soared to the Ninth Heaven," as Chinese poets have dreamed since ancient times. The only regret was that neither the graceful goddess Chang E nor the savory laurel brew the poets sought was found on the moon. Americans launched their first earth satellite on 31 January 1958, about four months later than the Soviet *Sputnik*. In 1969, Apollo astronauts Neil Armstrong and Edwin Aldrin Jr. landed for the first time on the moon. By 1972, six groups of American astronauts had made lunar landings. In April 1981, the first flight of the space shuttle Columbia was launched, making space travel easier.

While I am in Houston, the world is watching Columbia's fifth launch, scheduled for 16 November, 1982. The flight is important because the shuttle will carry two communications satellites into space and put them into orbit. Success will make satellite launching simpler and less costly than the conventional blast-off by multi-stage rockets. From *Sputnik* in 1957 to 1982, according to American press reports at the time, so many satellites have been launched, mainly by the United States and the Soviet Union, that there are now 1,277 operational ones whirling around the earth, to say nothing of 1,614 others that are still up there but have fallen silent. These "watchers and listeners in the heavens" have made inter-continental telephone calls as easy as a talk with the neighbors, brought live TV broadcasts of Olympic Games to homes in all parts of the world, and enabled scientists to see as clearly as the palm of their hand the morphology, geology, vegetation distribution and crop trends on our planet. They also mark a giant step forward in man's quest for a closer watch of the sun, the other planets and celestial bodies within and outside the Milky Way galaxy. The sad aspect of the story, however, is that many satellites are parts of the two superpowers' bulging arsenals. Reporting *Columbia's* latest launch, the American press gleefully says that the Pentagon's Big Bird, a spy satellite, "has the eyes of a hawk (the word is that it can read the license plates on the Kremlin's ZIL limousines)," and that the "ferret" satellites, or "electronic ears," can eavesdrop on Soviet military radio transmissions. And most recently, the "Star Wars" space program (named after the popular American science-fiction film) is being vigorously promoted and may someday become a reality.

This fast advance of space technology gives further explanation to the extraordinary economic growth of Texas. The state, and indeed the whole Sun Belt, has prospered on space-related, high-tech industries. These are lucrative businesses and each transaction may involve tens or hundreds of millions of dollars. One of the satellites to be orbited by Columbia on its fifth flight, for instance, is owned by Satellite Business Systems, a partnership of IBM and other companies. It costs $24 million plus the $9 million charged by NASA for the launching.

The fast growth of the Sun Belt, however, has led to many difficulties. In Houston, for instance, city construction is lagging. Public transport, schools, hospitals, and even underground water are in short supply. There are many new job openings, but the influx of unemployed from the northeast and the midwest, and the legal or illegal immigrants from Mexico and Central American countries by far outnumbers the vacancies. I have seen many newspaper reports on the subject. A couple who lost their combined salary of $70,000 a year for their jobs as a company vice-president and secretary in Michigan, have come to Houston to try their luck. The man gets a $385-a-week job but loses it again in five weeks. The wife has found no work at all. Many people end up at the door of the Salvation Army when their savings run out.

The swarms of unsuccessful job seekers are no boon to public security. *Texas Medicine*, a monthly journal of the Texas Medical Association, publishes in December an article on training medical students in the city's surgical wards where, it says, "the steady increase of gunshot and knifing victims...gives the public hospital a war zone atmosphere." "Current economic difficulties" and "general levels of frustration and anxiety in life" are among the factors that have resulted in "an urban war zone." Of the 1,545 patients admitted with wounds, eighty-one percent were found to be inflicted by firearms and knives. For future military doctors, the article says, the hospital provides good clinical opportunities because, as one doctor puts it, "We can show them virtually every type of gunshot wound known to man." The state capital of Austin isn't very happy, either. It used to be a tranquil college town. But in the 1970s its population increased by thirty-six percent as the town turned into a sort of "miniature Silicon Valley." Vexed residents put bumper stickers on their cars proclaiming "Keep Austin Austin."

Flourishing Third Industry

From Houston I fly on to the famous resort city of Miami, Florida, which protrudes like a huge toe into the Gulf of Mexico and the Atlantic. True to its nickname of "Sunshine State," Florida is warm. A week earlier I had to wear a woollen sweater plus a light coat in Iowa. In Houston a sweater was enough and now in Miami I have to change to a short-sleeved silk blouse. The sky is bright but then suddenly a rainstorm gathers and hailstones shower down. But no problem. I just take shelter under shop verandas for a few minutes and fine weather suddenly comes back. Banyan trees are seen everywhere. It is a queer plant with drooping branches which themselves strike roots into the ground. They then grow into new trunks so that the tree becomes a thick and gnarled cluster. Palm trees also abound and add to the subtropical atmosphere. Downtown Miami has a congregation of skyscrapers, many of them housing banks. The city is not only the financial center of Florida but is also known as "the capital of a financial empire" controlling the whole of Central and South America.

To help me economize, a friend has arranged for me to stay at the home of an old lady who offers a few unoccupied rooms for a short lease and charges twenty-five dollars a night for the lodging, plus a breakfast of coffee, an egg and toast. Hotels are much more expensive. Miami is a strip-shaped city facing the Atlantic and numbers its streets northward from the first to the 125th. The large number of senior citizens is a striking demographic feature. The areas from the first to the 29th streets, I am told, are inhabited mostly by septuagenarians and those even older, while people over fifty usually live from 29th up to the 65th street. The rest is occupied by young and middle-aged citizens. Another feature is the high percentage of Cubans. Miami is also a haven for "gays." Back in the forties, a University of Missouri professor was fired for homosexuality. Then considered a "terrible scandal," it was reported in the local press in closely guarded, euphemistic terms and people passed on the new word only in whispers. But by the 1960s, American "gays" had come into the open, and on my present visit I have even seen their "wedding" announcements. From a Chinese viewpoint, I find it a perplexing phenomenon, to put it mildly.

Because the number of Spanish-speaking residents has increased sharply, a plebiscite is being held on the day of my arrival to determine whether English or Spanish should be the primary language in the city. English-speaking citizens heave a sigh of relief when their language barely wins. I have also read in the press that Florida is suing the federal government claiming financial compensation for the losses it has incurred as a result of the influx of Cubans. The federal government, the state charges, should be held responsible for the trouble.

Historically, Florida had been fiercely contested by France, Britain, and Spain before its annexation to the United States in 1819. The state is one of the country's "fruit and vegetable baskets." There are numerous orange groves and vegetable farms in the suburbs of Miami. It is November but citrus fruits are still seen all around. My landlady who lives in town also has a fruit garden. One day I help her to cut clusters of bananas and then climb on a ladder to pick avocadoes. It is the first time I have ever eaten that fruit. About the size of a small Chinese gourd, it is quite tasty. Florida fruits and vegetables are sold far to the north, including big cities like Chicago. Principal money earners in the state, however, are service, trade, tourism, and electric and electronic equipment manufacturing industries. Out-of-state visitors spend as much as $20 billion in 1982 in Florida, and Miami alone attracts 13 million tourists a year.

For two successive days I go to visit Miami's "gold coast." It is lined with high-rises, almost all hotels. Eye-catching billboards feature different "selling points" of the hotels. Some emphasize luxury and comfort, some a variety of recreational facilities, and some claim low prices. Fine sands along the seemingly endless beaches are dotted with multi-colored sunshades and sun-bathers' folding chairs. Swimmers, though numerous, are thinly spread out and nowhere will you see the kind of crowds that throng the Beidaihe beaches near Beijing. The clear blue waters rippling in gentle waves look more beautiful with the yachts, sailboats, water skiers and surf-riders racing at a distance, I linger on till nightfall. On my way back to town I catch another beautiful scene which could well be called "automotive dragon lanterns." On one side of the expressway is a long, rolling stream of red automobile tail lights, and on the other side a flowing streak of white or yellow headlights. Where the road curves, the two "dragons" seem to be wriggling. The rows of fancy lamps in a Chinese lantern festival are exquisite, but the "dragon lanterns" here are grand. Often the cars seem to be running on causeways through lakes formed by the seashores. On the waterfront are super-chic houses, most likely the "winter palaces" of the super-rich. Wealthy oldsters, I learn, like to live in warm, scenic Florida and that is why the average age of its population is much higher than in other states.

Sights and spas are plentiful in the "Sunshine State." Apart from the Miami "gold coast," there are the Florida Keys, a hundred-mile string of islands resembling the curved spine of an enormous animal. The tropical sights on the island chain are fascinating. On the middle

Atlantic seaboard are the famed Kennedy Space Center (named after President John Kennedy, who was assassinated in 1963), and the Cape Canaveral launching site. When the first lunar landers were sent into space from the site in 1969, one million people came from all parts of the country and the world to watch the spectacle. While I am in Miami, Columbia's fifth flight is seen by half a million spectators. Events like this add considerably to Florida's tourism income.

In Miami I find an epitome of America's highly developed third industry which includes tourist and other service trades, banking, information and a wide range of other businesses. For decades we in China had believed that only material production could boost economy while service trades helped consumption and should therefore be kept to the minimum. This misconception had led not only to a neglect of people's legitimate desire for more comforts and convenience, but also proved to be a damper on the national economy as a whole. It is fortunate that our economic planners have discarded this wrong idea and fruitful efforts have been made to expand the third industry in recent years. I don't mean, however, that garish Miami should be taken as a prototype of Chinese cities because consumerism, as I see it, does not truly contribute to social well-being.

"Future World" or an Approaching Reality

The most-frequented place in Florida is perhaps Disney World in Orlando. Many Chinese know Walt Disney and still more know Mickey Mouse, the cartoon character he created. Disney spent a huge sum to build Disneyland, the world-famous amusement park in Los Angeles. There Mickey Mouse welcomes millions of visitors, particularly children, to innovative and fantastic shows every year. In 1971, the Magic Kingdom, a similar project, was carved out of a Florida swamp at a cost of $700 million. In October 1982, two major new additions, Future World and World Showcase, were opened; they cost $1 billion to build. The sprawling complex is known collectively as Disney World. Combining fun with education is its declared purpose. Its sponsors include giant corporations like the Bell System, General Motors, and Eastman Kodak. But I find none of the usual bombastic, self-glorifying advertisments for them on the side. Bigger

American firms often open their purses to help educational projects in order to establish a public-spirited and benevolent image for themselves. It is a clever way to improve "public relations" and win customers.

Disney World is a beehive of activities and tourists. The place is big and has so many dazzling shows that a lone visitor can easily get lost. I try to find companions on the tourist bus. All nineteen riders, except for me, are Spanish-speaking tourists. A Guatemalan couple and their four children gladly take me along because the husband, a worker, can speak some broken English. We go to the Magic Kingdom first. It is essentially a children's amusement park but the facilities are fancier and more sophisticated than usual. Children love to ride the swirling model airplanes, miniature race cars and brightly colored nineteenth-century train coaches. They can slide from a high platform into an artificial pool or board a submarine-shaped craft to see the undersea world. There is also a multi-tiered restaurant that looks like a ship. And the display of multi-colored light beams in the evenings is said to be more spectacular than ordinary fireworks. Funny creatures like Mickey Mouse can be photographed with you for a small fee. If you go for a "jungle cruise," your boat will descend into a tunnel and reach tropical waterways populated by large authentic-looking model elephants and other wildlife. The wandering animals suddenly growl or charge headlong at your boat. Startled children throw themselves' into their mothers' arms and begin crying. Then there is a futuristic monorail that whizzes by over the park at a speed that sends shivers up my spine.

The queerest of all is the "Haunted Mansion." It's a dimly lit graveyard with dilapidated tombs and tombstones. Further on, we run into the "999 ghosts, ghouls and goblins" occupying the "mansion." They are clad in most bizarre clothing and have absolutely the ugliest faces imaginable, often with sharp protruding teeth. They are moving, jumping, weeping, shrieking, howling or playing dirges on musical instruments. They are so close to you that you can see the whites of their glowering eyeballs. The loudest shout you hear is that "you will be the one thousandth (ghost)." Of course you know they are just so many automatons, but the sight is still terrifying. I wouldn't call all this recreation, still less an education.

Taking a hasty leave, we board an elevated train which rapidly moves visitors out of the complex. I ask some English-speaking fellow riders what they have found most interesting. All say it was the "Hall of the Presidents," where computer-controlled, life-like models of prominent statesmen in American history would come out to meet and address visitors. What a pity that instead of seeing the "presidents" we have wasted time mixing with "ghosts!" When I say goodbye to the Guatemalans, the small daughter wants her father to ask me how to say "I love you" in Chinese. I write the three Chinese characters with English pronunciation for her. She learns to say the words properly in no time. In fact, even before I do the teaching, her eyes are already speaking "I love you!"

On the next day, I go back to visit the newly opened EPCOT, an acronym for "Experimental Prototype Community of Tomorrow." One component is called "Future World." The most prominent structure is a colossal geosphere, eighteen stories tall and sheathed in a thousand triangular aluminum panels. It is called "Spaceship Earth." A track spirals through its interior and visitors in small open coaches can see the history of human communications from primitive cave paintings to the modern language of electronics. At the height of the journey, you see your own spaceship — the earth — far below and "descend" to the home planet at what feels like lightning speed. Another show is called "World of Motion." It traces the history of human movement from a footsore caveman just back from a hunt, to horse carriages and automobile traffic. There is an exhibit of new vehicle designs and prototypes which are near at hand. "The Universe of Energy" is also interesting. Visitors are taken on a drifting ride through a primeval swamp where they can see immense dinosaurs roaming free. Accompanied by earthquakes and fiery volcanic eruptions, the earth enfolds all forms of life to be transformed into the fossil fuels of our era. At the finale, you will see all forms of energy burst around you. "The Land" is the last section I have time to see. Interior canals take you on a cruise into history from the era when primitive men made the transition from hunting to crop cultivation, all the way to an "Amazing Future Harvest" in which tomatoes grow without soil, a wheat-like grain thrives in the desert, and lettuce grows alongside cane-size cucumbers in outer space. "Journey into the

Imagination," I am told, features an array of electronic devices. There you can write, paint, play music or lead an orchestra by operating laser and sensor devices, computers, and video projections. Within "CommuniCore" is the EPCOT Computer Central which helps control and monitor the wizardry that animates the far-flung complex.

The second component of EPCOT, the World Showcase, is a quiet and leisurely display of the architecture and culture of nine nations, consonant with the Future World because both emphasize mankind's inventive genius. The American pavilion is a replica of Independence Hall in Philadelphia. Actors portraying Benjamin Franklin and Mark Twain are the hosts escorting you through scenes recounting the three-century American saga. The eight other countries represented are Britain, France, Canada, Mexico, Italy, Japan, Germany and China. Each features a typical structure — replicas, for instance, of the Eiffel Tower of Paris, a tall Mayan pyramid for Mexico and an ornate six-tier pagoda for Japan.

I choose the Chinese pavilion as my last stop. It is a small replica of the Temple of Heaven, the Hall of Imperial Prayer for Good Harvest in Beijing. The structure is a wonderful reproduction and true to the original except that, unlike in Beijing, an arch inscribed with the characters *Chao Yang Men* (Facing-the-Sun Gate) is erected in front of it. It does no harm, though, because the arch is an equally typical Beijing structure. A plaque at the entrance bears Chinese characters proclaiming the show as "China Wonders — the Beautiful Ancient Middle Kingdom." In a large theater in the building, I see a circle-vision motion picture featuring panoramic Chinese scenes, from Mongolians lassoing horses on their prairieland, to snow-clad peaks on the Tibetan plateau, from the majestic Forbidden City in Beijing to the beautiful West Lake in Hangzhou. The announcer on the screen is none other than the Tang Dynasty romantic poet Li Bai (701-762 A.D.) portrayed by an actor dressed in period costume but speaking fluent American English as if he might have attended Harvard!

I fall into meditation while resting in front of the pavilion. A young American couple with children pass by. They tell me that from now on they plan to save every cent so that when the children are older they will have money enough for the whole family to tour China. I smile my thanks to them and fall back to musing.

We Chinese are rightly proud of our beautiful land and wonderful heritage. But I believe posterity will blame us if we fail to create something new to match or surpass what our forbears have left us. We have been trying to do just that in recent decades. But much precious time was wasted. For years we shut ourselves behind closed doors, parroting dogma as a panacea for our troubles, and engaging in follies like the "cultural revolution" and the "mass movement to criticize Confucius." Meanwhile, we closed our eyes to the scientific and technological progress in the outside world. As a result, a whole generation of young people grew up without proper education. And for intellectuals like myself, knowledge has grayed with our years. But science and technology have made unprecedented progress in recent decades. The Future World I see is not a distant illusion but an approaching reality. A sense of urgency seizes me as I ponder the meaning of the futuristic displays.

While writing this report, however, I feel relieved because Chinese leaders have emphatically put forward new guidelines that education must be oriented "to modernization, to the world and to the future."

SHADOWS IN THE SUNLIGHT
— A Youth Village and a Women's Prison

In Houston I meet Louise de Young, a U.S.-China Peoples' Friendship Association activist. She works as an officer in Community Unit IV of the Harris County Juvenile Probation Department. At my request she arranges for me to visit the County Youth Village outside Houston. There are thirteen-hundred registered delinquent youths in the county. Sixty percent of them have been admitted to the village and the rest remain home under the joint charge of the probation officers and their parents.

Director Ronald J. Niksich, a former policeman who came to head the village after getting his college degree, meets us. He shows us around and readily answers all my questions. He is a warm person, and seems to be dedicated to his work and to love the children here. The kids we meet show no sign of fear of the director and a few loudly ask him, "Ronald, when will you let me go home?"

The village occupies a fairly large tract of land. The buildings are not at all dilapidated, as I had imagined they would be. We see the dormitories. Large rooms for boys are shared by sixteen in each, and smaller ones for girls by two or three. The beds are covered with white sheets and there is a writing desk between every two beds. The young inmates put their belongings in prescribed places and the whole place appears neat and clean. The director shows us the indoor gymnasium and swimming pool, a carpentry shop with complete sets of tools and a repair shop in which a car is suspended from the ceiling. It is late afternoon. The kids are all playing outdoors. They observe a strict schedule, Mr. Niksich says.

The village was built in the 1920s and renovated in 1974, and a girls' ward was added two years later. Age for admission is ten to sixteen years, and the present average is 14.8 years. Most of the youngsters have got into trouble for shoplifting, petty larceny or other misdemeanors.

On the outdoor playground I find most of the teenagers are black or belong to other minorities and only a few are whites. They are dressed in the same colorful clothes as other American youths and one can hardly detect anything different from their appearance. Mr. Niksich points to a group of black girls and whispers to me: "Most of them have had babies or were once pregnant." They are so young! Birth out of wedlock is quite common in America and, unlike in China, is not considered an appalling loss of face for the girls or their parents. Louise tells me that white families often prefer their daughters to have an abortion but the black people, having a tradition of big families, often keep the illegitimate babies.

The director explains to me "the basic philosophy of treatment" in the village. "Attitudes, feelings and structure," he says, "should convey warmth and genuine concern" for the children and stress is laid on helping their "self-image and self-confidence," I find this very similar to the Chinese approach to juvenile delinqents because they tend to be desperate and "smash the whole pot since it's broken anyway." But, Mr. Niksich adds, the job is difficult as "most of the students have a closed, protective nature that impedes communication — the key to relationship." "One of our main goals," he says, "is to develop a trusting relationship that provides a basis for the sharing of feelings." This is again similar to the approach in Chinese "work-study schools" — our equivalent to the American youth villages.

The structure of the village seems to embody the goal of "developing a trusting relationship." There are no high walls or iron-spiked fences around it. The compound is separated from the outside by a small river and the students are required not to cross it. Those who do and fail to return in a month will not be eligible for re-admission. But freedom for such "truants" often leads to new breaches of the law and more severe punishment than confinement in the youth village. Those who refuse to obey rules in the village are grouped into "special classes." It means that they will be locked indoors and not allowed to speak, though they can read and write. Meals are sent to their rooms. Because children love to move around and speak, the "special class" treatment is often enough to make them repent. Those who commit minor mistakes are made to stand up facing a wall for a while.

Mr. Niksich gives me a detailed account of the education program, including math, reading and writing, physical education and health which are also to be found in ordinary schools. In addition, there is a wide variety of vocational courses ranging from home and community services, building maintenance, general construction and general mechanics. But apparently the inmates can take only a few courses because, according to the director, they usually stay in the village for only six months or at most a year.

If I could talk to some of the youngsters, it would perhaps enhance my understanding. But I am afraid that their "closed, protective nature" would make communication with a foreign stranger more difficult and the interview might not help their "self-image and self-confidence." So I decide to take leave after heartily thanking the hospitable director, who invites me to have a drink at his home.

On our way back I tell Louise that the village is much better materially than similar institutions in developing countries. And I appreciate the director's "basic philosophy," his sincerity and dedication. But is this village one of the common run or of a better type? I ask Louise. She smiles and tells me, "Of course I would want you to see one of the best."

Roots of Juvenile Deliquency

For years I have read in the American press alarming reports of growing juvenile delinquency in the United States. According to statistics for 1982 that I see later, more than 1.07 million males and 290,000 females under 18 years of age were arrested there. Figures for 1981 showed that among the prison population of 340,000 in all states, seven percent belonged to the age group of fifteen to nineteen and fifty-six percent to the group aged twenty to twenty-nine. This was the number of imprisoned convicts. Law-breakers not arrested, those arrested but not convicted, and those convicted but released on probation were not included.

What are the causes of the problem? I have discussed the matter with many Americans and take it up again with Louise. Some think that the root cause is poverty, others criticize the media for their eroding sex-and-violence influence, and still others deplore that the traditional values of "God-fearing and law-abiding" citizenship are somehow fading with each generation.

Louise, basing her judgment on long experience, thinks that lack of proper family education, especially in "single-parent households," is largely responsible for the problem. Her talk leads me to dig into some statistical data about American families.

In the decade from 1970 to 1981, the number of American families increased from 63.4 million to 82.4 million while the average number in a family decreased from 3.14 to 2.73. This trend underlines in a way the dissolution of not only the old-type extended families but also nuclear families. Late marriage, unmarried sons and daughters choosing to live independently of their parents and a drastic drop of birth rate are justifiable reasons for the reduced family size. But there are other reasons. The number of divorces was 1.2 million in 1981, compared with one million in 1975 (though it should be pointed out that many divorced Americans remarry.) The number of men and women living together as unmarried couples also rose sharply; such households increased from 523,000 in 1970 to 1.8 million in 1981.

These families were loose and could break in two at any time. Another reason is the drastic increase of births out of wedlock, resulting from the so-called "sexual revolution." Many unmarried mothers have to set up their own households, which are known as single-parent families. Single-parent (usually fatherless) households represented eleven percent of the total number of American families in 1970. In 1981 the percentage rose to thirteen which means one out of every eight families had a single parent.

A single-parent family has only one breadwinner (if he or she is lucky enough to have a job) and is therefore poorer. It gives less security to the child. In China, working parents are usually worried about the care of their children, known as "kids with keys hanging around their necks." The problem is obviously much more serious for children with a single parent who has to go out to work. Summing up the experience of her contacts as a probation officer with such families, Louise says that they are characterized by low income, low values and low morality. The single parents themselves are often juvenile delinquents and the "education" they give children is more negative than positive. Improper family education again results in the children's virtual lack of immunity against bad habits spread by other youngsters.

Louise's talk helps me to understand better a passage from Theodore White's best-selling book *America in Search of Itself** (I have a special interest in White's writings because I read and liked *Thunder Out of China*, which he co-authored as an American correspondent in my country in the 1940s.) That passage reads:

> ... And the chief victims of this growing dissolution of family were not the lonesome old people, but the children of the dissolution.
>
> Few figures are more poignant than those on one-parent households. The sterile term "one-parent household" conceals the anguish of mating breakups.... In the America of 1978, 22 percent of all children under eighteen were growing up in such

America in Search of Itself, published by Harper & Row, Publishers, New York, 1982.

homes. And as we sift the statistics, we come upon the tragedy of black children, a tragedy impossible to ignore. In 1960, 31 percent of all black children were growing up in homes with only one parent caring for them. By 1978, that figure had swollen to aching dimension — 56 percent of all black children were growing up in fatherless homes. For them, the street was school, the asphalt the jungle, the love that must warm children as the sun does flowers was generally absent.

Louise has visited China several times. She makes a few comparisons: Chinese parents make a point of helping with their children's homework, while many American parents don't. Chinese parents make strict demands on their children in their choice of friends while American youngsters, having a tradition of personal independence, often would not heed their parents' advice. Chinese residents keep an eye on their working neighbors' children and would report anything bad to their parents, but Americans doing so might be considered "nosy" and "meddling in other people's family life." That's why juvenile delinquency is more serious in America. I thank her for the compliments. In China, however, juvenile delinquency had also become an alarming question since the "cultural revolution." In those years, smashing and grabbing were publicly lauded as the traits of "revolutionary rebels." But fruitful efforts have been made in recent years to save the young lawbreakers, often referred to as "pest-infected flowers" because Chinese children in general are called "flowers of the motherland".

Sybil Brand Prison

Later on my tour, I have an opportunity to visit a women's prison in Los Angeles, the third largest American city which, like Houston, is flourishing in the "Sun Belt." It is named Sybil Brand after a rich woman who donated the land for it.

Professor Robinson of M.I.T. has introduced me to William Russell, his college schoolmate and an engineer in the aerospace industry, and Mrs. Marjorie Russell, a member on the Los Angeles City Council who represents a constituency of 200,000 people. Mr.

Russell takes me to the town hall to see his wife. Her secretary tells us that she is at a meeting. American city council meetings are usually open to the public, a good tradition, I think. We go straight to the assembly room and avail ourselves of the opportunity to listen to the aldermen discussing over a round-table. After the session, Mrs. Russell joins us and asks what she can do for me. Knowing that crime rate is high in major American cities, I request that I be allowed to visit a prison. Most helpful, Mrs. Russell tells her secretary, an ethnic Chinese, to make the arrangement for me.

Frank Pestana, one-time president of the U.S.-China Peoples' Friendship Association, accompanies me on the visit. The atmosphere at the prison, surrounded by high walls, is entirely different from the Harris County Youth Village. A male receptionist reports our arrival to the officers inside. We wait for quite a while before a uniformed woman guard comes out to meet us.

It is the time of changing shifts and many women guards are coming out. They go to a big room where they put away their uniforms, change into civilian clothes and each take out a pistol. Holding or tossing their weapons, the women walk to their cars, parked outside. It is strange that they don't carry weapons while working but get pistols when they are off. Their profession, I gather, requires added protection at home.

It is also time for visiting the prisoners. Many people are lining up for permits, most of them black. We see a hall partitioned into small compartments separated by a glass wall from the prison compound. Visitors talk by telephone to the prisoners behind thick, reinforced glass, through which they can see each other. We then pass by a telephone booth where prisoners having no visitors are queuing up to make phone calls to their families or friends.

All the prisoners wear uniforms, a kind of loose-necked gown that looks like a grocery bag. The uniforms are green, purple, yellow or brown. I am told they are made by the prisoners themselves and the colors are for identification of different cells. We are then shown a big sewing room with many dolls, made by the prisoners to sell. There are no other production facilities in this big prison. It seems that they don't attach as much importance to reform through productive labor as Chinese prisons do. There is a big laundry room with washing machines and dryers. The warden tells me that the inmates do all the cleaning work in the prison. We are then led to a library and a big mess hall. There are TV sets in the hall. Prisoners who behave well are allowed to read in the library or to watch TV.

From the hall we go upstairs to see the cells. One of the doors happens to be open and I see dozens of beds in the room. Some of the women inmates are sitting on the beds staring blankly at the wall and others are lying on pillows with books in their hands. The cells are not over-crowded, by prison standards. But the warden shuts the door before I can take a closer look. She says that there are small cells for solitary confinement. Feeling the tight security, I refrain from requesting an interview with prisoners. And I feel that without the powerful help of Mrs. Marjorie Russell on the City Council, a foreign stranger like me, having nothing much to do with the criminal justice system, would not have been granted the visit.

On our way out we see a new arrival, a fat, gum-chewing black woman. A warden is searching her body and asks her to open her mouth. She spits the gum onto the ground several feet away, apparently not caring a straw that she is in prison. The warden tells me that after the routine search a new arrival will be told to take a bath, change into prison uniform, go through a physical check-up, and then begin to serve her term.

Crime Wave

The atmosphere in the prison is oppressive. I feel relieved to see the bright sunshine again in beautiful Los Angeles. Why in this rich country, I wonder, should crime be so rampant that it is called a "wave"?

American crime statistics often do not tally, perhaps because of different criteria used in different surveys. A friend has given me a copy of *U.S. News & World Report* (12 October, 1981) and recommended a special report for me to read. The weekly is generally considered an authoritative one. I base this report of mine on its figures and analysis.

In 1980, according to the magazine, twenty three thousand people died at the hands of murderers, up from nine-thousand two decades earlier; eighty-two thousand women were raped, up from seventeen thousand reported in 1960; more than half a million people were robbed, up from 108,000; and more than 650,000 were assaulted, up from 154,000. During the same twenty years, crimes against property — burglary, larceny and car theft — tripled, causing billions of dollars in losses. With an eye-catching chart captioned "As the Clock Ticks," the report shows that there is one serious crime every two seconds; a murder every twenty-three minutes; a rape every six minutes; a robbery every fifty-eight seconds; an aggravated assault every forty-eight seconds; a motor vehicle theft every twenty-eight seconds; a burglary every eight seconds and a theft every four seconds.

U.S. Department of Justice statistics issued later show that the rate of serious crimes was 1,887 per 100,000 people in 1960, and had since soared to 5,583 in 1982. There were occasional drops in some years, but the overall trend is rising and rising again.

What are the reasons? Associate Editor Ted Gest of *U.S. News & World Report*, who has covered criminal justice subjects for many years, says: "There is no question that much of the increase is caused by economic factors, unemployment, drugs, poverty, ethnic friction and the decline in American family life. But a lot of respected analysts now say that the justice system itself is responsible for at least part of today's crime wave."

Police — Unlike TV's cop heroes, they make arrests in only nineteen percent of the serious crimes reported (many victims, molested women in particular, choose not to report). The reason for the low arrest rate, according to police claims, is that they are overworked and understaffed, and many have to juggle an array of non-criminal duties such as mediating family quarrels, directing traffic, and dealing with drunks.

Prosecutors — They typically reject or reduce the severity of fifty to eighty percent of the charges filed by police. The reason for this, the prosecuting attorneys say, is their manpower shortage. Besides, a lot of cases police bring them are "not worth pursuing".

Courts — American criminal proceedings are very complex. Many legal hitches (which I have to omit in this brief account) result in criminals' getting off scot-free or in inconsistent conclusions handed down from the judge's bench.

Prison — The situation is appalling. "The 329,000 prisoners in Federal and state penitentiaries are housed mostly in antiquated, crowded institutions, in which violence and drugs proliferate, opportunities for rehabilitation are skimpy and the exchange of tips on criminal techniques is a major pastime....Because of a shortage of funds and facilities, only one prisoner out of ten receives job training while in prison.... As prison cells overflow, parole boards make room for new convicts by releasing before the end of their terms inmates judged to be rehabilitated." Building new prisons requires money which is not easily available. Land is difficult to find, too. I have read reports about residents demonstrating or even filing suits in court to prevent building prisons in their neighborhood.

During my stay in America, I have found that public opinion often calls for sterner anti-crime measures. President Reagan has gone a step farther to voice the new conservative view that the "nature of man" is simply the root of crime. "Some men are prone to evil," the President declares, "and society has a right to be protected from them." But the "nature-of-man" theory is disputed by many people. A criminologist points out that this pessimistic view of man cannot explain why the United States has so much more crime and violence than other countries — why, for example, in 1977, ten American men died by violence for every Japanese, Austrian, German or Swedish male? "Are Americans just more wicked? If so, the 'nature of man' varies by national boundaries." It is a justified question, I think. And a newspaper columnist raises another sharp question: "If prison is the answer, why did crime keep rising from 1975 to 1981, while the rate at which people were being locked up rose by over a third?"

How can the crime wave be stemmed? Nobody seems to know the answer, because the problem, as a Department of Justice official in charge of criminal statistics puts it, is vast and complex.

Chapter X
PLYING SOUTH AND NORTH

After visiting the fairytale Disney World, I fly to Atlanta, Georgia. Now I am in that part of America known as the Deep South. According to what I knew in the forties, poverty and "blackness" were two salient features of the region.

I still remember a tale describing a funeral in the South. People cut through solid marble rock to make the grave for a poor man and yet the marble tombstone was bought from the North. They buried him in a pine forest and near an iron mine, and yet the pine coffin, the nails and the iron in the shovel all came from the North. The dead man wore a coat from New York and shoes from Chicago. In short, the South had nothing to contribute but the body and the hole in the ground. An exaggeration of course, the tale was meant to show the poverty of the South. Long years of cotton and tobacco cultivation had depleted the soil. Single-crop-economy and absence of mining and industry were causes of the impoverishment.

By "blackness" I mean the high percentage of black people in the population and the dark age they were living through. Racial discrimination and segregation were rampant. The blacks were not allowed in white schools and restaurants. They had to jam into the rear of a bus even when seats in the front reserved for whites were vacant. White-masked and robed Ku Klux Klansmen showing only their eyes and brandishing torches and weapons often went after black people in the night. Photographs of lynchings and cartoons flaying the white supremacists were seen from time to time in the press.

How is the situation now? I embark on the visit full of curiosity. To be fair, I find that great changes have come about over the decades.

The Deep South isn't all that poor and some parts of it are prospering in the Sun Belt. Significant gains have been scored by the blacks in their struggle against segregation and poverty, though their complete emancipation is still far off and new crises are brewing.

"I HAVE A DREAM"
— Paying Homage to Martin Luther King Jr. at His Grave

Atlanta is the state capital and the largest city in Georgia. After checking in at the downtown Ladha Hotel, I go out for a stroll in a drizzly rain. Imposing high-rises and glittering shop windows are largely the same as in other cities. But the sight changes drastically as I walk southward. Houses resemble the bare apartment buildings rigged up in Beijing during the "cultural revolution" when asceticism was equated with socialism. Staircases, not fire-escapes, are built on the outer walls. Shop and church buildings are also crude. The black community lives in the southern part of the city and whites generally live in the northern section. But the black pedestrians' manners appear different from what I knew in the forties. In those years they usually looked humble and hesitant. But now they stride on and hold their chins up in a way not much different from the whites. Blacks account for sixty percent of Atlanta's population. Its mayor is black, Andrew Young, the noted civil rights leader and former U.S. Ambassador to the United Nations.

Night Reading

Back in the hotel, I open a few history books which I have brought along for background information about American blacks. Some of the descriptions are ghastly.

In 1619, a mysterious ship flying the Dutch flag reached Jamestown on the Atlantic coast. Her "cargo" was 20 black slaves. Before that, large numbers of Africans had been shipped to the Spanish and Portuguese colonies in South America and the Caribbean. But the "cargo" unloaded at Jamestown was the first of its kind in

North America. Africans were usually captured in the interior of their continent and sold on the coast. The treks to the seashore, sometimes for 1,000 miles, with people shackled around the neck, under whip and gun, were death marches in which two out of every five blacks died. When they were put on sale on the beaches, ship surgeons would examine every part of every one of them, men and women being stark naked. The "good and sound" ones were set aside and marked on the breast with a red-hot iron, imprinting the mark of the slave-trading companies. Then they were packed aboard ships. The space between their "sleeping cots" was sometimes only eighteen inches, less than the breadth of their shoulders so that they could not turn over. And they were usually chained to the deck by the neck and legs. According to one historian, by 1800, ten to fifteen million blacks had been transported as slaves to the Americas, representing perhaps one-third of those originally seized in Africa. It is roughly estimated that Africa lost 50 million human beings to death and slavery in those centuries. In North America, most of the blacks were forced to toil on southern cotton plantations. The children of slaves were born slaves.

Wherever there is oppression there is resistance. Spontaneous and sporadic slave uprisings never stopped. After American independence, capitalism thrived in the North on wage labor while the South retained its plantation system based on servitude. Complex political and economic contradictions between the two parts of the country were exacerbated by a growing abhorrence of slavery, and burst into the American Civil War (1861-1865). More than 200,000 blacks joined the Union army and fought for their emancipation. The war resulted in the legal abolition of slavery. But Black Americans failed to win either economic freedom from want or social freedom from discrimination.

By the way, I wish to add that there is a "Gone with the Wind" museum in Atlanta. The novel and movie of the same title were once very popular in China and till today Scarlet O'Hara remains perhaps one of the best-known fictional American women among educated Chinese youth. The museum provides "a historic pilgrimage into the storied times." But I have heard caustic comments by some progressive Americans on the love story. They say it is a distortion of history, or even "racist," because the black slaves were portrayed by the author as devoted servants of their white masters and inveterate haters of the "Yankees."

Civil Rights Revolution

I have come to Atlanta mainly to pay homage to Rev. Martin Luther King Jr. Foul weather continues on the day when I go to the memorial gravesite. There is drizzle in the autumn wind, making the scene quite dreary. The tombstone is plain and a flame flickers in front of it. There are no other visitors around. I stand in silent tribute, recalling King's words which had once reverberated through the world:

> I have a dream that one day this nation will rise up and live out the true meaning of its creed, "We hold these truths to be self-evident, that all men are created equal".... I have a dream that my four little children will one day live in a nation where they will not be judged by the color of their skins, but by the content of their character.

The place is no majestic mausoleum. But King's life, short as it was, represented a landmark in the history of American blacks. At the side of the grave stands Freedom Hall, about the size of an ordinary meeting hall. There are no memorial exhibits except for about thirty groups of photographs and reproduced newspaper clippings on the walls showing the course of the civil rights movement led by King. I spend hours in the hall and take a lot of notes. But I can recount only some highlights here.

The century following the American Civil War had witnessed the adoption of several amendments to the U.S. Constitution which guarantee black rights. But in America as elsewhere, laws written on paper proclaiming social justice are more often than not hollow promises. The state and local authorities made their own laws to block the implementation of the constitutional amendments. Racial discrimination and oppression remained grave, doubly so in the southern states.

In 1957, there was a conflagration in Little Rock, Arkansas. Black children went to white public schools demanding enrollment. They met with police repression. Brutal treatment of the kids appeared on TV screens across the country and abroad. Public opinion was inflamed. The blacks, and those whites who supported them, won out in the end.

In another violent incident in Montgomery, Alabama, in the late 1950s, Martin Luther King Jr. began to emerge as a leading figure. One day Rosa Parks, a black seamstress in the city, took a seat in the "white" section of a bus because the rear was too crowded. She was manhandled by a policeman and taken to jail in handcuffs. Angry blacks went to a community church to consult their minister, who was Atlanta-born Martin Luther King Jr. The young minister, born in 1929, hated racism but was deeply influenced by Mahatma Gandhi's belief in non-violence. He advocated struggle by peaceful means and, together with his supporters, organized forty thousand blacks in the city to sign a pledge to boycott the buses. The protest action lasted for 382 days during which blacks were repeatedly subjected to police violence. But once again they won out. The entire black population in the south was elated and encouraged.

Little Rock and Montgomery were the opening shots heralding a civil rights revolution that overtook the whole country in the 1960s. I shall briefly recall the turbulent Freedom Rides and sit-in movements.

In those years blacks sitting together with whites on trains had to segregate when they reached the southern states which had laws requiring segregation. Challenging the vile practice, the Freedom Riders continued to sit together. They were beaten up by racists and hooligans and thrown into jails as lawbreakers. But more Freedom Riders showed up on trains and buses. Conflicts and fights broke out everywhere. Finally the federal government had to abolish segregation on interstate buses and trains. But public transport within state boundaries, with the exception of Montgomery, persisted in its adherence to the old tradition. The federal government couldn't do anything about it.

The sit-ins were spearheaded against segregation in public eating places. A few black students would take seats in a snack bar selling coffee and sandwiches to whites. They would be refused service. They wouldn't leave and would sit silently. When police came, they would resort to brute force to expel the blacks. But the next day more blacks would come and "sit-in." The movement spread and thousands ended up in jail.

Adhering to King's stress on non-violence, the protesters usually refrained from fighting back against police attack. This was believed to be a correct tactic. The racists were the ones most eagerly hoping that the blacks would use violence. It would justify their recourse to much more powerful force.

The non-violent Freedom Rides and sit-ins succeeded in building a mass following and winning national and international support for King and his supporters, who then decided to organize for a complete elimination of all forms of segregation. Beginning in March, 1963, mass demonstrations took place in Birmingham, Alabama, one of the strongholds of racism. The police chief, "Bull" Connor, sent his force to attack the demonstrators with clubs, tear gas, dogs and high-powered water hoses. King was arrested. But people continued to take to the streets. Finally King was freed and the Birmingham authorities had to abolish segregation.

In the year 1963, hundreds of protest demonstrations took place in many southern cities. Imprisonment became commonplace. Beatings were frequent. But ever more people came forward in defiance of the repression. Songs reflecting the spirit of the times were born in mass protest actions, one of which says:

> *If you miss me from the back of the bus,*
> *And you can't find me nowhere,*
> *Come on to the front of the bus,*
> *I'll be ridin' up there....*

> *If you miss me from the cotton fields,*
> *And you can't find me nowhere,*
> *Come on down to the courthouse,*
> *I'll be voting right there....*

People would alter the words to suit different situations. The struggle spread like a prairie fire.

March on Washington

Historic circumstances make heroes. The nationwide turmoil inspired King and other national civil rights leaders to plan a march on

Washington, D.C., in 1963 (a century after Abraham Lincoln's Emancipation Proclamation). The march took place on 27 August as 250,000 people rallied in the capital. It was at this historically unprecedented mass gathering for black rights that King made his "I have a dream" speech and became the recognized black leader of the country.

In the following year, 1964, the United States Congress passed an omnibus civil rights bill banning discrimination in voting, jobs, public accommodations, etc., the most comprehensive one in history. An American historian has told me an episode that preceded the voting on the legislation. Seeing the momentum of voting sentiment turning against them, opponents of the bill cleverly added the word "sex" to "race and color" in the anti-discrimination clauses. In addition to hard-core racists, there was no lack of male chauvinists among the lawmakers. The addition was designed to enlist their support and swell the ranks of those opposed to the bill. But the attempt failed.

The unity and struggle of the blacks were the primary reasons for this major victory in the civil rights revolution. But it must be remembered that many whites, particularly in the northern and western states, had joined the struggle from the very outset and their number kept increasing as the fight intensified. Another important reason was to be found internationally. The old nineteenth century form of colonialism had almost completely crumbled. The newly emerging African and other Third World countries, as well as fair-minded people all over the world, cherished a deep sympathy for American blacks. As scenes of cruel suppression continued to appear in the worldwide mass media year after year, the international image of the United States became more and more tarnished. Washington, which claims to be the leader of the "Free World" and champion of "human rights," pondered the implications.

After the 1964 legislation, King did not rest in euphoria. He pressed the fight forward, now for black voting rights. As early as 1870, the 15th amendment to the U.S. Constitution already barred the denial or abridgement of voting rights on account of race and color (sex was not included and American women were not given suffrage until 1920). But many localities had their own ways to block the implementation of the fifteenth amendment. All that would be necessary in some communities, for instance, was for the local Ku Klux Klan to pass the word around that it would "finish off any nigger" going to the polls. Also there were local laws requiring voters to pay a poll tax or be able to read and correctly understand the articles of the Constitution. The result was that large numbers of poor and illiterate blacks were denied the right to vote. Though the 1964 civil rights bill once again banned discrimination in voting, many southern localities went on obstructing black voter registration by various subtle means.

King and other leaders chose Selma, Alabama, as the site at which to stage a demonstration against the continuation of these abuses. A march from Selma to the state capital of Montgomery was organized. It began in the spring of 1965 with 25,000 black participants. More blacks and whites joined on the way and their number expanded to 150,000. They met with police attacks and one white woman participant from the North was murdered. The mass action, nonetheless, prodded Congress to adopt a new voting rights act which declared obstruction to black voter registration illegal. The last bulwarks of open segregation were toppled. And a lull set in gradually in the civil rights revolution that had spanned over a decade.

The Second Dream

But the problem has deeper roots. As a professor puts it: "What's the use of the right to dine with the whites if you don't have the money to foot the bill?"

The civil rights revolution did result in a minority among the blacks, usually skilled workers and professionals, rising to better positions. But job opportunities for the poorest blacks remained limited. College enrollment for black students rose rapidly but most of them were from middle class families. Great difficulties persisted for the black masses. In short, equal rights cannot be real when economic polarization prevails.

King felt the problem keenly. His vision began to accommodate another dream: poor blacks joining hands with poor whites to fight off poverty. To this end, the second march on Washington was organized in 1968. Calls were made for the U.S. Government to divert money budgeted for the Vietnam war to aid the American poor. A union of poor blacks and whites, if formed, would undoubtedly be an overwhelming force. But King, in this second dream, had gone beyond the pale. Some people reacted violently. On 4 April 1968, Martin Luther King was shot to death at the age of 39.

American blacks were infuriated and riots rocked more than one-hundred cities. To allay popular wrath, President Johnson declared 4 April a day of national mourning and the assassin was sentenced to a term of ninety-nine years.

In China, protest demonstrations were organized in many cities across the land. At that time the country was in the pangs of the "cultural revolution" and most people, including myself, were heartily sick of the endless political rallies and marches. But I voluntarily joined the massive turnout in Beijing, as did my colleagues, to voice solidarity with black Americans. Waving banners and shouting slogans, we marched from one end of the city to the other. Years have gone by but the moving scene remains fresh in my memory.

Dream and Reality

A man who symbolized the struggle of a people for basic human dignity and freedoms was slain. But as the great Chinese writer Lu Xun wrote: "Strong grows the grass on plains made rich with blood; in winter-frozen earth spring starts to quicken."

On 19 September 1981, half a million workers and their sympathizers gathered in Washington, D.C., for a solidarity day demonstration. The emblem of the gathering was a white hand joining a black one in a clenched fist. Then on 27 August 1983, another march on Washington took place on the twentieth anniversary of the first one led by King. I was already back in China and learned from news reports that over 200,000 people from 340 large and small cities joined the rally. The demonstration had the support of 715 national organizations, representing a coalition much broader than that of 1963. At the rally for "jobs, peace and freedom," Coretta Scott King

(Martin Luther King Jr.'s widow) said in her address: "We still have a dream." Black leader Jesse Jackson's thrilling speech brought the rally to a climax with calls to turn dream into reality. (Mr. Jackson later became a presidential aspirant seeking the Democratic nomination).

Before the 1983 march, a black American friend of mine, Richard Pendleton of Boston, sent me a number of pamphlets and leaflets prepared for the occasion. In one of them was written: "When white America catches cold, black America gets pneumonia." First fired, last hired, blacks were hit hard in 1982 when their average unemployment rate soared to 18.9 percent compared to 8.6 percent for whites. About fifty percent of black teenagers couldn't find jobs — again more than double the rate for white teenagers. One pamphlet contains some other interesting information. One example: "We're Only Number 19: The United States ranks a poor 19th in infant mortality on a list compiled by the Population Reference Bureau Inc.," because the high death rate of black and other minority babies had lowered the U.S. rating.

American blacks numbered 26,488,000, or 11.7 percent of the total population, according to the 1980 census. The impression I gathered is that the majority of them are not happy with their present situation. The current calm does not mean the volcano is dead. "Amid the silence comes the crash of thunder" — what Lu Xun once wrote about smoldering popular discontent might be true in America, too.

Still, it must be said that great changes have taken place since the 1940s. As noted before, the mayor of Atlanta is a black, Andrew Young, something hard to imagine in earlier years. A friend has introduced me to Mr. Young, who promises to meet me on Sunday. I go to the city hall and find him busy working. Many visitors are waiting their turn and I am fortunate to spend thirty minutes with him. He tells me that as early as 1964 King had publicly called for recognition of the People's Republic of China, and was attacked for saying so. The short interview does not permit any in-depth discussion. Nevertheless it gives me a sense of the black Americans' present situation which is, after all, quite different from decades ago.

In November 1983, President Reagan signed an order designating the third Monday of every January as Martin Luther King Day. It will be observed as a national holiday beginning in 1986. (King was born on 15 January and American holidays are usually set to make for a long weekend, hence the third Monday of January). Some sceptics have characterized the presidential move as a tactic to win support from blacks. Regardless, the great honor conferred posthumously on King means that his name is synonymous with the quest by black Americans for emancipation.

CHICAGO ELECTS A MAYOR

The Atlanta visit has heightened my interest in the problem of blacks. On 12 April 1983, a mayoral election, held once in every four years in Chicago, will take place. The Republican candidate is a white and the Democratic nominee a black. A fierce election campaign is attracting nationwide attention. Major newspapers and radio-TV networks have sent in reporters and writers to cover the campaign. Foreign correspondents from Britain, France, Canada, Italy, and Japan have also converged on the city. Chicago is the second largest American metropolis. If a black is elected mayor, the repercussions will spread far beyond the city itself.

In order to observe directly the election, I make a stopover in Chicago on my flight from the West Coast back to Boston. It is late March. Seattle, my point of departure, is already blossoming with flowers. But the plane runs into a whirling snowstorm over Chicago which almost forces it to land elsewhere. Charlie Fischer, husband of Sylvia, an activist in the U.S.-China Peoples' Friendship Association, meets me at the airport. They are a politically oriented couple. With their help I have the opportunity to witness some scenes of the election drama.

I lived for a while in Chicago in the forties and worked for some time in a Chinese restaurant there. On revisiting, I find the city more flashy and boisterous. The world's tallest building, the 110-story, 1,454-foot Sears Tower, has been built here. The city faces Lake Michigan, one of the five Great Lakes known as the "North American Mediterranean." As soon as the first signs of spring appear after the snowstorm, I go to the lakefront to enjoy again the view which once enchanted me. On one side of the drive is an endless expanse of rippling blue waters dotted with ships and boats, and on the other side is an architectural gamut of beautiful old buildings and newer steel and glass citadals. I used to like watching the small curls of white clouds floating in the clear sky over the lake, imagining that they were herds of lambs under the care of heavenly shepherdesses. They are still there, casting their images on the lake. But I am not that poetic now.

Reminiscences of Chicago, however, are not all pleasant. The color line was an annoying experience. There were plenty of apartment-for-rent notices in the classified ad columns in the 1940s. But when I found the house, the owner, often a lady, would peep out through a narrow opening of the door. Seeing an Asian, she would say curtly: "Sorry, it's been rented out." Finally I got two rooms, bare but expensive, in a mixed area between white and black communities.

But now it has become possible for a black to become mayor. I say "possible" because the competition is sharp and nobody is sure of the outcome.

Harold Washington

The Democrat nominee is sixty-year-old Harold Washington. He served in the U.S. Air Force for four years during World War II, saw action in the Marianas Islands and received numerous military decorations. After the war he went to college and earned a degree in political science and one in law. Then he served in the Illinois legislature as representative and later as a state senator. Elected to the U.S. Congress in 1980, he has voted against virtually every cut in social programs proposed by President Reagan. He was in favor of establishing a Select Committee on Hunger and called for transferring a sizeable part of defense spending to medicare and other programs.

On the day of my arrival in Chicago, Sylvia tells me that there is a women's rally for Harold Washington in the evening and asks if I would like to go. Certainly I would. The meeting is held in the conference hall of a big downtown hotel and attended by about one thousand people, including a number of men. Coretta King, widow of the assassinated black leader, is greeted with warm applause when she takes the floor. Among those seated on the rostrum is the wife of former U.S. Vice-President Walter Mondale. Harold Washington, however, is away attending another rally in Detroit. The meeting comes to a climax when he hurries back and delivers a speech at 9 p.m.

What amazes me is that Washington says in his speech that he would break the party machine and appoint people to public office according to their merits. I should explain briefly for my Chinese readers that the two major American political parties have powerful local organizations which, to quote a Chinese saying, "have deep, twisted roots and long, gnarled branches." They are called "party machines" and their bosses wield great influence on elections. Candidates who win under their sponsorship must reward their people with appointive public offices, a long-standing practice known as the "spoils system." It is detested by the public but has become so ingrained that to change it is exceedingly difficult if not impossible. But Washington is publicly challenging the "machine." This, I feel, shows a determination to appeal directly to the public in a bid to get rid of the "spoils" system.

A few days later, Sylvia asks me if I would like to attend a $25-a-plate banquet for Washington organized by ethnic Chinese Chicagoans. It is of course an even more welcome opportunity for me. The banquet is given in a restaurant called the "Hunan Palace" and there is a large attendance. Instead of reading a prepared speech, Washington talks extemporaneously. He says that the many Chinese in Chicago are a "wonderful stock of people" who have made outstanding contributions to the city. But they have been excluded from the "mainstream of life." It is unfair that there has not been a single Chinese alderman on the city council, he says. The blacks have been discriminated against over a longer period of time. Some people still believe it to be unimaginable, or even fantastic, to have blacks or other minority people in important offices, he says. It is high time to change the idea. At the same time, however, Washington stresses racial unity. He especially cites a letter an 11-year-old Chinese child has written him urging him "to bring people together." After the speech he comes around to every table and shakes hands with the well-wishers. When Sylvia tells him that I am a visitor from Beijing, he holds my hand tightly for a while.

Bernard Epton

The Republican nominee is Bernard Epton, 61, a white lawyer. He has also served in the Illinois legislature. Local press says that before the election campaign Mr. Epton was not a well-known public figure, nor was Washington. But Epton is a millionaire and "his personal wealth has been estimated at $5 million" as a report says. Epton's election platform, as I gather from the press, is rather vague and general. His main argument against Washington seems to be with the color of his skin.

Chicago newspapers in these days are dominated by campaign reports. The *Sun-Times*, the nation's eighth largest daily, with a circulation of 649,000, prints a series of articles criticizing Epton. Mike Royko, a columnist and winner of a Pulitzer Prize, the highest honor for American journalists, takes Epton to task in a *Sun-Times* article headlined "Blame for Campaign's Nastiness Dogs Epton." He writes: "The tone of the campaign was set way back in the opening minutes of the debate. That's when Epton decided that his long-range strategy was not to talk about specific issues concerning the future of this city and how he would deal with them." Instead, he launched personal attacks. "And when campaigns become personal, they inevitably become dirty," Royko says. The columnist cites many examples of racist literature churned out by the Epton staff. A raving hand bill says: "You, a white person, don't dare walk the streets or ride in the downtown area. Your car will be stoned. You will be robbed or killed, while white women will be raped. With a black police chief there will be absolute chaos in the city." It is Epton's forecast of the disaster if Washington is elected. I should add that columnist Royko is white. And he is not alone in his disgust with Epton and his racist tactics. The *Chicago Tribune*, the other major daily newspaper in the city, isn't friendly to Mr. Epton either.

Walking on Chicago streets, I often see people wearing election buttons. The most common one is a blue badge with the name *Washington* inscribed in white. Epton supporters wear fancier types, usually a pure-white one bearing no word, but conveying the clear message. Another type bears the phrase: "Epton — before it's too late." It simply means that you'd better elect Epton before a black man is elected mayor. By then it will be too late to save the white men from murder and the white women from rape. There are T-shirts printed with an imaginative slogan: "Vote Right, Vote White." It is not possible to render it into equal Chinese rhyme but the jingle reminds me of "might is right". Street demonstrations are frequent.

The debate sponsored by radio, TV, and the *Sun-Times* on the eve of the election day represents the climax of the contest. Professor Pingti Ho and his wife Shao Jingluo, my schoolmates at Qinghua University in the 1930s who now live in Chicago, invite me to dinner at their home to watch the debate. I attentively follow the exchanges between the two candidates from beginning to end, keen to learn where Mr. Epton argues specifically with his opponent's political platform. But I end up in disappointment. Columnist Royko's criticisms of Epton seem well-founded.

Victory

Chicagoans make their choice on 12 April. From 6 a.m. to 7 p.m., more than 1.6 million registered voters in nearly three thousand precincts go to the polls. Radio and TV give continuous coverage. People anxiously follow the news reports and analyses and wait for the returns as if they were watching a most exciting ball game. I, too, stay in front of the TV till midnight. Though exact final figures are not yet available, Washington's victory is a foregone conclusion. Scenes of ecstatic celebration at Washington's headquarters appear on the TV screen. A predominantly black crowd of ten thousand cheering, hugging, and kissing people chant again and again: "Harold, Harold, we want Harold." They explode into joy when Washington steps onto the platform, waving his hands and saying "thank you." People respond with louder cheers and once again he says "thank you." The process is repeated almost twenty times.

The mayor-elect delivers his victory speech after midnight. His keynote: "I want to reach out my hand in friendship and fellowship to every living soul in this city.... Our most important concern at this moment is unity." People generally approve of this approach because the bitter campaign has left the city population sharply divided and the conservatively inclined ones rancorous with a racially tinged hatred.

It is customary in American elections for the winner to make a "victory speech" and the loser to make a "conceding speech" to show statesmanship. But Epton leaves town that night without conceding—for a family vacation in Miami. At a "unity prayer luncheon" attended by the outgoing woman mayor, Washington, and other officials on the next day, Epton's brother attends as his substitute and reads a routine congratulatory telegram from the defeated candidate.

Washington inherits a Chicago government which is in dire financial straits. The newly elected mayor soon announces a twenty percent cut of his 60,000-a-year salary. As a U.S. representative in Washington D.C. he was paid 70,000 annually. The voluntary reduction means that he will get 22,000 less a year. Epton, on his part, tells the press that he is assembling a group to purchase the *Sun-Times*. And he says that if he acquires the newspaper, he would "immediately" fire Mike Royko and another *Sun-Times* columnist. The millionaire, however, fails to clinch the deal.

Dilemma

Harold Washington is not the only black mayor in the country. I have found no statistics prior to the civil rights bill of 1964. By 1970 there were 169 black mayors and the number has increased to 238 by May 1983. Most of them are running small towns but quite a few major cities, among them Los Angeles, Washington, D.C., Detroit, Atlanta, New Orleans and Cleveland, have elected black mayors. Washington's victory in Chicago is soon followed by another black victory in Philadelphia.

The significant political trend is undoubtedly a result of the 1964 civil rights legislation and the 1965 voting rights act. But there is another factor which should not be neglected. Many prosperous whites have been moving out from urban centers to outlying towns and far suburbs. This change in lifestyle has left inner cities populated more and more by blacks and other minorities. Thus it becomes easier for blacks to be elected. But it's not only blacks who vote black. Spokane, a fairly large city in Washington state, is only 1.6 percent black but has a black mayor. So does Abilene, Kansas, where blacks number less than one percent. Sylvia, my hostess in Chicago, is a white and on top of that a Jew like Bernard Epton, and her husband, Charlie, is Anglo-Saxon. But both of them are firm supporters of Washington.

I have read many press reports on black mayors confronting tough tasks. Their trouble, to put it in a nutshell, lies in their lack of money and power. "Old-guard business establishments," one newspaper correspondent writes, "tend to regard a new black mayor much like the Czar regarded Lenin." Without support of the white economic power, it is difficult to keep a city going, let alone improve it. So it is imperative to create a partnership with the white business community. Andrew Young, the black mayor I interviewed in Atlanta, once said: "What I did that turned out to be quite effective was just to have a regular breakfast for the chief executive officers of the twenty-five largest businesses.... I said to them, 'I can get elected without your help but I can't run the city without your help.'" The reason is clear. Blacks have enough ballots but not enough dollar bills.

The question of power is as much a headache for the black mayors. The deep-rooted party and bureaucratic machines are not pliable tools. The police chief, above all others, is a crucial figure. He can make the going very rough for the mayor if he does not cooperate.

Black mayors of northern cities are faced with an additional difficulty. Traditional industries there (often called "sunset" or "smokestack" industries) are declining. Unemployment is rising. City treasuries are draining and mayors are hard pressed to make ends meet.

As early as 1977 there was an academic study which concluded: "Black mayors do not have the power and resources to liberate black people." A co-author of the report again predicts after Harold Washington's election that he "will have to explain to his people that he can't create miracles." In Hartford, Connecticut, the black mayor put it more figuratively when he says: "I find myself in a fishbowl. People are waiting until I make my first big mistake." "Post-autumn harvest liquidators," a term we in China use to describe ill-wishers expecting a peasant's crop failure, are watching the black American mayors.

In spite of the hard time they are having and the pitfalls before them, the increasing number of black mayors is nonetheless an important sign of the progress of black emancipation. When I am leaving Chicago after the election, news spreads around that blacks have been inspired by the victory and are considering nominating a black vice-presidential candidate for 1984. Many people dismiss this as wishful thinking. But then it turns out that Jesse Jackson, a black leader, does win sufficient following to enable him to seek the Democrat nomination.

Chapter XI

THE HOSPITABLE
DEEP SOUTH

According to a pre-arranged itinerary, my short sojourn in Atlanta, Georgia, will be followed by visits in two other Deep South states, Mississippi and Louisiana. "Deep South" is a loose term. A dictionary defines it as "the southeasternmost part of the United States, especially the confederate heartland of South Carolina, Georgia, Alabama and Mississippi." A travel book lists Texas and Louisiana as parts of it. But some Americans tell me that Mississippi and Louisiana are more typical of the region. Climatically the two states should also be included in the "Sun Belt." But they have not prospered as Texas has and remain relatively poor and hence look a bit backward. Politically they tend to be conservative. In religion they are more pious, and are sometimes called the "Bible Belt" with Mississippi as its "buckle." Agriculturally, they belong to the "Cotton Belt."

We in China often describe unusually hospitable people as "warmhearted adherents to ancient ways." This is exactly what I find in the less developed towns and country of the two states. The reception accorded me is warmer because there are fewer Chinese students and visitors in these places. Though I don't envy official delegations who have escorts to help them, traveling as a private citizen is sometimes difficult. "You have parents' care at home but need friends' help going places" — this old phrase encourages Chinese children to be sociable. But I have no friends on this leg of the journey. My husband, as a foreign language publisher, often meets American visitors in Beijing and knows some people in this part of the United

States. But I have always been an "independent" wife and like to act on my own. Now facing difficulties, I have to write a member of the U.S.-China Peoples' Friendship Association in Mississippi whom my husband knows. But the gentleman happens to be ill and he passes on the letter to Margaret McLemore, another USCPFA member. As luck would have it, Mag is coming to Atlanta to attend a southwestern regional conference of the Friendship Association and has reserved a room at the Ladha Hotel, the very place I am staying. We meet as soon as she arrives. It turns out that I have more than "friends' help" because Mag treats me as kindly as she would a younger sister. Later, in our correspondence, I always address her as "my dear elder sister," and she and her husband, Mac, call me "younger sister" — the Chinese way. I fly with Mag from Atlanta to Jackson, the state capital of Mississippi. It is the first time I have a companion on long-distance travel. And how much easier it is now that I don't have to make inquiries at every step!

Pretty soon I hear from Mag's friends that she has a nickname — "iron butterfly." "Iron" means she is full of vigor and never tires in spite of her age. And "butterfly" dates back to her college days when she was chosen as "Queen" of the campus for her beauty and elegance (beauty queens in those years weren't like the flamboyant girls of nowadays, my informants explain). By the time I meet her, the "butterfly" has flown over the vast land of China four times as a tour leader — a testimony both to her vitality and love for my country.

Talking and laughing all the way, we reach Jackson, Mississippi, much sooner, it seems, than I would if I had been traveling by myself. Mag's car is parked at the airport and she drives me to her home at Hazlehurst in Copiah County. It's only thirty miles away and we are there in no time.

For several weeks I have been exploring the rise of the Sun Belt, tracing the ups and downs of the black emancipation movement and delving into unpleasant crime and juvenile deliquency statistics. My study is superficial, to be sure. But it's a nerve-racking job for a foreigner. Now in the two Deep South states, I decide to slow down my pace and leisurely observe the customs and mores of the people. For this purpose, "Iron Butterfly" is a godsend to me.

INTERESTING AND FRIENDLY PEOPLE EVERYWHERE

—Hazlehurst, Shreveport, and New Orleans

It is quite late when we get to Hazlehurst. Mac meets us at the gate. After "glad-to-meet-you" greetings, Mag makes me rest. Next morning at the breakfast table, the amiable couple tell me their life stories. Before retirement Mac was a government employee in charge of agricultural survey and soil conservation in Madison County, north of Copiah. For years he worked outdoors and walked the fields. This is why, I gather, he shows the qualities of a good workingman though he is also a college-educated specialist. Silver-haired now, he still walks at a light and quick pace.

Mag, after graduating from college, worked several years as a teacher of housekeeping in high schools. But there was a feudal-tinged state law barring women from work once they were married (the terrible ban lasted till 1946). This housekeeping teacher didn't want to be a mere housekeeper. So she became a florist in 1945, not only selling flowers but also providing decorations for weddings and funerals. The trade made her weekends busier than her weekdays. She didn't grow flowers herself, but placed orders with New Orleans horticulturists. You can't keep a big stock of the highly perishable goods. Mag had to keep in daily contact with New Orleans growers.

She worked hard for 25 years before finally selling her shop and retiring. Though there is much household work to do, she no longer has to keep a constant watch over the store. Feeling like a bird freed from a cage, she eagerly wanted to go places. So she became a "travel buff" and began touring China, her fondest hobby.

The couple own 235 acres of forested land left by Mac's hard-working parents in the thickly wooded state. They trust their woodland to a black lumberjack who takes care of the trees and shares one-third of the income with them. Quite unusual in business-minded America, their business arrangement is very informal, and they all get along very well together.

There is a big garden around Mac and Mag's house. A plot is reserved for growing fruits and vegetables and much of their jam and preserved fruits are homemade. There is a pool where ducks live and breed on their own. On the side of an antiquated-looking, thatched shanty hang a few metal strips which tinkle softly in the breeze. An elevated, latticed structure looking like a big basket is the place to rest on summer nights, a "cooling pavilion," we would call it. It keeps mosquitoes off, Mac tells me. While we are strolling around, there is a buzz in Mac's pocket. It's a device connected with the home telephone, a must for the couple, who are often out working in the garden. On another occasion Mag walks into my room and passes the device to me for a conversation with her good friend Sandra Vance, a professor of American history in a junior college in neighboring Hinds County, whom she wants me to meet.

Annals of A Small Town

Mac and Mag live in a two-story house. In this forested region most private houses are built of the best kind of timber and are very solid. The structure is an 1860 antique, *antebellum* or pre-Civil War as Americans would say. Mac's father, a vegetable farmer, bought it in August, 1907. It was already dilapidated and had to be thoroughly repaired before the family moved in. Mac was born one month later in the house, the youngest of ten children. All the brothers and sisters grew up to be vegetable farmers with the exception of Mac and his next elder brother who had the luck to go to college. Mac recalls that horses were their draught animals in those years and at most one farmer could work five acres. While speaking, he shows me an account book of 1899 and tells me that the annual cash income for his big family ranged from $200 to $400. His father managed to buy a car in 1920. But he still remembers distinctly how the family rode in a mule-drawn carriage to the church. There was no electric light here before 1945. It was the Great Depression of the 1930s and the "work relief" program introduced by President Franklin D. Roosevelt that created the gigantic TVA (Tennesse Valley Authority) project which finally brought electric power to many Deep South rural areas. There was no running water before 1962. Mac paid $15,000 to have pipes laid to the neighborhood and forty black families in the vicinity also benefited. Now, as I see it, the whole house has been thoroughly modernized and equipped with all kinds of electric appliances and facilities. Changes in their home generally reflect the development of the community. A detailed account could fill an absorbing volume entitled "Annals of A Small Town" — to borrow the name of a popular Chinese novel.

"Don't ask a lady her age and a gentleman his income." I have long since been indoctrinated with this American taboo. From my observation, however, I conclude that Mac and Mag are quite wealthy by Chinese standards and above average in American terms. To be frank, I have had frequent doubts as to whether China will be able to catch up with the American material standard of living. After learning that it has taken only half a century for Hazlehurst to modernize, I feel that my country has a good chance of closing the gap by the middle of the next century — a long-term goal set by our current development strategy. Americans are luckier to have a vast land and smaller population and their natural resources are far from being depleted. But China, too, has immense untapped land, in the great northwest for instance. Besides, the use of modern science and technology can help greatly to quicken the pace of development. The newly emerging small number of "modernized households" in China's poor rural counties may well be "swallows heralding the spring."

Mag shows me the program she has worked out for my visit. I am shocked to find it to be a tight schedule, with visits in the mornings, meetings in the afternoons and concerts in Jackson in the evenings. I have to depart from my Chinese principle of "doing what the host sees fit" and beg her to make drastic cuts. I appreciate her hospitality but insist that I just want to roam around. Hard bargaining results in an agreement to exempt me from all formal appointments with the exception of a cocktail party and a dinner in Jackson which have already been planned.

It's Sunday morning and I ask Mag to take me any place they will go. Of course they are going to church. I tell her I am not a religious believer but would like to accompany them. The couple dress up and we drive to the center of the town, about three miles away. Houses are few and far between and their closest neighbour is almost half a mile off. But they can readily tell who lives in which house. Most residents are old couples, or widows or widowers living alone. Practically all businesses in the town are family undertakings and have few employment opportunities to offer. Young people have left to find jobs elsewhere. Mac and Mag have two daughters and both of them have gone away.

The center of the town is a square with a church of a different denomination at each of the four corners. We enter the Baptist church where a few hundred people have gathered. It looks like everybody knows the others. The atmosphere is solemn and pious. I feel honored when the minister begins his sermon by expressing welcome to "Mrs. Wang from China." The choir of robed boys and girls is well-trained. After hymn-singing, they give a special performance with eight bells of different sizes. The harmonious tune sounds quite like Chinese *Bian* chimes (an assortment of sixty-four 2,400-year-old bells of different tones unearthed in 1978). When the service ends, friends and neighbors exchange greetings and then gradually leave. Religion apart, it's a good kind of social gathering, I think. We take a stroll on the main street. The town is small but complete with a hotel, a bank, a post office, some stores and a public library, too.

"Mass Media"

The next day, Mac and Mag take me to Canton, the Simpson county seat. The name "Canton" is identical with the old English name of the major South China port city now translated as "Guangzhou." The highway is well maintained and we reach the town much sooner than I expect in a rural area.

The first person we meet is Mac's friend Dr. M.G. Trend, a scholar in residence studying economics here. He says he is leaving for Alabama to survey one of the ten poorest counties in the United States. He offers to take me along if I wouldn't mind the hardships. Food and even drinking water will have to be carried in the car. It will take five days to go and come back. I say right away that I would like very much to go. My rash decision apparently worries Mag greatly. She insists that I mustn't go. She is not trying to cover up the seamy side of her country. "I must be absolutely responsible for your safety," she says, leaving no room for bargaining. And I have to yield to my "elder sister."

We then pay a visit to the weekly *Madison County Herald,* because I am a journalist. The paper's editorial office and printing shop are housed in one building, not large but spacious enough for its streamlined staff of thirteen editors and printers. For years I have been involved in foreign language publishing in Beijing and the linotype has always been my close "associate." It's a much more advanced process than setting by hand the thousands of complex Chinese characters in a composing room. But even the linotype has long since become obsolete in Western countries. In the *Herald's* printing shop, I find that the small newspaper has also switched to computerized composing. The noise, the molten lead and the ink-blackened hands are gone for good. It's fortunate that *China Daily* in Beijing, the first national English-language newspaper, edited by one of my Missouri Journalism School classmates, has introduced up-to-date printing process along with modern journalistic expertise. And a number of other printing houses are following suit. Meanwhile, rewarding results have been achieved in applying computer techniques to Chinese language typesetting and printing, and a quiet revolution is going on in the nation's printing industry. Without the policy of opening up to the outside world, the linotype would most probably be enjoying a unique longevity in China.

Madison has a population of 42,000, according to the 1980 census. Two papers are published in the county. The *Herald,* a thick bundle, mostly of advertisements, has a circulation of five-thousand. Another weekly newspaper in a smaller town called Flora, prints three-hundred copies.

Seeing my intense interest in statistics, the host gives me a telephone directory of "Mississippi News Media 1978-1979." "Media," by the way, is a more recent term denoting all forms of mass communications. But I still feel a bit jarred to be called a "media woman" which, if literally translated into Chinese, would sound like an old-type, clownish, matchmaking go-between. Later, I make a count of the entries in this directory and find 123 weeklies, twenty dailies, 150 local radio stations and ten local TV stations — all these in a state of eighty-two counties with a population of only 2,520,000! All of them are privately owned.

Why so many of them and how can they keep going? As I see it, they are used primarily for commercial advertising. Local news is also important but the media can hardly subsist on it. Apart from full-page and smaller ads, newspapers print a lot of "classified ads," including jobs wanted, employment vacancies, sales or lease of apartments or houses, weddings and funerals, lost and found, searches for missing cats or dogs, and other items of daily life. You feel the community pulsating in the columns. The media derive the main part of their income from advertisements, particularly those for local business establishments. Before every weekend you will find in newspapers a greater flourish of ads selling everything from crabmeat to ladies' underwear. Ads for "dime stores" offering special sale prices, that I remember seeing in the 1940s, no longer exist. I have seen, instead, some "dollar stores" — a testimony of continuous inflation.

Reporting local news is another important function of the media. Stories are never lacking because, by American standards, anything unusual makes news. Robberies and burglaries, traffic accidents, divorce suits, property disputes and all sorts of unhappy events often overshadow what we would call in China "positive reports." Sensation seeking, muckraking and even key-hole reporting, the unsavory part of American journalistic tradition, remain strong. But let there be no misunderstanding that American reporters can invent stories and sling mud as they please. The nation has a stringent libel law. The court may award damages that could ruin a journalist financially or even lead to a jail sentence if he should be found guilty of libel.

China used to be information-scarce. Now as a commodity-oriented economy emerges and news media grows, the volume of information is expanding quickly. Even once-banned commercial advertising is making a comeback as a booming business. I do hope, however, that we will not be flooded by an over-abundance of information as the Americans are. Since my college days in Missouri, I have subscribed to the axiom of "all the news that's fit to print" and refused to believe that only "man bites dog" stories make news. As for advertising, I was irked then, as now, by the commercial interruptions thrust into radio or TV programs. But what a pity that some Chinese programers seem to be following the American path!

A Surge of Maternal Love

Mag has arranged for me to visit a private grade school in Copiah County. All its pupils are white. The principal invites me to see a performance by fourth graders for the whole school to celebrate the forthcoming Thanksgiving.

After the performance he asks me to speak to the children. In the plainest possible language, I give a ten-minute talk on China. American custom requires that there be a question-and-answer period after a speech. Unlike Chinese children, the pupils here show no shyness. Many small hands are raised for permission to ask questions. "How many people do you have in your family?" "What is your religion?" "What are China's main industries?".... They bombard me with all sorts of questions. Then a particularly lovely girl stands up and asks: "What are Chinese children like?"

As I look around and see so many cute little faces, a maternal love surges in my heart and I answer as I would talk to my grandchildren: "Now listen. Chinese children are just like you. They wear diapers when they are very small. Then they learn to crawl. Then they toddle. When they grow older, they like to dream about a bright future and a better world." The clever principal chimes in, saying: "Right. Chinese children are like you. You are also dreaming about a bright future and a better world. Let's applaud to thank Madam Wang."

The meeting ends happily and is engraved in my memory. Thanks to the several hundred small "broadcasters," I become a "star" in Hazlehurst on the very next day. When I go to the bank to cash traveler's cheques, the teller smilingly greets me, saying: "You must be Madam Wang from China. My daughter was very happy when she came home from school, telling me about your visit." Then I go to a shop to have a Chinese scissorcut framed as a gift to Mag (it happens to be a large black butterfly with some colored dots), the shopkeeper also recognizes me right away as "Madam Wang from China."

In the afternoon, Mac and Mag drive me to neighboring Hinds County to see the community college, Mac's *alma mater*, and to meet

Professor Vance with whom I have talked over the telephone. The professor leads me to the library to look for some recent reports on American labor. But I can't read, having left my glasses behind. A good-looking young woman kindly helps me to find a number of magazine articles by computer and xeroxes them sheet by sheet for me. Throughout, she wears a charming smile.

When I later admire what a beauty the librarian is, Mac becomes nostalgic and recalls how boys and girls associated with each other when he was attending the college, in the twenties. They were allowed to have only one date a week. After supper on Friday evenings, the boys would line up and be led to the girls' dormitory by a proctor. The girls would also line up and be led out by their housemother. They were free to choose their partners and then led in pairs by the male proctor and housemother to the cinema. They saw a film together and that was all. Everybody had to go back to their dormitory. "The lights were left on during the movie, weren't they?" I ask jokingly. Everybody bursts into laughter. It looks like the American art of love-making has progressed as fast as their technology. What would take years to achieve in the past can now be done in a matter of hours or quicker.

There is a happy by-product of the visit. The college library has recently found a few fading photographs of early students and nobody can identify them. Learning that Mac is an early alumnus, the librarian asks him to help. They happen to be Mac's fellow students and he has such a good memory that he can write out every name without difficulty. A thorny problem is solved and everybody is happy.

Leaving Hinds College, we hurry on to Jackson for a cocktail party attended by more than thirty Friendship Association members. After the party I am invited to a "Dutch treat" dinner in a Chinese restaurant. I don't know why the Dutch are credited for the convenient practice of each paying his own expenses (I am of course exempted, as the guest of honor). The eating place is called "Golden Dragon," a truly golden hall with glistening decorations and the traditional "four calligraphed squares" which are now seldom seen in China — four red boards fixed on a horizontal beam inscribed with the words *fu* (felicity), *lu* (high position), *shou* (longevity) and *xi* (happiness).

After dinner I am invited to speak. Americans are not accustomed to the type of four-hour reports, divided into sections one, two, three, and four, that we often hear in China. Many times I have been invited to "report" on China at universities or on other occasions. Friends advise me to limit my talk to thirty minutes and leave more time for questions at the end. They also advise that the talk should have personal touches. Usually I give a brief account of the 1911 Revolution which ended the centuries-old monarchy in China, the 1919 "May Fourth Movement" for democracy and science which heralded the rise of Chinese communism, and other major events leading up to the nationwide liberation in 1949. Some personal experiences are helpful for understanding. For instance, how I began fleeing from gunfire as an unborn baby, as my mother moved from place to place to seek safety from the frequent wars fought between warlords backed by foreign imperialists, and how as a college student I joined in patriotic movements when Japan was about to conquer my country.

The Americans are a pragmatic people, they like "human interest" and detest abstract generalizations (I am of course not talking about scholarly seminars or official functions). I do not mean to be trite in saying that the Jackson meeting ends "in a very friendly and cordial atmosphere."

A Poor Farm Family

On another day Mag arranges for her friend, Mrs. Louise Reagan, to accompany me on a visit with the official in charge of Copiah County's agricultural survey and soil conservation. I simply want to get an idea of what Mac's work is like by observing the same post in Madison County. The official, a very friendly person, is Gene Martin. On a wheel-shaped slide projector, one image after another of land areas appear on a TV screen. Martin can tell me instantly what the vegetation is, how it is growing, and whether the trees are old or young. The photographs were taken by professional photographers who specialize in aerial photography, and from planes piloted by commercial pilots. The high degree of specialization and division of labor is a characteristic of the American society. The aerial photography, Gene says, is done at a 1.5-mile altitude. The pictures are clear and precise as the acreages can be readily calculated with a computer. Photographs taken by satellites can serve the same purpose but the acreage won't be as accurate. Mac has told me that he had to drive or even walk to all parts of the county to make surveys. Hearing this, Martin says with a shrug: "Ah, that's old stuff now."

Mrs. Reagan tells Martin that Mag wouldn't let me go to Alabama to see the poor farmers there. "Oh, that's easy. Come on, I'll take you to see one," he says. Knowing the land like the palm of his hand, Martin drives me straight to a ramshackle house about fifteen miles away from his office. A black couple, John and Mary, are owners of this log cabin built there on a plot strewn with wild grass and littered with garbage. They are quite indifferent when Martin introduces me. We enter their home and find a worn sofa to be the main furniture in what might be called a living room. There is a gas stove in the kitchen, but the place is scattered with used cans and odds and ends. They have a telephone, a TV set and two old automobiles. You couldn't call them poor farmers in China, where household durables are taken as a measurement of prosperity. But they are in fact terribly poor. Both in their seventies, they have to work as young people do, raising cattle, hogs and poultry and growing vegetables and sugarcane. They must work constantly to keep one step ahead of complete destitution. They are busy pressing sugar cane, having neither the time nor the mood to talk with me and only make terse replies to my questions. In pre-revolution China, "thirty *mu* (five acres) of land plus a cow" used to be the fond dream of a peasant family. John and Mary are faring much better than that. But toiling endlessly at their age is dispiriting. And what will happen if they fall ill or become too old to work? I feel sad at the thought and don't want to bother them any more. When we are leaving, the old man suddenly dashes out of the house and runs straight to his car. As he starts the engine, he tells us that his brother living near-by has phoned for help to halt a stampede of his cattle.

In the evening, the McLemores give a dinner to friends including me and Professor Sandra. Vance of Hinds College and her husband. The middle-aged couple are elegantly dressed. Mr. Vance, Mag tells me, is the owner of a clothing store. We chat freely after dinner. Deeply religious, Sandra asks me who, if not God, had created man. I tell her frankly that I believe in Darwinism and in the theory that labor created man and distinguished man from animals. She asks further who then created the universe and the earliest form of life. I explain that I believe in materialism and hold that the whole universe is cognizable. Though man's knowledge is as yet very limited, he will unveil the secrets gradually. There is no ground for agnosticism. "Haven't you Americans done very well in broadening man's vision and knowledge?" I ask. We both find the discussion so absorbing that Mr. Vance has to point to his watch, reminding Sandra it's midnight. My discourse on atheism in the very "buckle of the Bible Belt" is a good measure of American open-mindedness and their tolerance of differing views — a trait I have found on many occasions.

A Gala Thanksgiving Day

My visit in Hazlehurst culminates on the last Thursday of November — Thanksgiving Day. This is a peculiarly American festival of popular rejoicing. Both Thanksgiving and Christmas are occasions for family get-togethers. A family Mag knows very well invites us to join in their celebrations. Their house, called Shelton Estate, is antique looking but has modern facilities. Coming into the large living room, I notice a portrait of an elderly couple hanging prominently on the front wall. Bette Reno, our hostess, tells me that they were her parents. Like many other early settlers, they came here, felled trees and built a cattle farm. They sold milk to buy bricks and eventually managed to erect the house. Later they acquired four hundred acres of forested land and by hard work created their "estate."

Most early immigrants raised big families and the couple had eight daughters and two sons. They died many years ago and their second-eldest son has also died. With the exception of the eldest sister (born in 1907), who is not able to be here, all the siblings have travelled from different places to Hazlehurst for the Thanksgiving reunion, bringing along their offspring. It is a grand gathering of thirty people, old and young. Bette says jokingly that her generation has lagged far behind their parents in childbirth. "The ten of us have only seventeen children and the next generation will probably give a poorer performance," she says. The higher the level of economic and cultural development, the lower the birth rate — this is almost a rule.

Merry laughter rings in the house as the relatives, holding glasses of wine or other drinks, chat in small groups. I am of course busier, shaking hands and giving holiday greetings to everybody. The dinner begins. All adults sit at a long table and children are free to eat wherever they like. Mrs. Reno says the prayer. All listen attentively and then say "amen" together to thank God for the blessings. Food is plentiful and varied, and there is of course a turkey. A lady sitting at my side, one of the eight sisters, tells me of the hardships in the early days. Their parents, I say, don't look like poor people in the portrait. She explains that in those days people had photographs taken only once or twice in a lifetime and they would dress up in their best for the rare occasion. They could hire garments from the photo studio if they didn't have good clothes. Another sister recalls that when boys came to see them on Sundays, the first thing they would do was to help the eight girls clear the huge pile of laundry. "They worked real hard," she says. Why? "The earlier we finished the chore, the more time we would have to go out together." "It must have been a wilderness around here — what was the fun in going out?" I can't help asking. She smiles as shyly as a young girl and answers, "We would go to the woods."

"However lovely, a banquet must come to an end," as the Chinese saying goes. When we take leave, Mag suggests that I should see some less fortunate people. She drives me to meet one of her neighbors — a 104-year-old black woman. Sitting in a sofa, the centenarian speaks fairly clearly. Her house, not at all crammed, is equipped with the ordinary kinds of home appliances. The living room, however, is a mess, littered with clothes and objects. Her daughter-in-law has had a fierce row with her husband and is packing to leave. Intermittently, the old lady tells me something about her childhood. She had to start working when she was very small. The stove she worked at was too high and she had to stand on a bench to do the cooking. The story reminds me of the early tribulations of the American blacks. President Lincoln issued the Emancipation Proclamation in 1863, only fifteen years earlier than the birth of the old lady. At that time she and the other blacks were just emerging from slavery.

Then Mag takes me to see the black man who manages her forest. The family is doing well. Apart from working for the McLemores, the man is employed at a gas station and has another part-time job. In his younger days, he had wandered about the country as a vagrant worker in search of a high-wage job. But eventually he had to come back to Hazlehurst, convinced that going from rags-to-riches was just a dream, and there was no place like home. A robust man, he works hard at three jobs to keep the family going. Though his wife, a seamstress, has been unemployed for some time, she manages the family finances so well that the eldest daughter, one of six children, will soon go to college.

The whole family is pleased with the unexpected visit of a guest from faraway China. After having photographs taken with me, they ask me to give each of them a Chinese name. He is Carey Fultz and the wife is called Annie May. So I write for him the Chinese characters Fu Kairui (Fu the Triumphant and Lucky), for her Fu Anni (Fu the Peaceful Girl), and similar auspicious names for all the six children.

When we get back to Mag's house, I find I have left my bag with several hundred dollars in cash and more in traveler's cheques at "Fu's" home. Mag isn't worried at all, saying that she will go to pick it up the next day. Barely has she finished speaking when we hear an automobile drawing up at the door. All eight members of the "Fu family" have come in a station wagon to return my purse. Beaming with smiles, Lao Fu (Old Fultz, an affectionate Chinese form of address though he is only middle-aged) says that the whole family is glad to find an excuse for an outing, which makes their Thanksgiving a happier day.

Since my departure from Hazlehurst, I have been corresponding with the McLemores. They continue calling me "younger sister." Unlike Mag, Mac doesn't like to travel. But, in order to pay a return visit to the land of his "younger sister," Mac makes up his mind to fly with "Iron Butterfly" to China in 1983. I don't have a big *antebellum* house in which to receive them, but the reunion at my humble Beijing home after a roast duck dinner at the Quanjude Restaurant is so happy that they decide to skip the widely praised dance drama "Legend of the Silk Road" for more talk. We chat on and on till the chauffer waiting outside gets bored and pulls a long face at me when I see them off.

Fragrant Hill and Dianchi Lake

My next stop is Shreveport. The bus crosses the "Father of Rivers" into the neighboring state of Louisiana. What I see is a thickly wooded but thinly populated land. The bus is a much better transport for visitors because it zigzags through as many towns as possible to pick up more passengers. I find the towns looking poorer than in most of the other states. A sorry aspect of the otherwise interesting trip is the toilet facilities at bus stops. Lack of toilet paper or washbasin, and poor sanitary conditions make the lavatories unusually unpleasant in comparison with other parts of the country. Once in a while I see billboards of wayside inns prominently advertising "clean toilets," showing that the lack of proper facilities is perhaps more a rule than exception in this area.

Shreveport is the second largest city in Louisiana, with a population of 200,000. M.I.T. Professor Robinson has written to one of his old acquaintances, "Serv" Severinghause, asking him to take care of me in the city. Serv has sent a prompt reply to me, saying that both his parents had taught in China in the 1920s and he himself had served in Chongqing, Kunming and other Chinese cities for two years (October 1943 to October 1945) during the war. He is an engineer and his chief assignment as a U.S. Army major was to help build an arms factory at the edge of the Dianchi Lake near Kunming, in southwestern China's Yunnan Province. This makes me feel closer to him because my husband was brought up at the edge of the lake and he always talks about its beauty. Serv worked hard on the project in the belief that the weapons produced would be used to fight the Japanese. But the situation took a drastic turn with the end of the anti-Japanese war when the Kuomintang hurled its American-equipped forces against the Communist-led areas. Washington then gave full backing to Chiang Kai-shek in the fratricidal war. Serv recalls in his letter that he had talked with a colleague in China who later became an American corporation president. "I told him: 'Whatever the pressures, politics and positions at high levels, I do not feel there are serious differences between the people of China and the people of the U.S.A. They simply need to know each other. Bill (Serv's colleague) suggested I should be ambassador to China, thus showing his appreciation even though we both knew it was an unreal suggestion." What a pity, I think, that the bellicose Major General Patrick Hurley was made U.S. ambassador to China and General Joseph Stilwell, a good soldier who knew America's best interests, was relieved as commander of U.S. forces in China. Ordinary Americans like Serv were wiser.

Serv enclosed in his letter to me a detailed resume about himself, so I know much about him when we first meet at the bus depot. At sixty-two, he is already silver-haired and wears an equally white beard drooping almost to his chest. He looks a bit somber and doesn't talk much. Without any explanation he drives me through some dilapidated streets littered with waste paper. Only when we are at his home does he tell me that he has chosen to let me see the black ghettos, a district known rightly as "Bottom." The downtown center is of course a flashy place but I have probably seen enough of that elsewhere, he explains.

Serv has a house of his own and is apparently a middle-class man. But he is quite unfortunate because his wife, Sally, was struck with breast cancer in 1959. After a major operation, she was weak and somehow a hole developed in her lung. Now she can only sit around or lie down all the time. All their children have left to work in other places. It can well be imagined how lonely the old couple are.

Sally, too, has deep roots in China. Her father, Dr. Peter W. Claassen, was a biology professor at Cornell University and was invited to China in 1924 to help inaugurate a biology department at the National Qinghua University, my alma mater. Sally was six at the time and went with her father to Beijing, where she lived for one year. She recounts for me her fond memories of a visit to the Great Wall in a creaking mule-cart, and asks me if the giant bronze Sleeping Buddha at the Wofo Temple in the Fragrant Hills and that pair of Buddha's jumbo shoes are still there. I can sense her nostalgia for those happy days and describe for her as well as I can how the Great Wall and the Fragrant Hills have been renovated and are now bustling every day with Chinese and foreign tourists — no longer the secluded places of the early years. She then says that she was told the Sleeping Buddha would wake up some day, put on his jumbo shoes and walk out to spread blessings to the unhappy mundane world. She asks me if I believe that. "I only wish I could," I reply. "Ah, you're not as good a Chinese as I am," Sally says with a rare smile. "I believe the Buddha will stand up and you don't!" She further says that she had read in the press that the first Red Guards sprang up in Qinghua University. "I am sorry for that, for Qinghua is the only Chinese place I know well." The vandalizing Red Guards, in fact, first appeared in the Qinghua Middle School, but the university soon caught up and became one of the worst dungeons of "rebels" in the " cultural revolution."

Every morning Serv prepares for me a pot of Chinese tea and keeps it warm with a typically Chinese padded wrapper. I find him spending most of his time perusing one newspaper after another on a big table in the dining room, and ask him if he is doing some research. "Research?" he answers with a wry smile. " I'm reading the classified ads to see if I can find the right job. But who cares to employ a man of 62?"

Serv became a mechanical engineer after graduating from Cornell in the forties and later earned a master's degree in business management at Harvard. The resumé he has mailed me is one of many ready copies prepared for the purpose of seeking employment. Demobilized from the army, he worked in administrative posts with the Ford Company and a number of big hospitals and research institutes, and the references, according to the resumé, are quite favorable. Later he moved on to become associate director of the North Louisiana Health Systems Agency, Inc. For some reason he was compelled to resign in 1982, prior to the usual retirement age of 65. He is anxious to find a job, I surmise, not for financial reasons but because of loneliness. Besides, his "old companion" (the Chinese way of calling ageing spouses, after the popular saying "mating up young and keeping company old") is so sick. Small wonder Serv always looks so downcast.

The strange thing is that I find on an open piece of ground outside the house a yacht mounted on supports like in a shipyard. The body of the boat, Serv tells me, is custom-built according to his design. And whenever he has time, he climbs into it to install mechanical and electrical equipment and build such facilities as a bath and toilet. It's a hobby, he says. Besides, he can sell it when it's finished.

Taciturn Serv is nonetheless a good host. He takes me to visit a college and meet a black professor, see a high school, call his friends at their homes, and look around in the suburbs. The city is expanding, Serv says. The forests on its outskirts will soon give way to new buildings.

To express my appreciation for their hospitality, I invite Serv and Sally to dinner at the best Chinese restaurant in town. The place is called "Peking Restaurant." The Chinese waitress, learning that I am a true native of Beijing, is all the more obliging. I ask her in the extraceremonious, pre-revolution way: "May I know your venerable family name and your fairyland-like native place?" She says she is from Taiwan. "From which part of the country did your family move to Taiwan?" I ask further. "Sorry, I have to find out from father." The girl goes to the kitchen and comes back a few moments later to tell me that the place is Kaiping County, Guangdong Province. Kaiping is far away from Beijing, but I am glad to know that Chinese from Taiwan don't gnash their teeth at the name "Peking" as the Taiwan lobbyists would like people to believe. We are all Chinese after all.

When I prepare to leave Shreveport, Serv and Sally want me to write something as a memento. There is no Chinese writing brush and I leave the following words with a pen: "May the Chinese and American people's friendship be evergreen! For Serv and Sally whom I shall always remember." When shaking hands to say goodbye, all three of us feel a bit sad. The Tang Dynasty poet Du Fu's famous farewell verse passes through my mind: "After this parting, mountains will separate us. None is sure of what will happen, in this world of caprices."

Lord Guan Goes U.S.A.

The New Orleans-bound bus, after leaving Shreveport, races southeastward on a freeway cutting diagonally across the state of Louisiana. Forests abound but habitations are scarce all along the way. After a three-hundred-mile ride I arrive at the historic city of New Orleans (pop. 560,000) near the mouth of the Mississippi. Mag McLemore's sister has a friend here who is willing to help me. The man is Tom Deane and his wife is Maud. They appear to be quite comfortably situated and, unlike the Severinghause couple, are very active. Many curios are displayed in their house because they own a shop in town selling antiques and handicrafts. Tom is straightforward and tells me that the key to his business is to buy cheap and sell dear. He shows me an interesting example — a baby stroller which can be folded up as a high chair or converted into a rocking chair. It was made of high-quality wood by master carpenters in the early days of pioneers when people built home, family, and everything to last. Tom says that he won't sell it now but will keep it for use by his grandchildren. Only after that will he put it on sale. The older it gets, the more money he'll get out of it.

On the evening of my arrival, Tom and Maud take me to a pre-Christmas "potluck" at Magazine Street ("magazine" is the French word for shop). What's "potluck?" The *American Heritage Dictionary of the English Language* modestly defines it as "whatever food happens to be available for a meal, especially when offered to a guest." There are more than one hundred participants in this one, mostly businessmen, at the gathering in a French restaurant. Everybody brings along his or her best home-cooked food. So much so that it becomes a grand feast, a real exposition of American cuisine. The restaurant provides only the cutlery and drinks, which you buy at a counter. People gather in small groups, chatting while they eat. There is a piano in the banquet hall. A lady volunteers to play and many pairs start dancing. The atmosphere is easy and merry. I move around, shaking hands and meeting people. All of them are very friendly to a complete stranger like me. As a guest at the "potluck," I would change its definition to "all the best foods available for a banquet." There is so much to eat that a big turkey contributed by someone lies untouched and unnoticed. A lady insists that I must taste it. Americans must eat turkey for Thanksgiving and Christmas, mustn't they? I ask. So both of us cut a thin slice — just to make the forlorn bird feel a bit useful.

The next day is Sunday. Tom and Maud take me to the famous French Quarter. As I noted earlier Louisiana and an immense chunk of territory adjacent to it were bought from Napoleon at a dirt-cheap price. New Orleans, the state capital, has the strongest French atmosphere with much French architecture and a large number of ethnic French-Americans. There is a fair every Sunday in the part of the town called the French Quarter. It's a beehive of activity, like Beijing's Spring Festival fairs. At street bazaars there are stalls vending all sorts of goods. Musicians are playing not for money but for the fun of it. They keep on bowing and blowing even when there is no audience. There are artists drawing portraits of visitors. They do it very fast and charge only a little money. In front of some restaurants amateur bands are playing, and many passers-by dance to the music. I feel good to see some very old men and women twisting and turning together with toddlers, and marvel at the easygoing and fun-loving Americans. We happen to meet a friend of Tom's at a stall selling old magazines. The man is a professor of economics and the vending is a kind of hobby. He tells me that business is brisk. The Bell Systems, for one, are offering good money for all their old advertisements. There are people who, for the money or pleasure, sift through every old magazine for such advertisements. Some others are collecting pictures of Shirley Temple, the former child star who is even well-known in China. She was once so popular that practically every slick magazine carried her picture in one way or another. As an adult, Shirley Temple became American ambassador to the United Nations. All sorts of collectors are the scholarly vendor's customers.

When we get home, Tom leads me into a storeroom and asks for my help in identifying some of his oriental commodities. I immediately notice a Chinese statue as tall as a writing desk. "Phoenix eyes, silkworm-shaped brows, a face as red as a date and lips as crimson as painted" — such is the description of the warrior hero, Guan Yunchang in the classic novel, *Romance of the Three Kingdoms,* known to every Chinese household. There is no mistaking that the statue is him, moved here from some out-of-the-way Chinese temple. It doesn't look like an ancient work. In the briefest way, I tell Tom some stories about the man popularly called Guangong (Lord Guan) — how he, a loyal general, hung up the gold and high official seal bestowed on him by a rival kingdom and left to resume service for his cherished cause; how he, a brave warrior, didn't blink his eyes when a surgeon filed his bones to remove the poison of an arrowhead (anesthesia was of course out of the question seventeen centuries ago), and so on. Guangong's legendary virtues were so valued by subsequent generations that temples were built all over the country, even in some remote hamlets, to honor him. Doing a bit of advertising on my part, I suggest to Tom that he order one of the *Panda Books* published in Beijing which contains an English abridgement of the *Romance*. Tom is very pleased. With a few interesting anecdotes to tell the customers, he will have a better chance of selling the statue, and Lord Guan on his visit to the United States will make more money.

In America, you have to work to please customers. If you always shake your head when the buyer asks you questions as, unfortunately, some Chinese salespersons do, you'll go out of business and there is no "communal pot" anywhere you can eat from. ("Communal pot" is a popular way of describing the fool-proof wages employees in public enterprises get, whatever their performance.) Then Tom shows me some Japanese ceramics. I happened to have stayed in Japan for a few months in my young days and still know some traces of the Japanese language. With that little bit of knowledge, I am able to help Tom find in books the origins of that particular type of Japanese ware, thus enabling him to identify all the vases, bowls and pots by the characters on their bases.

To thank Tom and Maud, I invite them to dinner at a famous Chinese restaurant. We make a detour to see the mouth of the Mississippi River. It is as wide as a sea and you can hardly see the other shore, shrouded in a haze rising over rolling waves. The "Father of Rivers" is truly mighty as the name implies. Suddenly I remember the description in a history book of early settlers sailing south from the Ohio River into the Mississippi. "Hi-o, away we go, floating down the river on the Ohio," the boatmen often sang in husky voices as they moved on to open up new frontiers. Time flowed away swiftly and the land changed fast. Erstwhile virgin forests and primeval marshes have become prosperous cities and well-developed land within a short historical period. American achievements show that capitalism, in spite of the human sweat and blood it demanded for its growth, is nonetheless a great leap forward in the course of development of human society. It's like our Great Wall which, built with slave labor and causing so many Mengjiangnu-type* human tragedies, remains nonetheless a historic wonder that can clearly be seen from the moon.

MORE ABOUT AMERICAN ABCs
— From Thanksgiving to Uncle Sam

My chief purpose in the two "Deep South" states is to learn about American customs and mores. Throughout the visit I deliberately avoid discussing political and social problems, still less the worrisome international issues. Chats after dinner or tea have been very interesting and informative. Here I shall piece together what I have heard and seen in the two states and elsewhere into a chapter called "More About American ABCs," because a primary aim of my book is to provide Chinese readers rudimentary knowledge of America.

Legal or Public Holidays

The pleasant Thanksgiving Day I spent in Hazlehurst prompts me to look more into American holidays or "festivals," as we would say in China. First of all let me trace the origins of Thanksgiving. On 1 December 1620, a group of English pilgrims crossing the Atlantic landed at Plymouth in what is now the state of Massachusetts. Many of them succumbed to the bitter cold and hunger and only about half of the one hundred immigrants survived to see the next spring. They were lucky to meet a kind-hearted Indian named Squanto who taught them how to hunt, fish and grow corn for subsistence in the wilderness. One day in October 1621, when the autumn harvest was in, they gathered to thank God for his blessing, with singing, dancing

---

*There is a temple at the eastern seaside end of the Great Wall honoring a woman named Mengjiangnu. Legend has it that her husband was impressed into the slave labor force to build the Great Wall only a few days after their marriage. Years passed and the man never returned, so Mengjiangnu went to the foot of the 10,000-*li*-long wall, looking for him. There she learned that her husband had been killed in an accident. She sobbed and sobbed till part of the wall collapsed, and she jumped into the sea and drowned herself. The episode has been passed down through generations in folklore and folksongs known all over China.

and feasting on wild turkey and other foods. Then in 1623, a day of fasting and prayer in the midst of a drought was changed into a day of thanksgiving for the coming of rain during the prayers. This type of spontaneous celebration gradually spread to other places on the new continent. But it was not until 1864 that President Lincoln formally designated a Thanksgiving Day. Finally it evolved into a public holiday on the last Thursday of every November. Turkey has long since been domesticated but remains a favorite component of the holiday menu.

Thanksgiving is closely followed by Christmas, which falls on 25 December, and is celebrated by Christians worldwide as the anniversary of the birth of Jesus. Non-Christians in America also enjoy the festival with equal zest. The holiday season begins soon after Thanksgiving when shops vie with each other in offering all sorts of innovative Christmas gifts. Post offices are probably busier than the shops as hundreds of millions of Christmas cards and gift parcels pour in to be mailed elsewhere. It is also a season of the greatest flow of traffic as people travel long distances for family reunions.

Days before the festival, you'll see twinkling colored lights and beautifully tinselled Christmas trees. *Jingle Bells* , perhaps the best-known American song in China, is heard everywhere. "Jingle bells, jingle bells, jingle all the way/Oh what fun it is to ride in a one-horse open sleigh." The tune is so merry that many Chinese youth unfamiliar with its origins sing it in the heat of summer. There also are the sweet lyrics of a song for children which I have come to love since my first visit in the forties. "Better not shout, better not cry, better not pout — I'm telling you why, Santa Claus is coming to town."

Formal celebrations begin on 24 December, Christmas Eve. Exquisitely wrapped gifts bought by family members for each other are placed under a Christmas tree in the living room. What's inside the packages is kept strictly secret until after the family dinner. When they are finally opened, you hear exclamations like "how beautiful!" "how gorgeous!" and "how lovely!" as husbands and wives, parents and children, kith and kin hug and kiss each other. Americans express their joys and feelings much more freely in comparison with the reserved ways of Chinese holiday celebrations. Festivities last into the small hours. Small children still believe in the old tale that the Christmas gifts have been brought by Santa Claus who descends into every home through the chimney. But when they grow a little older they invariably ask why Santa's long white beard and red gown aren't scorched by the chimney smoke.

Christmas time continues through New Year's Day and is the happiest festival, equivalent to the Chinese Lunar New Year, now called Spring Festival. The American scene changes fast but I have found Christmas celebrations remaining much the same except that gifts have become more sophisticated and expensive, and commercial advertising has gained greater ingenuity and higher pressure.

In addition to Thanksgiving, Christmas, and New Year's Day, there are seven more legal holidays for the whole nation. They are: Independence Day (July 4, equivalent to our National Day on October 1), Memorial Day (the last Monday in May), Veterans Day (November 11), Columbus Day (the second Monday of October), President's Day (for the birthdays of George Washington and Abraham Lincoln, the third Monday of February), Labor Day (the first Monday of September) and Martin Luther King's Birthday (the third Monday of January, which will be observed beginning in 1986). The holidays are so arranged that each gives people a "long weekend" of three days including Saturdays and Sundays. Government agencies and commercial establishments have their own schedules which vary from place to place. Apart from the ten federal legal public holidays, there are a lot more days observed either nationwide or in different states. But people usually have to work on these days.

Soon after my arrival in America in May, 1982, I came across Mother's Day (the second Sunday in May). Many shop windows in New York City displayed goods with the sign: "Mom will like it." Even used goods stores were trying to cash in on the occasion. I saw in one such store a set of old furniture consisting of a long table and six chairs. They looked quite commonplace but were priced at $1,500! In people's homes I saw greeting cards to mothers displayed over the fireplace as well as flowers, bouquets, and fancy gifts sent by children. It dawned over me that the long list of American holidays has an important economic role to play — stimulating consumption which, unfortunately, has further promoted commercialization and consumerism.

From New York City I went to Boston. Another holiday, Memorial Day, fell on Monday, 31 May. For three days beginning Friday, the post office was closed and even steet cleaners stopped working. My friend Rita Gould accompanied me to the town of Natick in the southern part of the city to watch a parade. Led by veterans of the two world wars riding in open cars (only a few World War I veterans are still living), the marching column was composed of grade school boys and girls wearing scout-type uniforms, and then high school students beating drums and blowing trumpets. Many spectators lined the street in silent tribute and the atmosphere was quite solemn. It was a good form of patriotic education, I thought.

Rita then took me to the cemetery where her husband was buried. A small American flag had been planted on the tombstone. Rita told me that Gould had served as an army doctor during the war. Silently she removed the wild grass growing up on the grave. We proceeded further to a larger cemetery where a long row of small flags was planted on the graves. On Memorial Day, Rita said, there was a flag for every dead soldier who had served during the war, not necessarily those killed in action.

Later when I went to Weld, a tiny town up north in Maine, I saw a stone tablet in front of the town library on which were engraved the names of all the town's veterans, twenty-four in World War I and fifty in the second. A saddening high percentage for a town of four-hundred people! May man be wise enough to avoid another holocaust which might wipe out all of Weld and millions of other towns, I prayed. Memorial Day is more or less similar to China's "Clear and Bright Festival" on April 5 every year, an occasion for people to pay homage to all the deceased, particularly revolutionary martyrs.

Then on June 20, I came upon Father's Day (the third Sunday of every June) in New York City. Shop windows now feature many "Dad will like it" signs, while a deluge of greeting cards and gift parcels give post offices another hard time. Journalists, too, rack their brains to produce stories marking the occasion. On the previous evening, Hugh Dean, a writer and friend of China since the 1930s, and his wife, Beverly, took me to see an open-air show at Lincoln Center. While I was watching the colored fountains after the show, three women suddenly went up to Hugh. I saw spotlights shining and microphones thrust at his face. What was happening? I walked toward Hugh and when I got there the three women were saying thanks and leaving in a hurry. They were reporters, Hugh told me, and were asking fathers what they would like to be given on their day. Hugh answered that he hoped his children would each give him a phone call. The next day we saw on the TV screen Hugh and a number of other fathers making wishes. "Everything in America costs money," I joked. "A.T. & T. should pay you for the advertising."

July 4 happened to be on a Sunday in 1982, so Monday was made a public holiday. It was another "long weekend" for travel, outing, camping and all sorts of merrymaking. I was visiting Professor Philip Foner and his wife Roslyn in remote Maine country and saw no celebrations. When I came back to Boston, friends told me that there had been a grand display of fireworks for Independence Day and I felt sorry that I had missed it. Then in September, I saw the circus-like Labor Day celebrations in New York City.

October 31 was the eve of the once-religious All Saints or All Hallows Day, informally observed with masquerades and carved pumpkins. I did not bother to find out why there are the pumpkins because this year's Halloween, the eve of All Saints Day, was rather grim. Halloween used to be a traditional occasion for children to play pranks. They are allowed to go to neighbors or relatives to beg for treats, or to play a trick, called "treat or trick." It is a different kind of children's day from our June 1, when many public activities are arranged for them and even infants are given something new to suck on. I was in Iowa City at the time of Halloween. Excitement was dampened by continous reports of the poisoning of Tylenol, a painkiller found in almost every household. Some criminals had added deadly cyanide to the medicine, causing the abrupt deaths of seven people. They were trying to extort a huge sum from Johnson and Johnson, the Tylenol manufacturer, and threatening to poison more if their demand was not met. The horrible story hit the headlines and was prominently featured in TV reports for days on end. Johnson and Johnson had to take back all its unsold stock for a thorough examination and reintroduce Tylenol capsules in new safety-sealed packaging. The Tylenol trouble might be over, but who could tell that no other pill or food had been poisoned? There was public nervousness to the point that "every bush and tree looks like an enemy" as the Chinese saying goes. And things were made worse as reports circulated that some older youngsters had hidden tiny pins in cakes to "treat" their little friends. Parents had to take extra care of their kids, adding a grim note to this year's Halloween.

I spent St. Valentine's Day at Stanford University in Palo Alto, California. It falls on February 14, a day for lovers because it was believed in old times that on this day birds began to choose their mates. Incidentally, sweethearts or loving couples in China are also called "birds flying wing to wing" or "mandarin ducks locking their necks." But non-lovers also benefit from the day. I had happened to have arranged an interview with Professor Robert Hess, a specialist in educational psychology. He came to the office with several bags of chocolates for his secretary, assistant and student, my friend Zhang Zhimei, and one for me too. The sweets were all heart-shaped and wrapped in golden papers. And heart-shaped decorations were seen everywhere in shop windows advertising all imaginable gifts for lovers. These festivals make me feel strongly that Americans are shrewd businessmen, though they often complain that the Japanese are the smarter ones.

Then there is another religious festival called Easter — the first Sunday following the first full moon after each spring equinox, usually in April. Dyed or painted eggs or other egg-shaped objects are traditional Easter gifts. April 1, or Fool's Day, is better known in China and many believe that the day is widely observed in sensation-loving America as an occasion to pull strange tricks. Actually it is not. But friends have told me that some small town papers may print an amusing phony story that will harm nobody.

In the American "melting pot," many ethnic minorities still keep their own festivals intact. Chinese-Americans, for instance, observe the Lunar New Year, or Spring Festival, as warmly as in China itself and perhaps with greater ceremony because they still retain many pre-revolution customs.

In late April, 1983, I was in Chicago and was invited to observe Passover with a Jewish family. All the children and grandchildren were there, making a total of eighteen, plus me. Tradition requires that they eat unleavened bread. At the dinner table the family head took the lead in reading a passage of Hebrew Scripture and then passed the book on for others to read. People who don't know the language may read a passage in English instead. I did accordingly but knew little of what I read. The hosts told me that when their ancestors fled from Egypt to escape slavery, it was the unleavened bread that saved their lives, in the same way as turkey helped to save the English pilgrims. Passover is a grand festival which may last seven to eight days.

State, Counties, Cities and Towns

On my American journey I usually hop from city to city. But in less developed Mississippi, I have roamed from county to county — Copiah, Madison, Hinds, etc. Actually all America, with the exception of Alaska, which comprises twenty-three "divisions," is divided into counties. Vast Texas, for instance, consists of 254 counties, while tiny Delaware has three. What do the counties do? I have asked some Americans. But nobody seems able to give me a precise answer. A jocular professor shrugs his shoulders and tells me, "You've to go to the county to find a court or to sit in a jail. And that's all." I have delved into a few books but it would be tedious to go into details.

Briefly, America is a highly decentralized country. Each state manages the government within its boundaries. Every state has legislative, executive, and judicial branches modeled after the federal government. All of them have a separate senate and a house of representatives with the sole exception of Nebraska, which somehow has a unitary legislature. Within this general framework, however, no state is identical with another in the structure and jurisdiction of its government. Many things are perfectly legal in some states but explicitly prohibited in others. Gambling is an example. It is illegal in most places but not in Nevada where it is big business, and a main source of state revenue. In the forties I knew that people would go to Nevada for a convenient, time and money-saving divorce or marriage. It's still true today.

Another example is smoking. While I was riding a bus from San Francisco up north along the Pacific Coast, the driver warned through his megaphone as soon as we crossed the state boundary that Oregon laws forbid smoking in buses. The driver himself happened to be a habitual smoker. Every now and then he would announce a five-minute stop, to the delight of the smoking passengers and the chagrin of the others. Then when we entered the state of Washington further to the north, the driver didn't forget to announce: "Ladies and gentlemen, now you may smoke."

Smoking in America is no longer what it was in the forties, when professors and students could puff freely in some classrooms. Public awareness of the health hazard has been growing. Planes and restaurants now are usually divided into smoking and non-smoking sections. Trains and buses often require smokers to sit in the rear — a welcome new form of segregation. If you light up a cigarette while standing in a line, don't get offended if people glower at you, for you more than deserve it. No American would offer his guests cigarettes except perhaps those frequent China visitors who have assimilated Chinese ways. I only wish the Oregon law could be introduced all over China to stop the 300 million smokers puffing to pollute the air and slowly kill themselves.

Though, geographically, cities and towns are situated within counties and some bigger ones may even straddle counties, they usually govern themselves independently of the counties. Big cities are by themselves administrative entities. As three-fourths of the American population lives in cities or in suburban and outlying towns, there indeed isn't much left for the counties to do. But, I am told, cities and towns usually have neither court nor jail while the counties have both. That's why it's said that you have to go to the county seat when being sued in court or when sent to prison. The situation is vastly different from China with its pyramid structure of the central government, the provinces (or municipalities), prefectures, counties (or small cities) and then townships (formerly people's communes), each level governing the lower ones in all spheres of activity. Though emphasis is now being laid on decentralization, it would be altogether unimaginable for any particular province in China to pass a law banning smoking in public places, or legalizing gambling or expediting divorces.

Cities predominate in American life. New York City well-illustrates this dictum. For example: Only seven out of fifty states have a larger population than that metropolis. Consequently, it's often said that the most difficult public office in America next to the presidency is that of the mayor of New York. Municipal government structure varies greatly from place to place. Some cities have independent executive and legislative branches while others combine the two into a city council with a mayor. As urban administration becomes more and more a specialized field of science, many · smaller towns have introduced a "city manager" system. A popularly elected council would assume charge of the guidelines while hiring a specialist to manage the day-to-day business. The town manager can serve as long as the elected body wants to retain him.

All American states have nicknames, again with the exception of Alaska. New York in the east is called the "Empire State," California in the west the "Golden State," Washington (in the northwest) the "Evergreen State," and Florida (in the southeast) the "Sunshine State." Every state has its own motto, tree, bird and song. Rhode Island, with the smallest area, wary of being bullied by others since the time of independence, has adopted a motto: "Hope." The largest, Alaska, perhaps with an eye to its immense untapped territory, proclaims the state motto: "North to the Future."

National Flag, Anthem and Uncle Sam

America is a very young country but it seems to attach great importance to its own history. Books and papers on minute details of the country's past produced each year, to borrow a Chinese saying describing writing proliferation, would be "enough to make oxen carrying them sweat, and fill houses to the rafters." Take the origins of the "Stars and Stripes," for instance. I had read various arguments on the subject in the forties. In chats with Americans on my second visit, I learn that research is still going on.

The earliest documentary record of the national flag can be traced to a resolution offered by the Marine Committee at the Second Continental Congress on 14 June 1777. The resolution simply said, "Resolved: that the flag of the United States be thirteen stripes, alternate red and white; that the union be thirteen stars, white in a blue field, representing a new constellation." But nobody yet is sure who actually designed the Stars and Stripes, who made the first flag, or whether it ever flew in a sea fight or land battle of the American Revolution. Later, in 1795, Congress formally passed an act that the American flag should have fifteen stripes, alternate red and white, and fifteen white stars on a blue field in the union, as two new states had been admitted in addition to the original thirteen. With the fast westward expansion, many new territories gained statehood in quick succession. If a new stripe was to be added for each new state, the flag would obviously become an eye-straining medley. Congress decided that after 4 July 1818, the flag should have thirteen stripes symbolizing the original thirteen states and that whenever a new state was admitted into the union a new star should be added. The present fifty-star national standard was raised for the first time officially on Independence Day 1960, with the forty-ninth star representing Hawaii and the fiftieth representing Alaska, both of which joined the union in the previous year.

Uncle Sam as the image of the United States or of the U.S. government is known to the whole world, though he may look kind or ferocious as different cartoonists portray him. Before the thawing of Sino-American relations in the early 1970s, the old fellow appeared in the Chinese press invariably as a saber-rattling overlord. A formal portrait of Uncle Sam should be a tall, thin man with a white beard and wearing a blue swallow-tailed coat, red-and-white-striped trousers, and a tall hat with a band of stars. It originated during the second war against Great Britain (1812-1814) which occurred about thirty years after the War of Independence. During that war all U.S. army supply packages were stamped with the initials U.S. for the United States. There happened to be a supply inspector named Sam Wilson and nicknamed Uncle Sam. People joked that the U.S.-marked packages were the belongings of Uncle Sam, so the name spread and stuck as a symbol of the U.S. government. The image of Uncle Sam was first introduced by cartoonist Frank Bellow in the New York newspaper *Lantern* in 1852, with a long knife in the old man's hand.

Origins of the U.S. national anthem, the Star-Spangled Banner, are clear and I haven't heard much dispute. During the War of 1812, an American lawyer named Francis Scott Key, who was a volunteer in a light infantry company, tried to secure the release of his physician friend, Dr. Beanes, who had been captured by the British. Under a flag of truce and carrying a personal note from the then American President Madison, Key went to the British fleet to negotiate. Aboard a ship, Key witnessed a fierce twenty-four-hour British bombardment of an American fortress at Baltimore. As dawn broke, he saw the American flag still flying over the fort. In a surge of patriotic emotion, Key wrote a stanza on the back of an envelope. The poem was later passed into the hands of his brother-in-law, who suggested it could be set to the tune "Anacreon in Heaven" (Anacreon was a Greek poet noted for his songs praising love and wine). Soon the song found its way into a newspaper and became a popular ode to American patriotism. But it was not until 1931 that Congress formally designated it the nation's anthem. Key's manuscript was bought by the Waters Art Gallery, Baltimore, in 1934 for $26,400. The flag that Key saw flying is preserved in the Smithonian Institution in Washington D.C.

The Star-Spangled Banner is written in beautiful verses, the first stanza of which reads:

Oh, say can you see by the dawn's early light
What so proudly we hailed at the twilight's last gleaming?
Whose broad stripes and bright stars thru the perilous fight,
O'er the ramparts we watched were so gallantly streaming?
And the rocket's red glare, the bomb bursting in air,
Gave proof through the night that our flag was still there.
Oh, say does that star-spangled banner yet wave
O'er the land of the free and the home of the brave?

Chapter XII

MOUNTAINS AND DESERTS

Leaving New Orleans, I begin a long journey covering two-thirds of the American continent to the West Coast. I decide to take a bus back to Houston in order to see more of the Deep South and from there proceed to Nevada and California.

The Trailways bus runs fast and makes the trip to Houston in nine hours. In Louisiana, the landscape is more rural than urban, appearing poor and desolate in comparison with most of the other parts of the country I have seen. Forests abound but towns are few. Nature isn't always benevolent to America and disasters of all kinds are frequent. A rainstorm had hit Louisiana a few days earlier and caused a bad flood. Much of the forest along the highway is still soaked. New Orleans, at the estuary of the Mississippi, is low land and more vulnerable to floods. But the area has built four giant pumping systems. Local papers say that while one system is in constant operation to drain superfluous waters, the other three have been put into use after the rainstorm and barely saved the city from innundation.

The scene gradually changes after the bus enters Texas. There are more towns and they look quite affluent. The closer to Houston, the greater the difference. More and more factories and tall buildings come into view. Multi-decked superhighway interchanges appear, one after another. An endless stream of cars and heavy trucks speed along the expressways lined with advertising billboards. All are unmistakable signs of the growing prosperity of the Sun Belt.

From Houston I fly to Las Vegas, Nevada. The plane has more than two hundred seats but only sixteen passengers — a rare scene in a country where people are always on the move. But it is a good opportunity for me to freely change seats to get the best view, particularly because the day is bright and cloudless. Soon the plane is flying over a mass of mountains. They are the Rockies, known as "the backbone of the North American continent." The rugged range starts in the Arctic and stretches all the way down to Mexico. It is the watershed of the continent as rivers east of it drain into the Atlantic and those in the west into the Pacific. There is a saying that if you make two snowballs on the mountains and throw one to your left and one to your right, one will eventually reach the Atlantic and the other the Pacific.

Night is setting in. As the plane approaches Las Vegas, two dazzling clusters of lights connected by a less-bright corridor, apparently an expressway, appear against a completely dark background. I think they look like shining diamonds sewn on black velvet. But immediately I correct myself, for to my Chinese mind it is inappropriate teasing to liken a gambling den to the beauty of a diamond. The background is pitch black because Las Vegas is surrounded by deserts.

I see the deserts only later when I go further west from the city. It is brown all around — the ground is brown, the mountains are brown and the queer plants which look like neither trees nor grass are also brown. The continuous deserts stretch into eastern California, whose road map shows as few place names as that of China's undeveloped far west. What amazes me is that on the absolutely barren and uninhabited land the interstate expressway is so well built and maintained. And there are well-kept public lavatories and telephone booths on the way. As our car climbs, roadside landmarks give the elevation at 3,000 ft., 4,000 ft. and higher. When descending into valleys, I feel my ears singing and my own voice seems to be coming from a long distance away. As we continue gaining altitude, snow-capped mountains come into view and the landmark indicates their height as 8,000 ft., quite imposing, though they would be dwarfed by Mt. Qomolangma (Everest) in China's Tibet.

The Rockies, the Sierra Nevada further to the west, and the vast deserts lying between the two ranges combine to form a geographical region. But it is not completely desolate. Las Vegas, for example, is an "oasis."

A NOSTALGIC POET AND
THE GAMBLING CITY

— "Dream Journey," Slot Machines and a Casino Dealer

I have come to Las Vagas not to try my luck, but to meet a warm-hearted Chinese-American friend, Stephen S.N. Liu, and his wife Shirley (You Xiaoling). They have invited me to spend Christmas and say it will help keep me from becoming too homesick on a holiday marked by family reunions. For me it is a good opportunity to learn how they, as long-time residents, feel about living in America.

Shuning (S.N.) was born in 1930 in a mountain hamlet tucked away on the bank of the Yangtze River in Fuling County, Sichuan Province. He went to school in Chongqing, the largest city in southwest China, and there came into contact with modern ideas. During the later years of the Anti-Japanese War (1937-1945), he, like many other college students, was drafted into the Chinese Expeditionary Army and served in India. After the war he attended Nanking University as a student of Chinese literature. Becoming bored with campus life, he wandered to Taiwan and taught in middle schools there for a few years. Then he came to America and worked at a variety of odd jobs, as a dish-washer, hamburger cook, janitor, teacher, and caretaker of white mice. Finally, he worked his way through college and earned a Ph.D. degree. The year of his graduation happened to be a bad time in the cyclic American academic job market. It was not too unusual for the holder of a doctorate to be found eking out a living as a taxi driver or bartender. He was considered exceptionally lucky to find a teaching job at the Clark County Community College in Las Vegas.

A few years ago I had a chance to read some of Shuning's English poetry and was stirred by the depth of his feeling and refinement of his artistry. The New World Press in Beijing, of which I was a deputy chief editor, decided to publish a selection of his poems under the title *Dream Journey to China*. I admire Shuning because even though he was raised in a backwoods village, he has studied so hard that he can write poetry in a foreign language and, in addition, won a 1981-1982 Creative-Writing Fellowship Grant from the National Endowment for the Arts for his poetry. What has impressed me most, however, is the deep feeling he retains for his homeland.

Remember What I Have Said

One of Shuning's poems reads:

Remember what I've said:
if somewhere I'm found dead,
not a tear or coffin for me,
give me away to the sea;
but let not the sea be my grave,
let the white-horse wave
bear me to the other shore,
where I lived before.

Dear motherland, be thou my bed,
thy earth a pillow for my head;
and under the star-streaming sky,
while the sea sings me a lullaby,
I'll sleep like a sleeping child.
I'll sleep like a sleeping child.

In the preface to *The Dream Journey*, the poet writes:

"The Chinese verse says, 'The north-bred Hu horses lean upon the northwind, and the south-hatched Yue birds nest in the southern woods.' Transplanted into the American desert, I am, metaphorically, one of the tangerine trees in my father's orchard. Unaccustomed to the alien water and soil, it bears only bitter fruits, my rugged verses. My nostalgic reveries of home, however, came true in the summer of 1975."

"I entered China to find my native fields bleak under the demoniac blizzard created by the Gang of Four. Great scholars were buried, books were burned, and a deer was called a horse." Liu's second visit to China was in 1980. By then, he writes,

"Venomous clouds of the Gang of Four had been swept away." "I found myself treading the garden path of my father's house.... We lingered for hours in Liu's Hamlet.... Late in the night, bamboo groves sighed incessantly like surging streams. Unable to sleep, I sat by the window and watched the land I love." And the poet foresaw that over his homeland the "dazzling sunbeams of the 'four modernizations' will break through the season's nimbus. The day will come, must come. May I no longer moan upon a dark bough after a nightingale; like the lark in Shakespeare's sonnet, let me soar about the heaven's gate and sing hymns of praise for you, China, a country of boundless beauty and grace."

The Dream Journey has been well received. One reviewer wrote in the *North Dakota Quarterly* (spring 1984):

> "The core of the poetry, the central wound around which the poems wind their solemn dance, is the poet's loss of his homeland. Like the amputee groping for his ghostly limb, Liu forever feels the China that is not there. The wound itself, with its universal shapes and hues, mocks and teases, ever ready to ambush him with a reminder of what is and what is not. Picking up a pebble along the Tennessee, he plummets through the tunnel to a Yangtze that is not there; his daughter's face becomes a map that '... extends and leads me, all the way back to that time-obliterating village.'"

"I cannot judge the Chinese of this bilingual collection," the reviewer adds, "but the English (the language in which these poems were originally written) demonstrates he has made his way quite well."

I feel regret that Shuning is not widely known in China. We do need scientists to help in our modernization drive. But don't we also need "lark" singing for our ancient but rejuvenating land?

Shuning and I have been friends for a few years, but only by correspondence. Since my arrival in the United States, we have often talked over long-distance telephone. "You're traveling alone and must take good care of yourself. Keep warm and don't forget the aspirin...." Admonitions like this make me feel like I have a brother in this foreign land. But it is at the Las Vegas airport that we meet for the first time. I am even happier to find Xiaoling, his wife, to be a lovely woman. She went to Taiwan from the Chinese mainland as a child and came to settle in the United States after graduating from college. Like Shuning, she has a profound love for the homeland. And it is for this reason that they take great pains to teach their two American-born daughters to speak and write good Chinese. April, the four-year-old younger sister they have brought to the airport, speaks standard mandarin as fluently as English.

A Strange World

But Shuning is not happy with the city in which he lives. In letters to me he has called Las Vegas "a den of crime." He would have left if the Clark County Community College had not appreciated his work so much that he was given tenure after only two years of teaching instead of the usual four or five. As a poet, he is uncomfortable with the garish and vulgar qualities of a city which he describes as "not having an iota of culture." But I don't think it's all that bad because he lives quite far away from the big gambling casinos. Drawing the curtains to block off the dazzling lights, he can engross himself in his writing or fondling his five pet cats. But I do sympathize with him when he complains: "What can I show a guest except the casinos?"

So one evening, Shuning and Xiaoling take me to the glowing Las Vegas Boulevard, or "The Strip," to visit the M.G.M. Grand, a plush two thousand-room hotel. Older people in China used to know M.G.M. (Metro-Goldwyn-Mayer) as a leading film company. Apparently it has diversified into the gambling business because "hotels" in Las Vegas also mean casinos. A Nevada state law requires that all casinos must have hotel accommodations — a clever arrangement making it more convenient for customers to stay longer for the games.

The busiest section of The Strip is a cluster of tall buildings — M.G.M. Grand, Hilton, the Holiday Inn, etc. They are fighting an "optical war," each trying to outshine the other with dizzying neon lights. The so-called "entertainment capital of the world" not only features games of chance but claims to offer "the satisfaction of every conceivable desire." The Lido, for example, presents parades of hundreds of nude males and females. And there are a lot of other joints doing who knows what.

We go to M.G.M. primarily for dinner. The best and most reasonably priced restaurants in the city are all run by the casinos. As we enter, I find a strange world of lights and sounds in a building without windows, clocks or calenders — so that you can forget about the hours and days you have spent there, I suppose. Slot machines stand in wait in all the corridors, either singly or in rows. The restaurant gives bargains to gourmets. You pay only three dollars for the buffet and can eat as much roasted, fried, or broiled meat, fish, and fowl in addition to a wide variety of salads, desserts and fruits as you like. Xiaoling tells me that a few years back the casinos used to provide lavish, free breakfasts before seven in the morning so that customers after a night's "fight" could have a hearty meal and then a sound sleep in their rooms to prepare for a new round at the games of chance.

After dinner we go to see the gambling. I am a stingy customer and scrape my purse for all the quarters in it which add up to a modest investment of six dollars in all. The gambling tables are on the ground floor of the sixteen-story building; the second floor houses shops, and the hotel rooms are higher up.

Slot machines are for beginners like me. I throw in a quarter and pull the handle. What luck! A flood of coins rains down. I try another machine but this time only a few coins appear. As I go on, more often than not my quarter never returns and I lose all six dollars in a few minutes. There are plenty of coin changers around but I decide to "take my defeat lying down." Only now do I understand why slot machines are translated as "coin-eating tigers" in Chinese.

Cards seem to be a more advanced game. A male or female dealer stands behind a semicircular table where customers sit opposite. The money hunters place their stakes on the table as the dealer deftly and swiftly distributes the cards. When the cards are turned up, the dealer collects all the losing chips with a long-handled rake while paying the winners. Then another round begins and the game goes on and on in quick succession. I am told that the cards are fiercer "money eaters" than the slot machine "tigers" as desperate losers may stake everything they have.

Roulette is another sophisticated game. I don't know the rules at all but find the customers' facial expressions most interesting. Very solemnly they place their stakes on the checquered table and then, with

eyes wide open and mouths tightly closed, watch almost breathlessly
as the wheel turns and stops. They remind me of defendants standing
in a court as the judge begins reading the verdict.

Then there are the dice games. The crowds around the tables are so
thick that I can't get a closer look. Looking around, I see waitresses
moving about and serving red, white and brownish wines. Drinks
used to be free, in the past. Some people are sipping while watching,
and others quickly gulp down a glassful and go back to the game.
Neon signs keep flashing, twinkling, and moving, completing a scene
of revelry where, as the Chinese saying describes, "colors riot in the air
and wine flows on the ground.' All these must be quite stunning to the
budding senses of four-year-old April whom, having no baby-sitter,
my hosts have brought along. I also feel it is too much for my poor
.nerves and propose that we leave.

We then take a plush elevator to the top floor but see nothing
except closed hotel rooms. On the second floor is a hall where huge
portraits of old-time Hollywood heroes and heroines are hung on the
wall. There are also stores selling things ranging from expensive fur
coats and ornaments to daily necessities. Life has been made much
more convenient and comfortable for the present-day gold rushers, I
think, though the chance of hitting a fortune seems now much
slimmer, if any.

Shuning tells me that Caeser's Palace is generally regarded as the
top casino and he will take me to see it some other evening. "One spot
of the leopard is as good as the other," I say, declining a second visit.

Chance Encounter with a Woman Dealer

Shuning has a good friend in the city, a poet whose husband is a
senior engineer. The couple invites Shuning, Xiaoling and me to
dinner. One of the guests happens to be the poet's younger sister, a
casino dealer who has been recently laid off in the ongoing recession.
She has spent eight years of her young life on the job. I ask how she
feels about the work. "Absolutely boring" is her answer. I ask why the
dealers I have seen are all poker-faced, stern as granite. The question
somehow brings forth a flood of words. She explains that dealers are
not allowed to change their facial expression or make any motion

other than the routine distribution of cards, raking in and paying off. If the hair becomes dishevelled, it is not smoothed. If there is an itch, it is not scratched. There is not only surveillance on the spot but also closed-circuit television watching all the time. The worst thing is when the dealer fails to hold back a sneeze. It could be taken as a hint to some customer and could get the dealer fired. Dealers are so trained that they don't even lift their eyebrows. Hence the granite-like faces.

Dealing must be fast, the faster the better, she adds. For time is money. After a few months, the action becomes as much a part of you as your pulse and breath.

"Are the dealers handsomely paid for such a strenuous job?" I ask. No, they get the minimum wage prescribed by federal law. Luck does strike sometimes when an overjoyed winner gives the dealer a good tip. But then the boss will not be happy because his aim is to collect every penny from the customer's purse.

It should be obvious to all that chances for winning are much less than for losing. Why then do people flock to get fleeced?. The young woman says that the gambling habit can be a kind of illness, an addiction to the possibility of easy money and to the excitement of the game. Winners won't quit because they want to get more. And losers won't stop because they want to get their money back. She tells me some examples of people whom she knows personally. A couple, who had sold their house on the East Coast and were going to resettle in the West, passed Las Vegas on their way. They came to her casino just to have some fun and lost a small sum. Gambling then seized them psychologically. They went on trying to recover their loss but ended up with their house money gone, and not knowing what to do next. On another occasion, a man playing at her table had lost an enormous sum. She happened to know that he had a wife and children to support and felt a strong urge to hint that he stop. But how could she do it? Her job was to be silent.

She says that gambling psychology is a branch of science and the casino bosses know it well. The slot machines are a good example. They can be adjusted to control the ratio of intake and outflow. If a machine eats up money too wildly, it can be made less greedy. When the delightful sound of coins raining down is heard more often, players will feed the machines more readily. Then the machines can be readjusted again. Whatever the gimmick, she says, the players are bound to be the losers. If they are the winners, she asks, how could the gambling business keep going? The newspapers help the business a lot by publicizing a few lucky winners while not mentioning those who have gone bankrupt.

I ask her to tell me some strange stories which I believe must be numerous in this "adventurers' paradise." But she seems to have become so benumbed that she doesn't feel that anything is particularly strange. After a brief pause she merely says that sometimes there are tense moments when a customer wins an especially large sum. The boss, the manager, and the senior staff might come to watch and by clever maneuvers keep the winner playing. Luck is fickle and at some point the winnings will begin to drain away.

She also says that dealers are always wary for their personal safety. Some losers also lose their temper. When going off work, she habitually looks around to see if there is anyone glowering at her. The dealer is an easy target of the revengeseekers. I remark that I saw some hefty men prowling around the casinos, apparently plainclothes guards who should be able to protect at least the women dealers. She explains that it all depends on who the malcontent might be. If a frequent and wealthy customer, the casino wouldn't want to offend.

On our way back from the party, Xiaoling tells me that the young woman is from the state of Wyoming, up in the north. Her husband is a drunkard and often beat her. She got a divorce and her sympathetic sister helped her come to Las Vegas to find work. But now even that unenviable job is lost. Xiaoling says that the woman is usually melancholy and speaks very little and this is the first time she has heard her talk so freely.

Something About Tycoons

Over four decades ago Las Vegas was a small town of fifty-six-hundred inhabitants, many of them newcomers. It is now a city of three-hundred thousand and riding an upward trend.

Las Vegas owes its growth partly to gambling and partly to the United States Government. Nearly one million acres of barren desert land in its vicinity has been restricted for military training or nuclear weapons testing. The Energy Research and Development Administration (formerly the Atomic Energy Commission) employs some ten thousand people at its Nevada test site. Many are professional scientists experimenting and perfecting nuclear engines that power rockets and space engines and doing biological research on the effects of radiation on animal and plant life. And an air force base near Las Vegas is the biggest training center of pilots in the United States. More than seven thousand people make up its military and civilian components. The government employees are important consumers whose money helps to fuel the growth of Las Vegas.

The other important source of revenue is gambling. The business can be traced to the building of Hoover Dam in the 1930s which brought about an influx of laborers, and the subsequent construction of military installations after World War II. At first there were only a few hotels with attached gambling facilities. Then the Flamingo, a big casino-hotel, was erected. But it was a legendary billionaire who made Las Vegas "the gambling capital of the world." So many stories have been circulating about the man that to this day his life is still shrouded in mystery. How he died remains a riddle and one version of the story says that he suspected poison in all foods, wouldn't eat anything, and starved himself to death. He wasn't married and had no children. The legal battle over the inheritance of his enormous fortune was a grand drama but failed to establish an heir. Then his property went to the public. Later, while travelling in Los Angeles, a friend points out to me a vast tract of land and tells me that it belonged to the man — Howard Hughes.

How Hughes boosted the Las Vegas gambling business will give my Chinese readers a glimpse into the ways of American multimillionaires. So far I haven't mentioned any of the barons, tycoons, magnates, or the super-rich, as Americans admiringly or disdainfully call them.

One night in 1967, Hughes was secretly carried on a stretcher to a resort hotel called the Desert Inn. In typical Hughes style, his aides booked the entire ninth floor so that his privacy would be inviolate during his convalescence. Hughes liked the setting so well that he stayed on and on. This caused serious problems for the owner, who needed the luxurious rooms for "high-roller" guests who could be counted upon to drop many thousands of dollars at the gambling tables during their stay. Faced with eviction, Hughes solved the irritating impasse by making the owner an offer he couldn't refuse — $13 million in hard cash for the entire hotel. Just because he didn't feel like moving.

In fact the matter was less dramatic but more in keeping with the pattern of Hughes' financial wizardry and penchant for new ventures. Hughes had just sold his controlling interests in Trans-World Airlines for $566 million. Before that half-billion could be consumed by taxes, he had to reinvest the money quickly. Hughes was no stranger to Las Vegas. In his younger, playboy years, he had made many quiet visits to the gambling mecca. The town, at the time of Hughes' convalescence, had over-expanded in the building of resort hotels and private construction. Hughes solved the problem by buying up five more hotels in addition to the Desert Inn. In rapid succession, he also bought about $30 million worth of undeveloped land, the North Las Vegas airport, an airline, and a television station. He expanded his empire northward to Reno and bought the gambling casino that had started it all — Harold's Club. Hughes' powerful presence gave Las Vegas a shot in the arm both in economy and morale. "Respectable" hotel chains, previously hesitant because of the taint of organized crime in Las Vegas, had their doubts dispelled. They bought or erected some of the biggest resort hotels in the world. Hilton came. M.G.M. got into the business. Others followed suit. New innovations and powerful publicity further boosted the business. The desert city's fame, or notoriety, as "the gambling capital" was firmly established.

NO WINDFALL WEALTH
— Hoover Dam and Other Projects

Shuning's family remains strongly Chinese. They celebrate Christmas, but not as warmly as other Americans do. We retire quite early on Christmas Eve, having decided to visit the Hoover Dam, not far from Las Vegas, the next morning. The dam is an engineering feat and the lake it created has become a tourist resort.

We drive southeast from the city and see bald and strangely shaped hills all the way. Their colors are even stranger — reddish brown, yellowish brown, or of hues that are difficult to describe. Desert plants cling tightly to the sand rocks and look like decaying twigs. Xiaoling says that they will show a little sign of life only in spring and summer. The highway, as usual, is well-paved but there are few cars as most people are staying home because of the holiday. This adds to the bleakness of the landscape.

Hoover Dam, on the border of Nevada and Arizona, is built in the Black Canyon on the Colorado River. The brochure distributed to visitors says that the dam is a colossal structure 726 feet high and 1,244 feet long on the crest. The reservoir formed behind the dam is the largest of its kind in the United States and called Lake Mead. A year-round season attracts more than five million visitors for swimming, boating, skiing, and fishing.

We take a stroll at the lakeside. The waters are sparkling clear and stretch as far as the eye can see into a hazy distance. Xiaoling has brought along a bag of bread crumbs to feed the waterbirds which look like seagulls. Accustomed to easy living, they boldly circle over our heads and even dart down to our arms to seize the food .

We then go to see the power plant. It has a generating capacity of 1.34 million kilowatts. Quite modest in appearance, the installation is nonetheless one of the largest in the United States and an important source of energy for industrial, agricultural and daily use in many parts of Nevada, Arizona and southern California, including Los Angeles. Hoover Dam has brought irrigation to large tracts of land along the Colorado, and turned unproductive wilderness into "fruit and vegetable baskets." That's why Americans proudly call it one of the country's "Seven Modern Civil Engineering Wonders." A bronze plaque mounted on a concrete pedestal records the honor as well as the names of people who lost their lives during construction of the project.

The Colorado River originates in the Rocky Mountains. It gathers massive melting snows in the spring and summer and descends southward to drain into the Pacific Ocean. For centuries it flooded the low-lying land along its route yearly. Then in late summer and fall it would dry to a trickle. Crops and livestock withered and died when the river ran too low. History records that in 1905 the wild Colorado cut through a new outlet on its way and formed a forty-five-mile long lake, submerging farmhouses and railroads in murky waters, and making thousands of farmers and ranchers homeless. Something had to done. In 1931, when President Herbert Hoover was in office, construction of the multi-purpose project began. In 1935, President Franklin Roosevelt personally dedicated the dam, which was named after his predecessor.

Construction of the hydro-electric plant followed and the last generating unit was commissioned in 1961. Hoover Dam set an example and a number of projects of comparable scale were initiated. Later, when I visit the state of Washington, I hear people recall how the Columbia River was likewise tamed after the completion of the Grand Coulee Dam in 1942. Grand Coulee is twice as long as Hoover Dam and yields great benefits in irrigation, power production, flood prevention and navigation. The large lake it formed is named after President Franklin Roosevelt.

Lake Mead is indeed an attractive resort. Many brightly colored boats and yachts are moored at the docks. It would be fascinating to take a ride and enjoy the scenery. But business is closed on holidays. We return to Las Vegas for lunch. The brief visit, however, has aroused my interest in American efforts to remake nature.

Taming the Tennessee

Discussing America's economic development, many Chinese stress its rich natural endowments. They are right, but not completely so. I believe we should also take into full account the American people's gigantic efforts, strengthened by their science and technology, to transform nature.

In this respect, the usual example is TVA. Many Chinese know the abbreviation but not the full name — Tennessee Valley Authority — nor its full story. The Mississippi, the mightiest river on the continent, has two main tributaries, the eastern one known as the Ohio, and the western one, as the Missouri. The Ohio River has a main tributary called the Tennessee, which flows through the state of the same name and has branches in a number of neighboring states. The Tennessee used to flood frequently, destroying crops and houses, drowning people and livestock, and washing off precious topsoil. The river was very shallow in many sections and navigation was impossible. For generations inhabitants in the valley lived in abject poverty.

Bad things can turn to good account, as we say in China. The devastating Great Depression in the United States of the 1930s yielded a few good results, too. To contend with the crisis, President Franklin Roosevelt adopted a number of emergency measures collectively known as the New Deal. Part of the New Deal program was "work relief" — hiring the unemployed to work on public projects. TVA was one. The plan involved the building of dozens of main dams for flood prevention, irrigation, improving navigation, developing hydro-electric power, reforestation and soil conservation. Many years of arduous work turned the Tennessee River into a string of long clear lakes — reservoirs of different sizes. As a result, agriculture and commerce grew, and people's livelihood improved markedly in the valley. The project has brought benefits to a much larger area beyond. In Hazlehurst, Mississippi, my friends Margaret and Bryan McLemore spoke highly of TVA. They used to live an old-fashioned life in an *antebellum* house lit by candles. Thirty-four years ago, in 1945, the advent of electricity changed their whole lifestyle. It was a blessing from TVA. I have read a book saying that the U.S. has gained in TVA "a herculean servant" giving as much as 1,400,000 million hours of human energy each year (calculated on the basis that one kilowatt hour equals 13.5 hours of human energy). Only 37,000 people had to be employed by TVA in 1983 to produce this great energy.

The Missouri was another unruly river. While studying in that state in the 1940s, I often read about its devastating floods. Back in China, I read again in 1951 news reports that another flood had made 200,000 people homeless. There was speculation that thermo-power business was lobbying against a river-harnessing project which would produce cheaper hydro-electricity. In actual fact, a plan was afoot as early as 1944 and was later put into execution. On my return to Missouri in 1982, my host Roy Fisher told me that the menace had largely been removed. True to the motto of the "Show Me" state, the Journalism School dean drove me to see some once-distressed rural areas. The car ran up and down low hills, sometimes through dense bushes, and then reached a flat land where farm houses were scattered here and there. Automobiles and agricultural machinery were parked in front of almost every house. The cars were usually of a large type, looking like mini-buses. Some houses had two of them. Dusk was setting in. The farmhouses were brightly illumined with locally produced power. Apparently the Missouri River has become more of a blessing than a scourge.

From Deserts to Ranches

The San Joaquin Valley in California is another example. Once a desert, it has now become one of the world's most fertile areas for agriculture and animal husbandry. My visit there reminds me of the vast deserts in north and west China. If they can be transformed into San Joaquins, my country will have acquired enormous new wealth.

I have travelled from Las Vegas to Clovis, near Fresno in central California, soon after my visit to Hoover Dam. My hosts in Clovis are Dr. M.E. Ensminger, president of Agriservices Foundation, and his wife, Audrey, a nutrition specialist and photographer. On the second day of my arrival in the small town, Dr. E. and another scholar of the foundation, Dr. Richard Parker, take time out to accompany me on a visit to two ranches.

Though Clovis is not part of the green coastal valley of California, the climate is similarly mild. On the way I see many orange farms and well-cropped vineyards. Plenty of fruits still hang on the orange trees and many fallen ones cover the ground like a golden carpet. Harvest season is over and they are surplus left to rot or to be plowed under.

We first visit the Souza Dairy. It is owned by Joe Souza, his wife and two sons. The dairy employs twenty-five people and has a herd of twenty-five hundred cattle, mostly milk cows, raised on two thousand acres (twelve thousand *mu*) of grazing ground.

They raise cattle here in a different way than I saw in Iowa. In that midwestern state the herds leisurely graze on pasturelands. In this dairy they are kept in large pens fenced off with wooden rails. The cattle have to stick their heads through to get their fodder in troughs outside. The pens are densely populated and the trodden dung has turned into muddy pools. This prompts me to make a casual remark:

"The cattle here are not as happy as those in Iowa." Dr. E. disputes my comment, saying, "Oh, they have such fine feed here. They are happier." It seems we are picking up the debate of ancient Chinese agnostic philosophers. When one sage said that the fish in the pond were happy, the other retorted, "You are not fish so how could you know they are happy?" But of course Dr. E. knows. He is an internationally known animal scientist. Besides, Iowa is much colder than California. Who knows if there is still any green pasture left up there? Anyway, the doctor's quick reaction to my comment impressed me as a sign of his dedication to his work, of his love for the ranch and the cattle. So much so that he doesn't want me to think that the cattle here are unhappy.

We are led to see the milking parlor. Two men are working, each attending to eight cows, four standing on one platform and four on the opposite one. The machinery is efficient and it takes only six minutes to milk each eight cow batch. After the ground is washed with a water hose, eight more animals are let in. The work goes on round the clock, divided into two shifts. Each cow is milked twice a day. The milk is cooled to forty degrees Fahrenheit and deposited in a big stainless steel tank. The container is equipped with a device that automatically records the temperature at one-minute intervals. I am told that the milk must be strictly examined before shipping. The meticulous care they pay to food hygiene leaves a favorable impression on me and I ask especially for a copy of the temperature record as a souvenir. The current milk output, my host says, is fifty-seven hundred gallons (one gallon equals 3.785 liters) per day.

The Souza Dairy looks like a thriving business. The host tells me that the milkmen are the highest paid workers in the dairy, getting $1,000 a month plus above-quota bonuses ranging from $50 to $150. They are provided free lodging on the farm but have to pay their own water and electric bills. They get free beef and milk for the table. The employer pays for the workers' medical insurance. All employees have five days off each month and a one-week vacation each year. Those who have worked for five years or longer have a two-week annual vacation.

The Harris Ranch, which we visit next, is more than a ranch. It is an integrated enterprise of twenty thousand acres (120,000 *mu*) of land, growing cotton, vegetables, and fodder grass. It also operates a fodder processing mill, a slaughterhouse, and a restaurant. The cattle-raising division alone employs 125 people. The owner is John Harris.

We see the fodder plant where machines are humming and the sweet smell of ground corn pervades the air. A worker shows me a big shovelful of hot corn being processed. Most of the men working here, and at the Souza Dairy, too, look like Hispanics. I ask the superintendent showing us around if he speaks Spanish. "It would be fine if I could," he replies. He says so obviously because most of the workers don't speak English. There may even be very low-paid "undocumenteds"—illegal immigrants from Central and South America—among them, I suppose.

We end our visit with a meal in the Harris Restaurant. The tall wooden counter and the antiquated copper kettles and pots hanging on the walls as ornaments are to give the impression that it's a time-honored restaurant. Its advertisements claim that it is one of the ten best in California.

My Chinese readers should know that though this part of the American West raises a lot of cattle now, it is not the setting of the "Westerns" familiar to Chinese film-goers. The "cowboys" generally were men active on the Great Plains east of the Rockies in the later part of the last century. They herded long-horn cattle from Texas and other parts of the old southwest to railway heads in Kansas on epic "cattle drives." From there the cattle were shipped to the great Midwestern meat packing centers. The long horns were believed to have descended from six young cows and a bull that had come to Mexico with the Spanish in 1521.

The tough long-horn cattle of the nineteenth-century American ranches were scattered over the range and had to be rounded up by cowboys who knew how to ride their horses and would drive the steers across the plains. Men who often possessed strength and courage, the cowboys had to be on guard for bands of robbers, fierce storms, and flooded river crossings. To keep the nervous animals calm at night, they had to circle the herd and often sang ballads to them and to each other. The romantic scenes, woven by writers into plots of love, gallantry, and violence, were a source of countless, enchanting themes for films of the "Wild West." They were in vogue for a long time and were a basis for many of the myths that became a part of popular American culture.

The cowboys on horseback no longer exist nowadays. In 1887, the famous Great Blizzard struck the Great Plains with wind, ice, and snow. After the storm countless buffalo and cattle were left dead or dying. In some places the snow blew into drifts nearly one hundred feet deep, burying houses, animals, and men. After two months, the ice and snow melted and flooding rivers added new terror to the old. The Great Blizzard ended the era of open range. Ranchers replaced the wandering cowboys. Today the Great Plains have become a base of modern animal husbandry. Clovis, where I am, is on the edge of the San Joaquin Valley, a long way off from the Great Plains.

At the Harris Restaurant, I pick up a brochure about the valley. It says that the U.S. Congress established the Central Valley Project in 1935. Under the plan engineers built three large dams, 366 miles of canals, giant pumps and hydroelectric plants to produce the power for controlling and pumping the water. The project turned the San Joaquin, which at best could only graze a few sheep in its grassy places, into the presently rich agricultural area. This again shows that America has not attained all its wealth only by windfall.

The Friendly Ensmingers

Today tens of thousands of American agricultural and animal experts are continuing the efforts to blaze new trails and scale new heights. Dr. Ensminger is one among them. His works *Animal Science* and *Feeds and Nutrition (Abridged)* have been translated into Chinese and favorably received by his Chinese colleagues. *The Foods and Nutrition Encyclopedia*, a two-volume work co-authored by Audrey, Dr. E. and two other scholars, is being excerpted for *Encyclopedia Britannica*. The Agriservices Foundation, of which Dr. E. is president, is a non-profit organization supported by voluntary private donations whose purpose is "to foster and support programs of education, research and development which will contribute toward wider and more effective application of science and technology to the practice of agriculture, for the benefit of mankind." The foundation has rendered services to more than fifty countries around the world.

An outstanding scholar, Dr. E. is still modest. He invites me to the foundation headquarters, surrounded by attractive gardens, for a lengthy conversation. I know little about agronomy, but he explains to me like a natural teacher. I need some figures, for instance, on the number of American farmworkers and the breakdown in different categories. He phones the U.S. Department of Agriculture in Washingtion, D.C., to find the latest figures for me.

He does not do all this merely as a token of personal hospitality to me. He and Audrey are friendly to China and the Chinese people as a whole. The doctor has made five lecture tours in China and done much for Chinese animal science and practical husbandry. He has also arranged for Chinese animal scientists to come to America for further studies, and is always ready to be consulted by his Chinese colleagues. On his latest lecture tour in 1984 he was awarded the title of honorary professor by the Huazhong Agricultural College in the central China city of Wuhan.

Why are the Ensmingers so friendly? A beautifully illustrated book they give me as a present provides an answer. *China — the Impossible Dream* was written by the couple after their first visit to China in 1972. In the preface they say: "We went as people-to-people, as two American farmers (peasants) visiting the peasants (farmers) of China." Then they go on to introduce themselves. Dr. E. "grew up on a Missouri farm; his family was very poor. In the great depression of the early 30s, his father lost the family farm. There wasn't enough money to buy gasoline; so, the car was left in the garage and the family went to church in a big wagon drawn by mules. As a freshman at the University of Missouri, he hauled garbage to feed hogs as a means of working his way through college." The junior author, Audrey, "grew up on the Canadian prairies; earned her way through college by tutoring students and by winning scholarships for academic achievements. She was too poor to have a dowry when she married, in the old China, she couldn't have wed." So the authors have "a kindred feeling for the Chinese peasants, having experienced the same deprivations."

I am particularly moved by what they say in the last chapter entitled "The Chinese Medley". The concluding paragraph reads:

Our Reaction and Prediction. — After seeing the Great Wall, which was constructed by slave labor and without mechanization; after reliving, ever so little, the deprivations of the Chinese peasants throughout history; after seeing the present enthusiasm of the Chinese people as they tug their way, with chin up and quickened step, into a modern sophisticated world — after experiencing all these, we came to the inescapable conclusion that the Chinese people had to be good genetically. Otherwise, they would never have made it; they wouldn't have been able to suffer all the insults that have been heaped upon them and yet endure. Without doubt, in the transition some fine people were hurt and some injustices were wrought. But few countries have escaped similar events....

In China, as in the United States, the past is prologue. We predict that soon after the year 2000 A.D. history will record that ushering the new China into the twentieth century was one of the great feats of world history; that "China - the impossible dream" will have come true.

Re-reading the passage in my Beijing home, I look up to the east and silently send my best wishes to Dr. E. and Audrey on the other side of the Pacific, wishing them happiness and success in promoting friendship between the people of our two countries.

THE LOVELY AND LOVED
— Children in Denver and Elsewhere

Apart from Las Vegas in Nevada, the only other city I have visited in the sprawling geographical region of mountains and deserts is Denver, Colorado, on the eastern foothills of the Rockies. I had been there once in June 1947, and was left with the indelible impression of its severe coldness. When I got off the bus at night, the freezing temperature found me in a summer dress. For years afterwards, whenever I thought of the night drive through the Rockies, I felt shivers down my spine.

Economically, Denver's temperature has risen sharply. According to newspaper reports, it is one of the two American cities — the other being Houston in the Sun Belt — which expect the fastest growth of population in the next few years. The reason is that petroleum and coal have been discovered in the area. A mere assembly point of cowboys before the 1880s, Denver is now vying with Houston as "the energy capital of America."

I have flown in from Seattle on a fine and cloudless day and got a good aerial view of the American Northwest — the snowbound mountains, meandering rivers and dense forests. It seems that Wyoming is covered with the thickest snow and is even more sparsely populated than Idaho. The landscape is strikingly similar to parts of China's Northeast, once called "Manchuria." A fellow passenger tells me that among the 50 American states, Wyoming ranks forty-ninth only above Alaska, in population density and Idaho is not much higher. We run into a blizzard near Denver. The stewardess urges passengers to put on warm clothes as Denver has had an eighteen inch snowfall. This time I am prepared for the cold. But my stay in Denver turns out to be very warm in human terms. A memorable meeting with American children changes my memory of the city from shivers to smiles.

Carol Robinson of Boston has introduced me to her eldest daughter, Shelley Schreiber, who is working for her master's degree at Denver University. Shelley, in her turn, introduces me to her good friend Monica Lobato, a school teacher, because I hope to see more American children. Apart from teaching, Monica works as the "hostess" in a luxurious restaurant two evenings every weekend. We go to dine at the place and find her clad in an elegant evening gown and ushering customers to the tables — a service not available in smaller restaurants.

Beijing — Denver

Monica takes Shelley and me to the Smith Public School where she teaches and invites us to attend a class. More than twenty children seat themselves around Monica on a carpet and listen with intense interest to the ordinary string of stories about princes and princesses. The classroom is a cheerful place. On one side is the teacher's platform with a wide blackboard behind it. On the opposite wall the children's handiwork hangs — human caricatures cut out of cardboard with movable heads, trunks, and limbs. American diversity and pluralism seem to begin with the children, as no work is similar to the other in dress, color or facial features. A few figures wearing beards are particularly funny. The children's short compositions are also on display.

After the stories, Monica tells the kids that Mrs. Wang from Beijing has come to meet the class and asks them to go back to their desks and welcome the guest. Meanwhile, Shelley distributes pieces of chocholate candy wrapped in golden paper on each desk and gives me one, too. I mount the platform and say, "Let me teach you a few Chinese words. Would you like that?" "Yes!" comes the unanimous reply. I write out on the blackboard the two Chinese characters for *Mei Guo* (America). Monica asks the children to copy them down. Then I lead the class to read the words ten times and ask a blonde girl to read them aloud. She pronounces the words correctly and says, as I have explained, that *Mei* means "beautiful" and *Guo* means "country" and that Chinese call America "the beautiful country."

Then I add one more Chinese character, *Ren*, which means "people." The children are excited to learn that they are *Meiguoren* (Americans), "people of the beautiful country." Trying to test further their patience and aptitude, I write out in Chinese the numerals from one to ten with corresponding Arabic figures. I again lead the class to read, ten times, "*yi, er, san, si, wu, liu, qi, ba, jiu, shi* (one...ten). To learn ten strange sounds at one time is obviously quite difficult, but to my suprise most children are able to pronounce them. Then I ask them to copy down the numerals. All of them conscientiously draw the difficult ideographs on their writing pads. I find that one boy has done it beautifully. Thrilled, I put my piece of chocolate on his desk.

There is a whisper behind me: "Look, he's got two." How interesting! American children, like Chinese kids, always like to compare themselves with each other. I feel I must explain why he's got two. Raising the boy's pad, I say, "His writing is the best. Shouldn't I give him a little prize?" "Yes," comes the loud reply.

Finally Monica proposes that I give everybody a Chinese name. The kids, each holding a piece of paper in hand, come up to me in all seriousness. Most Chinese names consist of three monosyllabic words, the first one being the family name and the other two the given name. Accordingly, I take out the first syllable of a child's surname and two from his or her given name, and write out three Chinese characters of approximate sounds to create a name. It's not easy work for me, though, because the traditional Chinese way of translating foreign names is to select words of identical or approximate sounds which bear the best possible meaning ("Beautiful Country" for America is an example). And I have to rack my brain for nice names.

The next day, Monica hands me a scrap-book with a handpainted cover as a gift from the pupils. Each page carries a few words of thanks to me written and signed carefully by a child. Some pages have hand-drawn designs or paintings on the back, all free creations by the children. A portrait of me is a most interesting one. The black hair, the brown purse, and even the colors of my clothes and the frames of my glasses are true to the original. The girl painter surely has sharp eyes and a wonderful memory. A boy has drawn a sketch map of the world showing China and America separated by the Pacific and with Denver and Beijing represented by two distinct stars. It's a very imaginative work for a child of seven.

The Smith School, according to Monica, is comprised of three grades, the first grade is divided into seven classes and the other two grades are divided into six each. There is an attached kindergarten of two classes, one class divided into three and the other into two groups. The whole school has a faculty of twenty-five, and a student body of 625.

Monica also tells me that the school is multi-racial and has white, black, and Asian pupils. The fierce struggle which took place throughout the country in the 1950s-60s did achieve, in law, the desegregation of schools. But *de facto* segregation still persists in many districts, and indeed, is actually spreading in all parts of America. In Chicago, for instance, I visited the Shoesmith Public School, which is almost completely black and Asian. My friend Sylvia Fischer, who once taught there, told me that Shoesmith used to be a white school. After the desegregation legislation, white pupils gradually withdrew to private schools and some white parents even took the trouble of moving the whole family out to predominantly white suburbs to escape school desegregation. It is sad to see that racial prejudices die so hard and that legislation alone appears inadequate to solve a complex social problem.

But Shoesmith is well-equipped by Chinese standards. It has a big playground which many Chinese urban schools would envy. Pupils like to come early and are skipping rope and playing on swings. They are as noisy and naughty as Chinese children. But there is a striking difference. American kids are not shy at all before strangers. Seeing me taking their pictures, they rush forward and make funny faces at the camera.

I saw another Chicago public school, William Rye, which is predominantly white and has some black pupils, perhaps as a sign of its compliance with law. According to the headmistress, the school has "special classes" for retarded and linguistically handicapped minority pupils. In addition there are "quick" and "slow classes." I remember some newspaper articles describing the practice as a "tracking system" and a disguised form of segregation.

The headmistress told me that all teachers in the school were being sent on rotation to training classes in computer education, a program sponsored by the municipal authorities. American schools, like most other organizations, have streamlined staffs and demand high efficiency. The rotation puts pressure on the teaching load, but employing substitutes costs money. Moreover, government appropriations for education are being slashed across the board and the headmistress said she had to solicit private donations.

Education Through Recreation

Apart from schools, American society which, on the whole, shows a tender love for children, has created many facilities to educate them. Any city of a good size has its own museum or museums which have special programs for the young. There are amusement parks like Disneyland in Los Angeles and Disneyworld in Orlando which are children's paradises. They provide them with generally educational tours and displays.

I visited the Children's Museum in Boston where the kids were having great fun. The smaller ones came with their mothers. There were plenty of toys and space for them to play. Parents didn't worry about the kids making a mess of their clothes. Washing machines have become a household item since the 1940s and a little extra laundry is no problem. So the kids were allowed to crawl and roll as they pleased. I found that American parents and teachers usually adhere to a "policy of non-interference." They believe that too many "don'ts" will hamper the initiative and creativity of children.

Toddlers everywhere like to play with water. I saw in the Boston Children's Museum a special indoor pool in which they could splash with hoses and throw plastic balls in the water. I have seldom seen a merrier place. There was another place for soap bubble lovers. Bubbles were blown to the size of balloons. A guide explained to the kids the basics of the physics involved and a number of volunteers, aged eight to sixteen, assisted.

Older children had more sophisticated games to play. I saw a "production line." The little workers, just like grownups, would check in with a card on which a machine recorded the precise time. They took up their places on the line, each doing a part in making rolling tops. A quality controller carefully inspected every finished product, throwing the rejects onto a scrap heap and letting the others go on to become toys for smaller visitors. After one shift, the process began all over again and the children would swap jobs. I saw another game called "classification." The players selected from a mixed heap of turtle, frog, bird, rabbit and fox bones and restored them into skeletons of the various animals. Though there were illustrations to follow, it was no easy job.

"Granny's Home" was another instructive game. It was a cross-section of a house from basement to the second floor, complete with underground plumbing, telephone wires, furniture, hearth and chimney, and of course the Granny—an automaton. The aim of the game was to give children an idea of the structure of an ordinary house. This game is "education by the principle of discovery," as the guide called it. In Chinese terms, we would say it was to "observe and understand the world."

As I have already observed, even small town libraries have special reading rooms for children and organize a variety of extra-curricular activities for pupils. I have also read in *The New York Times* a report on "toy libraries" for handicapped children. The library in Rye, New York, which was opened in 1982, inspired several states to follow suit. It lends sophisticated toys like remote-control robots, cars, and trucks. Two may be borrowed at a time and for a period of two weeks. The children are of course free to come and play in the library.

In Miami, I had a chance to visit a kindergarten with a group of students from the nursing school of the University of Miami. Teacher Claudia Houari took ten nursing students to the Happy Day Nursery, in the far suburbs, to do physical checkups on the children. For them it was practice, while for the school, which enrolls poor children, it was a welcome free examination. The checkup was meticulous and time-consuming and I spent almost a whole morning there. But it was interesting to watch how the students, guided by their teacher, first learned how to calm the nervous kids and then proceed with one test after another. I then took a stroll on the playground and saw a worker "mowing" the meadow with a vacuum cleaner. The lawn was actually made of synthetic fiber and was laid out like the *tatami* in Japanese houses. While it looked like real grass, it could stand all the wear and tear of the children.

The school principal at Happy Day Nursery was an older man devoted to his work. He explained to me that most of the children were from "single-parent families" headed by divorced or unmarried mothers. To qualify for enrollment, the woman must have a job but her income must not be above the official poverty line. The school provides only day care and the children get practically free meals on public money. The principal showed me his account books, saying that though money was tight, he was doing his best to give the kids adequate nutrition.

When we took our leave, the children had already had their lunch and were playing on the "meadows." They were excited to see me snapping pictures of them. When I followed the student nurses and got on the bus, the kids surged forward, pressed their smiling little faces against the fence, and shouted: "Come back! Come back!" They were mostly black and yellow, mixed with a few whites. Whatever their color and race, children are equally lovely. I felt glad to learn from teacher Claudia that the checkup showed these poor children to be in pretty good health.

"A Single Hair from Nine Ox Hides"

But it's not all sunshine for American children. Apart from the errant type I saw in Harlem and the Houston youth village, the luckier ones going to school regularly are faced with troubles, too. Deterioration of the quality of education is a topic often discussed in the press. At Stanford University in California, I interviewed Professors Robert Hess and Paul Hurd. Both are specialists in education who deplore the shortage of educational funds. They point out that teachers of primary and high schools are underpaid. The brightest college graduates, particularly in the natural sciences, are attracted by higher salaries to private businesses. The University of California, Los Angeles, has just published a survey of 1982 freshmen, showing that most students chose engineering, business, and law, and that educational programs for future teachers have the fewest applicants. The end result is that the best minds are taken away from the important work of training the younger generation. A similar problem has existed in China, but fruitful efforts have been made in recent years to halt the trend. What do the present teachers in America think of their jobs? The National Institute for Education, research arm of the Federal Department of Education, has answered the question in a report published in July 1982. In 1961, according to the study, 49.9 percent of all teachers interviewed said that if they were given a chance to begin again their careers, they would choose teaching. But in 1980 only 21 percent of the teachers held that view.

Family education is also causing worries. Another authoritative report I have read in the press says that one out of every four American children live in "single-parent" families and half of these families are poverty-stricken. The age group of three to five spends an average of thirty hours a week watching TV, while the six to eleven-year-olds spend twenty-five hours. The pity is that even programs made especially for children are not always educational, not to mention the diet of sex-and-violence which abounds on "prime time" programming. The time consumed by TV watching has drastically reduced children's reading abilities and affected their homework.

Then there is the problem of the glaring disparity between public and private schools. I know some parents who are spending $3,000 to $4,000 a year on tuition alone to send their children to private schools. These lucky few, apart from regular lessons, are given expert after-school guidance in music, painting and other creative arts, to develop their talent. Frequent visits to museums, art galleries, and other cultural institutions are organized for them. In short, the wealthy can get a much better education from the very begining. To my egalitarian-oriented Chinese mind this is unacceptable.

· Many Americans take pride in the fact that public schools were first introduced in their country and they believe that American equality should be manifested first and foremost in equal educational opportunities. I hope that all the lovely American children will some ·day enjoy that equality. It should not be too difficult for a rich country like the U.S.A. which has an annual federal budget of close to a trillion dollars, not to mention the local outlays. To divert a bit more money into education would be like "lifting a single hair from nine ox hides." And that "single hair" will give education a boost and may bring equality to a lot of "unequally born" children.

Chapter XIII

A 4,000-LI TRIP ALONG THE PACIFIC COAST

From Nevada I travel further west to the Pacific Coast. Geographically the narrow strip of land along the ocean is called the West Coast valley, formed by the coastal range which has mild slopes but is prone to earthquakes. Further inland are the roughly parallel and more rugged Cascade Mountains and Sierra Nevada in the south. Lying between the Cascades, Sierra Nevada and the Rockies is a vast triangle of deserts where "oasis" cities like Las Vegas and natural wonders like Death Valley and the Grand Canyon are situated.

Early immigrants who came from the East and the Midwest wrote of the West Coast: "To our great delight we beheld a great valley.... The valley of the river was very fertile, and the young tender grass covered it like a field of wheat in May." That was about 150 years ago. At that time it usually took the settlers at least four months to trek to the Pacific coast in covered wagons. Many fell sick or were so worn out that they died on the way. Graves were a common sight on the trails. In earlier days, traders seeking to establish trading posts on the West Coast had to sail all the way down to Cape Horn at the tip of South America and then turn west and sail north. The several months' voyage, on often stormy seas, was a risky proposition. Natural barriers, however, couldn't daunt the enterprising Americans. By the mid-nineteenth century, in the period approximate to the Opium War which reduced China into an emaciated semi-colony, the Americans took another giant step forward in building the country as large numbers of settlers poured into California and Oregon to open up the last frontiers on the continent.

I start my trip from San Diego at the southernmost point bordering Mexico, travel northward through Los Angeles and San Francisco in California, reach Portland in Oregon and stop at Seattle in the northwestern state of Washington adjacent to Canada. The distance is thirteen-hundred miles, equal to about 2,000 kilometers or 4,000 Chinese *li*. In the south the climate is subtropical or temperate. Up in the north, on the same latitude as China's freezing Northeast, the climate is also mild because of the warm "Japanese Current" which runs down the Pacific coast. It is February and March, but Oregon and Washington are covered with profuse vegetation and riotous flowers. Cities and towns are well built and bustling with activity. The early settlers, if any of them could see the place now, would certainly marvel at a world so changed. To me, the history of the American westward expansion is always a source of inspiration as I visualize the development of China's vast but as yet untapped great Northwest.

SAN DIEGO, LOS ANGELES AND SAN FRANCISCO

— The Land and the People

I have selected San Diego as my starting point not merely because it is a tourist attraction, but because it has been listed by some American economists as one of the ten most promising cities in the Sun Belt. In 1900, the city had only 17,000 inhabitants. The number rose to 697,000 in 1970 and 875,000 in 1980, leaping to the eighth place among American cities. Its proximity to Mexico has resulted in an increasing influx of Spanish-speaking immigrants who now account for one-seventh of the population. The city has both old-fashioned Spanish architecture and ultramodern American high-rises. Industries centered around aerospace industries and other high technology have been mushrooming and the rapid increase of population is expected to continue.

Wise Investment

A senior staffer of the Space Theater and Science Center to whom a friend has introduced me, kindly helps me to work out a program of visits. The theater itself is of course on top of the list. It is equivalent to our planetarium, featuring shows of the mysterious universe. I see an interesting show on a hemispherical screen, produced by a starfield projector with no less than ten-thousand lenses! The Science Center has many displays but not the usual "Please don't touch" notices. It is a fascinating place for children, who are encouraged to play with the exhibits. Some are operating radio communications equipment, some are peeping through real submarine periscopes.

My next stop is the natural history museum, with the ordinary run of dinosaur bones and other fossils. In the vicinity there are close to a dozen institutions including two art galleries, a museum highlighting the physical and cultural development of man, an aerospace museum and the "Hall of Champions" honoring San Diego athletes who have won national and international recognition. It would take days to just go around to all these "tourists' musts" and I have to skip most of them. Hurrying to the zoo, which claims to be the world's largest, I have time only to join a guided tour and take a quick look. The guide says that the one-hundred-acre park keeps a collection of thirty-four hundred animals. I see none of them in cages; all live "freely" in simulated canyons, mesas, and other natural surroundings. After the forty-minute tour on the slow coach, visitors can take a cable car ride to get an aerial view of the whole place.

The next day I go to Sea World, also one hundred acres in area. It is a marine life park featuring many shows. I see big and small dolphins "dancing," darting out and then back into water to the sound of music. Like bears in circus shows, they have to be fed again and again during the performance and some stubborn ones would refuse to go on without an adequate "incentive." Then I see a glass house with man-made ice in which funny-looking penguins are staggering around. The scene makes me homesick because it is exactly like what I would see with my grandson in my Beijing home when his favorite TV program "Animal World" is on.

San Diego further confirms my impression that American

museums, art galleries, zoos and similar institutions are both numerous and imaginative. They enable visitors to have a look at man's past and future, at outer space and the deep sea, at a whole spectrum of natural wonders and human creations. They help to enrich people's knowledge, broaden their vision and cultivate their minds. I believe the Americans are wise and far-sighted to spend so much money on these "intellectual development projects," as we would call them.

San Diego has nice beaches, too. Strolling around, I find an almost endless expanse of fine sands gently washed by rising and ebbing ocean waters. Small lakes have been formed here and there on the seashore. Rowboats, yachts, surf-riders and water-skiers dot the sparkling blue waters. The modestly-priced Holiday Inn, my lodging, is also a beautiful place. I can see water on all sides and clusters of lights and neon signs in every direction at night.

Las Vegas is said to offer "satisfaction to every conceivable desire." But San Diego can boast a lot of sensible things to see and enjoy. The only trouble is that everything is so expensive. I pay $52 a night for the hotel and $10 including tip for a simple dinner at a restaurant. Admission to the zoo is $7.20 for adults and $2.90 for children from six to sixteen, excluding the cable car fare. Sea World charges $8.95 for an adult visitor and $2 for children from five to fifteen . Back in Beijing, I can take my grandson to visit the zoo and see the pandas for 10 *fen* , less than an American nickle. The Americans, of course, earn much higher wages but the price scale is also high, particularly in such cities as San Diego. The temptations to spend are very strong and you always feel the pressure of consumerism. Work more, earn more and spend more — that's the formula. But it's so much easier to spend than to earn. Credit cards have made spending all the easier and you can even spend more than you have on your bankbook. But the credit card interest rate is twenty percent and thus you pay $120 for every $100 you spend in advance.

"A City of Cities"

Boarding a train from San Diego to Los Angeles, I ask a fellow passenger when we will arrive. She seems nonplussed, replying that it depends on which part of Los Angeles I am going to. The third-largest American metropolis next only to New York City and Chicago, Los Angeles is known as "a sprawling city" or "city of cities." Its area is three-fifths larger than that of New York City but its population (100,000 in 1900 and 2.96 million in 1980) is only half as large. Along twisted lengths of expressways, one finds the city to be a conglomeration of distinct, virtually independent boroughs, mountains, deserts, beaches, worldly market places and secluded, self-styled paradises. Even those born and bred in the city have not seen it all. There are two Chinatowns, the old one plus another built in recent years by Chinese from Taiwan. Ethnic Japanese live in a compact community called Little Tokyo. And then there are Black and Hispanic ghettos.

A relative of mine who has lived for years in Los Angeles, fearing that I won't be able to find his home, has told me over the phone that he would meet me in front of the Dinghao Supermarket in the new Chinatown. This gives me an opportunity to look around the streets. A Chinese *dimsum* shop arouses my curiosity. I look at its menu and am amazed by the wide variety of *dimsum,* small refreshments or snacks distinct from regular dinner courses. They include noodles with spareribs, beef or sliced chicken, dumplings with or without soup, glutinous-rice doughs for the Dragon Boat Festival, and cakes for the Lunar New Year, to name a few. Most customers are non-Chinese. The liberal-minded Americans are at the same time liberal-mouthed gourmets. *Dimsum,* in the wake of chop-suey, has become a new entry in newer American dictionaries. On the spiritual side, there is a World Bookstore which sells publications from Hongkong and Taiwan including fairly complete works of modern writers like Lu Xun and Guo Mojo, some of which are "pirated" editions from mainland publishing houses. Later, in the old Chinatown, I see a bookstore selling mainly publications from the mainland including English-language magazines and books put out by the Foreign Languages Publishing Bureau in Beijing. *China Pictorial,* a large-format monthly popular on the mainland, is on sale in both Chinatowns. The different stock at the two bookstores makes me feel sorry that an ideological gap still divides the two Chinese communities even in the same American city.

My sightseeing trip in Los Angeles takes me first to Beverly Hills, the home of the affluent and celebrated, and Hollywood. In movieland, however, I only have time to join the Universal Studios Tour said to be a "must for tourists." Visitors board a small train which runs through different movie scenes, now an eighteenth century street and then the "killer whale" darting out from water and charging at the coach. The train seems to be capsizing. Women start shrieking and children are crying in mothers' arms. Suddenly the "killer" vanishes and the train goes on as usual. Another shock comes when a house bursts into fire and flames are licking at the train. The fire goes out as suddenly as it appears and calm is restored. Then the bridge under the train breaks with a terrifying crack and the coach seems to be falling into the waters. But the horror is soon over. The program is purported to show how thriller scenes in famous movies are mere tricks pulled by prop-men with the aid of audio-visual devices. Much of the sensationalism is not to my taste. Most American visitors, however, appear to enjoy the program heartily as they loudly exclaim at scenes they recognize from films they know.

The movieland is now actually an empty shell, as most studios have moved to the suburbs. Much of the remaining business belongs to the "recreation and entertainment" trade. A travel book makes a special point to warn women visitors: "Don't stick around Hollywood at night; you'll either be propositioned or arrested as a prostitute."

Los Angeles boasts another world-famous sight — the Disneyland built by the creator of Mickey Mouse and cartoon film wizard, Walt Disney. There is no need to describe the amusement park since I have written on Disneyworld in Orlando, which is a newer and bigger model.

My hosts in Los Angeles are Frank Pestana and his wife, Jean Kidwell, both founding members of the U.S.-China People's Friendship Association. They are lawyers practicing independently and therefore Jean keeps her maiden name as Chinese women do. Frank has toured China more than a dozen times beginning in 1957. As old friends of my country, they are exceptionally warm to me.

Frank and Jean moved to Los Angeles thirty years ago when the city's population was below the two-million mark and real estate was not so expensive. They bought a small hill in a place now called Mulholland and contracted with a building company to bulldoze the slope into a flat site for a house. The company flattened a much larger area for them without additional cost because another customer was buying dirt to fill a hollow plot. On that hill Frank and Jean worked hard for years to build themselves a lodging, beginning with a bedroom and kitchen. So much so that Frank has become almost a professional builder. Now a beautiful house has been erected, the trees they planted have grown up and the children they brought up here have left and are working elsewhere. I find the story interesting because it is typical of the hard way many Americans have built themselves a decent life with their own hands.

Frank and Jean know my country well and understand America much better, of course. They are ever ready to answer my questions from law to politics, from income taxes to living expenses. I jokingly call them an open "Encyclopedia Americana." And I appreciate even more their candor and ardor in discussing political issues.

Frank accompanies me on my visit to the woman's prison. Jean takes me to a public housing project on which I shall report in the next chapter.

Another part of Los Angeles I visit is Pasadena, where the California Institute of Technology, a school quite well known in China, is situated. Professor David Elliot shows me around the quiet and antiquated-looking campus. He has xeroxed a page from the institute's alumni book for me. On it Professor Hsui-shen Tsien is listed. The Chinese jet propulsion specialist overcame many obstacles to return from the United States to the Chinese mainland in the 1950s and has made outstanding contributions to China's technological progress. Dr. Tsien, according to the listing, earned a M.S. at M.I.T. in 1936, came to Pasadena, got his Ph.D. at Cal.-Tech, and became a research fellow and professor at the institute.

Mrs. Elliot drives me to visit the Huntington Botanical Garden donated by a railway magnate of the same name. It is a vast complex and I choose my favorite beat, the library. The Huntington Library is unique for its collection of original logs and dairies kept by settlers during the westward expansion, and other rare historic materials. The librarian who shows me around says that a woman scholar, Lillian

Schlissel, did extensive research in the library and wrote a book, *Women's Diaries of the Westward Journey* (published by Schocken Books, N.Y., 1982). It happens that I have read parts of the book which, as its preface aptly says, gives the reader "a clearer idea of what has gone into the making of American woman, and what women have contributed to the making of America." Another point that strikes me is that the native Indians as seen by the women on the westward journey were often disposed to be friendly and not the "savages" depicted in Western stories.

From Los Angeles I proceed north to San Francisco, a city well-known in China as the gateway to America. With a population of 340,000 in 1900 and 678,000 in 1980, it now ranks fourteenth among American cities. San Francisco has an area only one-tenth that of Los Angeles and is a compact city. Facing the Pacific on one side and the San Francisco Bay extending inland from the ocean on the other, it is surrounded by waters. The mouth of the bay is called the Golden Gate and the bridge spanning it called the Golden Gate Bridge. It is an imposing structure built in 1937. A powerful earthquake hit San Francisco in 1906 and the subsequent fire left four-fifths of the city in ruins. But it was quickly rebuilt and in a few years had a new grandeur.

San Francisco is always known in China as *Jiujinshan* (Old Gold Mountain). The name evoked illusions of gold nuggets all around and attracted many poverty-stricken Chinese to the land in the later half of the nineteenth century. The city is truly hilly, like Chongqing in southwest China, and you have to be very careful driving down the steep streets.

San Francisco, my friends tell me, is liberal and receptive to different things and lifestyles. The University of California at Berkeley, adjacent to San Francisco, was a harbinger of the campus riots of the 1960s. Today, not only are homosexual people accepted with little question in the San Francisco Bay Area, but they wield significant power in the city's government and politics.

Dedicated Artists

I wish to meet some American artists. An American woman working with my publishing house in Beijing has written to introduce me to the Mime Troupe of San Francisco. Strictly speaking, mime should be silent. But it has broken into articulate language with dramas, musical comedies, and open-air shows similar to Chinese skits. Diverse in form, its repertoire is politically progressive in content.

Director and leading actress Sharon Lockwood invites me to see a rehearsal. It is noontime when I get to the predominantly Hispanic neighborhood where the troupe is housed. I buy a "taco" (Mexican cake with meat and onion inside) as lunch and take it to the rehearsal hall. The place is quite bare. The actors and actresses greet me, a guest from socialist China, warmly but informally. I feel easy with them and take a seat at the side to watch the rehearsal while munching on my taco. The director seems to be very demanding and frequently orders repeats. During the noon break, they go upstairs for lunch in a few dilapidated offices. While drinking coke and eating a sandwich from a simple lunch box, Sharon talks to me.

The Mime Troupe was founded in 1959, declaring explicitly its purpose as "dealing with important social issues in an entertaining but thought-provoking way and reaching out to the broadest possible audience." The troupe is now collectively run by fifteen actors, actresses, musicians and writers representing many races and cultures. In addition, there are three administrators. Its performances take three forms — indoor runs in the winter, a yearly summer season of free performances in parks, and tours in other cities and countries. The Mime Troupe openly proclaims itself to be "political theater." Box office receipts account for seventy-five percent of its income, and the deficit is made up by fund-raising events and government grants. They proudly declare that they "do not go to American corporations for funds — perhaps the only independent theater group that follows the policy."

Why would the government help finance such a political theater? The reason, I am told, is that the Mime Troupe during its twenty-four year history has won a certain prestige. They show me a stack of newspaper clippings — reviews by drama critics printed in *The New York Times, Los Angeles Times* and other leading papers. There are also foreign press comments as the Mime Troupe has performed in Cuba and Canada and made three European tours. Beginning in 1982, it launched a new venture by bringing theater to predominantly working-class communities around the Bay Area. In the popular outbursts against the Vietnam War in the 1960s, the Mime Troupe improvised many shows including street-corner skits called "guerrilla theater". Over the years many leftist organizations have disintegrated and fallen into oblivion. But the Mime Troupe has held out and is called by *The New York Times* "America's longest-running and most outspoken political theater." Its quite shabby rehearsal hall and offices help me understand why the *San Francisco Examiner* writes: "They are all miserable at home. But onstage the troupe is invincible. They create happiness."

I am invited to a formal performance of *The Uprising of Fuente Overjuna,* a play by Lope de Vega (1562-1635), the so-called "Spanish Shakespeare." It depicts a peasant uprising at "Sheep Well" (Fuente Overjuna) in the fifteeth century. The rebels killed the feudal lord. Under torture, men, women and children refused to single out the guilty, saying only "Fuente Overjuna lo hizo" (Sheep Well did it). A broadsheet prepared by the Mime Troupe says that when a journalist asks the Sandinistas in Nicaragua who killed dictator Somoza, the reply he gets is "Sheep Well did it." Mime's political message is clear.

The Mime Troupe's current repertoire includes shows which satirize fanatics for nuclear weapons, those who say the poor shouldn't have abortions, and CIA agents meddling in "San Martin" (obviously meaning El Salvadore). The plots are cleverly contrived and the dialogue is at once caustic and amusing. Though script writers invariably declare that "the resemblance between the people and events of the play and actual people and events are entirely coincidental," Mime's arrows are clearly aimed. While I watch the actors and actresses wisecracking amid the laughter of the audience, I sense an undertone of popular protest.

When I take my leave, my hosts show me a self-portrait by Wu Xue, a well-known Chinese dramatist. It shows an old-fashioned aristocrat dressed in a long gown and brocade vest. Captioned "landlord," it is obviously a wealthy villain Wu once played. I am glad to learn that the Mime troupe has established contacts with Chinese dramatists. To run such a theater in America requires exceptional courage and dedication.

Respectable Old Friend

Back in 1952, while working at the Asian Pacific Region Peace Conference in Beijing, then Peking, I made the acquaintance of John (more often called Bill) Powell and his wife, Sylvia, who attended the meeting as members of the American delegation. Bill was then editor of the English-language *China Monthly Review* published in Shanghai. Thirty years later, Bill and I met again in Beijing. We had Mongolian hot-pot mutton together but didn't have enough time to talk. Bill and Sylvia live in San Francisco and of course I must call on them. They own a modest house and run a store of used home furnishings on the ground floor. There is a spare bedroom upstairs which has become a sort of hostel for their frequent Chinese guests. A few of my colleagues and friends have stayed in the room and I, too, become a temporary tenant. As old acquaintances, we don't have to stand on ceremony. I help them with cooking and making jam while talking with them. I have heard about the main points of their sad experience and try to learn the details.

Bill's father, John Benjamin Powell, was a professor at the Missouri University School of Journalism. In 1917, he took over editorship of the *China Weekly Review* in Shanghai. The journal was an outspoken critic of Japanese aggression against China in the 1930s and became quite influential in Chinese intellectual circles. For instance, it gave objective coverage of the December 9, 1935, patriotic Chinese student movement demanding resistance to the Japanese invaders while the Kuomintang government imposed a tight news blockade on Chinese papers. As an activist in the movement, I became one of the *Review's* devoted readers. After Pearl Harbor, the Japanese took over the once-safe foreign "concessions" in Shanghai and old Powell was thrown into prison. He suffered terribly and lost both feet as a result of frostbite and gangrene. Repatriated to the United States in 1942, he died five years later. Politically, he supported Chiang Kai-shek.

The young Powell was born in Shanghai in 1919 and later

graduated from the Missouri School of Journalism. After the war, he inherited from his father the Shanghai weekly and changed it to a monthly. During China's War of Liberation (1947-1949) against the Washington-backed Kuomintang dictatorship, the *Review* often highlighted KMT inefficiency, corruption, cruelty and press censorship. It also criticized the U.S. policy of alignment with Chiang Kai-shek as well as the witch-hunting "un-American activities" probes at home. In early 1949, associate editor Julian Schuman (a longtime colleague of mine in Beijing who is better known by his Chinese name Shu Zizhang) ventured into the liberated areas and reported that the communist rule was honest and efficient in contrast to the corruption and harshness of the Kuomintang. After the outbreak of the Korean war, the *Review* was a critic of American aggression in Korea and hostility toward China. It later accused U.S. authorities of stalling the Korean armistice negotiations and reported Korean and Chinese charges of U.S. germ warfare and relevant investigations by some international organizations and foreign correspondents.

As American companies stopped advertising in the *Review* and U.S., British, Japanese and some other governments banned or interfered with the import of the journal, Bill found it financially difficult to carry on and closed the paper in 1953. The farewell issue praised the progress of the new China, declaring that more had been achieved in the four years since liberation than had even been imagined during the previous thirty-two years of the *Review*'s existence.

For this political record Bill courted the disaster which was to plague him for years to come. Before the *Review*'s closure, a CIA man had offered to "work" for the paper without pay. Bill refused him. In August 1953, while Bill was traveling home from Shanghai, the CIA man, waiting for him in Tokyo, offered to recruit him. He would get an annual salary of $15,000 (not a meager sum at that time) simply by attending more peace conferences and coming back to report "who said what." Bill rejected the offer. When he landed at San Francisco, the customs and FBI tried to pump him for information. The two thousand books he brought back from the *Review*'s library were held at the Customs Service for their "political nature." Visiting friends and relatives, he was always tailed by FBI agents.

In September 1954, Bill was summoned to testify before the Senate Internal Security Subcommittee. Prior to that, the chairman of the subcommittee had "revealed" a so-called "wartime conspiracy" of John Fairbank, Owen Lattimore, John Service and other China specialists (the "conspiracy" meant their disapproval of the official U.S. policy of all-out support for the Chiang regime and animosity toward the Chinese Communists). The security investigators pursued the "conspiracy" further and "uncovered" "a little cluster in Shanghai" centered in the *China Weekly Review* in the postwar years. The new subcommittee chairman William Jenner declared that Powell, "this renegade American," had come back to the United States "to soften up the American people...so we will agree to trade with the Soviet bloc and keep quiet if Red China is admitted to the U.N." He demanded that the United States Attorney General press treason charges against Powell. In retrospect, Mr. Jenner could have waited some years for a much stronger case against Dr. Henry Kissinger and President Richard Nixon! The investigation spread further to Bill's wife and Julian Schuman.

Much fuss was made before a grand jury in San Francisco returned thirteen counts of sedition against Powell, Sylvia and Schuman in April, 1956. The core of the charges was the *Review's* reports on U.S. germ warfare. From the outset the defense lawyers maintained that vital evidence had to be obtained in the People's Republic of China and North Korea. The Chinese government, on its part, had declared its readiness to provide fifty witnesses. But there was a great hitch — United States refusal to recognize the People's Republic and to issue passports for travel to the Chinese mainland and the Democratic People's Republic of Korea. To enable the "trial" to proceed, the State Department had to give, reluctantly, a passport to lawyer A.L. Wirin. Meanwhile, Secretary of State John Foster Dulles emphatically declared that the decision in no way affected the policy of forbidding travel to the two countries. In January 1958, Wirin came to China. He interviewed the fifty witnesses. Some of them claimed that they saw American planes drop containers of insects while others were prepared to testify that the insects carried fatal diseases. But Wirin reported that no witness would appear at a trial unless the United States and China negotiated a judicial assistance agreement. The State Department of course sneered at it.

It was also difficult for the United States Government to provide evidence to prove its case. If the court demanded examination of documents relevant to germ warfare and truce-stalling charges, the hearings would very likely touch on "highly sensitive" materials. The Pentagon wanted to drop the case. But the State Department somehow sharply disagreed. Looking back, the Defense Department had good reasons to be prudent. The "Pentagon Papers" revealed years later during the Vietnam War were an object lesson in government suppression of factual evidence. Information about the Korean War also was restricted. In fact, the tidbits already leaked through the American press before the Powell trial, if pursued further, might lead to highly damaging revelations.

Legal and political complexities delayed the trial until January 1959. But how to obtain evidence remained a thorny problem. After many twists and turns, U.S. Attorney General Robert Kennedy finally in 1961 ordered the sedition indictment dismissed and closed the investigation of treason charges. "Because of the existing conditions on the Chinese mainland," he lamely explained, it was impossible to obtain the requisite witnesses. The eight-year travesty of justice sputtered to an end.

Eight years! It is a lot easier said than lived through. Still in anguish, Bill recalls that even with the help of sympathetic lawyers and friends, he had spent his savings of $40,000 on the legal battle. When money ran out, he had to raise funds. His opponent was none other than the powerful U.S. Government, which had in effect deprived him of a livelihood with the treason charge. No employer dared give him a job. No publisher would risk publishing his writings. He was even denied the right to explain his case to sympathizers as thugs often disrupted his scheduled speaking sessions. In spite of the harassment, Bill managed to speak out at small gatherings arranged by friends. After speaking, he would move around to collect donations, like a vagabond minstrel. "I feel miserable whenever I recall begging for money, hat in hand," Bill says.

"How did you pull the family through?" I ask. By renovating houses, he says, a trade he learned while doing it. Altogether he had bought fourteen dilapidated houses, repaired them one by one, and then sold them, thus earning some money to tide them over the crisis.

History is vindicating Bill, Sylvia, and Schuman. The Japanese later admitted that they used bacteriological warfare in northeast China. Following the release of a Japanese TV documentary in 1976, the U.S. Army finally acknowledged the Japanese crime. U.S. involvement began to filter out when documents released later confirmed its own cover-up and use of Japanese germ warfare personnel in postwar years.

I feel sad while listening to Bill's account and at the same time admire him, Sylvia, and Schuman for their moral courage. There are many Americans who share my feelings. Soon after my return to China, Bill mailed me a xeroxed copy of a chapter from a book called *The American Inquisition*. In that chapter entitled "This Renegade American — The Sedition Trial of John William Powell," the American author gives a detailed and factual account of the case which proves it to be truly an inquisition.

Far-Sighted "China Hand"

Upon Bill's introduction, I meet John Service, a well-known expert on China. Mr. Service is busy at his San Francisco home revising a scholarly work on the history of the Qing, the last monarchic dynasty in China. He agrees to an interview.

Service's parents were missionaries working in West China. Born in the city of Chengdu, capital of Sichuan Province, in 1909, young Service learned to speak fluent Sichuanese. After college education in the United States he entered the foreign service and was posted to a clerkship at the American Consulate in Kunming, capital of southwestern Yunnan Province. Transferred to Peking in 1935, he mastered mandarin. From 1938 to 1941, he worked at the U.S. Consulate General in Shanghai and then joined the U.S. Embassy in China's wartime capital, Chongqing. His outstanding ability won the esteem of the then American ambassador, Clarence Gauss. In 1944,

Service was sent to Yanan accompanying the U.S. Army Observer Section posted at that northwestern city, which was the headquarters of the expanding Communist-led revolutionary movement.

Service wrote a series of reports on China for the ambassador to transmit to the State Department as a reference in making policies. In February 1945, a policy recommendation authored by Service won approval of all the political officers of the U.S. Embassy in Chongqing. They collectively signed it for delivery to the State Department. Their observations had convinced them that China was rushing toward a civil war in which the Communists would be the certain victor. They urged the necessity of freeing the United States from a position of exclusive support for the Kuomintang. Such support, they held, both increased KMT intransigence and disinclination either to reform itself or compromise with the Communists, and ensured that the Communists, when they ultimately triumphed, would have every reason for "unremitting hostility toward the U.S."

To be objective, Service had no particular love for the Chinese Communists. He was merely proceeding from the best interests of the United States and recommending a sensible and realistic China policy. At the end of 1944, however, Major General Patrick Hurley took over as ambassador to China. He clung to the policy of exclusive support for Chiang Kai-shek and got support from Franklin Roosevelt in the last months of the President's life. When the Service policy recommendation reached Washington, D.C., Hurley was already there for consultation. Infuriated by the report, the general immediately had Service recalled.

In early 1949, four years after the Service recommendation, one million Communist-led troops swept across the Yangtze River and the Kuomintang regime crumbled like a house of cards. In Washington, D.C., the pro-Chiang conservatives were dismayed and hurled angry charges at the State Department for the "loss of China." I still remember the hue and cry and also the angry Chinese response: How could the United States "lose China," when it never had it in its possession?

The situation got out of control and Hurley had to resign. He offered a typical explanation for the debacle when he charged that the professional diplomats "sided with the Chinese Communist armed party and the imperialist bloc of nations whose policy it was to keep China divided against itself." By "imperialist bloc" he obviously meant the Soviet Union and other socialist countries then sympathetic with the Chinese people's cause.

From 1945 to 1951, loyalty and security hearings became almost an annual event for Service. The State Department board, however, repeatedly returned rulings favorable to him. Whatever his views, Service was only fulfilling his official duty to report to his superiors, and confidentially, too. This seemed to be common sense.

But the McCarthyite hysteria was sweeping the United States at the time. "Pro-Communist" or outright "Red" labels were freely pinned on American liberals. And the State Department was a main target of the red-baiting. In early 1950, for instance, Senator Joseph McCarthy spoke in West Virginia. Holding some papers, he shouted, "I have here in my hand a list of 205... names that were made known to the Secretary of State as members of the Communist Party and who nonetheless are still working and shaping policy at the State Department." The next day, speaking in Salt Lake City, he claimed that he had a list of fifty-seven (the number kept changing) such communists in the State Department. Shortly afterward, he appeared on the Senate floor with photostatic copies of about one hundred dossiers from State Department security files. He read from them, and invented or changed the contents as he read. For example, he changed the dossier's description of "liberal" to "Communistically-inclined," "active fellow-traveller" to "active communist," and so on. In retrospect, the senator's performance bore a striking resemblance to that of Jiang Qing, the hysterical leader of the "Gang of Four" in China's "cultural revolution."

In this onerous atmosphere, the Civil Service Loyalty Review Board offered in December 1951, the verdict that "there is reasonable doubt as to Service's loyalty." Secretary of State Dean Acheson dismissed Service. But Service refused to yield and pressed on with his case.

The political climate in the United States gradually changed, as McCarthy had made too many enemies. Many in high positions had also come to believe that the senator had gone too far. In December, 1954, the Senate voted to "censure" him. The man died later silently, leaving his "high aims" unachieved.

In 1957, the U.S. Supreme Court in the case of Service vs. Dulles ruled unanimously in favor of the victim. He regained his work and got his pension upon retirement. But Service tells me that four of his colleagues dismissed along with him never got back their jobs and are still experiencing difficulties.

Probably out of modesty or reluctance to reopen old wounds, Service doesn't want to talk much. He gives me a book and writes on the flyleaf: "To Wang Tso-min, a formidable interviewer. With warm regards." I am not all that "formidable" though I must admit my keen interest in his story.

The book, entitled *Lost Chance in China — the World War II Dispatches of John S. Service,* was published by Random House in 1974. I have read some reviews but not the book yet. The editor is Joseph Esherick, a professor of Chinese history at the University of Oregon.

The Service dispatches are valuable historical evidence. Part I of the collection comprises reports on Kuomintang China. One of them deals with the famine in Central China's Henan Province. It says inhabitants are eating grass, bark and roots and the relief workers have seen corpses of starved refugees along the roads. The price of women (a common index of hard times in old China) had fallen to one-tenth of the original and even the price of the much-needed conscripts pressganged into the Kuomintang army had fallen by one-third. The cool and factual account reminds me of the nightmarish years I knew personally. Other reports cover the plight of the peasants in general, the state of the Kuomintang army, the KMT dictatorship, Chiang Kai-shek and "the Royal Family," etc.

Part II consists of reports on the Communist areas, including people's life, the Chinese Communist leadership, the strategies of the Chinese Communist Party, the CCP policy toward the KMT and the U.S., and a personal interview with Mao Tse-tung (Mao Zedong).

Part III is captioned "Debate with Hurley." Of particular interest are summaries of another interview with Mao on 13 March 1945 and conversations with Chou En-lai (Zhou Enlai), Chu Teh (Zhu De),

Tung Pi-wu (Dong Biwu) and other Chinese Communist leaders. One evening in 1945 at Yanan, the peasant-like commander-in-chief of the Communist-led armed forces Zhu De patted Service on the knee in his jovial, avuncular way and said, "We don't really expect any arms from you. Ultimately we'll get them from the KMT (Kuomintang) anyway." This episode showed that the Chinese Communist leaders at that early date already foresaw Washington's intentions but were nonetheless confident of victory. When the civil war broke out later, Chiang Kai-shek, as Zhu De predicted, earned the honor of "chief supply sergeant" for the People's Liberation Army when it captured huge amounts of U.S. arms and ammunition from the routed KMT troops.

Editor Esherick writes in the introduction that had Service's advice been heeded, "instead of Nixon in Peking in 1972, we might even have had Eisenhower going there (and not to Korea) two decades earlier." Another lesson, he goes on, is that "if the United States, or any other power, ignores again the popular strength and appeal of Asian peasant revolutions, it will do so at its own peril." Then, in the epilogue, the editor adds that without Korea and Vietnam the correctness of the policy recommended by Service and others would be far more difficult to demonstrate. "Such is the tragedy of the policy and career of John S. Service: only in rejection could there be vindication." To put it in a Chinese way: "You will realize the necessity of mending the fold only when the sheep are lost."

Having recapitulated all these unpleasant memories, I wish to end with what Mao Zedong said in his interview with Service on 13 March 1945:

> Between the people of China and the people of the United States there are strong ties of sympathy, understanding and mutual interest. Both are essentially democratic and individualistic. Both are by nature peace-loving, non-aggressive and non-imperialistic.

I believe this brief statement voiced the popular sentiment in China, then as now. Let bygones be bygones. And let the future be warned.

JOYS AND SORROWS
UNDER DIFFERENT ROOFS
— Public Housing and Poverty Line

Los Angeles is one of the few American cities familiar to the general public in China. The older generation knew it through Hollywood because movie theaters in pre-liberation China were flooded with films made there. The younger generation saw Los Angeles often during the last Olympics in 1984 which it hosted. Its image on the TV screen is one of affluence, modernity, and glamor.

But there are many dark corners in Los Angeles, too, as in other American cities. My hostess, Jean Kidwell, has a friend, Jane, working in the city's "summer employment program" for the poor. Jean asks her to guide us on a visit to a public housing project. Without a proper escort it would not be safe to go, Jean explains. It is not that the people are bad, but because there is much social volatility which strangers might unintentionally wander into.

The place is called Pueblo Del Rio Housing Project. It is part of "the other Los Angeles" where trees and lawns are rare and garbage litters the streets. Many Blacks, obviously bored, unemployed and dispirited workers, sit on old benches and stare blankly at passersby. The project, I am told, has 670 apartments of which ninety percent are occupied by Blacks, ninety-five percent by "single parent families."

Jane seems to know everybody here. Mothers we meet in the streets would tell their children, "Ask Jane to find you a job." Jane tells me that job applicants must meet a number of requirements — they must be fourteen to twenty-one years of age, be Los Angeles residents, have a family income below the Federal defined poverty line, etc. The nine-week employment begins on July 1 but applications have to be filed between mid-March and the end of April, leaving ample time for strict examination. It's not easy to get a job, Jane says.

We ask for permission to see a few apartments. An extraordinary thing is that all the rooms inside the apartments have only door frames but no doors. Jane explains that they were omitted to save building costs. Each apartment has a living room, bedrooms, a bath and a kitchen with a gas stove. But the furnishings are bare and upkeep poor. Still, it can hardly be considered cramped and bad by the standard of Third World cities plagued with housing shortages.

I learn that Pueblo Del Rio has a rule which seems to me incomprehensible and even cruel. All children above the age of eighteen are forbidden to stay any longer in their parents' home because it is thought that they should be living independently. But many of them cannot find work. Consequently, they have to rove the streets, sneak back occasionally for a bite, and steal sleep at home under the cover of night. This takes place so often that the administrators can only keep their eyes half-closed to the rule violations.

Who can qualify for a place in the government-subsidized public housing projects? The qualifications are complex. To put it in the simplest way, they are the poor who cannot afford to pay normal rent. Rents in America vary greatly in different localities but are generally high. Statistics for 1980 showed that an urban family of four in the lower income bracket had to spend an average of $220 for rent every month. Public housing is therefore in great demand. I have been astonished by a news photo showing a fairly large public square in Chicago jammed with applicants. Public housing is not free housing. In Los Angeles, the tenant families have to pay one-third of their income as rent. What about those who are destitute? The bureaucratically managed U.S. Social Security and welfare programs are very complicated. Many Federal departments and agencies have a hand in them and different states have added their own provisions. I am told that only people running the programs are able to read through the bureacratic jargon and gobbledygook and determine who qualifies for what.

Leaving the apartments, we go to see a public dining room which provides meals to children under twelve. The food looks nourishing. A total number of 278 children are qualified for the free meals. As for the qualifications, they are again very involved and I don't have the time to dig into the legal complexities.

Dusk is setting in. As we are leaving, a police car sounding a shrill siren rushes by. Jane says that it has come to nab drug traffickers who are particularly active in the poor districts. Meanwhile, a kind-looking, black-robed priest is coming up the street, bringing consolation to the unhappy souls.

On our way home, Jean points to two sections of the street and tells me that here the "human market" is held, where many jobless people gather daily to get temporary employment. If you need somebody to do an odd job for a few hours or days, you can easily find one. But the place is now empty because it is getting late. Many of the job-seekers, Jean says, are vagrants who have to look for temporary lodgings, under bridges, for instance. But you see them sleeping there only late at night as cops can easily round them up if they go to sleep too early.

Chinese readers having housing difficulties may wonder how public housing residents, living in apartments with hot baths as they do, can be called poor people. Poverty, of course, is not measured by housing alone, nor is it entirely a question of a material living standard. It is also a state of mind. Hot baths and other facilities notwithstanding, the atmosphere pervading the public housing is oppressive.

Apart from housing there is the question of food. I wouldn't say that the American poor are starving to death. But one can easily imagine how they feel when they can buy only the cheapest groceries at the richly stocked supermarkets. When even the cheap stuff is beyond their reach, they have to rely on food stamps doled out by the government. As the food stamps run out, they end up standing shame-facedly in front of soup kitchens run by charitable institions. Breadlines are not a rare sight even on festive holidays like Christmas.

Clothing and transportation are problems, too. There are plenty of fashionable clothes on sale, but the poor can only admire them in show windows. Beautiful new cars are moving on the streets, while many public housing residents have to stagger along carrying heavy grocery bags home. How do they feel about the stark constrast? Moreover, every family will at one time or another encounter the problems of childbirth, disease, senility and death, which are particularly expensive in America.

Last but not least, there is the question of social attitude. In

American society, wealth is honor and poverty is shame. Imagine yourself being one of the poor. The personal resignation of adults to their fates and acceptance of hardships and snobbery is one category, but it is much harder for them to accept the same fate for their children. Lacking proper education, they may be loafing in the streets, acquiring bad habits, and facing an ever-dimmer future. A woman administrator at Pueblo Del Rio tells me in a sad tone, "Many children here are clever and talented, but..." Poverty itself is, of course, grinding, but I feel that in the polarized American society it has been made worse by a sharp sense of ineqality among the poor. This accentuates my conviction that while China must increase its social wealth, measures must be taken to prevent social polarization. An inequitable society, however rich, is not a happy society.

Polarization

No country in the world has yet achieved complete equality of personal wealth. But in America the disparity is increasingly glaring. In the "land of plenty" the number of poor is far too large and, worse than that, is steadily mounting in proportion.

Poverty statistics can be traced back over the years. By 1964, relevant Federal departments had worked out a unified criterion to adjust the poverty index to such factors as family size, sex and age of the family head, the number of children under eighteen and rural/urban residence. The often-cited poverty line has since been defined yearly. According to the authoritative *Statistical Abstracts of the United States* (1981), there were 25.34 million people below the poverty line in 1979, representing 11.6 percent of the American population. A four-person family on an annual income of less than $7,412 were defined as poor. *The U.S. News and World Report* (16 August 1982) reported that the rate of poverty had increased to fourteen percent in 1981 when the line was drawn at an annual income of $9,287 for a four-member non-farm family. The latest news reports I have seen quote figures released by the U.S. Bureau of Census on 2 August 1984, showing a further increase of the poverty rate to 15.2 percent in 1983. It means that no less than 35.26 million Americans were living below the line in that year. Poverty statistics don't always tally, but they appear fairly consistent in their implications.

Who are those on the poor and "have-not" side of American society? A foreign visitor like me can hardly make a field study so I rely on Professor Ian Robertson's *Sociology* (1981 revised edition) for basic information.

The American poor, according to Robertson, comprise the following five categories:

— Fatherless families — more than half of the families living in poverty have a female as head of the household, with no husband present;

— The children — more than ten million children live in poverty and half of them in fatherless homes;

— The minorities — about a third of the Indian families, a quarter of the Chicanos (of Mexican origin) and nearly a third of the Black families live in poverty while, in contrast, less than one white in 10 is poor;

— The aged — people aged sixty-five or over represent thirteen percent of the poor;

— And the regional poor mainly in decaying inner city neighborhoods and pockets of rural poverty.

On the other side of this materially divided society, a tiny minority owns the bulk of the nation's wealth (assets). The richest fifth of the American population posesses seventy-six percent of the total wealth, while the poorest fifth owns only 0.2 percent. The next poorest fifth owns only 2.1 percent.

Mr. Robertson cautions the reader that "we know much less about the very rich than about the very poor, a fact that probably reflects the ability of the wealthy to keep inquisitive sociologists at arm's length." In the meantime, he points out that the great disparity notwithstanding, there has been a general rise in American living standards and that, allowing for inflation, the median income of Amercians has more than doubled in the past quarter of the century. Comparing what I have seen on my present visit with the 1940s, a general rise in the living standard is obvious. But I have also read many analyses, some calmly factual and others vehemently critical, pointing to a rich-get-richer and poor-get-poorer trend. At any rate, the term *median income* is a tricky yardstick to measure the general well-being of highly complex American society.

Every society educates its children in ways which perpetuate the nature of the social system. In America, for example, people are inculcated from early childhood with ideas of equal opportunity and free competition and of the acceptance of personal responsibility for one's successes or failures. Children are told that Abraham Lincoln was born in a log cabin but made it to the White House, and that early-American capitalists like Andrew Carnegie, John D. Rockefeller and J.P. Morgan began with little but became millionaires. This "gospel of wealth" sustains a still widespread belief that hard work and ability are the key to success while the poor have only themselves to blame. That is why people languishing at the lowest rung of the social hierarchy are so demoralized.

In the fiercely competitive American society, there are indeed people rising from humble beginnings or slipping down the social pole. But Robertson cites the surveys of many sociologists to show that dramatic vertical mobility has progressively declined since the 1920s. To put it in a popular way, only a few "soar like swallows" while most are bound to the earth.

Robertson writes that the general pattern of American society is one of moderate upward mobility which involves only minor changes of status — usually a rise from blue-collar worker to white-collar middle-class positions. The reasons for mobility are: First, the growth of the economy has created many more white-collar occupations. Second, the higher classes have lower birth rate and fail to supply the personnel needed to fill the increasing higher-status positions. And third, immigration of unskilled workers from other parts of the world and from rural areas of the United States has tended to "push" existing urban groups into higher occupational statuses.

Robertson is most interesting when he produces statistics to explode "the peculiar American myth" that the poor are poor because they are idle and prefer not to work. An analysis of those on welfare reveals the following about their compositon:

— children under fourteen, making up 34.4 percent;

—elderly, sixty-five and over, making up 18.2 percent;

—ill and disabled, making up 4.7 percent;

—young people in school, aged fourteen and over, making up 6.6 percent.

In other words, the above four categories add up to nearly 64 percent of those on welfare and they are incapable of working anyway. Of the remaining 36.1 percent, 23.8 percent are working but their income simply cannot make ends meet, and 12.3 percent are not working. Of this 12.3 percent who could have worked, 10.9 percent are female, the vast majority of whom are at home caring for small children. Thus only 1.4 percent of all those on welfare are able-bodied unemployed males, many of them lacking skills or living in areas of high unemployment.

Robertson's views appear convincing to me. But many Americans who believe uncritically in the perfection of their "free enterprise" system would not agree. I cite Robertson not as the incontrovertible truth but in a "let one hundred flowers blossom, let one hundred schools contend" spirit.

Figures make for dull reading. I remember an Americn song called *Money Is King*. It was popular for some time after World War II as a reflection of widespread discontent with Mammon. One stanza goes:

> *Now a man with money can go to the store,*
> *The boss will run to shake his hand at the door.*
> *Call ten clerks to write down everything*
> *—suits, hats, whiskey and diamond rings!*
> *They will take it to your home on a motorbike,*
> *You can pay for it whenever you like;*
> *Not a soul will ask you a thing,*
> *They know very well that Money is King.*

The lines continue even more bitterly. For instance, "now if a man has money to spree, people do not care if he has leprosy" and "a man has money and everything nice, a woman might call him sugar and spice."

TWO HUNDRED YEARS OF VICISSITUDES
— The Past and Present of Chinese in America

As a Chinese travelling in America, I have naturally come into contact with many Chinese living here. Some occasions are reunions with old friends from whom I have been separated for decades and more are meetings with new acquaintances.

Chinatowns

Back in China, many people still call the Chinese communities in America by the old name *Tangrenjie* (literally "Streets of the Chinese"). Chinese-Americans now call them *Huafu* or "Chinatown."

I have been to the Chinatowns in Boston, New York City, Chicago, Los Angeles, San Francisco, and Seattle. "Uniqueness and prosperity" are my general impression. They are unique first for the street scenes. The buildings often have Western inner structures but keep such salient Chinese architectural features as pavilions, towers, and corridors. They are also painted in bright reds, greens, or other folksy colors. Ornaments like golden dragons and colorful phoenixes — the usual symbols of China in Western eyes — are seen here and there. The names of shops, public institutions, and streets are written in both English and Chinese. The Chinese characters remain unsimplified, as in old China. The settings remind me of the bustling shopping centers in pre-liberation Shanghai. By prosperity I mean first the numerous and well-stocked shops. You can find precious deer antlers, ginseng, and tremella and all the usual medicinal herbs in the pharmacies. The groceries sell practically all foods that are available in China, from soy sauce and egg noodles to expensive seafood and wild game. As for the restaurants, most of them are exquisitely decorated with gauzy palace lanterns and gold-inlaid sandalwood screens. Waitresses clad in brocade and waiters wearing bow ties receive customers with traditional Chinese courtesy. Handicraft shops display a wide assortment of goods ranging from expensive jade and ivory carvings, moderately priced cloisonne and lacquerware to cheap embroidered slippers and painted fans. Few American sightseers or foreign tourists would miss the chance of having a Chinese dinner and buying some souvenirs. The streets are narrow, and so the hustle and bustle becomes more conspicuous.

Of all Chinatowns, the one in San Francisco seems to me to be the busiest. I have spent the Chinese Lunar New Year's Eve with a Chinese couple working at Stanford University in Palo Alto. Early in the morning of New Year's Day I go to the San Francisco Chinatown and find the sidewalks covered with a thick layer of red paper shells of exploded firecrackers — a sign of the gala festivities the previous night.

I attend the Spring Festival (Lunar New Year) shows at the Chinese Cultural Center. For days on end there are performances of folk dances, music played on Chinese instruments, displays of martial arts and gymnastics, plus a lantern exhibit. Master craftsmen invited from the Chinese mainland demonstrate culinary sculpture by quickly cutting a carrot into a long-tailed pheasant and other such feats. Other chefs show how to make Shanghai-style round pastry and how to knead and stretch dough into extra-thin "dragon-beard noodles." The most attractive performance is micro-engraving by Yang Zhou, from the ancient city of Xian, who produces paintings and calligraphy on pieces of ivory and turtle shell smaller than a rice grain. A TV screen at his side enlarges the work he is creating. Organizers tell me that many more orders for his pieces have been placed than he can produce during the show.

Apart from Spring Festival and other age-old traditions, some customs already forgotten on the mainland are still uphheld here. I have, for instance, received an invitation to a red-egg and ginger buffet to celebrate the one-month birthday of the hosts' baby daughter. The red-painted eggs and the gorgeous invitation card inscribed with the golden characters for "longevity, wealth and felicity" are exactly like those I saw half a century ago, but the banquet has become a Westernized buffet.

In addition to commercial establishments, the Chinatowns have practically all the Chinese trades and professions and are a complete society in themselves. I am told that for many years in the past the Chinese in San Francisco were confined to Chinatown, the first compact Chinese community in America. Any Chinese who ventured outside the ghetto would be assaulted or at least have his windows smashed by white racists. With the rise of Chinese in social status, many have moved out. Celebrated scholars and professionals, in particular, often live in better residential areas.

How They Came

How did these Chinese communities come into being? In 1980, a well-documented exhibition, "The Chinese in America — 1785-1980" was held in San Francisco. But I am too late to see it. I solicit help from H.M. Lai and Jack Chen, two of the main designers of the exhibit. Jack Chen is a writer who has worked many years on the Chinese mainland, and Lai is a lecturer on the history of the Chinese in America and vice-president of the Chinese Historical Society of America. Mr. Lai has compiled for the exhibition a pictorial entitled *Two Hundred Years of Vicissitudes*. On the basis of the pictorial and other materials I shall try to give here a brief account of the growth of Chinese communities in the United States.

The arrival of Chinese in America could be traced to the years immediately after American Independence. In 1785, three sailors by the name of Ah Sin, Ah Chuan and Ah Cun landed on the East Coast. But it was only in the 1840s and 1850s, the period of the Opium War in China and of the Taiping Revolution, that large numbers of Chinese came to the United States, particularly California. Most of them were impoverished people from the Pearl River Delta in south China. They left their homeland reluctantly because life was unbearably hard, especially in rural areas, as the oppression and exploitation by foreign imperialists and domestic rulers became harsher. Meanwhile, America was vigorously opening up its west and needed an abundant supply of cheap labor. By the later years of the nineteenth century, the number of Chinese in America had reached 320,000 plus 50,000 in Hawaii, which had not yet been annexed. They included contract laborers and coolies abducted by fraud or force in a business cynically called the "pig trade." It was the period of the Gold Rush when Chinese arrived in California in large numbers. So San Francisco, the main port of entry, was called *Jinshan* (Golden Mountain). Honolulu, the largest Hawaiian port, was named *Tangxiangshan* (Sandalwood Mountain) because the British were cutting lumber there for export to Canton. Many Chinese joined the search for gold in America but they were heavily taxed or edged out altogether.

By the 1860s, Chinese laborers had become an important force in building the transcontinental railway. When the eastern and western sections of the line were first joined in 1869, there were twelve to fourteen thousand Chinese on the construction sites. They lived in shacks in the snowbound wilderness and did the heaviest and most dangerous work. I have seen a vivid painting showing Chinese laborers standing in a basket suspended from an almost vertical precipice and drilling holes on the cliff to place explosives. It was estimated that one out of every ten Chinese workers died of accident or illness. Afterwards the Chinese turned to equally back-breaking labor, building the California railways, fishing and shrimping on primitive wooden boats, cutting firewood and collecting junk.

But what the Chinese got in return for their labor was an outburst of racist hysteria. In the 1870s, economic depression spread to the American West and the jobless were incited by demagogic racists to expel, beat, and even murder the Chinese as scapegoats for their unemployment. The anti-Chinese agitation led to the adoption by the U.S. Congress, in 1882, of the Chinese Exclusion Act banning Chinese immigration. The number of Chinese in America sharply decreased in the subsequent decades. By 1920, only sixty-two thousand remained, doing menial jobs at small restaurants, laundries and groceries, or as domestic servants. It was not until World War II when China became an American ally that the U.S. Congress saw fit to abolish the Chinese Exclusion Act and bestowed on China a token quota of 105 immigrants a year.

Angel Island

In the decades when the Chinese Exclusion Act was in force, many Chinese, despairing of the chaotic situation at home, kept on coming to the United States. Under the Act, entry permits could be given to a few categories of people including merchants, children, and grandchildren of naturalized Chinese-Americans. All Chinese seeking entry were subjected to a strict screening. The main point of inspection was set up in San Francisco Bay on a small island ironically named "Angel."

Mr. Daniel E. Chu, former president of the Chinese Historical Society of America, and his wife Vyolet L. Chu, vice president of the same organization, have given me generous help in my work. They invite me to their home for a lengthy talk with historian H.M. Lai. Through their arrangement the California State Park Service dispatched a motorboat to ferry me and a number of my Chinese comrades working at the San Francisco Consulate General to visit Angel Island.

It is a fine day and a walk on the small road around the island would be a pleasant outing. But we are in no mood for sightseeing and walk straight to the large two-story wooden building where Chinese immigrants were detained. Not far from the structure a monumental tablet has been erected bearing a fitting Chinese couplet: "Away we wandered from home and got locked up in this wooden house/Hard we toiled and blazed new trails on the Golden Mountain." The building, resting on a low hill, overlooks the bay. From 1910 to 1940, large numbers of Chinese immigrants were kept here for examination. Those denied entry were also kept here waiting for deportation. Living conditions were bad and the examination was arrogant and often unreasonable. If, for instance, a boy claimed to be the son of someone already naturalized as an American citizen, he had to answer a barrage of questions like: How many steps are there at the front door of your house? Who lives in the third house on the second row (of houses) in your village? Of what material is the floor of your bedroom? And where is the rice bin located? The same questions would be put to the father and any discrepancy in answers (which were likely to occur because of the father's long absence from home) might lead to denial of entry. Hence the immigrants were kept in a cruel state of uncertainty.

Chinese have a propensity for poetry, and painting or carving a few lines on walls was an ancient tradition. Consequently, a profusion of verses were left on the walls of the detention building in which the inmates expressed their sorrows and hopes. Some years ago, the state authorities decided to tear down the place of confinement. Vigorous lobbying by the Chinese communities resulted in its preservation as a historic site. A number of Chinese-Americans still versed in classical Chinese put in much effort to record the increasingly illegible wall poems and other writing. H.M. Lai made an extensive collection and study of them and interviewed more than thirty elderly Chinese who had survived the Angel Island experience. On this basis he edited an interesting book entitled *Poetry and History of Chinese Immigrants on Angel Island 1909-1940*. It contains sixty-nine poems in English translation by Lai, plus an appendix of all other such writings he had been able to collect.

The "poets" were mostly poor peasants from the Pearl River Delta and they could hardly be expected to comply with the rigorous demands of rhyme and pattern in traditional poetry. But the works are nonetheless moving for their simplicity.

One of them, lamenting the long detention with no end in sight, reads:

> As a rule, a person is twenty before he
>   starts making a living.
> Family circumstances have forced me to experience
>   wind and dust [the rigors of travel].
> The heartless months and years seem bent on
>   defeating me.
> It is a pity that time quickly ages me.

Another one expresses sorrows over the fate of the motherland intead of personal woes:

> I lean on the railing and lift my head to look at
>   the cloudy sky.
> All the mountains and rivers are dark.
> Eastern Mongolia is lost [to the Japanese] and the date
>   of her return is uncertain.
> The recovery of the Central Plains [a loose reference to
>   lost territories] depends on the youth.
> Only the tongue of Changshan* can slay the
>   villainous.

To kill the bandit we must wave the whip of Zu Di*
I am ashamed to be curled like a worm on this Island.
I grieve for my native land but what else can I say?

We look around carefully at the inside of the building. The detention cells are upstairs, including a big one crowded with narrow berths, and small ones for solitary confinement. A single cell has only a wooden plank for the inmate to sit on and he could hardly turn around in it. Downstairs is the former mess hall, now empty except for some wooden boards displaying photographs of the life of early Chinese immigrants. Comparing the eerie scene with the prosperous Chinatowns, I recall the saying that "the force of wind tests the strength of the grass." — We Chinese are a sturdy people who can weather all storms and stress.

A Turning Point

Improvement of the situation of Chinese in America began in the 1940s and 1950s. As the world colonial system began to crumble in the aftermath of World War II, the United States, out of political and other considerations, took a milder attitude toward the Chinese minority. Many Chinese gradually moved into such fields as science, technology, academic research, medicine, arts, and education, which were, in fact, closed to them in earlier years. Meanwhile, the political and social upheaval in China brought about a change in the occupational composition of Chinese in America as a great number of people of political and intellectual circles left their country to stay in America. In 1965, the U.S. Congress revised immigration laws and abolished the system of quotas based on national origins. This further enabled many more Chinese to immigrate to America from Taiwan and Hongkong. The civil rights movement of the 1950s and 1960s also inspired Chinese-Americans to work for racial equality.

Many ethnic Chinese have distinguished themselves in different fields. There are, to name a few widely known in China, Nobel prize-

*Historical allusions to an ancient official who kept on reviling the enemy while he was being executed by his captors and a brave general who swore to recover lost territory.

winning scientists Dr. Cheng Ning Yang, Dr. Tsung Dao Lee and Dr. Samuel C.C. Ting, the outstanding architect I.M. Pei, and computer manufacturer Dr. Wang An.

In 1970, the number of Chinese in America totalled 435,000, representing an increase of eighty-three percent over that of 1960 and 0.2 percent of the American population. By 1980 the number had increased to over eight hundred thousand, about 0.3 percent of the American population. Tens of thousands of senior scientists and engineers have come to the fore — "a galaxy of talents" as some Chinese-Americans proudly say. Their numbers are large, though they represent a small part of the American demographic chart. Chinese have also entered into American politics and the public offices they hold are increasing in number and rising in rank. Among those better known in China are California's Secretary of State, March Fong Eu, and Delaware's Lieutenant Governor Shien Biau Woo. A forty-seven-year-old professor, Woo was elected in 1984 by the people of that small but highly developed state on the East Coast.

In 1970, according to H.M. Lai, professionals, scientists, technical experts, and managers accounted for 35.4 percent of the total Chinese-American population; technical workers, 20.2 percent; service and other workers, and farmers, 23.3 percent; and salespersons and clerks, 21.1 percent. The first category had expanded and the latter two diminished markedly compared with 1950 statistics. And the trend is continuing. Gone are the days when Chinese could only toil in small laundries, and chop-suey restaurants, or work as domestic servants.

The progress has been achieved the hard way. An old friend has told me, "All of us here know that we have to put in ten times as much effort as the whites to win a position for ourselves or for our children. Every one of us takes great pains to encourage and help our children to study hard."

While I write of progress, I don't mean that it is all smooth sailing in the Chinese communities. Unemployment, crime, and the other maladies plaguing the American society also exist among the Chinese-Americans. The influx of newcomers has caused more difficulties in housing, employment and public security in the Chinatowns. And it would be naive to believe that racial prejudices against Chinese, though less obvious now, have been uprooted. Besides, the Chinese communities remain divided by political and ideological differences, and fratricidal strife — "bean stalks burning to cook beans," as the ancient poem puts it — have not ended. On top of all these problems, there have been shocking incidents like the murder of patriotic writer Henry Liu by Kuomintang agents in San Francisco in early 1985.

Looking to the future, however, I agree with what H.M. Lai has written in *Two Hundred Years of Vicissitudes:*

> Today, the 800,000 Chinese in America are not a homogenous whole. Some are American-born whose families have lived here for generations. They no longer speak Chinese fluently or don't know the language at all. They are entering the mainstream of the American society. Some are old immigrants who have been here for a long time but still adhere to many customs they brought from Chinese villages. Some are new immigrants, among whom many had lived in cities for long periods before they came and have brought with them the customs and mores of Hongkong, Macao, Taiwan, or the Chinese mainland. They are less possessed with localist and clannish ideas. As for the Chinese of academic circles, many of them are non-Cantonese. Most of them live off college campuses and are only loosely connected with the Chinatowns. Then there are the refugees from Cuba, Vietnam, and Cambodia who have their special historical experiences. But, wherever they may have come from and whatever their background, they are all ethnic Chinese living in the great family of Americans. They are confidently forging ahead toward the future, together with Americans of other racial origins.

Fond Memories

I have been back in China for some time but memories of meetings with my Chinese compatriots remain fresh.

Kew Wong of San Francisco, a man in his late seventies, was born at Houwei Village, Wenchang County, on Hainan Island. His impoverished father went to Thailand to make a living and died in a place the family never knew. Wong's widowed mother brought him up by toiling on a tiny family farm. In the 1920s, when China saw an upsurge of anti-imperialist and anti-feudal revolution, Wong and his cousin, a primary school teacher, joined the Communist Party. In 1927 when the Kuomintang, allied with the CCP, turned on the Communists in a White Terror and began its mass arrests and murders of revolutionaries, his cousin was beheaded. Wong hid himself in a dungeon and contracted sores from head to toe and became swollen all over. His mother begged people to take him in disguise to Guangzhou Bay across the strait. There he again got involved in revolutionary activities and was wanted by the authorities. He escaped to Thailand but kept on with his revolutionary work. Hunted again, he fled to Singapore and became a sailor plying between that British colony and America. This gave him the chance to settle in America in 1938. Once more he joined progressive activities and FBI agents frequently observed his home and interrogated him for information. A good friend of his, a member of the U.S. Communist Party, was so persecuted that he lost his mind, and Wong too went through a mental crisis. Then the war broke out. He joined the U.S. Army and served until he was thirty-eight. After demobilization he worked four years as a welder in a shipyard making war vessels. Then he became a janitor and a cook. To keep his job as a chef, he had to plough through thirty cookbooks to improve his proficiency.

As he gained in years, he felt more and more urgently the need to build a secure life. To open a restaurant seemed to be the only feasible way. By virtue of hard work he saved some money and started a small restaurant on a shoestring. His meager knowledge of the English language was a handicap to his business. Luckily, he married a white woman of mixed Jewish, Norwegian and Spanish blood, who could help him. Besides, she shared his political inclinations. The loving couple worked twelve hours a day and seven days a week for two whole decades. Always living on a tight budget, they saved enough money for a down payment on a house and struggled month after month to pay the installments. Then they got a mortgage on the house to buy another one. This finally laid the financial foundation for their retirement. After telling me his life story, Wong asks me to convey a message to the Chinese youth: "Don't look only at the glitter of the American life. It is not easy to make a living out here. Besides, human relations are cool."

Wong retains a deep love for his homeland. In 1981, soon after

China opened its door to foreign tourists, he went back to visit his native Hainan Island. In 1983 he joined a tourist group and traveled to Beijing and many other cities. Back in San Francisco, he wrote saying, "China has truly made great progress. Everywhere I have seen new workers' dormitories replacing old thatched huts, and also newly built shops and department stores, roads and bridges, dams and power plants. My heart is filled with joy and excitement as I, having lived in distant foreign lands for so many years, suddenly see the new sights." But his love for the homeland also makes him bitterly critical of its shortcomings. He wrote, for instance, that he could never accept any explanation for "toilets stinking to the high heavens at historical sites unrivaled in the world."

When I met Wong in San Francisco, a political incident was attracting much attention. A man named Wang Bingzhang, sent from the mainland to study in Canada, declared that he would forego his medical studies for political activism aimed at curing China's "political illness." He came to America from Canada and rigged up a group called "China Spring," whose declared purpose was to stir up a revolution on the mainland for "human rights." A section of the American press made an issue of the matter. Kew Wong is enraged and shows me a poem he has written denouncing the man as a "souless living corpse," a renegade against his motherland. The much-publicized "political dissident," by the way, found few who would follow him and soon fell into obscurity, as Wong predicted.

I also met an equally patriotic woman, Doris Lee. She wouldn't tolerate any criticism of the People's Republic. Doris left her distressed Guangdong Province and came to America as a small girl. The ragged and hunched ricksha pullers and the arrogant foreigners seemed to have left a particularly strong impression on her young mind. Several times I hear her retort to critics of China, saying: "I saw all that with my own eyes. Do they still exist now?" Brought up in a poor peasant family, Doris certainly knew how life was for most Chinese, particularly women villagers, in the old days. She has visited China twice in recent years and seen the difference. Many working people of the older generation seem to share the feelings of Wong and Doris.

What about the intellectuals and professionals? I have met a number of them who are mostly middle-aged or young people. In Los

Angels, Wayne Y.H. Ho, an eye, ear, nose and throat physician, and his wife, Rose, invited me to stay overnight at their comfortable home at scenic Redando Beach. Dr. Ho came from Shanghai in 1945 to study in the United States and has since been a resident here. Rose is a fourth-generation Chinese-American. The hospitable couple often play host to Chinese visitors from both the mainland and Taiwan. Rose showed me their guest book and I saw the signatures of some well-known medical specialists and scholars from Beijing. In the hall hangs a photograph of Dr. Ho holding up hands with one of his classmates at the missionary St. Johns University in pre-liberation Shanghai. The other gentleman, they said, was Yan Jiagan, a leading politician in Taiwan. The Ho family, by American standards, belongs to the middle class. And many Chinese are rising to that social status.

Another couple I met in Palo Alto near San Francisco are likewise comfortably situated. They are Professor John C.Y. Wang, head of the department of Asian languages at Stanford, and his wife, Connie, who holds a technical job at Lockheed, the aircraft manufacturer. Both of them are from Taiwan but are very friendly to me, though I am from the mainland. Connie cooks a wonderfully rich Chinese dinner for me. We chat heartily about family life and state affairs. They show an intense interest in China's quest for prosperity and progress, and are proud of its rising international prestige.

A younger couple I met in Iowa City, Iowa, are also from Taiwan and equally friendly. The husband, Lu Jiaxin, teaches computer software at University of Iowa and his wife, Tan Jia, is a specialist in academic tests for college applicants. She is so young and warm that I soon began calling her "Xiao Tan" (Young Tan) in an intimate Chinese way. They have a family swimming pool and are quite well off. Our free-wheeling conversations rambled from the present situation and future prospects of the mainland and China as a whole to family budgets and how to find good and cheap things at supermarkets. I had dinner at their home and it was the computer expert who did all the cooking. Cheerful Young Tan, learning that I was going to Nevada, phoned her parents in Reno right away and told me that I was very welcome to visit them. I remain thankful for her hospitality though it turns out that I have not enough time to visit another gambling city in addition to Las Vegas.

In Iowa City, a college town, there are more than four hundred students and teachers from Taiwan, ten times as many as from the mainland. During my stay there, a chinese writers' delegation led by the writer Feng Mu and novelist Wu Chiang was visiting the city. On October 1, Chinese National Day, the delegation gave a reception at a small hall at the Universtiy of Iowa. The place was crowded because quite a few young people from Taiwan were present. Several girls, so young that I jokingly called them something like "chits" in Chinese, struck up a conversation with me. I invited them to dine and chat more on some other evening. They readily accepted. In the course of the dinner, one of them suddenly popped up with a question: "I think the Three People's Principles are good. Why not unify the mainland and Taiwan on that basis?"

The Three People's Principles — the Principle of National Rights, the Principle of Political Rights, and the Principle of Rights to a Better Livelihood — were enunciated by the great democratic revolutionary Dr. Sun Yat-sen, who led the overthrow of China's last feudal dynasty in 1911. Chiang Kai-shek took over the doctrine but did not practice what he preached. Driven to Taiwan from the mainland, Chiang and his succesors have insisted on "unifying China with the Three People's Principles" — an obviously impossible demand that the mainland revert to the old social order. And they have been inculcating children with the slogan.

The innocent girl followed up her question with some quotations from Dr. Sun Yat-sen's writings, trying to elaborate her argument. But she faltered because apparently she had not memorized them well. Her serious look made me smile. I said: "I can repeat a lot more quotations from Dr. Sun Yat-sen. The Three People's Principles were a compulsory course when I went to schools in old China. But the question is whether Mr. Chiang Kai-shek really put them into practice. Take the People's National Rights for example. Do you know the song *On the Sungari River?*" The girls nodded. The song, expressing the sorrows of the Chinese who had lost their homes on the Sungari River in Northeast China occupied by Japan, was once very popular.

"We used to sing the song in the 1930s, with tears in our eyes," I continued. "I was going to college in Peking. The Japanese were approaching the city and about to take the whole of North China, too. Have you heard about the December 9th (1935) students' movement? We took to the streets and demanded resistance to the invaders. But we were met by police swinging water hoses and swords. We had to risk arrest and bloodshed because we refused to become the slaves of foreigners. That was how the People's Principle of National Rights worked in the old days."

I had expected some debate but, to my surprise, the girls listened to my personal reminiscences with great curiosity. The stories must be very new to them. Then I enjoined them that whatever special fields they were in, they should study some Chinese history, and particularly, modern and contemporary history. The dinner was very pleasant and the girls said that they would like to come again for "more teachings"—a courteous Chinese way of saying another visit. I like the girls very much for their adherence to the traditional Chinese politeness to elders.

During my journey I have met a number of other Chinese from Taiwan. Our political and ideological beliefs may differ, but there is always much common language once we come into contact. Frankly speaking, over three decades of absolute separation has made me feel that Taiwan is remote and strange. Actually it is not.

SILICON VALLEY, PORTLAND AND SEATTLE
— The Land and the People

With the immense interest in Silicon Valley among Chinese readers, I would fail my mission if I didn't write something about it. Being "scientifically-illiterate," I ask my friend Eugene Ying-che Wang, a laser specialist studying at Stanford University, to help me during the visit. The Santa Clara Valley, near San Francisco, stretches from Palo Alto to San Jose. Since the 1960s, a micro-computer industry has thrived in this narrow valley which soon came to be dubbed "Silicon Valley" because silicon chips are the soul of the industry. Don Hoefler, an engineer (now publisher of *Microelectronics News*), put the name in print in an article published in 1971 and it has since spread far and wide.

Silicon Valley has not grown because of natural endowments. The place used to produce plums, pears, apricots, and cherries — anything but silicon. Its rapid rise is due to a "talent bank" in the vicinity. Palo Alto is the site of Stanford University, which boasts, among other things, a 3.2-kilometer linear accelerator, the world's largest. It shoots electrons at nearly the speed of light. In addition there are the prestigious University of California, Berkeley, and a number of research institutes nearby which form a major source of Silicon Valley talent.

I had imagined that Silicon Valley must be dotted with huge factories. But it turns out to be a quiet place of sparsely located, two-story buildings with big glass windows on all sides. Even street names bear an electronic imprint as, for instance, Semiconductor Drive. The name-plaques on the front of the buildings read Intel, Intersil, Siltec, Synertek and the like. None bears the familiar Chinese kind of name as, say, "No. 2 Semiconductors Parts Factory." But people in the trade know that there is high-tech wizardry behind each plaque.

John Calhoun of Intel, who has visited China, receives Ying-che and me. He shows us around a workshop which looks like a glass house. Several technicians in snow-white overalls are engrossed in work there. Sixty or so machines in the shop are welding and testing silicon chips. When the micro-circuitry (of course invisible to the naked eye) is found to be correct, the chips are moved on to be sealed. The whole operation is computer-controlled. Whenever there is a hitch, the computer automatically stops the work while red lights and buzzers call the attention of supervisors. We hear several such alarms during our ten-minute observation of the shop.

Then we proceed to the design section, which comprises several darkrooms, each equipped with a large-sized "coordinatograph" with two operators, a man in his thirties or forties (all having doctorate degrees, I am told) and an assistant, usually a young woman. The tiny chip is projected on a large screen. The engineer and his assistant check the circuits and determine the corrections to be made. I am told that the design of a chip often requires hundreds of revisions.

"Micro-engraving" Which Changes the World

Mr. Calhoun explains it all in English and Ying-che then translates into Chinese for me. Still I cannot fully understand the process. After reading the Intel brochures and a gift copy of *National Geographic* (October 1982) — a magazine I have long respected for its popular presentation of difficult subjects — I begin to understand something about the mysterious Silicon Valley.

The earliest computer was created at the University of Pennsylvania in 1943. It had 18,000 electronic tubes and was a colossal object costing $3 million. But today a computer with the same capacity is only as large as a typewriter and costs $300. A key to the progress was the appearance of silicon chips in 1959 on which highly complex integrated circuits can be "engraved." This ushered in microprocessors and micro-computers which have become ever smaller, lighter and cheaper. And Intel is a pioneer in this field.

The "era of micro-computers" began. Wristwatches that also work as a calendar, alarm clock, and calculator are now mere toys. The progress is so rapid that NASA has just scrapped a computer bought in 1972 for $30 million, and is installing a smaller and more efficient one costing $11 million. Small American dairy owners are installing sensors and calculators around the necks of their cows and in their feed bins so that the animals can be fed the proper amount of fodder, no more and no less. Crippled people are being equipped with electronic arms and the deaf helped with "bio-ears" about the size of a coin. More and more tireless robots are working in factories. Cars are equipped with micro-computers which help the driver to find the shortest route with the least flow of traffic. Newfangled "tricks" keep appearing in laboratories and then go to the market. Silicon chips are behind all these miracles. I see in *National Geographic* two illustrations, one of a chip being carted off by a large ant and the other an enlarged picture of its circuitry which reminds me of the aerial view of the labyrinth of New York City streets.

All this means that human society is going through a technological revolution, a transformation from the present industrial society to the so-called "information society."

The management of Intel may be of some interest as China is now absorbing not only the advanced science and technology but the worthy aspects of business management in Western countries. Intel was founded in 1968. Its annual income jumped from $10 million in 1971, to $855 million in 1980, and its net profit from $1 million to $97 million in the decade. Intel's "secrets" include "snake-biting" and plenty of meetings. Company Vice-Chairman Robert N. Noyce said, "We are an intensely competitive industry where change is very rapid. There is no resting on your laurels because you will get wiped out next year if you just sit back." David House, general manager of the company's development systems operation, coined the phrase "snake-biting." He says that managers are constantly, consciously looking for problems — looking for "snakes." "When a good, solid problem is discovered," he says, "we study the daylights out of it. How big is it? What color is it? How much does it weigh? Everybody studies, looks, jabbers about the problem and admires it, like putting it on a pedestal. Finally, somebody breaks the code, grabs and stomps it to death. Everybody cheers." This means, in plain Chinese, a never-ending search for shortcomings in the products. When customers complain, it will be too late.

Chinese government offices and enterprises are often criticized for their counter-productive "mountains of documents" and "seas of meetings." Intel, too, has often been accused of being a company where everybody is always at meetings. Intel Vice-President Eugene Flath, in a typical week, spends a day in major staff meetings, three days in management review meetings or one-to-one meetings, and only one day doing everything else, including telephone calls and activities necessary to follow up the meetings. The Intel way, however, seems productive. Ying-che tells me that private American companies cannot afford to do it the Chinese way. The "sea of meetings" being criticized in China means endless, inconclusive sessions at which leading officials read out long-winded and empty reports, ghost-written by their secretaries, to be followed by equally long-winded and empty discussions. As for "one-to-one meetings," they would be called "individual talk" in China, often between a departmental head and his subordinates. Under the Chinese system a work unit is obliged to take care of all the personal woes of its staff. Anybody can go to the "boss" and plead or push for, say, a better apartment, a place in the nursery for his child or a pay raise. But Intel executives, I suppose, don't have to care so much.

Ying-che tells me that Silicon Valley is rich, has a higher level of education, ranks among the fastest growing urban areas, and has often been cited as the place "with the best quality of life" in the United States.

But the valley is no paradise, either. *National Geographic* prints a well-balanced report including a section entitled "pressure spawns drug abuse." It quotes an instructor at the San Jose drug rehabilitation center recounting her experience: "You start on drugs because the job's so boring, hour after hour, and you don't even know what the board is for (her job used to be soldering chips to the circuit boards). You take 'crank' (an amphetamine) and you feel a flash of energy — zzt, zzt, zzt — and do your work! You do twice as many boards! Then the technician standing behind you says, 'Hurry up, you did one-hundred boards last night.'" Theft is another problem. The integrated circuits are small but expensive, and someone can walk out with a fortune in his fist.

Another worry is known as "technological Pearl Harbor." The highly competitive Japanese have staged quite a few "surprise attacks" and edged American products out of world markets. Silicon Valley leaders have bemoaned the lack in the United States of a national industrial policy similar to that of Japan and are lobbying in Washington, D.C., for it. They refuse to yield, saying: "They (the Japanese) have won the skirmish, but we'll win the war." But the pressure is increasing. All in all, it seems that what the "information society" holds in store will not be all roses, as some futurologists predict.

The visit to Silicon Valley recalls to my mind unpleasant memories. As early as 1959, I reported as a journalist on the program-controlled machine tools being developed in Qinghua, China's leading polytechnic university. I was told that only a few countries were at the time pioneering in that field. But since then, as the ultra-leftist tendencies grew in politics, Chinese scientists, already discriminated against as a section of the untrustworthy "bourgeois intelligentsia," further sank in social status. When the "cultural revolution" came, they were, together with other intellectuals, regarded as the "stinking ninth category" after eight other categories of "class enemies." The pseudo-Marxists of those days degraded intellectuals as virtual ignoramuses who "did not know how to grow their own food grains" and as remnants of the Confucian-blessed elite of "rulers by mental work," living on the labor of the working people. Their book knowledge was said to be so much feudal, bourgeois and "revisionist" rubbish. The dire result was that many scientists died and most of the survivors' knowledge grayed with their years. I still remember the propaganda stories deliberately belittling scientists under such sensational headings as "Revolutionary Grannies Produce Monocrystalline Silicon, With No Equipment but Cooking Cauldrons." What was the use of those bookworms since grannies could do all that? Thank heavens that folly is gone! I cannot help saying to Ying-che: "Don't tell me the Chinese hands that can engrave the twelve famous Jingling beauties on a tiny chip of ivory will not be able to make a sophisticated silicon chip. What we need is knowledge of modern science. Work hard and catch up!"

The Rich and Super-Rich

I leave San Francisco for Portland and Seattle. Susan Padgett, an enthusiastic member of the U.S.-China People's Friendship Association, has arranged for other association members to help me at my stopovers. The bus first drives along the Pacific Coast on Highway 101 (U.S. federal highways are numbered) and soon makes its way into thick forests. The trees, mostly redwood, are huge, the biggest as thick as the wooden pillars at the Hall of Supreme Harmony in Beijing's Palace Museum. The taller ones are sixty meters or more in height, an awesome sight. There are several national parks in the forests with camping facilities, adding to my impression that the Americans know how to enjoy themselves.

It is dusk when I get to Eureka, on the northern boundary of California. Claire Courtney is at the bus depot to meet me. She works as a local government employee helping the jobless to find work. Eureka, a timbering town, has been hard hit in the recession year of 1982, with an unemployment rate of 18.5 percent against the national average of ten percent. "Talking shop after three opening sentences," as we Chinese describe people who are devoted to their work, Claire soon begins to complain about the difficulties she is encountering. The lumberjacks have been cutting wood all their lives and are not trained to do other types of work. Even if they get new training, the town cannot offer enough job openings with its principal industry in decline.

I cannot help asking why the government does not do something to alleviate the situation, because we in China are accustomed to blaming the government whenever something goes wrong. Claire says offhand that I should read a book entitled *The Rich and the Super-Rich*** and will find an answer there. She takes a copy from her bookshelf and gives it to me as a present. In fact, a few Americans have recommended the book to me and I have already bought one.

The book used to be a best seller. Published in 1968, it saw eight printings in two years, and a Bantam edition put out in 1969 has been reprinted many times. The author is Professor Ferdinand Lundberg. An earlier work by him, *America's Sixty Families,* was translated and published in China in the 1940s. He wrote the latter volume after three years of extensive research. The book purports to answer the questions: "Who really owns America? How do they keep their wealth and power?" With a mass of facts the author tries to prove that there are 200,000 very wealthy individuals in America, most of whom belong to some 500 "super-millionaire families" and sixty-one percent of them inherit their wealth. They are wealthier than ever before. The book tries to unveil "the real truth behind the five-hundred families who rule our lives today." They are the "silent rulers" "whose names you may never have heard of or seen in print before." Some book reviewers seem to think highly of the work. The *Los Angeles Free Press,* for one, writes: "It is probably the most important book in print in the United States today, and you will go on reading it for a long time."

Carlson and Avshalomov

I bid farewell to Claire early next morning and set out for Portland. The scenery on the route is unique. At first the bus runs through the

---

*A Bantam book published by arrangement with Lyle Stuart, Inc, New York, 1969.

redwoods on an expressway which has only one lane in each direction. Cars are few and there is a primitive atmosphere. Coming out of the forest, the bus travels very close to the Pacific coast. The blue waves roll away till they turn into a misty white expanse of water merging with the sky. The yellowish sand beaches are dotted with strangely-shaped black rocks. The bus turns away from the coast when it approaches Portland, on the northern border of Oregon.

Paul Morris, who has just come back from a visit to China, and his girl friend Janet Malloch greet me at the bus depot. The first thing Paul says is that he had met my husband and had a good talk over beer in my home in Beijing. It is nice to meet somebody just back from my home. Paul and his friend entertain me with a Chinese dinner they have prepared. I feel happy that Americans and Chinese are visiting each other's homes, a sign that exchanges are maturing beyond the stage of formal toasts at official banquets. Chatting with them, I learn that Portland (pop. 360,000) is known as "a city of roses" and holds rose festival parades every year. It has the largest number of fountains of all American cities. The municipal authorities strictly limit the height of buildings so that views of the Cascade Mountains in the east and the Coastal Range in the west will not be impeded. A wise decision, I believe, as many people are worried by the disorderly arrays of high-rises shooting up in many ancient Chinese cities.

Only 50 miles north of the city, Paul tells me, is Mount St. Helens. A violent volcanic explosion on 18 May 1980 blew away its northern face, leaving a crater one mile wide and two miles long, and reduced the mountain's elevation by 1,370 feet. The blast devastated an enormous area around it, flattened vegetation and filled streams with hot mud. Ash rained down on nearby cities, turning skies dark at midday. Three more eruptions occurred in May, June and October, 1980, and left an inch of ash in Portland. I am given a packet of the ash as a souvenir.

There are many friends of China in the city. Mrs. Bryan Sweetman is a Friendship Association activist. Her husband was taken to China by his missionary parents when he was six months old. The family stayed until 1927 when chaos once again reigned in China as the Kuomintang rightists turned against their one-time ally, the Communists, and murdered tens of thousands of them. There is a picture of the young Sweetman dressed in typical Chinese clothes in a large frame hanging in the sitting room. I almost mistake him for a Chinese boy.

I also meet Dr. Charles M. Grossman and his wife, both members of the Friendship Association. Dr. Grossman is also chairman of an organization called the Evans F. Carlson Friends of the People's Republic of China. Progressive Chinese intellectuals of my generation may know something about Carlson, but not the details.

Carlson first landed in Shanghai in 1927, a young Marine officer with all the prejudices of white America. He wrote home that "the only effective policy is to teach these Chinese a lesson." Ten years later, he arrived in Yan'an in northwest China's Shaanxi Province, site of the headquarters of the Communist-led liberation movement, and became the first Western military officer to observe the Communist Eighth Route Army's effective tactics against the Japanese invaders. He spent much of the next two years with the guerrillas and met Mao Zedong, Zhu De and many other Chinese leaders. In Hankou in central China, he was introduced to Zhou Enlai by Agnes Smedley, Zhu De's biographer. After his return to the United States, Carlson spoke about the successes of the Chinese Communists, the corruption of the Chiang Kai-shek government, and the error of U.S. policy to sell scrap iron to Japan for weapons which ultimately would be used to kill Chinese. Carlson had to resign in 1939 from the Marine Corps, which could not tolerate his political views. But he continued to speak about China and published *Twin Stars of China* and another book, as well as a number of magazine articles. Dr. Grossman strongly recommends that I read *Twin Stars*.

Patriotic, Carlson rejoined the Marines in 1941 in anticipation of a Japanese attack on the Philippines, Guam and Wake Island. After Pearl Harbor he organized a battalion known as Carlson's Raiders, modeled after Chinese guerrillas. He led two very successful operations behind Japanese lines in 1942, on Makin Island and Guadalcanal. His raider battalion received so much favorable publicity in the United States that the Marine Corps, which would not tolerate such individual acclaim, removed him from his command. Carlson served as a staff officer until he was wounded at Saipan. He retired as a Brigadier General and died in Portland in 1947 at the age of 51.

Writing this brief account, I feel sad at the thought that if Brig. Gen. Carlson had lived to the age of eighty-eight he could have come, together with Bill Powell (editor of the English-language *China Weekly Review* whom I interviewed in San Francisco) and other old friends, to Beijing in 1984 to join the celebrations of the thirty-fifth anniversary of the People's Republic and witness the grand parade of the Chinese People's Liberation Army—whose predecessor was the Eighth Route Army with nothing more than "millet plus rifle" that Carlson saw. "The Evans F. Carlson Friends of the People's Republic of China," Dr. Grossman says, "is a group organized to keep alive the memory of this great American."

Dr. and Mrs. Grossman invite me and Mrs. Sweetman to lunch at a Chinese restaurant. There we chance to meet Dr. Grossman's friend, composer and conductor Jacob Avshalomov. When Mr. Avshalomov learns that I am from China, he invites me to a musical drama, *The Great Wall*, in the evening.

Why Great Wall? There is another story of friendship. Jacob was born in China's coastal city Qingdao, and grew up in Tianjin and Beijing. He came to America in 1937 and has served many years as music director and conductor for Portland Youth Symphony and become one of the country's prize-winning composers in the international circle of musicians. His father, Aaron, was born in Siberia and later moved to China. As a musician and a friend of the Chinese people, Aaron felt sorry that the Shanghai Symphony, China's leading philharmonic orchestra at the time, was conducted by an Italian, and did not have a single Chinese player. Moreover, its repertoire was European from beginning to end. To counter the trend, he composed many works on Chinese material and *The Great Wall* is one of them. At its premiere, he asked a Chinese to play the first flute and the musician's European teacher to play second.

It is tradition in China never to forget old friends. Almost two decades after Aaron's death in America in 1965, an unexpected invitation came to his son to visit China from Jiang Chunfang, Aaron's friend. Mr. Jiang is a well-known scholar and editor of the Greater Chinese Encyclopedia. When I met him in early 1983, Jacob has just returned after three memorable weeks spent in China. He has had extensive contacts with Chinese musicians and attended concerts of his father's works. In Shanghai, a large tea party was given in his honor and more than sixty friends and colleagues of Aaron attended. One by one they came up to tell him how much his father had cared about Chinese music and Chinese artists. "They poured over me these reminiscences to the point that I could no longer hold back the tears," says Jacob.

I regret that I cannot attend *The Great Wall* performance because I have to leave. Jacob gives me a copy of the newspaper *Oregonian* which features a lengthy account of his China visit. A color photograph splashed across the page bears the caption: "Back to the source — Jacob Avshalomov pauses before the Great Wall of China, inspiration for one of his father's greatest musical works." And a banner headline says: "The Sounds of China — Portland conductor Jacob Avshalomov returns to his roots." Jacob's root-searching tour will probably strike some new roots of friendship for China among the Oregonians.

Continuing my trip northward, I arrive at Seattle in five hours. The scenery on the way is unique for the numerous clear rivers and beautiful bridges spanning them. Seattle (pop:490,000) is on the shores of Puget Sound, linked with the Pacific. It has close maritime connections with the Orient. Its symphony orchestra, opera and ballet companies are famous throughout the United States. I choose to pay a visit to Weyerhaeuser, a giant lumber company eager to do China trade, whose headquarters is near Seattle. On the way is the largest building in the United States — the forty-seven-acre Boeing 747 manufacturing plant in Everett. On the open field outside the plant are a number of passenger airliners on which Saudi Arabian flags are being painted.

Friendly Divorce

David "Mac" Shelton, a young lawyer in charge of the local chapter of the friendship association, and his wife Frauke are my hosts in Seattle. The couple have twice led bicycle tours to China. The groups included some versatile artists who occasionally performed for Chinese pedestrians, on street corners. The pictures they took show smiling Chinese audiences apparently admiring the easygoing and fun-loving Americans. Mac says that he will be my "temporary secretary," meaning that he will do everything to help me know Seattle.

The lawyer's family gives me a chance to tell Chinese readers something about how the Americans handle their divorces. Mac parted from his former wife seven years ago and Frauke was widowed at about the same time. They got married recently. They display on the wall a wedding card, with the design of two hearts linked, drawn by Frauke's daughter. The child was apparently pleased to have a new dad. Mac has a son and a daughter who are now living with their mother. Mac lives with Frauke and her two children. Every Saturday Frauke drives to the home of Mac's former wife and takes his son and daughter to Mac for the weekend. The couple and their four children live in harmony and happiness. Once I invite the family to dinner at a downtown Chinese restaurant and propose that Frauke pick up Mac's two kids for the occasion. But Frauke declines, saying that their mother may be displeased because the agreement is only for Mac to spend weekends with his children. This may seem a trifle but I see in it a good spirit of honoring promises.

The Shelton family reminds me of a younger Boston couple, the son and daughter-in-law of Rita Gould I have mentioned earlier. Widowed, Rita loves her granddaughter as if she were, to use a Chinese phrase describing pampered girls, "a pearl on the palm." One day Rita gave a large birthday party for the "pearl." I saw the father and mother happily pose with their daughter for photographs, and, after the party, leave together. I was surprised to learn that they were divorced and wondered why they would not remarry since they seemed to be getting along very well. But a friend told me that it was not possible now because both of them had "steady friends." Then Rita explained to me that theirs was a "friendly divorce," a very new term for me. It aroused my interest because the number of divorces has been rising in China in recent years — not a sign of family dissolution but rather a reaction against the feudal tradition which regards divorce as a terrible sin and the once-prevalent "revolutionary" idea that divorce is bourgeois decadence. It is a necessary evil that couples without an affection be allowed to part, but in China the divorced people often treat each other like enemies and the children are caught between the two "belligerents" and suffer. "Friendly divorce," I think, is something we can learn. But I am told that in America, too, many divorces are "unfriendly."

The Story of "Skid Road"

I often hear Americans quote the saying that "a good picture is worth more than a thousand words" and attribute it to the Chinese. Not well versed in classics, I have failed to trace its origin. Chinese or non-Chinese, the saying can be used aptly to describe the book, *Seattle — A Pictorial History* , which Mac shows me. The album, with some three-hundred pictures, records the 130-year pageant of Seattle, its growth from a barren beach to a modern city. It includes pictures of the railroad years, showing Chinese workers digging routes for Northern Pacific tracks through snowfields, the Great Depression days with the Hoovervilles, and of the Boeing boom fueled by orders for B-29s during the war, and the imminent collapse of the company saved by a bold gamble on the postwar 707 jet transports.

Mac finds me engrossed in the book and suggests that I go to see Murray Morgan, one of the editors of the pictorial. A veteran newspaperman and octogenarian, Mr. Morgan has witnessed much of the history of Seattle. The other editor of the book is his daughter Lane Morgan and their collaborator is Paul Dorpat, a collector of historic photographs.

Mr. Morgan and Mr. Dorpat receive me in a studio and give me an autographed copy of their book as a present. Mr. Morgan gives me another book, *Skid Road* .* A young assistant tells me that the book is a classic, revised five times and reprinted again and again since it first saw the light in 1951.

Mr. Morgan talks with me at length on the history of Seattle with special reference to the labor movement. It is after my return to Beijing that I have found time to read *Skid Road*. Its vivid narrative, plus Mr. Morgan's talk, helps me gain a graphic understanding not only of Seattle but perhaps of all the American Far West.

Seattle abounds in forests. Early settlers chopped down trees and pushed them down the road to Puget Sound for transportation. Hence

* Published by University of Washington Press, Seattle and London, 1982.

the name "Skid Road." More and more settlers poured in. Skid Road became a place with men sitting on curbs and sleeping in doorways, houses padlocked for nonpayment of rent, signs that read "beds, twenty cents" and "oatmeal, five cents," cheap taverns and cigar stores which also sold second-hand nudist magazines. The "fame" of the dilapidated Skid Road spread as quickly as that of the prosperous Silicon Valley today. There were and are Skid Roads in Seattle and elsewhere. So the proper name has become a common noun. As the *American Heritage Dictionary* defines it, "skid road" (or "skid row") is "a squalid district inhabited by derelicts and vagrants." In today's Seattle, the Yesler Way (named after an early owner of a timber mill) is still a dividing line of sorts: to the left are big new buildings on steep streets, and to the right, in Morgan's words, "The red brick buildings untopped by neon, along the unswept sidewalks where the rejected men stand and stare, are the symbols of the past, the monuments to men who dreamed the wrong dreams."

But *Skid Road* is not just a muckraking book. It tries to present a balanced picture of the city's growth. Reading it makes me feel strongly that China, with its numerous historic cities, with its literary world being rejuvenated now, and with such memorable ancient works as the *Dream-like Days in Dongjing* (now Kaifeng in central China's Henan Province) to emulate, should publish a series on city histories.

Skid Road starts with vivid images of the early settlers. Doc Maynard was one. They were not legendary heroes, but hardy, warm human beings. Doc liked to drink, and his worst faults grew out of his best virtue, a desire to help the unfortunate. Generous Doc found himself saddled with debts. When his children were old enough to look after themselves, he bade farewell to them and his wife, mounted his gray mule and rode off from Ohio toward California in 1850 to pan for gold nuggets. Having no cash, he relied on his profession to pay his way.

By firelight or in the early dawn he wrote entries into his diary. A few quotations, I hope, will give Chinese readers an idea of the hardships the early American settlers encountered, and that the present prosperity of the country is not luck. Doc wrote: "Passed the grave of A. Powers. . . was called to visit three cases of cholera," "took sick with the cholera," "found the mosquitoes so bad that it was impossible to keep the oxen and ourselves on that spot. Oh, God!" "...left Brandy and Polly to die on the road," "bought a fine spotted horse, which cost me $55... this night I had my horse stolen," "I was taken about sunset with dysentery," "we buried a child we found upon the bank of the river, drowned...."

On the way Doc attached himself to a caravan of wagons bound for the West. He met a widow with whom he fell in love and decided to go with her to her brother at Puget Sound instead of to California. The widow's train edged westward, four miles, ten miles, occasionally twenty miles a day. They reached Puget Sound in August (Doc left Ohio in early April).

Much happened before Doc finally settled in what is today's Seattle. The place, with only a few households, had no name yet. Doc became a good friend of an awesome-looking but friendly Indian chieftain named Sealth (pronounced *See-alth* and sometimes *See-attle*). At Doc's suggestion the residents agreed that the town be called Seattle. During the American Civil War, Congress enacted the "Homestead Act" by which Doc acquired 640 acres of land free (a huge estate of 3,886 *mu* by Chinese standards), half for himself and half for his new wife.

Doc warmly welcomed others to come and settle in Seattle, sometimes ceding his cultivated land to others in exchange for poorer lots. A Mr. Yesler came and set up a timber mill and the town prospered. Later, a war broke out between the white authorities and local Indians. As a friend of the Indians, Doc did his best to mediate, but was sneered at as an "Indian lover." After the hostilities ended he went into retail trade, served as a town official, worked as a lawyer, and practiced medicine. Because he also treated Indians, white clients were few. Doc drank more than ever, and became an alcoholic. Kinder when drunk than sober, he regained much of his old popularity. In 1873 he died, and the city held its largest funeral for him, as he was a founder. In brief, this was the life of Doc Maynard, an American with virtues and faults, bent on seeking a personal fortune, but at the same time ready to work for the common good.

Morgan shows deep sympathy for the Chinese laborers. He writes: "The Chinese had been popular once. They had been imported in large

numbers by the railroad builders when cheap labor was needed....
The Chinese, one and all, were called 'John,' and the stories of John's
prowess as a construction worker almost reached the status of folk
legend. John could work twelve hours on a handful of rice; impassive
John could handle blasting jobs that other men were too nervous to
carry out; brave John would work all day at the end of a hundred-foot
rope, chiseling notches for trestle supports; inscrutable John had the
best poker-face in a poker-loving nation. Good old John." But
immediately after the Golden Spike was driven in the final section of
the transcontinental railroad, an anti-Chinese hysteria swept over the
American West. Morgan describes the Chinese expulsion from Seattle
so vividly that the shouts of "go home, John" seem to be still ringing
in my ears.

Morgan is sympathetic with all underdogs, labor in particular. The
Industrial Workers of the World, a labor union, was active in Seattle.
It was popularly called the "wobblies." The name, Mr. Morgan tells
me, came from the Chinese whom I.W.W., unlike other unions, would
accept as members. Unable to speak English, the Chinese laborers
supposedly mispronounced I.W.W. as "wobblies."

From February 6 to 11 in 1919, a general strike occurred in Seattle.
Truly general, it brought about a complete cessation of business. "At
ten o'clock Thursday morning," Morgan writes, "whistles sounded in
the mills and on the ships at the docks. With that signal the industrial
activity of the city came to a halt. Streetcar service stopped. Schools let
out. Banks locked their doors. Restaurants shut down. The movies
closed. Presses and linotypes went silent and lead cooled in the
pots.... Maids stopped making the hotel beds.... People suddenly
heard the chirp of sparrows and the moaning of the doves that nested
in downtown buildings." "A hearse rolled slowly down the street,
carrying a placard which read: 'Exempted by the Strike
Committee'.... Labor guards, wearing red armbands but vested with
no real authority, patrolled the industrial district." At the same time,
heavily armed policemen stood at the street corners, and at dawn that
morning a convoy of trucks had rumbled in with fifteen hundred
soldiers aboard, alert for trouble.

There were no newspapers and rumors were afloat: the water
system had been poisoned, the city outskirts were being pillaged,

private property was being confiscated, the strike leaders had set up a soviet.... The mayor, however, had access to the national media and he fed stories everyday to the local United Press bureau. The UP dispatches stirred the whole country with a theme which was to be the title of a book written later by the mayor — *Americanism versus Bolshevism*. In fact, the whole thing had nothing to do with the Soviet Union, which was still in its birth pangs.

The strike came with the force of a storm, but labor leadership lacked a clear idea as to what to do next. Pressures from without and dissension from within dampened the morale of the workers. The strike ended in a week. The exhilarated mayor declared: "I am a great man." He became a Republican presidential aspirant but failed to get the nomination. He had to sell his property and moved out of Seattle.

Morgan strikes a responsive chord in my Chinese mind for his admiration of the Seattle journalist Anna Louise Strong. Strong is well-known in China because she had visited the Communist-led liberated areas in the 1940s, listened to Mao Zedong declare, in an exclusive interview with her, that "imperialism and reactionaries are paper tigers," and wrote several books on revolutionary China.

In Seattle at the time of the general strike, Strong was editor of the daily *Union Record*. She wrote a number of editorials. The one published two days before the strike was best known. She wrote: "LABOR WILL FEED THE PEOPLE.... Twelve great kitchens have been offered, and from them food will be distributed by the provision trades at low costs to all.... LABOR WILL CARE FOR THE BABIES AND THE SICK.... LABOR WILL PRESERVE ORDER.... Labor will not only *shut down* the industries, but Labor will *reopen*.... UNDER ITS OWN MANAGEMENT." "And this is why we are starting on a road that leads — NO ONE KNOWS WHERE!"

Strong was obviously talking about the unlimited possibilities to be opened by the strike. But the editorial also reflected that the labor leaders had only a vague idea about what the strike was intended to accomplish. The Seattle mayor repeatedly quoted the "No One Knows Where" editorial, always implying that it meant "straight to Moscow." This "Moscow hat" (hat in Chinese also means stigma) still seems to be in use to besmirch and intimidate American radicals or even liberals today.

Nobody could lead Seattle, or America, "straight to Moscow." But Anna herself, for one reason or another, later did go to stay in Moscow, where she was branded a "spy" after the war, came back to Seattle for a while, and then spent her remaining years in post-revolution China.

In 1984, a "Smedley-Strong-Snow Society" was established in China to promote research into the lives and works of the three respected American writers. The founding of the "SSS Society," as it is affectionately called, is also a tribute to many lesser known American friends of China, who foresaw the viability of the Chinese revolution in its embryonic stage.

During my interview, Mr. Morgan said that he was a "burnt-out radical." American society is complex indeed. There are people, like Iowa farmer Wheeler, who sincerely believe in capitalism. He could be called "a capitalist roader" in China (the abbreviated designation for "persons in authority taking the capitalist road," a label willfully pinned on officials during the "cultural revolution;" the omission of "in authority" makes it more appropriate for Mr. Wheeler). There are, at the same time, equally sincere radicals like Mr. Morgan. On the one hand, many people accept the views expressed in *The Rich and Super-Rich* that the United States is a financial oligarchy. And on the other, there is the widespread belief that America is a country dominated by the middle class. Again, I am in no position to judge which is right and which is wrong. A firm believer in the proposition that revolution cannot be exported, I feel it best to leave it to the Americans themselves to give the decisive answer.

"Adou" Finds His Father

Another interesting person Mac Shelton has introduced me to is Otto Sieber. His father, Professor Chow Chuan Ru, is a contemporary of my teachers. He was a research student at Qinghua University in the early days, later went to Britain for advanced studies, and married a German woman named Sieber. The couple and their son Otto returned to China. Professor Chow taught in a university in the

southwestern Sichuan Province. While the civil war against
Kuomintang rule was raging, the mother and son went from Sichuan
to Hongkong, hoping to return as soon as the fighting was over. But
then came the long years of blockade. They came to the United States.
And Professor Chow, sharing the fate of many talented Chinese
intellectuals, was branded a "bourgeois rightist" in 1957, deprived of
his teaching job and given a meager pay to live on. Despairing of a
chance for reunion, he remarried.

Then came the thaw of Sino-American relations. Otto Sieber
appealed to the late United States Senator, Henry Jackson, a friend of
China, for help in finding his father. The senator referred his request to
Leonard Woodcock, then head of Washington's Liaison Office in
Beijing, who in turn asked Chinese leader Deng Xiaoping to help.
Before long Otto was back in China and met his father.

The happy reunion was reported in *China Pictorial*, a multi-
language periodical with a big circulation. I happen to see the story in
which Otto's name was translated rather queerly into a Chinese
homonym *Adou*. *Adou* is a household word in China because it is the
name of a character in the popular classical novel *Romance of Three
Kingdoms*. An heir to the Kingdom of Shu, Adou was a weakling and
reveler who eventually lost his kingdom in spite of the support of the
wisest strategist Zhuge Liang. Hence the phrase "Adou who cannot
be propped up" is used to criticize those who cannot be saved by even
God's help.

When I call Otto at his home, Professor Chow happens to be
visiting his son. Otto is amused by the story of Adou. Perhaps to prove
that he is no Adou, he tells me a story about himself. A self-employed
film maker, he and several colleagues rushed to Mt. St. Helens to make
documentaries after its first eruption in 1980. They met with another
volcanic burst. Otto narrowly escaped death and was seriously
injured. And he shows me a photograph of two sheriffs escorting him,
with bandages on his forehead, off the scene. The film he made became
invaluable material. He has sold many copies for $500 each. Somebody
from the Federal Republic of Germany, his mother's homeland,
wanted to buy one, and he charged $10,000 for it. As a token of his
gratitude to Woodcock and Deng Xiaoping, he presented them each
with a copy.

But Otto got into trouble with the film. The sheriffs asserted that he had intruded into an out-of-bounds danger zone and had to pay a $500 fine or be imprisoned. He flatly rejected the charge, citing many maps to prove that it was the authorities who, in their eagerness to help the lumber companies extend their operational areas, failed to mark out the danger zones as they should have. As a result, he counter-charged, lumberjacks were unaware that they were working in hazardous places. It was fortunate that the first eruption occured on a weekend. Still, a number of workers lost their lives while earning overtime pay at the spot. It was the same area Otto entered. He was indignant over the authorities' collaboration with big business in disregard of people's lives, and angered even more by the charges against him. He decided to sue the authorities in court. Lawyers cautioned him, saying that a fine of $500 is nothing but going to court would be costly. "Are you crazy?" they asked, but Otto would not budge. After spending $20,000, he won the suit. The truth was out. The families of the victimized lumberjacks have filed suits for compensation. Court proceedings are still dragging on.

Our conversation then turns to Professor Chow. I ask him what he thinks of the years when he was "wearing the hat of a bourgeois rightist." He did not complain, merely saying with wry smile, "It is a pity that more than twenty precious years were wasted." It seems to me that Otto is endowed with his father's Chinese patience, his mother's German tenacity, plus the American spirit of adventure. It is a misnomer indeed to call him Adou! And particularly so because, Professor Chow told me, he had given Otto upon his birth an ambitious Chinese name — *Jiapeng. Jiapeng* means "roc of the family" and the Chinese roc is a legendary bird that can travel 10,000 *li* (three-thousand miles!) in one flight. I would like to stay longer in interesting Seattle. But I have to leave for Yakima to meet the American Indians.

THE REAL NATIVE AMERICANS

— A Visit to Yakima Indian Reservation

While discussing my itinerary with M.I.T. Professor Robinson soon after my arrival in the United States, I suggested: "A visit to an

Indian reservation would be wonderful, if possible." I immediately regretted saying that, believing it was difficult to arrange. Quite unexpectedly, the professor said: "Oh, that's easy. You can go to Yakima while you are in Washington State. It is my native town and there is an Indian reservation there."

From Seattle I travel southwest to Yakima. It is early February but flowers are blossoming in Seattle. The landscape changes drastically as the bus enters the Cascade Mountains. The warm Japanese Current is blocked off by the peaked range and the hills along the expressway are all snowbound. Piling up week after week, the snow appears in layers of different colors, making the hillsides look like multi-tiered Chinese cakes. The scenery also reminds me of the Changbai (Ever White) Mountains in Northeast China.

Yakima, about 125 miles from Seattle, is a small town of fifty thousand. Professor Robinson has written to his high school teacher Ray Miller, asking him to take care of me. Though 83 years old, Mr. Miller is in perfect health and comes with his wife, Ruth, to meet me at the bus depot. They drive me to the hotel for a short rest and then take me to their home for lunch. The fresh clam chowder Ruth makes is the best of its kind I have ever tasted.

In the afternoon the couple invite a number of Professor Robinson's old acquaintances to tea. Chatting with me, all seem to hold the professor's late father in esteem. One guest tells me that Dr. William D. Robinson was highly commended by the most famous citizen of Yakima — former U.S. Supreme Court Justice, William Douglas (in office from 1939 to 1975). Douglas, known for his liberal inclinations, wrote in a book that Dr. Robinson, as a Congregational minister, truly applied the teachings of Christ to the itinerant workers who came every year to the Yakima Valley in great numbers to pick fruits, even though these people were generally regarded as the underside of society. Family tradition seems to explain partly why Professor Dick Robinson is also a liberal.

The next day, the Miller couple drive me to the Yakima reservation. An Indian friend of theirs, Mrs. Naomi Shephard, accompanies us as a guide because she is a retired worker of the local agency of the Federal Bureau of Indian Affairs. Mr. Miller is at the wheel and drives at high speed as effortlessly as a youngster. He tells me that he used to be a teacher of architectural drafting and physical education. In his spare time he designed and built his own house. After retirement he has kept on doing physical work and often takes his grandson out on long fishing trips. I have seen many American elders as healthy and active as Mr. Miller. In 1980, life expectancy in America was 73.6 years while in China it had lengthened from 35 years in 1949 to 69. But I have not seen as many doddering elders in America as in China. Better nutrition, of course, makes for better health. But I feel that the American senior citizens' love for physical labor, as work or hobby, may also be an important factor.

The Town of Wapato

The car crosses a river and enters the Indian reservation. Before European immigrants set foot on the New Continent, the Indians had been masters of the land for many centuries. After repeated Indian wars, the whites finally succeeded in herding the surviving Indians onto reservations. Statistics for 1981 showed that there were over 260 confined Indian communities scattered across the country. Yakima is one of the larger reservations, with an area of 1.4 million acres. It is sparsely populated. We see very few people working on the land, probably because it is the slack farming season. West of the plain of farms, ranches, and fruit and vegetable gardens, towers snow-capped Mt. Adam. Naomi says that there are many small, sparkling lakes and meandering brooks in the dense forests on the mountain slopes where fish and wildlife abound. The reservation actually is no longer reserved for the Indians as close to one-fifth of the best land has been sold to the whites. There are altogether twenty-seven thousand inhabitants within the confines of the Yakima reservation, of whom only six thousand are Indians. The rest are mostly whites.

We soon arrive at Wapato, one of the two small towns on the reservation. It is comprised of a number of scattered one-story houses. At the heart of Wapato is its largest building complex, the Heritage House, Cultural Center for the Yakima Indians, opened in 1980. I see a strange-looking building there which, Naomi says, is a modern version of a teepee, the cone-shaped tent of skins or bark used by early American Indians. The teepee houses a museum of Indian life and culture. A large number of exhibits are on display, ranging from fishing canoes and pottery for daily use, to exquisite handicrafts like silver and embroidered and woven articles. One of the vessels is so finely woven that it can hold wine. Around the teepee are a library and research center, a meeting hall and a restaurant.

Mrs. Shephard takes us to visit an Indian family she knows. The man, Wapt Bassett, is out and his wife, Sah Tayuse Rosalie, is glad to visit with a guest from China. She explains that her husband, a carpenter, has lost his job and left to look for work. She stays home, not only doing the housework but sewing a kind of brightly colored Indian costume for sale, to earn the family some money. Our hostess is very hospitable. After a brief exchange of greetings, she hurries to the kitchen, takes from the refrigerator some wild fruits that look like cherries, defrosts them in the micro-wave stove, and insists that I eat some. Naomi explains that it is considered a treat. The Indians here try to retain the way of life of their ancestors. They go to the mountains every spring and autumn to gather wild fruit and plants, and preserve them for guests. Mrs. Bassett then shows me her Indian holiday costume and insists that I put it on for a souvenir photograph.

When we have walked quite a distance from the house after taking leave, we see a boy running after us. He is Mrs. Bassett's son, just back from school. While gasping for breath, he hands me a bag of full-grown Indian corn. He says that he has just learned from his mother about my visit and decided that there must be a gift for the Chinese guest. The episode reminds me of the description in a history book of Columbus' arrival at the Bahama Islands in 1492. The native Indians, the book says, hurried out from their village and brought food, drinking water, and gifts to the sword-carrying strangers. Columbus himself later wrote of the landing in his log:

> They willingly traded everything they owned.... They were well built, with good bodies and handsome features.... They do not bear arms, and do not know them, for I showed them a sword, they took it by the edge and cut themselves out of ignorance. They have no iron. Their spears are made of cane.... They would make fine servants.... With fifty men we could subjugate them all and make them do whatever we want.

The hospitable Indians had no inkling of what the Europeans had in store for them!

Naomi then takes us to meet an Indian artist, Leo Adams. He is obviously one of the lucky few, having been educated in Paris. His comfortable home has a good view of the land and Mt. Adam. All the furniture is peculiarly shaped and made of trunks, branches and roots of big trees. The artist is also hospitable. He does not treat the guests with wild berries, but with famous brands of liquors and wines stored in a cabinet. I feel sorry that I cannot drink at all.

In the Yakima reservation, all Indians I see wear the same informal dress as other Americans. They all speak English without accent. The heirloom outfit of beaded buckskin and feather plumes and the colorful tribal costume, I am told, are worn only on holidays and ceremonial occasions, and in dancing competitions. The Indians have their own spoken language and some linguists are devising a written script for it.

Let Bygones Be Bygones

How did the Yakima reservation come into being? A pamphlet published by the tribal council and entitled "The Land of the Yakimas" provides a brief answer.

There were Indians living in the eastern part of what is now the state of Washington about fourteen thousand years ago. They were nomadic bands roving the great plains hunting wild game, catching salmon, and picking wild plants. By the early eighteenth century, they acquired horses and became skilled horsemen, which made possible expeditions to the plains east of the Rockies to hunt for the then plentiful wild buffalo.

In 1805, closely following the "Louisiana Purchase," the first expedition sent by President Jefferson to eastern Washington came into contact with the Indians there. The captain entered into his diary this impression: "These people appeared of mild disposition and friendly disposed." The expedition was immediately followed by other explorers, fur trappers and traders. The Indians received them all as guests. In 1850, the U.S. Congress adopted an act inviting settlers to occupy the Pacific Northwest. The Yakimas began to sense the danger of losing their land but had no idea of how to prevent it. In 1855, Governor Isaac Stevens of the Washington Territory (not yet a state) began negotiations for land cession with Yakima tribal chiefs at Old Fort Walla Walla.

While visiting the teepee Heritage House at Wapato, I bought a copy of a special "documentary collectors' issue" of the *Yakima Nation Review*, a fortnightly publication of the tribal council. It contains the detailed minutes kept by a secretary who assisted Governor Stevens in the negotiations from 28 May to 11 June 1855. The valuable document vividly records how the Indian and white representatives entered a blockhouse, how pipes were smoked several times prior to talk, how interpreters were sworn in to ensure honest translation, and then the negotiators' statements. The special issue is made livelier by sketches showing the grand sight of Indian tribal leaders arriving on horseback and the sites of the talks. Altogether three thousand Indians gathered at Fort Walla Walla, representing fourteen different Yakima tribes and bands.

The negotiations were difficult and often charged with emotion. One year earlier, Yakima Chief Kamiakin had said: "We wish to be left on the lands of our forefathers. . . . Where can we go now? There is no place left. . . . Better to die like brave warriors on the battlefield than live among our vanquishers, despised." One of the interpreters, according to the special issue of the *Review*, recalled in his memoirs that on the day of the treaty signing Governor Stevens lost his patience. Holding up the treaty text, he said, "If you **do** not accept the terms and sign the paper, you will walk in blood knee-deep." Kamiakin was the last of the chiefs to sign. He was in such a rage, the interpreter wrote, that he bit his lips until they bled profusely.

According to the treaty, the Yakimas ceded more than ten million acres of land, or a quarter of the present area of the state of Washington. More than one million acres were reserved for the Indians. Minor clashes broke out between the settlers and the natives less than five months after the treaty. Both sides sustained casualties. Emotions ran high. A conciliatory Indian chief went to talk under a flag of truce, but was killed and dismembered. War broke out. Some minor Indian leaders were hanged "as examples." After three years of fighting, the Indians were subjugated by the numerically stronger and much better armed white settlers.

At the end of the nineteenth century, the U.S. Congress adopted the Allotment Act requiring that the Indian land be divided into individually owned plots. The natives balked at the idea because since time immemorial their land had been open to all, owned by all, and used by all. But they were finally pressured into compliance. As the common property was turned into individual plots, free sale became possible. Richer white settlers soon bought up much of the fertile land.

Cragg Gilbert, a fruit farm owner whom Mr. Miller introduces me to, meets us at the Yakima reservation. His grandfather was probably one of the purchasers. He owns as much as six hundred acres (3,642 *mu*) and his storehouse is packed with big crates of the famed Yakima red apples. Mr. Gilbert, incidentally, has visited China twice. In 1976, he made his first trip to attend a seminar on horticulture. He tells me frankly that he had a pretty bad impression because the Chinese he met all seemed wary of speaking to foreigners. Then in 1982 he went again as a tourist and found the atmosphere quite pleasant because people were much more relaxed and open. It is interesting that even such a casual observer could accurately feel the difference when the strains of the "cultural revolution" were removed from the Chinese people's minds. Mr. Gilbert is doing a profitable business and he employs as many as two hundred workers in the busy harvest season.

After the Allotment Act, the Yakimas still kept part of their land as tribally owned. Deriving some income from the real estate, they gradually built a number of irrigation projects and started a lumbering industry and other trades. They went through a hard period of readjustment to the new way of subsistence, a way which was completely different from their age-old traditions.

The history of the Yakimas is more or less the epitome of what all American Indians have endured. The whites drove them step by step into reservations. One glaring example of their brutal practices was Wounded Knee — an incident in which about three hundred Indian men, women, and children were massacred by U.S. army regulars at a creek of that name in South Dakota in December 1890. Some historians estimate the original number of Native Americans in North

America as one million. But their population had dropped to 300,000 by the end of the last century. Author Dee Brown, after extensive research, wrote a best-selling book called *Bury my Heart at Wounded Knee*. It is a history of the white conquest of Indians and the subsequent genocide in the American West.

Organized resistance by Native Americans has long since been quelled. On a positive side, the U.S. Congress finally passed a bill in 1924 granting citizenship to them. The Federal Bureau of Indian Affairs and its local sub-agencies have given the Indians some help in employment, credit and financing, soil and water conservation, road building and maintenance, forest management and social services. It is, however, primarily the efforts of the Indians themselves that have slowly improved their situation. But even today, the rate of unemployment, alcoholism, drug addiction, and disease remains appallingly high among these people.

Heartfelt Wishes

By 1960, the Indian population had risen to 800,000. The official U.S. census lumps them together with the Eskimos and Aleuts and the combined number of all three was 1,418,000 in 1980. Most of the Indians now live on reservations scattered throughout more than twenty states. In 1981, Oklahoma had a larger number of Indians than any other state — 156,000. But the state had no reservation because, in the words of a yearbook, "many of the Oklahoman tribes are unique in their high degree of assimilation to the White culture." To my Chinese mind, a complete loss of cultural identity is deplorable. Official statistics show that in 1981, the Indian unemployment rate was as high as fifty percent in the state of Washington and the highest in Colorado — fifty-four percent.

Yakima has a governing body, the Tribal Council of representatives of fourteen tribes and bands. Council members are elected by all Indians aged eighteen and above. Beginning in 1947, their life tenure on the council was changed to a four-year term and half of them are re-elected every two years. Led by the council, Yakima has set up some logging companies, an "industrial park" of light manufacturing, a jewelry-making business, a plant processing frozen and smoked salmon, and a twenty-four hour air taxi providing ambulance and other services. A number of educational and cultural institutions have been established. Naomi takes us to look at Mt. Adam Furniture Company, the largest component of the industrial park. It employs 112 people and the upholstered furniture it makes for sale in the northwestern states appears to be of high quality.

As a Chinese, I have a natural feeling of affinity to the American Indians. My people, like them, have lived through a long and sad period as objects of bullying and massacre. Taking leave of the Yakima reservation, I look at snow-capped Mt. Adam, which is regarded as divine by local Indians, and make three wishes for all American Indians: May their population continue to grow, their livelihood get better, and the worthy part of their traditional culture be preserved and flourish. They deserve a better lot because, after all, they are the first Americans.

Chapter XIV
MYSTERIOUS ALASKA

I have made many inquiries about Alaska before my trip to that mysterious outlying state. Most Americans seem to know about as much of Alaska as most Chinese know about Tibet. In conversations here and there, I have gathered the impression that it is a vast, cold, rich, and strange place.

Alaska is truly expansive. Its total area is 586,412 square miles, the largest of all the American states and only slightly smaller than the Xinjiang Uygur Autonomous Region in China's far west. But Alaska is very sparsely populated, having only 438,000 inhabitants. The territory was "discovered" for the Russian Czar by a Dane named Vitus Bering (hence the Bering Strait). In 1867, the Americans bought the territory from Russia for $7.2 million — about twelve dollars a square mile. The U.S. Secretary of State who closed the deal was William Seward. Many Americans at the time sneered at the purchase and called it "Seward's folly" because they believed Alaska contained nothing more than icebergs and polar bears.

Alaska actually is both cold and mild. The smaller part of it within the Arctic Circle is covered with a 300-foot layer of permafrost. Even the never-setting sun from May to August can only melt the icy soil a little more than two feet down. Temperatures in the inland region can be as low as 40⁰ below zero Centigrade. Worrying about my health and distrustful of the soothing words in travel books, my friend, the poet Stephen S.N. Liu of Las Vegas, repeatedly advised me against going, but I have booked a ticket in Seattle. It turns out that the "Panhandle" where I am to visit has a milder climate than Beijing. Like Seattle, this part of Alaska is kissed by the Japanese Current.

Alaska is rich but the Alaskans are not necessarily so. It is true that they earn much higher wages. A friend tells me that primary and high school teachers are paid close to $30,000 a year in Alaska, one-third more than in the "Lower 48" (the forty-eight continental states lower in latitude). But prices are very high in Alaska. I spent $75 a night at Juneau, the state capital, for modest hotel accommodations and $15 for a meal at the hotel restaurant. The unemployment rate is also high. I see in Seattle a big poster over the window selling ship tickets to Alaska which reads: "Going to Alaska to find a job? If you are, DON'T!" The "DON'T" is in extra-large boldface type.

Alaska is considered strange or exotic primarily because of the native inhabitants, the Eskimos in the north, the Aleuts in the southwest, and the Indians in the southeast. I have a chance to meet only the Tlingit Indians at Ketchikan and find them to be fellow human beings as likable as the other Americans. If there is anything extraordinary about them, it is their hospitality. But I would not deny that the Alaskan landscape, the glaciers, mountains, and tundra, is unique.

TRAVELLING UP THE "PANHANDLE"
—Ketchikan, Tlingit Indians and Juneau

Reporting on my journey to Alaska, I have to begin with Boston, where I made the acquaintance of Regina Lee, a young ethnic Chinese woman. As a lawyer she has been giving legal help to the poor in Boston's Chinatown. While I was in Boston, she was studying in an M.I.T. program training minority leaders. I told her that I wanted to go to Alaska. She was pleased and promised to write to her good friend Jean Kollantai, who was working in Ketchikan. A friend of China, Jean would surely welcome my visit, she said.

There are both air and sea links between Seattle and Alaska. To get a fuller view, I choose the "Marine Highway," so-called because passengers can drive their cars straight into the ship and disembark at the other end in their cars. Knowing that things are expensive in Alaska, I have brought a big sack of fruits and coffee as a gift to Jean. But I don't have a car in which to carry it straight onto the ship. In addition, there is a rule that non-passengers are not allowed aboard, and the sack is much too heavy for me to carry alone. I am lucky, however, to have the help of the young and able film-maker Otto Sieber. He drives me to the dock and talks the steward into allowing him to carry my bags all the way to my cabin.

I am a bit late and the lower berth in my double cabin has been occupied. My roommate is not there and has left a thick volume on the desk. She must be a scholar, I think. But a closer look shows it to be a crossword puzzle book. I go out to see the ship. Apart from the cabins there is a large salon where the soft seats will recline with the push of a button so the passengers can sleep. I see many sacks heavier than mine in the salon and learn that they are food supplies brought along by jobseekers. The salon is quite spacious. Many passengers simply cover the floor near their seats with blankets and let their small children curl up comfortably and sleep there. By American standards the sleeping salon is in the economy class and has only a public washroom. The cabins are either single rooms or shared by two. Mine has a double-deck bed, a small table and an attached bath. My cabin fare is $109, fifty percent higher than the sleeping salon.

On top of the ship is an observatory with glass windows on all sides, swivel chairs in which you can turn in any direction, and a number of small card tables. The ship has a self-service cafeteria and a bar. Films are sometimes shown in the sleeping salon. I wonder why they take the trouble because few passengers would skip the grand views from the observatory for the run-of-the-mill films.

I find my roommate back in the cabin. The stout middle-aged woman readily tells me the main points of her life story. She lives in Houston, worked ten years as a bus driver, got bored with the job, and became a beautician. After spending ten more years in the beauty parlor, she got bored again and switched to a new job as a baker-cook. Every spring she travels to Haines, Alaska, to visit her son. In the tourist season there is not much difficulty in getting short-term employment as a baker-cook. At the same time, she helps her son, a good hunter and fisherman, to make bacon and can fish. She concludes her story with a comment: "It makes no difference what your job is. Your tombstone will have only the dates of your birth and death on it. Who cares what you've done?" During the voyage I always see her playing cards in the observatory or solving crossword puzzles by herself.

Ketchikan, where I am bound, is a town on the Alaskan Panhandle. The nickname has been given the narrow strip of coastal territory extending from the Alaskan mainland hundreds of miles to the southeast. On the map it does look like a handle on the pan-shaped Alaskan mainland. The "Panhandle" is adjacent to Canadian territories.

All along the way one can see Canada's coastal mountains, the immediate ones lower and dark brown, and the distant ones higher peaked and snowbound. On the other side is the ocean dotted with islets which are covered with spruce, fir, and cedar forests. The sea is heavy at times and the crests of the waves leap and bound like blowing cotton. Seagulls constantly circle over the ship and "escort" us on the whole voyage. When the sea is calm, it is quite comfortable to be out on deck. Though a sudden gust of wind may make you huddle up a little, the greyish blue sea has an enchanting wildness which makes me reluctant to retreat.

The Totem World

After a forty-hour voyage we arrive at Ketchikan, noon of the third day after departure. Jean Kollantai is waiting for me at the dock. She already knows me quite well from Regina's letters, and drives me to her house after a brief exchange of greetings.

Ketchikan is the fourth-largest town in Alaska, with a population of twelve-thousand. Juneau, the state capital up north on the Panhandle, is the third largest, with a population of eighteen thousand. A fishing and gold-mining community in its earlier years, according to sarcastic Alaskans, Juneau's main industry now is bureaucracy. The second largest city is Fairbanks. On the mainland, it is located on the knob of the pipeline pumping oil to the Alaskan gulf. The largest is the port city of Anchorage, also on the mainland. It has 200,000 inhabitants, almost half the total population of the state. In early years, Anchorage was a tent camp for two thousand railroad construction workers, but it has now become a trade, financial, and communications center, and also an important air and naval base because of its strategically menacing proximity to the

Soviet Union. Oil discoveries in the early 1950s have made Anchorage one of the fastest-growing American cities. Tourists to Alaska often confine themselves within the loop formed by the four cities. Outside the loop, especially north of it, there are as yet no highways and only explorers and surveyers venture into the mysterious land.

Ketchikan is known as a "strip town" built along mountain slopes looming behind it and with the sea in front. Some houses nestle on hillsides while others are erected on seaside trestles and pilings. They look quite like the riverside houses in China's "mountain city" Chongqing, though the buildings here are few and far between. The house Jean rents is on the waterfront and seagulls are always circling outside the windows. On the side of the gate is a big pile of short logs for heating. They would be precious timber in China, but are very cheap in forest-rich Alaska. Though much oil is produced in the state, Jean explains, it has to be refined on the continent and would be too expensive if shipped back as heating fuel. Jean is a pleasant young woman and we become good friends almost at first sight.

Ketchikan is also known as "a totem world," totem being an animal, plant, or other natural object serving as the emblem of an Indian or other tribe. The strange bright-colored symbols are painted on walls and more often carved on thick poles. They are seen everywhere in Ketchikan — on roadsides, in living rooms, and on the wall of the airport lounge. Totems have become an object of art appreciation instead of a symbol for worship.

Jean has arranged a tight program for me. The first visit is to a pulp factory, a division of the large Louisiana-Pacific Corporation. Its wood pulp is sold in many countries and I am shown a product called "Tongacell dissolving pulp." It looks like cardboard but can be dissolved to make cellophone, pharmaceuticals, rayon, and other goods. The factory is highly mechanized and only a few workers are seen in the shops. Bark, sawdust and other residues are burnt to generate electricity to power the plant. I am impressed by the technological level achieved even in such a small backwoods town. The factory manager, Mr. Mountain, tells me that Louisiana-Pacific's president will soon visit China as a member of a trade delegation and the company places high hopes on the China market.

I then go to a factory processig frozen salmon. It is an inopportune visit as the factory accountant has just absconded with some of its funds. But the young factory owner, Clifford Phillips, takes time out to show me around and talks confidently of his plan to expand the business he has just inherited from his father. In a workshop he asks a worker to "get some of our thirty-pounders and let Madam Wang see them." The man soon comes back with a cartload of salmon of almost uniform size. Their heads and tails have been chopped off and scales removed. Learning that the fish heads are dropped back into the sea, I feel it is quite wasteful because some kinds of meaty fish heads are considered a delicacy in China. Phillips explains that the other fish and marine life in the sea need good food, too. He then tells me frankly that he is facing difficulties because the strong dollar has made his salmon too expensive for more and more European housewives. His plant is overstocked with a highly perishable commodity.

In the few days I spend in Alaska, I have seen several local newspaper reports with headlines like: "Alaska forest products gain interest in China" and "China eyes Alaska seafood." I don't want to disappoint the enterprising young boss but know that though we do need forest products, few Chinese housewives would be able to purchase the expensive salmon.

During the Gold Rush at the turn of the century, Ketchikan saw an influx of adventurers. A busy red-light district had come into being. The brothels are still there for sightseers, but it is said that legalized prostitution no longer exists.

Grand Welcome by Saxman

Jean works in a small town called Saxman, first as its finance director, and now as the administrator. The popularly elected mayor and town council members have their own jobs and are not paid for their public posts. Some of them are longshoremen, as loading lumber is a principal business here. The council takes charge of the guidelines of administration and employs specialized personnel like Jean to conduct the day-to-day business. Saxman has 343 inhabitants, of whom ninety-five percent are Tlingits, an Indian tribe. They like Jean, a white woman, for her devotion to the town's general well-being. The love extends to Jean's friends and that is probably why the town decides to hold a welcome meeting for me — a grand reception by the none-too-rich minority community.

The reception is held on the ground floor meeting hall of the town office. Nearly fifty people come, including the mayor and two of the most respected citizens — a man and a woman in their seventies. The Indians, like the Chinese, have a tradition of respecting the old and say they never "talk back to the elders." So the presence of the two senior citizens is intended as a special honor for me.

The meeting begins with a dance. Everybody puts on the colorful Indian costume — a black robe with red borders embroidered with white flowers, and a hoop-shaped hat with a bird embroidered over the brim. I am told that the patterns on the robe and headgear vary from tribe to tribe and with different ages and social status. My hosts clothe me in their costume. Then everybody begins dancing to the beat of a tambourine with a totem pattern on it. I don't know the proper steps but the jovial atmosphere prompts me to dance as vigorously as they do.

Tea begins. Everybody takes off the costume and the mayor invites me to cut a big rectangular-shaped cake with the words in the frosting: "Welcome Madam Wang to Saxman." There are no speeches but the hosts' simple hospitality is heartwarming. Later when some American friends see pictures of the party, they say that the ceremony signifies that I have been admitted as a member of the Tlingit tribe. I know that the Indians are a proud and noble-minded people and feel it is a great honor if I was really "adopted."

The Indians and other natives had lived in Alaska for ten-thousand years before the Czar of Russia suddenly became the owner of the territory. They worked as hunters and fishermen, had developed many languages, diversified cultures and a way of life based on cooperation and sharing among people. Then Uncle Sam took over as master of the land. The natives, like the American Indians elsewhere, have suffered a lot. One consolation I find is that their population, after a sharp fall caused by displacement and by such diseases as smallpox and tuberculosis, is now close to what it was a century ago, a total of eighty thousand.

Jean shows me a copy of Saxman's annual progress report and two-year plan. According to the report, fifty percent of the town's 343 inhabitants are the potential labor force. But only thirty-four of them have "reasonably permanent, full-time jobs" and the rest are "employed either marginally, seasonally, or not at all." The report requests government help to develop tourism and to build a small boat harbor in order to increase employment opportunities and "maintain and enhance the identity and cultural heritage of the Tlingits."

It looks as though money is hard to get. In spite of the upturn of the American economy in 1984 and 1985, Jean tells me in her letters that Saxman remains in pretty bad shape. She has written a complaint to President Reagan and enclosed a copy of the letter for me to read. The "naughty girl" (as I sometimes call her because she is the same age as my elder daughter) writes sarcastically. Saxman inhabitants, she says in her letter to Reagan, "would like to be the ones to invade Nicaragua and overthrow its government" and "guarantee that the job would be done in no more than six months, at a cost of no more than $300 million—a saving to you." The money could be used to finance Saxman's development and "we would be willing to share the remainder with any other communities in Alaska or in the whole country that might have some needs." And if it is not possible to approve the proposal, "we have an alternative. . . .We would like to auction off an MX missile and believe we could get at least $200 million for it." "Time is urgent in these matters," she concludes, "so we hope to have a reply at your earliest possible convenience." I am amused by her humor but doubt if the letter will reach that high a level.

Like Saxman, Ketchikan is also hospitable in its way. The mayor, town leaders, and the director of the Chamber of Commerce and their wives give a "Dutch Treat" dinner for me. We chat freely while eating in an informal atmosphere. Often these dinners for me are so pleasantly informal that it has made me think we Chinese should try to emulate them. Though much simplified now, banquets for *wai bin* (foreign guests) often remain very formal. Even when the boss of a small unit entertains some foreigners, he has to stand up to make a speech, with an interpreter in attendance. I, for one, don't like the stiff way, nor do I believe it adds to friendship. Diplomatic functions, of course, are a different matter.

The owner of a local air tour service in Ketchikan is equally hospitable. He has two seaplanes and charges $120 for a one-hour cruise over the Ketchikan area. The city's visitors' bureau introduces me to him and he readily agrees to fly me and a guide from the bureau in a plane that seats only two passengers. And he says that the cruise will be free as his welcome to a rare Chinese visitor. Ketchikan is a rainy city but that day happens to be clear and bright. The views of the Canadian coastal mountains are a real sight. Never in my life have I seen such a mass of snow covering peaks and slopes, and filling the ravines. I also was impressed by the immense virgin forests. They revealed the fabulous wealth of the North American continent still waiting to be tapped. We then turn in the other direction and fly over the ocean. A galaxy of small islets comes into view. All of them are densely forested and shrouded in mystery. While I am wondering what wild animals are living down there, the plane suddenly descends for a closer look at a small isle. It has no trees but is crowded with hundreds of sea lions. Playing for the fun of it or perhaps struggling for *lebensraum*, they keep edging one another into the waters. The pilot circles twice over the isle so that I can get a full view of the rare natural circus.

The State Capital

Jean accompanies me on a visit to Juneau. It is not far from Ketchikan, but the trip is time-consuming as the plane hops from island to island to pick up passengers. There are inter-island boat services but the ride is too slow. I never like publicity and feel uneasy on arrival when I see posters at the airport lounge announcing: "Wang Tsomin, writer / editor from China, will give lecture / discussions, at 2 p.m. Saturday, March 12 at the Alaska State Museum. A tea will follow." The ten host organizations include the museum, the University of Alaska, Juneau, and the Juneau Adult Education Center. The "naughty girl" obviously has pulled a trick on me through her wide connections in the state capital. Nonetheless I appreciate it not only as a personal honor but, more important, as a sign of American open-mindedness and eagerness to see somebody from China and hear something new.

More than one hundred people of different trades and professions come to the lecture. I write on the blackboard the dates 1840, 1911,

1921, 1949 and 1978 and speak briefly on these landmarks. They represent the Opium War which turned China into a semi-colony, the democratic revolution that ended monarchy, the birth of the Chinese Communist Party, the nationwide revolutionary victory and the historic Third Plenum of the Eleventh Central Committee of the Chinese Communist Party which brought the country back onto a correct track following the disastrous "cultural revolution."

During the discussions, an immaculately dressed gentleman rises to ask a question. I suspect he may be a "bourgeois" disliking communism and expect a polemical question. But it turns out that he is quite radical and asks emphatically about the past depredations of imperialists in China. I mildly give some pointed information. When tea begins, he comes to talk with me and appears interested in the copy of the English-language *Beijing Review* I used as reference while speaking. I tell him that a subscription can be taken at China Books & Periodicals, a distributor in San Francisco, and thank him for his interest in my country. I would like to continue the conversation but have to move around to meet more people, all of whom are friendly.

At the time Juneau is preparing a banquet in honor of Dr. Alfred Widmark, an American Indian who is outstanding for his participation in political, educational, and Indian institutions. I receive an invitation. About 150 people including the state governor and other notables are present. Jean tells me that Widmark was a member of the American Indians' delegation, accompanied by her and Regina Lee, to visit China in 1979 at the invitation of the Chinese State Nationality Affairs Commission. Widmark got so excited on arriving in Shanghai that he broke into tears. Back in the 1920s, he had been a sailor and saw in that city the miserable life of the working people. On revisiting after half a century, he was amazed and moved by the change. Jean introduces me to him before the banquet. Trying to avoid attention, I ask Jean to find a table far from the platform. One dignitary after another takes the floor. The Americans like humor and keep making jokes on an occasion which would be considered quite solemn in China. One speaker, for instance, presents Widmark a key to Juneau, adding, "You may open everything except the city treasury." Merry laughter bursts out. Dr. Widmark is the last to speak. He catches me by surprise when he says, "I understand that there is a guest from the People's Republic of China. Will she please stand up and meet us?" I rise obligingly and nod to the friendly gathering.

While in Juneau I try to get some facts about the Alaskan economy. Timber, fishing and oil are the three principal industries. Petroleum was discovered in the early 1950s and tapped to the maximum in the 1970s. The income from tourism is considerable. In 1982, out-of-state visitors spent $277 million in Alaska, which would mean a per capita income of $640 for Alaskans. But per capita income is an easily misleading term in discussing the American economy because income here is never distributed per capita. There is an exception in Alaska, though. As oil revenues rose sharply, the state, after putting $2.5 billion into capital projects, had "salted away" $4 billion in a permanent fund against the inevitable day when the oil runs out. Then things seemed so prosperous that the state gave each Alaskan a $1,000 dividend from the fund in 1982. The "red-eyed" (a Chinese epithet for jealous people) in other states called the Alaskans "blue-eyed Arabs." Local people got irritated. To be fair, $1,000 in Alaska is no fortune.

It is generally estimated that oil output will drop by 1995 to half of what it is now. Economic forecasters are dismayed by the prospect. But optimists say that there is much else Alaska can do. The forest and fish resources are vast and renewable. The seals will continue to supply precious furs. The plentiful sunshine, if properly utilized, could be a boon to agriculture. And heaven knows what is buried under the vast frozen ground. If predatory exploitation like the Gold Rush is avoided and the ecological balance is improved, the real estate bought at the price of $12 a square mile will yield astronomical profits.

But that is only a future possibility. The present reality is a slow economy and high unemployment. A travel book advises job-seekers: "Don't come unless you have plenty of money to support what could be a long search. No one strikes gold in Alaska anymore." But Alaska is a haven for summer jobs. If you can stand working sixteen hours a day, the canning boom provides lucrative temporary jobs. Women can generally find work more easily than men — especially outside Fairbanks and Anchorage, the only places that have a balanced ratio. Waitressing and bartending are particularly easy for women to secure.

The question of the unbalanced ratio of men to women helps me

understand why the magazine *Alaska* carries many classified ads like:
"Japanese girls make wonderful wives. We have a large number of
listings. Only $2 brings application, photos, names and descriptions,"
"Beautiful girls, all continents, want correspondence, friendship,
marriage," "Attractive Mexican girls seek friendship, marriage,"
"Free, six pages of photos of marriage-minded girls," and
"Lonesome? Need romance?" The "red-silk industry" seems to be a
flourishing trade in Alaska. Chinese legend has it that the
matchmaking god ties the feet of prospective husbands and wives with
invisible red silk thread so that they will be drawn to each other
whatever the distance. China, by the way, has set up many
matchmaking agencies in recent years after getting rid of the ultra-
revolutionary idea that love-making is somehow "bourgeois." But I
have heard that they are not very successful in uniting spinsters and
bachelors. Alaska has more attractive advertisements, if not girls!

America on the whole has a rich natural endowment but lacks
social harmony. So does Alaska. On our way back to Juneau from a
visit to the glaciers, Jean takes me to see a maternity center. There I
hear a minor but revealing instance of discord in a society based on
competition rather than cooperation. A midwife shows us around.
The place is clean and has fairly complete equipment including oxygen
therapy for emergency. On the wall hang photographs of robust
children born here. In America, pregnant women usually visit private
obstetricians and then give birth at maternity hospitals. I am told that a
normal delivery, including the pre-natal checkups, can cost as much as
$2,000, plus hospital fees. American medical schools require a longer
period of study and charge high tuition. That is probably why it is
costly to visit doctors. Maternity centers are staffed by midwives who
have received proper training but have no college diplomas. They can
do the work at a much lower cost. Besides, the midwife tells me, they
make it clear that in case of any complication they are responsible for
transferring the expectant mother immediately to a regular hospital.
But, she says, college-trained obstetricians are campaigning for a
government ban on these midwives and the question is becoming a
nationwide dispute. To my Chinese mind, there seems to be nothing
wrong at all in having more maternity centers like this and saving
money for the mothers. A "multi-tiered and multi-channeled"

structure, from neighborhood clinics to specialized hospitals, is exactly what we are building. This structure also extends to the other service trades.

WOMEN HOLD UP MORE THAN HALF THE SKY
— "Rebel Girl," Campus Riots and Feminism

There is little "generation gap" between Jean Kollantai, who was born in 1949, and me. I like the young woman very much and the feeling seems to be mutual. She has a pretty face and a *svelte* figure but is never gaudily dressed and cares little about fashion. She has a thoughtful mind and talks intelligently. And she is frank, telling me her life story without self-glorification though she can be proud of her pursuit of high ideals.

Jean was the daughter of a wealthy doctor in California and has two sisters and three brothers. A bright student, she went to the University of California, Berkeley, in the early 1960s. Her personal album shows that she was even more beautiful at that time. The parents were proud of Jean's admission into a prestigious university and pinned high hopes on her — not as a promising career woman but as a prospective wife and mother of a wealthy and "respectable" family. Jean's next younger sister is a different type. She didn't like going to college and got married very young. The disappointed parents spent the money set aside for her college education to build a family swimming pool.

Jean, however, has not lived up to her parents' expectations. Under the influence of the ideals which inspired the campus revolt of the 1960s, she became a progressive, pursuing social progress instead of personal economic advancement. She rebelled against the traditional values which regard women merely, or primarily, as loving wives and devoted mothers. National and international affairs were always on her mind. Her parents did not understand, imploring and admonishing her to change her ways. After much friction, she broke with her family.

Upon graduation, Jean became a social worker in San Francisco, handling applications of the poor living on welfare. While in college, a schoolmate had often talked with her about China and gradually she accumulated a good feeling for the Chinese people. This prompted her to move to Boston and work at the local chapter of the U.S.-China Peoples' Friendship Association. The association is a non-profit organization functioning on small and voluntary membership dues. It employs only a very limited number of people at low wages. Jean didn't care and worked conscientiously. Her mother, having learned of her whereabouts from others, came especially from San Francisco to visit her. Jean's colleagues addressed the woman as "Mrs. Kollantai," making the mother and daughter feel awkward, for Jean had changed even her surname to show her complete rupture with the family.

From Boston she moved on to Alaska and worked for the Tlingit town of Saxman. Her promotion from financial director to town administrator shows the Indians' trust in her. At Saxman she works seventy hours a week and is dedicated to the town's general well-being. It appears to me that she has more common language with Nora, her Tlingit colleague, than with her own sisters. In 1980, together with Regina Lee of Boston, she organized and accompanied a delegation of more than twenty American Indians to visit Beijing and the minority regions of Xinjiang and Inner Mongolia. The delegation received a brotherly welcome from the Mongolians, Uygurs, and other minority Chinese. They brought back a lot of lantern slides. Many Indians, after the shows, said that they had seldom seen such esteem for their people.

Jean even tells me the details of her personal income and expenditures. She is paid $1,900 a month and the "take-home pay" (American term for after-income-tax net earning) is $1,398. Rent alone takes a quarter of her salary. She can barely keep going on the pay but works on without complaint.

After breaking with her family for five years, Jean finally resumed correspondence with her parents. As an elder, I try to encourage her to understand and appreciate their parental love. In mid-1984 when I was back in Beijing, Jean sent me a letter saying, to my great delight, that she was going back to California for a reunion with her parents and five siblings — the first one in years.

But Jean's letter is as political as ever. She laments the rising level of crime. A few days earlier, she wrote, an unemployed worker had walked into a fast food restaurant in San Diego, levelled guns against the customers and killed twenty-one, including old people and children. She discussed the forthcoming American presidential election, Palestine, and nuclear disarmament. She said that she was considering going back to California to work for a newspaper in order to play an active role in the peace movement and other activities against the Reagan Administration, for which she had little love. But the Saxman Tlingits had repeatedly asked her to stay, and it was difficult for her to make up her mind.

Jean further told me in the letter that her parents had "mellowed out" and taken a "more liberal attitude" toward her. Her brothers and sisters are working or studying in America or Europe. All of them have entered or are entering the ranks of the American middle class. They will build families, rear children and live a "respectable life" according to "traditional values." The way she said all this revealed her continuing disapproval of the beaten track of middle-class life.

Jean also told me that she had finally found a man for herself. For years smart, intelligent young men have been attracted to her. But she has chosen to remain single. One reason has been her busy preoccupation with work and another, as she told me in Alaska, is her strong dislike of the "sex-at-first-sight" ways of many American males. But she was in her thirties and I felt relieved to learn from a subsequent letter that she had married. My congratulations, however, do contain some criticism. In her letter she told me that her husband had promised to make her happy and "I have promised not to make him too unhappy." "Your promise," I wrote, "is not reciprocal and sounds imperialistic and hegemonic."

A Generation in Revolt

In the 1960s, as the civil rights movement swept across the country, American students and youth in general also rose in revolt. Jean's school, the University of California, Berkeley, witnessed the first outburst of student unrest. In 1964, white student activists who had gone to the South to join civil rights demonstrations came back to organize protests on campus. The school authorities forbade radical students to use the area for speeches and political activities, and prohibited the distribution of political pamphlets on the campus. This led to sit-in-strikes and other student protest activities that lasted for several months. Hundreds of the students were arrested.

Opposition to the Vietnam war came to be a significant issue of the campus movement. At that time the United States was sinking deeper and deeper into the quagmire and an ever-increasing number of American soldiers were being flung into bloody battles to save the tottering, corrupt South Vietnamese regime. Draft deferment for college students was abolished, and schoolmates felt they might be called to die a meaningless death in the southeast Asian jungles. Protests spread far and wide and reached their climax by the late 1960s. Statistics for the first half of 1969 covering 232 of the nation's two thousand institutions of higher education indicate that over 215,000 students joined in campus protests, almost 4,000 were arrested and close to a 1,000 were suspended or expelled. The protests even percolated down to the high schools where there were reportedly about five hundred "underground newspapers" agitating against the war in the late 1960s. Then in 1970 the war was expanded dramatically when U.S. troops were thrown into Cambodia. Students at Kent State University in Ohio organized a demonstration on May 4 against this new escalation. National Guardsmen were ordered to the scene. They fired into the crowds, killed four students, and paralyzed one for life.

The protests were not confined to campuses. In 1968 there was a mass student intrusion at the Democratic National Convention in Chicago. The students shouted in unison: "Peace now! Peace now!" "Stop the war! Stop the war!", and "XXXX you, LBJ! XXXX you, LBJ!" (LBJ was the Democratic President Lyndon B. Johnson.) A fierce clash took place as the police used clubs and tear gas against the demonstrators. In London, while the U.S. ambassador was holding an elegant Independence Day reception, two young Americans crashed into the compound and suddenly appeared in the reception hall, calling out a toast: "To all the dead and dying in Vietnam!" The protests gathered greater momentum as more people of various social strata came out against the war.

The students wanted not only an end to the war, but raised many other demands, such as curriculum reforms and democratization of school management. Many of these were met.

Increasing numbers of youth became disillusioned with traditional values underlying a rapidly changing American culture. Counter-cultural activities became popular. Some young people even retreated from the world and sought nirvana through Buddhism or fulfillment in other religious beliefs. In Chicago I met and became a friend of Finnie Ziner, author of fourteen children's books. She told me that her son in those tumultuous years left home to live in virtual isolation in the wilds of British Columbia, Canada. There was only a Buddhist monk living near him. Finnie's search for her son finally led her to the forests. She wrote a perceptive and intimate book about this experience entitled *On This Wilderness*. I treasure the autographed copy of the book which she gave me.

The Problem That Has No Name

Jean Kollantai hasn't said she is a feminist. Nor have I heard of her involvement, if any, with the women's movement which also surfaced in the 1960s and which has surged forward to change so many traditional features of American life. But her attitude to life is drastically different from that of my female schoolmates in the America of the 1940s. In those years, many "coeds" openly declared home-making as their ideal occupation, and college as a place to become better educated so that they could find better husbands.

The American women's movement has a long history. Universal suffrage used to be the heart of the issue for many years. The Nineteenth Constitutional Amendment in 1920 granted women the right to vote. But the ballot alone could not solve all their problems. Most women remained lifelong housewives, doing the home chores, bearing and rearing babies, and virtually working a seven-day week. But they continued to be regarded solely as "helpmates" to men, who were considered the "bread winners." That fortunate minority born "with a silver spoon in their mouths," as in old China, were often treated as Nora was in Ibsen's *The Doll House* before she walked out that door forever.

During World War II, however, large numbers of men went into the armed services and more and more women left housekeeping to go to work. By 1960, a total of 23 million of them or 36 percent of the female labor force above 16, were working for paid wages. But only a few of them held leading posts in government and business. Unequal pay for equal work was prevalent and it was estimated that their median wage was only one-third that of men. After work they had to carry much of the load of housework. And much of society continued to regard wifeliness, motherhood, feminity, beauty and housework as essential elements of ideal womanhood.

In 1963, a book called *The Feminine Mystique* (Dell Publishing Inc. N.Y.) raised the question in a powerful way. Author Betty Friedan wrote:

Just what was the problem that has no name? What were the words women used when they tried to express it? Sometimes a woman would say "I feel empty somehow... incomplete." Or she would say, "I feel as if I don't exist." ....Sometimes she went to a doctor with symptoms she could hardly describe: "A tired feeling...I get so angry with the children it scares me.... I feel like crying without any reason."

The problem that Friedan spoke of is the image of the American woman as mother, as wife, of living through her husband, through her children, giving up her dreams for theirs. Her answer to the unnamed problem is:"The only way for a woman, as for man, to find herself, to know herself as a person, is by creative work of her own."

In the rebellious 1960s, many women rose in revolt, too. They demanded equal opportunities for employment, and abolition of all in American culture which relegated most of them to roles of secretaries, typists, receptionists, salespersons and cleaning workers. They wanted equal pay for equal work. They campaigned for more daycare for their children and freedom of abortion. They demanded mainstream American society to see women as individuals with their own inherent potential. Many female activists emerged in the civil rights movement and the anti-war protests. Women's organizations mushroomed, including NOW — the National Organization for Women.

Different social strata became involved. A typical voice from the lowest rung was heard when Johnnie Tillmon wrote in 1972: "I'm a woman. I'm a black woman. I'm a poor woman. I'm a fat woman. I'm a middle-aged woman. And I'm on welfare." Her sorry plight was complete and she was certainly not the only woman immersed in it.

Some seemed to have gone too far in their revolt. In the fall of 1968, a group of women radicals hit the headlines when they protested the "Miss America" contest. They threw bras, girdles, curlers, false eyelashes and other things they called "women's garbage" into a "Freedom Trash Can." They crowned a sheep "Miss America." I, too, shared their view of the "Miss America" contest, particularly after reading a highly interesting talk by one of the beauty queens in Studs Terkel's *American Dreams: Lost and Found*. But bras and curlers seem innocent. Then members of WITCH (Women's International Terrorist Conspiracy from Hell) actually dressed as witches and suddenly appeared on the bustling floor of the New York Stock Exchange. These activities may seem ridiculous to Chinese. But in sensation-loving America, people often feel forced to stage extraordinary stunts to get public attention for their cause.

Like other forms of unrest, however, women's revolt became quiescent in the 1970s. Their situation has improved somewhat. According to 1982 statistics, there were 43.25 million women among the nation's 99.52 million employed workers. To facilitate their careers, women had raised the median age of marriage from 20.3 years in 1960 to 22.1 in 1980. And the birthrate has dropped markedly. Fast food industries have grown correspondingly, and housework has been further socialized. College enrollment registered a historic change when in 1980 female students totalled 5.9 million and outnumbered the 5.48 million men. Trades and professions formerly considered closed to women have been opened to them, at least symbolically. West Point and other service academies have admitted their first women cadets. The White House Guard now includes women in the same uniform as men and with the same weapons training. The number of women governors, judges and congress members has increased. According to reports preceding the 1984 presidential election, while women accounted for fifty-one percent of the American population, they were 52.3 percent of the voters. The nomination of Geraldine Ferraro as Democratic vice-presidential nominee was generally interpreted as a move to gain female votes.

Complying With the Times?

Still, women's problems have not been solved in America. We in China often say "women hold up half the sky" in recognition of their supposedly equal role, though much remains to be done to give full meaning to this phrase. In America, women are holding up more than half of the sky in some respects — their numbers, their votes, their college enrollment, and median life expectancy. But there are more areas where they also share far less than half the sky. There are still too few women in leading posts in relation to their population. For every dollar earned by men, women get only sixty cents, and other examples run *ad infinitum*.

Perhaps most symbolic, the Constitutional amendment American women have sought for decades (known as the Equal Rights Amendment, or ERA, which prohibits sex discrimination in employment, wage, pension, social security and other areas) was placed before the Congress as early as 1923. It has yet to be adopted. Constitutional amendments require ratification by two-thirds of the fifty states to take effect. As a result of the backlash of conservative opposition in recent years, ERA is dead in the water.

With the advent of the 1980s, many Americans believe that conservative ideas are gaining ground in young people's minds, men and women alike. A *Washington Post* columnist has written that the students of the 1960s — the fanatic and angry generation of rebels burning flags and occupying schools — has given way to a generation of conformists. Other writers also see a comeback of "traditional values" — stress on family life, hard work, religious belief and respect for authority — among young Americans.

Are they really a generation complying with the times? I believe it all depends on how the times are. They will comply if the times are good. If economic troubles get out of hand and more "dirty wars," let alone a nuclear holocaust, threaten their existence, it could be a different matter. Writer Howard Zinn may be right when he says in *The People's History of the United States:* "... though the great tide of the sixties had receded, it left on the beach millions of moving organisms, pockets of energy, in an atmosphere calmed down, but electric with possibility."

Jean Kollantai's story is a reflection of the American youth and women's movements. Though simple, it does provide an additional dimension to any perspective of American culture.

Chapter XV

SUNSET OVER
THE GREAT LAKES

—Transformation from an Industrial to an Information
Society

It is late March when I conclude my Alaskan visit. My one-year
reporting trip through America should end by early May. I have
experienced a kaleidoscope of impressions. Still, a question mark
looms over the mercurial patterns: Where is American society going?
Politics are hard to predict, but technological trends are more clearly
seen.

Since my arrival in the United States, I have often talked with
Americans about prospects for the future, in serious discussions or
after-dinner chats. The "Third Wave" theory put forward by
futurologist Alvin Toffler in 1980 seems familiar to many people. His
concept of a "First Wave" that characterized a major transition of
early human society was of the agricultural revolution which replaced
primeval hunting and fishing; the second transition or "Second
Wave" was the industrial revolution creating industrial society —
already in existence for three hundred years. The "Third Wave" is the
shift which began in the mid-1950s from the industrial to the
"information" society. In China, the transformation is called "a new
technological revolution" by scholars. In 1982, John Naisbitt's
Megatrends: Ten New Directions Transforming Our Lives (Warner Books,
N.Y.) appeared and has been a best-seller for two years running (A
Chinese edition has been put out by the Chinese Social Sciences
Publishing House, and is quite widely read). I find in discussions that

the first of Naisbitt's ten "new directions," i.e., the transformation from the industrial to an "information" society is generally accepted, but views vary greatly on the other nine directions.

The transformation from an industrial to an "information" society has broad meanings, but a basic element is the emergence of "sunrise" industries like electronics, information, robotics, biological engineering, space and oceanic development, all collectively known as "high-tech," and the simultaneous decline of traditional industries like steel, auto, construction, textiles, and related branches which are called "sunset" industries.

Handwriting on the Wall

I decide to go to Detroit, the famous automobile city on Lake Erie, to have a firsthand observation of the "sunset." M.I.T. Professor Robinson's brother-in-law Donald Kuhn and his wife, Rae, meet me at the airport. Donald happens to be in a "sunrise" business, the Burroughs computer company. Burroughs, one of the biggest producers of computers in America, has branches in many countries. It wants to send Don to work abroad but he prefers to stay on in Detroit where he was born and raised. Rae is affected, however, by the "sunset" nature of Detroit's economy. She is a qualified teacher but cannot find a job after staying home a few years to care for their small children. She is now doing some "special education" of handicapped children and teaching a cooking course. Education in itself is not a "sunset" profession but the decline of the principal industries has rippling effects on many occupations.

Don makes special detours to show me more of the city. We first drive through flat farmlands. The landscape is idyllic as the green winter wheat stretches to the horizons to mix with the blue sky dotted with drifting white clouds. As we get closer to the city, tall buildings and houses apparently out of repair and no longer in use begin to appear. Don drives me around a big General Motors plant. It is Saturday afternoon and no visitors are allowed in. Don says that there is not much to see in present auto plants anyway. In the past, almost the whole process of production was done in one main plant. But now there is a much higher degree of specialization. The plants, each making a few parts, are scattered around the country or even abroad. You no longer can see automaking at any one place.

We then drive past a fenced area. Don tells me that it is "Pole town." GM insisted on buying the area to build an ultra-modern plant where robots can work more conveniently in single-storied and contiguous workshops. The Polish people did not want to move and the city government was also reluctant to see the change. But GM warned that it would close its two remaining plants in Detroit if it could not acquire the site. The Polish and the city government had to give in because the unemployment rate had already reached double digits.

Detroit remains plush and prosperous in appearance. Many high-rises are being erected. But any newspaper reader knows that a high percentage of the population is suffering from, or menaced by, unemployment. Chrysler Corporation, the third largest automaker after GM and Ford, is an example of retrenchment. In 1979 the Detroit-based firm was on the verge of bankruptcy and was barely bailed out by a Congressionally-approved $1.5 billion Federal loan guarantee. An entrepreneur, Lido Anthony ("Lee") Iacocca, took over as Chrysler president. The now famous executive had formerly been president of the Ford Motor Co. After clashing with Henry Ford II and being fired by his billionaire boss, Iacocca assumed office, and immediately closed sixteen of Chrysler's fifty-two plants and cut the employees from 157,000 to 74,000. Chrysler survived and finally began to profit in 1982. Sales that year totaled $10 billion and profits, $1.7 billion, a meager sum for giant American companies. Moreover, the profit came mainly from defense contracts for the tank division, not from automobiles. After the drastic retrenchment, according to one press report, "there are dozens of eerily silent rooms with long rows of empty desks at company headquarters" where Iacocca works. There must be many more "eerily silent" homes, I guess, where those who lost their jobs are pondering their future.

The entire American auto industry, not just in Detroit, is in decline. In 1973, the United States manufactured 12.3 million automotive vehicles. By 1980 the number had dropped to nine million against Japan's eleven million.

What are the reasons for the slide? Some Americans say that

shopping, bank transactions, inquiries and much other personal work can now be done by computers and even some office routines can be handled at home terminals. Hence people don't have to go out so often and fewer cars are needed. My obervations, however, tell me it will be a long time before computers, though coming to homes in increasing numbers, begin to have an effect on auto usage.

Others say that the oil price hike some years ago has made fuel expensive and people are buying fewer cars as a result. There is some truth in the argument but it cannot explain the whole question. Oil prices have gone up everywhere but why, then, are Japan and a number of other countries producing more cars?

Still others hold that the high wages of American auto workers plus the increasing obsolescence of their plants have made American cars less competitive. This is a fact that is proven by the influx of Japanese cars to the American home market. In 1982, a total of 1.8 million were imported and the trend appears to be an upward one. I have read a report saying that it takes the Japanese, who use more robots, an average of nine hours to turn out a car, against 31 hours spent by the Americans. "The Japanese have taken away our jobs" is a much-publicized theme which has engenderd an undisguised anti-Japanese sentiment among the auto workers. In and outside Detroit, I repeatedly see "Buy American! Help solve unemployment!" splashed on huge billboards. Left unspoken is, "don't buy Japanese cars," or, "don't import steel from South Korea."

While I am in Detroit, the local Chinese community is indiganant. A court has just handed down an obviously unfair sentence — only a suspended three-year prison term plus a $3,000 fine — for the brutal murder of a young Chinese-American engineer, Vincent Chen. I see angry editorials and a picture of the victim's mother crying bitterly, printed in Chinese-language newspapers. The murderers were two unemployed white auto workers, father and son.

The circumstances surrounding the crime and trial seem to be clearly indicative of a particularly ugly form of racism that often surfaces in economically difficult times. Nine months earlier, on 19 June 1982, Chen went to a bar to celebrate with friends his coming wedding. Two whites mistook him for a Japanese, insulted him, and in the ensuing quarrel, beat him to death. The racist-tinged verdict has aroused strong protests from all Chinese communities in America. I, too, feel better when I see a news report two years later that the sentence is changed to twenty-five years for the chief culprit, after a re-trial.

I try to find out why the American capitalists, with their enormous financial power, do not upgrade the auto plants or build new ones to save an industry that has long been considered a pillar of the American economy. Some scholars have pointed out that consortia have foreseen an inevitable withering of the automobile industry. They argue that the history of railroads reveals the pattern of rise and decline. In its prime, rail transportation was one of the largest and most lucrative of American industries. But it has now been driven into the corner by automobiles and aircraft. Financial giants prefer to channel their money into more profitable fields, particularly "sunrise" industries. They are literally heeding the old Chinese adage that "all vehicles should be warned by a capsized cart ahead."

Some American economists I have interviewed stress that American multi-national corporations have "exported" jobs to the detriment of automaking and other traditional industries. Professor Barry Bluestone of Boston College cites figures to illustrate his point. Between 1950 and 1980, direct foreign investment by U.S. business increased sixteen times, from almost $12 billion to $192 billion. Of all U.S. imports in 1976, almost twenty-nine percent came from overseas plants and majority-owned subsidiaries of American multi-national corporations. He quotes the well-known American saying: "We have met the enemy and he is us!" Many of the imported goods flooding the American market are actually products of American capital operating abroad.

Modern capitalist economy is a highly intricate phenomenon. The auto industry, for instance, needs steel, rubber, textiles and thousands of other products as parts. These products come from many firms in many countries which often are owned or run by Americans. A car finally assembled in any one country is not necessarily completely, or even primarily, an indigenous product. The professor's remarks call to my mind the old Chinese love vow: "I am in you and you are in me. We are inseparable." Only the love here is for profit. Capital will move to wherever greater profits are available. Wages are high in America.

Many big corporations prefer to establish plants in countries where there is a large pool of cheap labor. Mexico is an example. In 1979 its automobile production had increased to nearly 300,000. But a considerable number of them are actually GM and Ford products assembled by low-paid native workers. Thus more and more American employment opportunities have been exported to the detriment of the traditional industries.

A Retiring "Generalissimo"

Since the 1950s, China called the steel industry the "generalissimo" of the industrialization march, whose pace was considered decisive in economic development. This one-sided emphasis on steel and other heavy industries has proven to be counter-productive and has now been revised. But it was a fact that before the emergence of new materials and other "sunrise" industries, steel was the backbone of any industrial structure. I still have a faint memory of the "steel capital" Pittsburgh and the "steel valley" of Youngstown that I saw on a railway trip to New York City in the 1940s. Towering chimneys were emitting heavy black smoke and waste gas was burning like torches in heaven. The furnaces and molten steel of the giant mills turned the early night into an inferno of fire and sparks. The sky was lit with a brilliant orange-red glow and the air smelled of sulfur. The scene, symbolic of industrial might, was spectacular and I had wished that someday my undeveloped motherland would have similar steel cities. Environmental pollution had not attracted much attention in those years and that issue began to cause urgent concern only in the 1960s.

Youngstown now has changed drastically. When I get there from Detroit, I see only one chimney pouring out wisps of thin smoke and learn later that it is not a steel mill but a thermal power plant. The orange-red evening glow, the black dust and "black rains" are no more. The air is much fresher. This is a result of many years of effort to reduce environmental pollution. But, more important, it is an indication that the mighty "steel generalissimo" is ageing and retiring.

My friend, historian Philip Foner, has suggested that I seek the help of labor attorney Staughton Lynd in Youngstown. A well-known historian, Lynd was a Yale professor who lost his job for opposing the Vietnam War. But he is out of town. Knowing nobody in a strange city, I feel lost. After all, I am no tourist who can just look around, take some snapshots and leave. An idea hits me: why not phone the local newspaper and ask if there are any Missouri Journalism School alumni who may care to help? The answer I get from the *Youngstown Vindicator* is no, but the man answering the phone is a senior editor who promises to assign somebody to help me gather materials in the paper's library. They are short-staffed, he apologizes, and cannot arrange interviews for me.

Labor reporter Michael Braun receives me cordially. The young man, thirty at most, shows me many clippings, including his own stories, and xeroxes all that I need. I then ask him what he thinks can be done to ease the unemployment situation in Youngstown. He says that most of the unemployed workers will probably find their way into expanding service industries. How can they expand when the principal industry in the city is going downhill, I ask. Braun is very frank and says that he doesn't really know the answer and proposes that I see his teacher, Dr. John Russo, director of labor studies at the State University of Ohio, Youngstown. And he will accompany me. The interview with Dr. Russo in the afternoon, plus Braun's reports, helps me greatly to understand the troubles of the city.

Youngstown is situated in the Mahoning Valley, long since known as the "steel valley" for the concentration of furnaces and mills there. The steel industry in the valley dates back to over a century ago and many residents are fifth-generation steelworkers. Like auto workers, they get high wages comparable to those of the middle class. In spite of the cyclic economic recessions in the country, steel invariably recovered and gained new strength. It looked as though people in Youngstown could live indefinitely on the lucrative business.

Then came "Black Monday" still fresh in the memory of local inhabitants — 19 September 1977, when the Youngstown Sheet and Tube Company's Campbell Works suddenly announced its closing and laid off forty-five hundred workers forever. The ensuing years saw more plant closings, including the Ohio Works of U.S. Steel.

Only a small number of mills survived the wave. Rippling effects rolled through the trucking companies, railroads, retail and other businesses, forcing them either to close or retrench. The city government has also been dealt a staggering blow as corporate and personal income tax revenues decreased drastically while social security and welfare expenditures soared. As a result, schools have lost one-third of their operating budget and even the police force has had to be cut. In the five years since 1977, 57,000 people have lost their jobs, among whom 23,000 are steelworkers. The unemployment rate has reached 18.3 percent against the national average of 10.4, and Youngstown now places third among American cities hardest hit by the ongoing recession.

Many of the unemployed have spent the past five years moving from job to job, facing an increasing chance of layoffs due to their loss of seniority when joining another company. They have to accept jobs that pay less, or retirement. It is harder for those who are too young to retire, but too old to be hired. And the path is toughest for a core of workers who are unskilled and, in many cases, minorities. Relief recipients are mostly young people between the ages of eighteen and twenty-five. The job market is all but closed to them due to their complete lack of experience.

The social consequences are grave. Marital discord, child abuse, alcoholism, depression, and mental illness have increased markedly. The population is down by ten percent as more and more people have left to find work in other places. But the crime rate is up. According to FBI statistics, the biggest increases have occurred in robbery, buglary, and aggravated assault, all of which have nearly doubled since 1977. I do not say Youngstown is dead. People are eagerly looking forward to the opening of a commuter aircraft company and other new businesses under preparation. But as we would say in Chinese, they have been "hearing a lot of thunder but not seeing any rain."

Dr. Russo is a learned scholar. In addition to the factual briefing, he presents a theoretical basis for his views. He holds that the American economy, having moved from free capitalism to monopoly capitalism, and then to "welfare capitalism," has been torn all along by contradictions. Dr. Russo believes it is unrealistic to think that most of the unemployed workers, as some people fondly hope, will find a place in service industries. I ask why America does not direct new investments into the traditional industries or at least into the more viable enterprises in those fields. The decline of traditional industries may be inevitable in America, I say, but I don't believe they can be dispensed with altogether. The professor explains that it is a tiny minority of people who own the bulk of American stocks and they are primarily concerned with profits. Only seven to eight percent of the American population have savings accounts over $4,000 or $5,000, and even among those only a very few can afford to buy any sizable amount of stocks. So it is not America as a whole but a wealthy few in the country who can decide the direction of investment. Braun joins in and frankly cites himself as an example. He earns $25,000 a year and as a bachelor had to pay $7,000 or $8,000 in income tax. There are some deductions now that he is married and has children. But he has to save money for the family and prepare for any eventuality. "I don't buy stocks because I can't afford to."

The "Rustbowl"

During the Great Depression of the 1930s, many midwestern farms lay in waste and were called the "Dustbowl." American journalists, always bent on coining eye-catching new terms, now dub the traditional industrial areas a "Rustbowl." In a series of interpretative reports (beginning 25 April 1982), the *Los Angeles Times* writes "What is happening here [Youngstown] also is happening across the Great Lakes, once the nation's great crucible." "The Rustbowl includes parts of New York, Pennsylvania, Ohio, Michigan, Indiana and Illinois." One report quotes Dr. Russo as saying, "It's a nightmare for the industrial belt of America."

Dr. Russo is not exaggerating. The whole American steel industry is in bad shape. American output of crude steel was as much as 137 million tons in 1978 but had rapidly dropped to 74.51 million tons by 1982. Total employment in the industry decreased from 627,000 in 1970 to 512,000 in 1980. The United States used to lead the world by a wide margin in steel production, but now Japan and Western Europe are exporting steel products to America in increasing quantities.

What are the reasons? Much discussion has been going on. I have read an analysis in an American steel trade journal pessimistically headlined: "Decline of Steel Industry Was Inevitable." It cites three factors. One is that American steelworkers want high wages. *Time* magazine has printed a chart comparing their wages ($23.99 an hour) with steel workers, earnings in Japan ($11.80 an hour) and South Korea ($2.39). Figures from different sources vary but all point to a striking disparity. The second factor is that the American stock holders want high dividends. And the last factor is that the American government requires environmental protection, which costs the manufacturers much money. The result of the three factors is that American steel products have lost much of their competitiveness. I have read another article stressing that the emergence of more and more new materials has lessened the demand for steel. The explanation seems one-sided because more steel is being produced elsewhere, not only in Japan and West Germany, but also in developing countries and regions like Brazil, South Korea, Argentina, Mexico and Venezuela, proving that more steel is needed worldwide.

It seems to me that the American steel industry is sharing the same fate as the automakers. The consortia have foreseen its gloomy prospects and don't want to spend the huge sums of money required to upgrade it. But they also know that steel is still needed and a more profitable place to produce it is in Third World countries where labor is cheap. Not only are U.S. corporations making the transfer but the Japanese are reportedly embarking on a similar course. The futurologist Naisbitt has praised the Armco Steel Company for its foresight. He writes in *Megatrends* that a dozen years ago, when big steel was riding very high, Armco looked around and decided that the good times were not going to last long. It decided to "get out of the steel business," which sounded crazy at that time. But Armco has proved itself wise. I had a chance to talk on the phone with a senior Armco official, Walter G. Smyth, in Middletown, Ohio, who told me that though Armco was still called a "steel producer," it had widely diversified and is now a conglomerate. This is to say what one loses in steel, one gets back from other businesses.

From Youngstown I proceed to Pittsburgh. That city, I remember, was blackened with smoke in the 1940s. Unlike Youngstown, however, it now appears even blacker and dirtier. Even in the suburbs, you can hardly find any of the green vegetation abundant elsewhere in America. There are trees, but they are anything but green and you wonder whether they are still alive. The specter of steel imports is stalking the once-prosperous steel capital. Along the expressway I see many more billboards calling on people to "Buy American and help create jobs." I chat with an American passenger on the bus and tell him that I have seen a more radical sign hanging on a lamppost in Youngstown declaring: "U.S. Navy must sink all ships carrying foreign cars, steel, TVs, cameras, shoes and clothing!" He sneers at the slogans as "nonsense," saying that if America builds trade barriers, others can do the same. All businessmen want to make money and they will buy whatever is good and cheap no matter who the maker is. Besides, he also says, a lot of imported goods are the products of American capital operating abroad.

Though I've seen the "sunset" over the Great Lakes, it is a complete misconception to conclude that vast areas in America are in dismal ruins. That is not true. The traditional industries are declining but not yet dying, and there may even be occasional upward turns in their overall downward curve. In the meantime, "sunrise" industries are growing fast. The third or tertiary industries are highly developed. Catering, retail, entertainment, tourist and other service trades, in particular, create an appearance of prosperity—an extravaganza of lights and sounds, a pageant of material civilization. Even in deeply distressed cities like Youngstown, you cannot readily see the human tragedies happening behind the abstract unemployment and crime statistics.

A New Opportunity, A New Challenge

What, then, does the future hold in store?

There are optimists. I regard writer John Naisbitt as one. "Economists predict gloom because they focus on industrial companies [the "sunset" economy]," he writes in *Megatrends*, "That's like predicting a family's future by watching only the grandparents." The "information society" Naisbitt visualizes involves great changes in economic, political and cultural areas as well as in human relationships and lifestyle. In short, the optimists foresee that in the "post-industrial" or "information" society more and more people will be employed in the third industries, providing services for other members of society, rather than extracting materials or manufacturing goods. Work will require more skills but will become more pleasant and less boring than in the present first and second industries. The workers will no longer labor on assembly lines, but will become technicians periodically checking the computerized and automatic equipment to ensure their correct functioning. Their work calls for greater responsibility but will become lighter and cleaner. Computers and robots will greatly increase productivity and lessen the demand for human labor so that people will have far more leisure time for personal development and fulfillment. As for agriculture, genetic engineering and other high technologies will create astonishing new varieties of plants and set off a great new round of the "green revolution." As office work becomes computerized, people will be able to "go to work" in their own homes. Personal computers will provide a family with all kinds of information and conveniences at their fingertips. People can do their shopping, consult with their doctors or even attend international conferences in their own living rooms.

There is an old Chinese saying that "scholars can know the world without going outdoors." It seems that in the so-called "information society" non-scholars can do that, too, and indeed everybody can discharge all his worldly duties without going out. I don't dismiss all these predictions as science fiction. In fact, some wild dreams are coming true faster than expected.

Then there are pessimists. Sociologist William Ophuls has described a "scarcity society" in which depletion of natural resources leads to a lower standard of living and a strong, authoritarian state to regulate conflict among groups struggling for their piece of the diminishing pie. Many people are concerned with the high-speed growth of world population and the serious disruption of the ecological balance, and the implications for our whole planet, America included. Far more people are worried about the prospect of a nuclear holocaust and the possible "nuclear winter" that will follow.

What is the way out? "One hundred schools of thought are contending," as we would say in China. Leaving international politics and economics aside, and insofar as American industry is concerned, economists have offered many different diagnoses and prescriptions, including an interesting strategy of "reindustrialization."

In his talk with me, Professor Barry Bluestone of Boston College observes that the "sunset" industries are indeed declining, and that the "sunrise" industries are inevitably playing a greater role in the economy. But the process has to be viewed in human terms. With deep sympathy for labor, he points out that during the past decade more than 30 million jobs have been lost as a direct result of plant closings and the number of workers indirectly affected is greater. While talking, he draws curves on a writing pad showing the trends of re-employment of the laid-off workers. Some of them do find a place in the third industries but are paid far less than before. Another portion has gone into the "sunrise" sector. But don't believe that a high-tech company pays everybody a high wage, he warns. The senior staff and specialists do earn good money, but ordinary technical personnel get much less than auto, steel and similar blue-collar workers. Besides, re-employment requires re-training, which costs money. The professor stresses that plant closings, like in Youngstown, have resulted in "community abandonment," and cause much human suffering.

Bluestone zealously advocates a new strategy of "reindustrialization with a human face." Allowing for my over-simplification, his program calls for government participation in developing the "sunrise" industries so that their swelling profits will not completely drain into private pockets but will at least partly flow back to the national treasury to alleviate the stress experienced by the dislocated. His strategy also requires government assistance in updating and restructuring the traditional industries. Finally, it calls for government investment in public utilities like mass transit and neighborhood health clinics, which can hardly be expected to make profits. The whole program envisages not only government involvement but community and worker participation.

The professor gives me an autographed copy of a book he co-authored with another economist, Bennett Harriman, entitled *The Deindustrialization of America — Plant Closings, Community Abandonment and the Dismantling of Basic Industry* (Basic Books, N.Y.). The book cites a wealth of data to urge the necessity of a "reindustrialization" strategy. But is the proposal a visionary or a realistic one? There has been a conservative backlash in America. A basic tenet of the ultra-conservatives remains *laissez-faire* — the less government interference with business, the better. "Free enterprise" is their nostrum. And in their view, mass unemployment in the basic industries is an inevitable, or even desirable, part of economic "restructuring."

I am neither an economist nor a futurologist. And I do not possess a crystal ball. But I am never a pessimist. I believe it is good for mankind that a new technological revolution is gathering force and bringing great change to society. One can feel the changes more easily in America, which is still leading in the world's technological progress. Having witnessed some manifestations of the revolution on my visit, I feel relieved that China has opened its doors and seen the ongoing transformation. Our theoretical scientists and policy-makers have recognized the "new technological revolution" as a "new challenge and new opportunity" for the country in its modernization drive, and are exploring corresponding development strategies. I believe that for the Americans, who are in the forefront of the revolution, it is also a new opportunity and new challenge. How should Americans meet the challenge and utilize the opportunity? I don't pretend to know. But one thing seems certain to me: Without corresponding social reforms, high technology will not, by itself, bring about "high happiness."

Chapter XVI.

FAREWELL, AMERICANS!

Writing this book in Beijing, I seem to be reliving the one year I have spent in America as I peruse my notebooks, look at the photographs and listen to the tapes. If I am asked what has impressed me most it is not the magnificent landscapes, nor the highly developed material civilization, but the Americans, the many Dicks and Janes I have met. All of them have something interesting to my Chinese eyes. Is it possible, then, to find some common points in their characters and answer the question my Chinese readers will probably ask: "What are the Americans like?" It is a difficult task. But I shall try, as the Chinese saying modestly puts it, "to survey the sky through a bamboo tube and measure a sea with a gourd ladle" (*guan kui li ce*). And I do this in the belief that "even the slow-witted might hit upon some good ideas as the wise may flounder once in a while" (*qian lu yi de*).

Deadline and Lifeline

I appreciate the hard-working spirit of the Americans. When I arrived in the United States in 1947, my first impression was of the quick tempo of life, particularly in my field — journalism. At the first class I attended in Missouri, all the professors stressed the absolute importance of meeting the deadline. Stories, however well written, could only go in the waste basket if they were late. And I remember distinctly a talk given by a press photographer, an alumnus invited back to discuss his experience. He described how he raced to the spot of a traffic accident, climbed to a "commanding height" thanks to a pedestrian who readily lent his "helping shoulders" and thus got a scoop. Dollar bills kept in your pocket, he advised, were always helpful. You could pay any temporary helper a small fee without waiting for change.

On my second trip I met many professors. There is a saying that American professors are faced with the choice to "publish or perish". The fast rattling of their typewriters to produce publishable manuscripts — their lifeline — has left a deep impression on me because, though lifestyles in China are changing too, I have not completely rid myself of the traditional Chinese image of scholars reading leisurely in their secluded studios or pacing slowly in their chrysanthemum gardens.

During my journey I have seen people everywhere working in earnest or "like mad". Farmers don't have to observe a strict work schedule but they seem to be working from dawn to dusk. Self-employed workers should be able to take things easier. But a taxi driver in Washington D.C. told me that he had been roving the streets for sixteen hours in order to earn the daily quota he set for himself. Another taxi driver in New York City asked me the date of the month because he had been working round-the-clock and got all mixed up. Except for the old and unemployed sitting on park benches and the browsing tourists, everybody seemed to be on the run. Old-fashioned Chinese gentlemen must speak in a slow and measured tone and walk at an easy pace to match their status. Not so the Americans. In China, I regret to say, work discipline remains lax in some units and you often see young ladies nibbling at sunflower seeds behind sales counters or knitting and chatting in offices. Not the Americans. They work while they work.

In a highly competitive society where there is no unbreakable "iron rice bowl" as we have for all wage workers in China, the Americans have to work in order to live and work harder in order to live better. But this does not completely explain the situation. Hard work, I believe, has become a trait of the American character since the early immigrants. The trait has not changed with the rise of productivity and living standards. In fact, the tempo of life seems to be quickening with the fast advance of modern technology. Otherwise, it would be difficult to understand why some senior citizens I had met keep on working in their carpenter shops or vegetable gardens, though they have money enough to spare. Work is their hobby. A very important reason for the rapid development of America, the transformation of a primitive continent into a highly modern country in a short period of history, I believe, is the American people's hard work.

To say that the Americans work harder in order to live better, however, does not mean that they can surely live better by working harder. In the early days of immigration the law of free competition did play a great role. Up to the turn of the century, there were many true "rags-to-riches" stories. But in present-day America, many sociologists believe, social stratification tends to ossify and the usual upward social mobility is a rise from blue-collar status to the middle class. Within the general framework of the existing social classes, however, people do fare better by working harder. As for the millions of unemployed or semi-unemployed, it is certainly not because they lack the American spirit of hard work that they have to sit around or idle about.

Skiing Craze and Arts Festival

The Americans play as vigorously as they work. This, of course, especially applies to people who can afford to play. In early spring, 1983, I ran into a fierce snowstorm in Denver. It recalled to my mind the lines from Mao Zedong's poem: "North country scene: A hundred leagues locked in ice. A thousand leagues of whirling snow." I expected that most people would have retired to their warmly heated homes. But, instead, I found the Denver airport as crowded as Beijing's shopping center, Wangfujing, a rare scene in America. People were coming from all parts of the country with ski equipment to vacation in the nearby mountains. When I was leaving the city for Chicago, I saw for the first time an airline getting into trouble because it had booked more seats than it had available (customary in America because passengers who have reserved seats often fail to show up.) So many vacationers were leaving that the company had to announce the over-booking of the flight over the public address system and offer $200 to anyone willing to wait an hour for the next flight. Two young men in the milling crowd dashed to the booking window and got the money.

Tourism is becoming an important part of American "play." In the 1940s, the dominant craze was sports. People also liked to travel but they usually went to nearby places. A housemother at the international dormitory where I stayed had traveled around the world by sea with her husband, and this enviable experience became the daily topic of her conversation. Now the Americans remain great sports fans, but long-distance travel has come into vogue. At home, the sunny Miami beaches attract as many as 13 million tourists a year. Many are going abroad. Passport holders numbered 853,000 in 1960 among whom 350,000 were tourists. The number had increased to 3.22 million in 1981, among whom 864,000 went abroad as tourists, and many travelling on other missions were part-time tourists. The annual income of all American hotels, including camping facilities, soared from $10.5 billion in 1972 to $25.1 billion in 1980, a sign of the growth of tourism.

American "play" also includes visits to the Las Vagas casinos I have described earlier and voyeurist dens in practically every major city. Many of these dens boldly call themselves "sex shops" and others prefer such euphemistic names as "adult theaters." Pornography is an increasingly grave social problem. Its rampancy in America helps me realize the necessity and timeliness of the stringent measures being taken in my country to prevent its intrusion.

But I feel I should clarify a misunderstanding. Some people in China believe that all recreational activities in America are more or less "yellow-tinged" (pornography is known in China as "yellow culture," a type of "spiritual pollution"). That is not true. Americans have amusement parks like Disneyland in Los Angeles and Disneyworld in Orlando, Florida, for "education through recreation." They have all sorts of wholesome folk music and dances, festivals and fairs, the kind I saw in the French Quarter in New Orleans. They also have a wide assortment of classical performances accessible to the general public. I spent a month in Iowa City, Iowa, in the autumn of 1982. Even in that small college town I had the opportunity to attend a concert by the Chicago Symphony Orchestra, an opera from Broadway, a typical American ballet and a performance by seven versatile Chinese artists of minority songs and dances from the Silk Road. In any country in the world that month could be rated as an arts festival.

Grade School and Capitol Hill

I am impressed by the American people's democratic tradition. Speaking of democracy, one must first of all have the habit of expressing oneself freely. I have visited many American grade schools and given brief talks about China, and found that free expression is part of the children's training. There should be a question-and-answer period after each talk, according to American custom. Many children raise their hands, vying with each other to raise questions. And they speak up loudly without the shyness Chinese children would show on similar occasions. I feel that this is not merely a national characteristic, but a difference between a democratic and feudal tradition. China has overthrown her centuries-old feudalism as a social system, but old ideas die hard. Feudal tradition demands that subordinates be blindly obedient to their superiors, and the young to the old. Its vestiges still remain as a mental shackle on many Chinese. But Americans don't have that shackle. Many Chinese find that their American friends are more frank and outspoken than they are. This, I believe, also has something to do with the democratic tradition established by the early immigrants, many of whom came to America because they were disgusted with the feudal order of the Old World.

Practicing democracy, one must also have the habit of accommodating differing and opposing opinions. From my contact with M.I.T. Professor Robinson upon my arrival, I have found that many Americans are open-minded. In Jackson, Mississippi, a number of U.S.-China Peoples' Friendship Association enthusiasts gave a party for me. A lady from Oklahoma who had just visited China gave me an article she had written about her impressions. One of her observations was that most Chinese intellectuals had fled China since 1949. In my talk at the party, I made passing reference to the question and, citing myself and many of my friends as example, showed that Chinese intellectuals had not left, but had rather returned to join the revolution since 1949. I did not name her article, but to my surprise, the lady rose after my speech and thanked me openly for correcting her wrong impression.

On another occasion I spoke to a group of students at the University of California, Los Angeles. A young man asked me a "loaded" question: "We have no political prisoners in America. Will you be allowed to write that in your book?" It so happened that I discussed the question with two lawyer friends a few days ago. They said that in a strict legal sense the United States government could not imprison anybody for political reasons. But in actual life everybody knew that there were people jailed for political reasons, and worse still, they might be assassinated or die in mysterious "traffic accidents." The woman lawyer recalled that she was jailed in the 1960s when she participated in the "Freedom Ride" movement, technically for violating a state law on segregation. "But wasn't I a political prisoner?" she asked. I briefly answered the young man's query along similar lines. Two students in the back seats loudly joined in :"You're right, Mrs. Wang. " The questioner did not seem to be offended. Tolerance of opposing views is a good American characteristic.

Another daily life manifestation of the democratic tradition is that Americans seldom address their superiors by official titles. It would be unimaginable to call somebody, for instance, "Board Chairman Williams," "Manager Smith" or "Director Brown." In China this form of address still persists, though it has been severely criticized as a residue of feudal hierarchy. Americans call each other, in polite way, Mr., Miss or Mrs., and more often by abbreviated forms of people's first names, like Dick and Lizzie. They do say "Mr. President" "Professor Robinson." or "Senator Jackson" when referring to people in their public positions, or as a way of expressing respect. But that does not seem to imply a sense of veneration for those on upper rungs of the social ladder. Dignitaries would not mind if you called them by their first names if you met them more than once. In short, common etiquette prevails rather than dictates of social or professional hierarchy. Service workers everywhere in America are polite and never rude. Customers, on their part, are also polite, and even the wealthy and powerful say "thanks" to waiters and attendants as politeness is considered by all to be a sign of gentility. All these, I feel, are the result of a rupture from the feudal tradition and welcome signs of people treating each other, at least nominally, as equals.

While appreciating the American people's democratic tradition, I don't mean to say that I believe the American political system is truly one "of the people, by the people and for the people." Nor do I believe that the American social system truly embodies the ideal that "all men are created equal." People do speak freely and exercise "majority rule," as the word "democracy" implies, at New-England-type town meetings. But that democracy is of necessity confined to debate and decisions on local and minor issues. Major issues of national and world import are a different matter. I attended, for instance, a town meeting in suburban Boston where an overwhelming majority voted for a "nuclear freeze." Later I saw a million-strong demonstration in New York City against the nuclear arms race. But what has happened since? The nuclear race has been accelerating and U.S. military expenditures continue to increase astronomically. Poverty and unemployment also increase despite widespread social concern. In 1982, according to official statistics, there were 12 million unemployed. Thirty-five million Americans were living under the official poverty line. Their sympathizers number many more millions. But there seemed to be not much that the government or official policymakers were doing about correcting the source of this social suffering.

Many Americans proudly tell me that they can elect their President and mayors. And that is true. But what surprises me is that it will be considered a good performance if sixty percent of eligible voters turn out to cast their ballots in any election. When I ask people why they vote Democratic or Republican, I often get answers like:"It's my family tradition" or "He (the candidate) appears to be a good guy." People talk about world affairs, most frequently about the Caribbean crisis, during my stay. But I have found that many don't know whether Washington is supporting the government or the anti-government forces in Nicaragua and El Salvador. When the United States intervened and sent its troops to Grenada, I was amazed to find that many people considered it a good show of "American strength," without stopping to think how they would feel if a foreign power landed its troops on American soil. It is, of course, unrealistic to expect that ordinary people in any country should know of the complexities of the international situation, but I do think that the Americans, with such an efficient media providing mass information, should do better.

Going to the roots of the question, the power of money undercuts the American democratic tradition. I had an opportunity to hear debate in the Senate on school prayer. It seemed free and heated. But I have also heard and read much about how numerous lobbies spend huge sums of money to influence Congress and about the dubious role of private donations in elections. The apparent equality among people cannot obliterate the inequality of wealth. In Chicago, I witnessed the election of Harold Washington, a Black American, as mayor. But I also read a press report that his defeated opponent, millionaire Bernard Epton, publicly declared his intention to buy the Chicago newspaper, the *Sun Times*, and to fire two columnists who criticized him in print during the election campaign. Though Mr. Epton did not succeed in the purchase, the power wielded by money over the press is all too obvious. Another black mayor, Andrew Young of Atlanta, once said to a number of big business executives: "I can get elected without your help but I can't run the city without your help." This oft-quoted statement is also revealing as to what money can do. Americans, I have found, can freely criticize their President, but not their bosses. The Chief Executive is far away, but the boss can terminate employment relatively easily.

I am not saying, however, that Capitol Hill and the White House always fail to be responsive to popular demands. The ending of the Vietnam war is an example. The military quagmire was an important reason why the United States decided to back out, but public pressure played an equally important role. President Nixon had proved this when he wrote in his *Memoirs*: "Although publicly I continued to ignore the raging antiwar controversy....I knew, however, that...American public opinion would be seriously divided by any military escalation of the war."

Regardless of how one tries to assess the American political and social system, I believe the American people do have a solid democratic tradition. They cherish democracy and abhor anything they have come to realize as being anti-democratic. The fact that the civil rights movements in the 1960s had such a mass following of both blacks and whites was a recent proof.

Dolls and Grannies

The American spirit of personal independence is as distinct as the democratic tradition. I have visited a number of families and seen how they cultivate this spirit in their children. Kids usually have their own rooms and are given complete charge of their "family" of dolls, teddy bears, toy puppies and bunnies, each bearing a name given by the young "master of the house." When children are naughty, parents might ask them to go to their own rooms and often will not scold them lest their self-dignity be hurt.

American youngsters are encouraged to contend with difficulties on their own. I heard an interesting story about a children's contest. A group of ten-year-olds were to ride young bulls and race across a field. One child met with a particularly stubborn animal and was struggling with it when all others had reached the finish line. Instead of giving the child a helping hand or advising him to quit, young and adult spectators cheered him on. Finally he brought the bull under control and ran the course. An ovation greeted the youth.

In New Orleans, my host was Tom Deane, owner of a curio shop. His children are encouraged to design and make handicrafts on their own, restoring, for instance, the skeleton of an ox from a heap of bones or carving out sculptures from tree roots. Their works are displayed in the shop with a name tag of the maker attached to each piece. When they are sold, all the money goes to the young craftspeople.

American youths, married or unmarried, regard it as a matter of course that they will leave their parents and live independently when they come of age. Old people, widows and widowers alike, prefer to live on their own and don't want to become a burden on their sons and daughters. We in China tend to believe that Americans don't care very much about their aged parents. There is some truth to this belief, but I must add that many American old people I knew insist on living alone out of personal choice.

This spirit of personal independence, I think, can also be traced back to the early immigrants. Fighting the elements on a primitive continent, with no relatives, friends and neighbors around, they had to rely on themselves. This way of life grew into a habit entirely different from the centuries-old Chinese tradition of living in extended families and clans, three or four generations under the same roof in crowded towns or compact villages.

Treasuring personal independence is a virtue, of course. But anything pushed to the extreme is likely to yield adverse effects. For me, a Chinese accustomed to the traditional family life marked by parental love and filial piety, by grannies' *han yi nong sun* (a very ancient saying describing the happiness of grandmothers "handing out candies and playing with grandchildren"), the loneliness of the American elderly is anything but enviable. I was shocked, for instance, to hear on my way to Iowa farmer Wheeler's home that his wife's ill and lonely uncle had shot and killed himself. I feel very sympathetic when reading discussions of "graying America." "The number of Americans sixty-five and older had been only 12,334,000 in 1950; the number in 1980 had grown to 25,544,000," writes Theodore White in *America in Search of Itself*. "The number would be half as large again twenty years hence.... By 1980, the life expectancy of an American female had grown to an unprecedented seventy-seven years. These old ladies could be expected to grow in numbers and unhappiness.... If the system could not provide for the love and warmth of children and grandchildren, it nonetheless must care for the aged. Grandmother care would become one of the saddest problems of the eighties and nineties."

Another adverse effect of personal independence is the issue of private ownership of guns. Out of an early need for an armed militia and personal safety, the Second Amendment to the U.S. Constitution in the Bill of Rights provides that "the right of the people to keep and bear arms, shall not be infringed." But times have changed. One reason for sky-rocketing crime statistics, some Americans tell me, is the large number of privately owned arms. Guns in the hands of irresponsible people, drunks, the mentally deranged, delinquent juveniles, and criminals are a menace to society. After the attempt on President Reagen's life a large segment of public opinion called for banning or limiting private arms, but to no avail. Even the President himself did not approve of the idea. This type of personal independence seems anachronistic.

Searching Waste Baskets and Visiting a Professor

A particularly pleasant experience for me is the American readiness to help. What the Chinese press lauds as "good people and good deeds" also abound in America.

When leaving Las Vegas, I got to the airport only minutes before the plane's departure. I rushed aboard frantically but found that I had not checked in my suitcases and had left them to a porter. I felt sick because many of my notebooks were in one suitcase. After landing, I hurried to the inquiry office for help. The gentleman asked me to try my luck at the luggage conveyer. I stood there and soon saw them coming. I still don't know by what magic the kind black porter rushed them to the plane.It must have been a split-second operation. In Santa Ana, California, I forgot to get off the train when I should have. Fellow passengers were very sympathetic. A working man asked me seriously if I had the money to pay the fare back and said he could help me. Learning of my problem, the conductor wrote a note on a slip of paper for me. With it I got off at the next stop and rode back without the least difficulty. In Indianapolis, I lost the receipt for my air ticket which I needed to report my travelling expenses. When I phoned Delta Airlines about my problem from Detroit, where I had landed, they called back after a while saying that they had searched even the waste baskets on the passageway but promised to continue the search if I could provide some clues. I was embarrassed when I found the receipt tucked away in my overcoat pocket. In Youngstown, Ohio, a lawyer whom I wished to meet was out of town. I had no acquaintances and had to phone the local paper *Youngstown Vindicator*. Labor reporter Michael Braun not only helped collect materials for me, but he accompanied me to see his professor, John Russo, for an in-depth discussion. After the interview, Professor Russo, in his turn, introduced me to Professor Barry Bluestone of Boston for a further discussion. If Delta Airlines had taken my problem as part of their business, Mr. Braun and Mr. Russo were certainly in no way obliged to take time out to talk at length to a complete stranger from another country.

American readiness to help is manifested on a mass scale by numerous volunteer service organizations. Some work for the welfare of the handicapped, some specialize in preventing suicide among the lonely and depressed, and some are devoted to the protection of birds and rare animals. When giant pandas in China were faced with starvation as a result of the flowering and withering of arrow bamboo, their staple food, many American pupils and students organized themselves to raise funds for panda relief. All volunteer services are rendered in spare time and usually without remuneration.

My friend Louise De Young in Houston, a probation officer in charge of juvenile delinquents, told me that each probation officer was responsible for a large district and had to enlist the help of volunteers. They would not accept just anybody who cared to help; he or she had to apply and prove themselves eligible after a trial period. Volunteer help had enabled Louise to do her job so well that she won an official commendation. It had also enabled her to be a volunteer in another field — supporter of the U.S.-China Peoples' Friendship Association. If all volunteer services were to discontinue, Louise told me, she just did not know how the nation could carry on.

But, on the other hand, some friends have told me that Americans, living in an intensely competitive society, have to take care of themselves all the time. As a result, they say, people often feel lonely deep in their hearts and *anomie* is prevalent. "Everyone for himself and God helps all" — how can this be reconciled with the ever-readiness to help others? An explanation, I think, might also be found in the life of the early immigrants. Starting with little, they had nobody but themselves to rely on to eke out a living or accumulate a fortune. Individualistic rather than collective efforts were the key to success. But everybody was bound to meet with some mishaps, major or slight, at one time or another, and to go through the agonies of sickness, old age, and impending death. At such unfortunate moments, help from others was necessary. Such help, in a way, was also reciprocal because someday the helper might need to be helped, too. So, on condition that one's basic interest was not harmed, people were willing to help others. It was like depositing goodwill in a "social bank" which one might later need to draw upon. Meanwhile it was a counter-weight to the loneliness caused by constant struggle for survival and self-improvement, and a consolation to feel that men were, after all, not living in a Darwinistic world where survival of the fittest was the primary law.

My analysis might be overly simplified, but the paradoxical phenomenon of fierce competition for self-interest coupled with a prevalent readiness to help others is easily visible in America.

"Water-Fall Cave" and Former Imperial Kitchen

I must emphatically convey to my Chinese readers the American people's friendliness to the Chinese people. It was evident everywhere I travelled.

In June 1948, my husband and I graduated from the Missouri School of Journalism. After commencement, each graduate was given an alumnus form to fill out. Those were days when the United States government was helping Chiang Kai-shek to fight an anti-communist civil war in China and my long-suffering motherland was engulfed in bloodshed. We were indignant when it became apparent that the U.S. government was inevitably becoming a foe of the emerging People's Republic and that the chances for us to come back to America were slim. So my husband wrote wryly on the form a "home address" — "c/o Sun Wu-kung, Shuiliantong, Huakuoshan." This combination of letters means nothing to ordinary Americans but it actually is the "address" of the legendary Monkey King Sun Wu-kung in the widely read classic novel *Journey to the West*, meaning "Water-fall Cave in the Flower-Fruit Mountain."

We returned to China one year later. The two countries were completely estranged in the subsequent decades, and our memories of our alma mater faded. My husband's queer address was no handicap because the school for many years did not communicate with any graduate in China, probably because of the prevailing political situation. Then, in the early 1970s, "ping-pong diplomacy" began. Mr. Kissinger came to China, President Nixon followed, and many American visitors arrived on their heels. One day, several Missouri Journalism School graduates living in Beijing received letters from the school, forwarded through *People's Daily*. The sender tried *People's Daily* obviously because it is the largest newspaper in China and we are journalists. We were happy to find that it was Dean Roy Fisher of the school who wrote us, expressing his deep hope that connections could be restored. We replied. Soon afterwards, Associate Professor Jane Clark of the school, coming to China as a tourist, was entrusted by the dean to talk to us. We had a very pleasant meeting in Beijing.

In 1980, my publishing organization joined two journalistic institutions to invite Mr. Fisher to make a lecture tour in China. Roy and his wife, Anne, came. On the afternoon of their arrival in Beijing, my husband, as the host, accompanied them to visit the Summer Palace. Strolling in the long corridors along the picturesque Kunming Lake, Roy brought up the idea that since Edgar Snow was a Missouri J-School graduate and a respected friend of the Chinese people, an Edgar Snow Scholarship could be set up for young Chinese journalists from the mainland to study in the Missouri school.

One evening, a number of Missouri graduates working in the Chinese capital gathered at a dinner in the former Imperial Kitchen restaurant to welcome Roy and Anne. Though the guests were our new acquaintances, the atmosphere was as congenial as a reunion of long-separated friends. Before long, exchanges under the Snow Scholarship began, and one more link was added to many others being rebuilt between the Chinese and American peoples.

Revisiting my alma mater, I was received by Roy and Anne with great hospitality. The dean introduced me to Professor Ernest Morgan, who had a party for me to meet the J-School students. Roy also introduced me to Professor emeritus Douglas Ensminger who spent two whole afternoons with me recapitulating the major changes in American society in the past three decades. Douglas then wrote to introduce me to his brother, M.E. Ensminger, an internationally known scholar in the field of animal husbandry, and his wife, Audrey, whom I met later in Fresno, California. This was the way my friends and acquaintances spread over larger circles.

While in America, I was frequently asked the question: "What have you found changed?" And I often answered: "Everything— with only one exception. The American friendliness to the Chinese people remains the same and, indeed, seems to have broadened."

In my mind's eye, I see American friends of China in several circles, each larger than the last. The smallest comprises those veterans, like Susan Warren and Hugh Deane in New York, and Bill Powell and John Service in San Francisco, who have worked for understanding between the two peoples since the 1930s and 40s. A larger circle is represented by the U.S.-China Peoples' Friendship Association founded in the early 1970s. I must acknowledge that apart from Professor Robinson, it was the association members who gave me the greatest help on my trip across the country. Another circle, larger still, includes the increasing number of Americans of all trades and professions who have recently established relations in one field or another with their Chinese colleagues, like the Fishers and Ensmingers. The largest circle is almost boundless, represented by all the Americans I have met, including the blacks who talked to me so freely in Harlem, and the Indians who welcomed me in Yakima Washington, and Kechikan, Alaska. Though most of them know little about China, they are all exceedingly friendly to me as a Chinese.

On the last leg of my journey I returned to Boston. Dick Robinson, an old friend by now, showed great concern for me. The first thing he said was that I looked tired and should rest. And the first question he asked was whether I had met with any unfriendly and provocative people on the trip. "No. Everywhere I have met with friends," I hastened to reply. I was saying this not out of courtesy but simply to tell the truth.

What is the source of this friendship? I cannot explain exactly. But it seems that American appreciation of China's ancient civilization is an important reason. Besides, since the U.S. steamer *Empress of China* called on my country two hundred years ago, contacts and connections between the two peoples had been frequent, close, and friendly in spite of the painful pages in the annals of government relations. During World War II, many Americans came to China to fight the Japanese invaders and everywhere met ordinary Chinese throwing up their thumbs and greeting them with the words: *Ding Hao* (superb) — a spontaneous expression of popular and deeply felt goodwill on the Chinese side. These happy memories are being revived though they had been over-shadowed during the years by massive American involvement in the Chinese civil war, the subsequent military confrontation in Korea, and then the Vietnam war.

"Testing Machine" and Space-suit

On my second trip I have been more impressed by the Americans' never-ending search for the new than I was in the 1940s. When I studied at the Missouri J-School, I must confess, one thing that vexed me very much was the "testing machine," a new-fangled trick I had called it. "The History and Principles of American Journalism" was a course required for all students, and had the most frequent quizzes. The questions, to be answered by underlining the correct dates and names, included, for instance: When was the first American newspaper founded; when was Joseph Pulitzer born and when did he die; what was the name of the first newapaper he owned, etc. With a long list of questions and hundreds of students attending, it must have been a headache for the teachers to mark all the papers. So a sort of testing machine was put into use. Each student was given a special pencil to underline so that the machine could pick up the pencil mark through a covering sheet punctured at the right places. This made it easier for the teachers and the quiz became almost a weekly affair. I was annoyed by these uncreative teaching and testing methods. But I also appreciated the Americans' continual quest for the new and innovative.

When I revisited the University at Columbia, Missouri, I found much had changed. A brand new building has been added to the J-School. The international dormitory where I stayed was nowhere to be found. TV was rare in the 1940s and the school offered no TV course. But it now boasts a full-fledged TV curriculum. A small town in the past, Columbia had only a local radio station (whose call, "KFRS, in the heart of Missouri," remains a pleasant memory for me.) But now it has a TV station as well. Linotype still ruled the day in newspaper production in the forties and we had to pay a special tuition for a typography course teaching the use of "advanced" linos. But now the *Columbia Missourian*, the school paper which is one of the town's two papers, has long since switched to computerized composition and done away with the molten lead and the clattering of the machines. Linotypes, I was told, have become "museum pieces."

Many more memories came to my mind. Once a Chinese girl student, Margaret Cheng, from a wealthy family in Shanghai telephoned her mother from Columbia and paid about $30 (a good sum in those days) for the call. I wrote a "human interest" story about it and *Columbia Missourian* printed it in a box. Some ingenious editor added the headline: "Homesick Coed Phones Mummy, Call Costs 30 Dollars." This showed that a trans-Pacific call at that time was "newsworthy." But by present standards, I guess, even a phone talk with an astronaut in space would not be worth a box. Students of press photography then were encouraged, not required, to try color photos. I had to think twice because film and processing were expensive. But now black-and-white pictures are made mainly for professional purposes and amateur photographers have all switched to color.

On the eve of my departure from Columbia this time, Anne pushed some buttons in her kitchen and the next morning coffee and toast had been prepared automatically. This again reminded me of the past. My husband and I had a double wedding — together with a Missouri University schoolmate and her fiance — at Overland Park, Kansas City, Missouri. On the morning of the wedding day, I remember, I had breakfast at her home and saw her mother cooking coffee in a blackened pot over a coal stove. This reminiscence, however, had a sorry note because I was not able to locate that schoolmate and her family on my second trip. The address book I used in America had been scrapped during the "cultural revolution" lest it would be taken by "Red Guards" as evidence of "illicit overseas connections" — a common stigma in those witch-hunting years.

Elsewhere in America, I felt the change, too. In Washington, D.C., I touched the moon rock displayed at the National Space Museum. In Houston, I saw a real space suit at the Johnson Space Center. These objects made the space age more real to me. Sightseeing at San Francisco Bay, I remembered *S.S. General Gordon*, rated as a fast steamer in the forties, aboard which I went home. If the Gordon is still sailing now, its passengers would really be "On a Slow Boat to China" as a popular song in those days went.

I was aware of not only the technological progress, but the enormous political changes, too. While we were sailing on the Pacific aboard the *S.S. General Gordon*, the U.S. State Department announced a ban on American ships calling on "Communist-occupied Chinese ports" including Shanghai which was our destination. We were forced to disembark at Hongkong. My husband and I, with a baby daughter born seven months earlier in Chicago, had to run the tight blockade imposed by the Kuomintang with American-made warships and eventually got to "Communist-occupied" Tianjin in north China, worn out and ill. What a sharp contrast to today!

But it is the material progress which has impressed me most deeply. Since the victory of their War of Independence, the Americans have pushed westward and opened up new frontiers at an amazing speed. They reached the last frontiers on the continent by the turn of the century. U.S. government efforts to open up "new frontiers" overseas have met with setbacks. But the American people have channeled their great vitality into a search for "new frontiers" in the field of science, technology, and material production, in the macro as well as micro-world. Their achievements are truly remarkable.

American efforts to open up "new frontiers" in the field of social progress, however, seem more problematical in their results. Many social problems remain, or, indeed, have been aggravated over the past decades. Things were especially bad in 1982, a year of deep recession. Though an upward turn came in 1983-84, none of the Americans I have met is sure that a recession will not recur along with the accompanying mass unemployment and suffering. The decline of the "sunset industries" may be unavoidable, but is the subsequent community abandonment equally inevitable? In an affluent society, why should one out of every seven people be living below the official poverty level? And then there is the troubling phenomenon of an ever-widening wave of crime. I quote Theodore White once again. "In 1967, one in three people had reported that they dared not walk alone at night within one mile of their home," he writes in *America in Search of Itself.* "A decade later," he continues, "that figure had grown to forty-five percent; and by 1980, for which data is not yet available, the figure was probably approaching half." Is crime bound to rise and not to subside? Many similar questions puzzle me as I try to evaluate the American scene. But of one thing I am sure. Talented and never self-complacent, the Americans will sooner or later find a solution to these distressing problems.

In 1840, the French writer Alexis de Tocqueville wrote the classic *Democracy in America.* One of his conclusions remains completely valid today: "They (the Americans) all consider society as a body in a state of improvement, humanity as a changing scene, in which nothing is, or ought to be, permanent; and they admit that what appears to them today to be good, may be superseded by something better tomorrow." This is exactly what I mean when I tell my Chinese friends that the Americans are a people who "know no last frontiers."

It was in a July evening that I left San Francisco for China in 1949. Looking back at the Golden Gate Bridge, as beautiful as a rainbow with its colored lights, I felt sad. A second visit would be very unlikely in my lifetime, I thought. When bidding farewell to Dick Robinson and Carol at the end of my second trip, however, I felt quite different. There was a reluctance to part but a lyrical saying often used in old Chinese novels immediately came to my mind: "As long as mountains remain green and rivers blue, we shall meet again." True enough, Dick was visiting at my Beijing home less than a year after my departure from Boston.

A grand bridge has been erected across the Pacific linking the People's Republic of China, the world's largest developing country, and the United States of America, the largest developed nation in the world. All indications are that traffic on this bridge will become busier with each passing day. If this book of mine can play the role of a tiny rivet helping to fasten the bridge, I shall feel more than rewarded for the laborious days of my journey and the many sleepless nights I spent in the course of writing it. Friendship is based on understanding. It is in this conviction that I have in this book truthfully reported to my Chinese readers my observations and reflections, and that I have agreed to publish the present English edition as a "feedback" to the American people who may like to know how their country looks in the eyes of a friendly but often critical Chinese.

Photo by Paul R. Schell
Staff photographer of *Youngstown Vindicator*

ABOUT THE AUTHOR

WANG TSOMIN, after graduation from the Department of Foreign Languages and Literature, Tsinghua University, in 1937, taught English in wartime Chungking for a few years. In 1944, she attended the Chungking Post-Graduate School of Journalism sponsored by America's Columbia University and graduated with honor. She earned a second bachelor's degree in 1948 at the School of Journalism of the University of Missouri in the United States and returned to China on the eve of the founding of the People's Republic.

Since 1949 she has been active in the publishing field. She was editor/translator at the Foreign Languages Press for a decade; editor/writer on literary and art subjects for the multi-language weekly *Beijing Review* for another decade; and Deputy Editor-in-Chief of the New World Press up to the time she was "loaned" to the Chinese Academy of Social Sciences to re-visit the United States (1982-83) to collect impressions and materials for the present volume *American Kaleidoscope*.

She married Duan Liancheng, her classmate at the Missouri School of Journalism, at Kansas, Missouri. They have two daughters, the elder one born in Chicago and raised in Beijing.

美 国 万 花 筒

王作民　著

段连成　编译

*

新世界出版社出版

北京外文印刷厂印刷

中国国际图书贸易总公司发行

（中国国际书店）

北京399信箱

1986年　第一版

编号：17223—190

01140（精）

00980（平）

17—E—2076

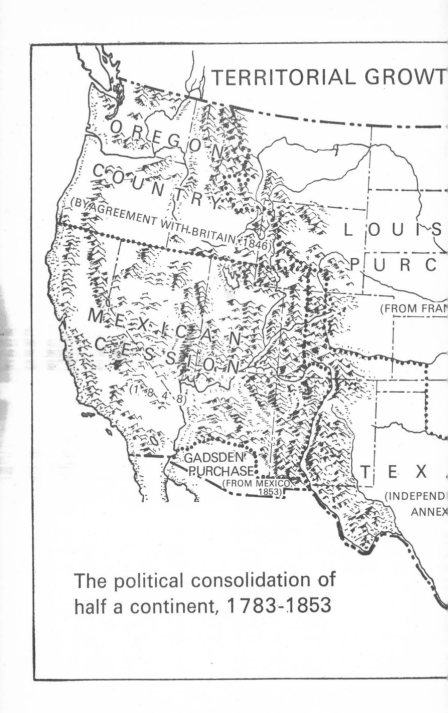

TERRITORIAL GROWT

O R E G O N
C O U N T R Y
(BY AGREEMENT WITH BRITAIN 1846)

L O U I S
P U R C
(FROM FRAI

M E X I C A N
C E S S I O N
(1 8 4 8)

GADSDEN
PURCHASE
(FROM MEXICO,
1853)

T E X
(INDEPEND
ANNEX

The political consolidation of
half a continent, 1783-1853